THE LITERATURE OF ENGLAND

A.D. 500 – 1942

BOOK
PRODUCTION
WAR ECONOMY
STANDARD

THE
LITERATURE OF ENGLAND

A.D. 500–1942

BY

WILLIAM J. ENTWISTLE

AND

ERIC GILLETT

*A Survey of British Literature
from the Beginnings to the Present Day*

LONGMANS, GREEN AND CO.
LONDON ❖ NEW YORK ❖ TORONTO

LONGMANS, GREEN AND CO. LTD
OF PATERNOSTER ROW

43 ALBERT DRIVE, LONDON, S.W.19
17 CHITTARANJAN AVENUE, CALCUTTA
NICOL ROAD, BOMBAY
36A MOUNT ROAD, MADRAS

LONGMANS, GREEN AND CO.
55 FIFTH AVENUE, NEW YORK

LONGMANS, GREEN AND CO.
215 VICTORIA STREET, TORONTO

First published 1943

CODE NUMBER: 18110

PRINTED IN GREAT BRITAIN
BY WESTERN PRINTING SERVICES, LTD. BRISTOL

PREFACE

THOUGH there are many introductions to and histories of English Literature, there has not hitherto been one which covers in detail contemporary writers up to the present day (1942) and also provides a brief survey of earlier literary history from its beginnings. The authors hope that this short book will appeal, not only to those readers who are primarily interested in present-day writing, but also to those others who have found stimulus and refreshment in the great literary classics of the past, and are now feeling their way among the dangerous shoals and quicksands provided in full measure by some contemporary writers, who have the strange belief that a thing is good merely because it is new. The book is designed also for foreign readers and students of our literature, and their difficulties have been borne in mind by the authors, who have spoken not unacceptably about British culture at places as remote as Lima and Singapore to minds of the Far West and East. It is now the business of one of them to mediate between a great foreign civilization and British pupils. In these circumstances they have found it profitable to approach English literature on lines rather unlike those followed in the majority of histories of literature.

The authors feel that many readers, British and foreign, want to be told as concisely and comprehensively as possible what is English literature, what is British culture, here and now. Many readers, depressed and disheartened by their first introduction to Shakespeare and other great writers during their schooldays, feel that they never want to read or see acted another English classic. Their reading is now confined to what the young lady at the circulating library recommends to them. For entertainment they go once or twice weekly to the cinema. They have not even made the acquaintance of the masterpieces of the English drama, because millions of young and middle-aged people living now have never been inside a theatre in their lives.

To the majority of present-day readers the approach to English literature lies through the portals of the present. The space allotted to the writers of the past fifty years is, therefore, much larger than in most manuals. Previous historians have wisely brought their books to an end ten or twenty years before the time when they wrote, feeling that there are no established, and therefore no teachable, judgments on the literature of the immediate past. The English reader has a certain knowledge of contemporary writing and he gathers opinions from the atmosphere around him. These opinions are necessarily inadequate because the output of books which came out annually from the English presses up to the outbreak of the war of 1939 was so enormous that it was clearly impossible for any reader to keep pace with this great flood of productivity. For the English reader and for the overseas student alike, therefore, should be available an historical summary of present-day authors and their books, and the latter part of this history is an attempt to provide one. The other way in which we hope to meet the demands of both British and foreign readers is by the perspective we offer of the older literature. We have taken the contemporary standpoint. We wish to display the mental furniture of a cultured English man or woman of to-day. Though his reading is, in fact, mainly contemporary, in newspapers, fiction, poetry, learned works, and belles-lettres, yet the most powerful influences on his mind, the springs of his deepest emotions, lie in the past. An extract from the Bible or from Shakespeare leaps more quickly to the mind and tongue, and is more conducive to action, than the sayings or writings of the most admired contemporary; the best of these, indeed, to drive home an appeal, are wise when they take a weapon from the old armoury. The older literature is best set forth in order of time, since that is the surest; but we have not thought it proper to attempt a strict chronology. We have tried to place books in groups conveniently read together as recognizable parts of the British heritage of to-day. Contemporary literature is displayed under subject headings, so that it is possible to read the survey of any literary form from the eighteen-nineties to the present day without interruption. All prose books difficult of classification have been grouped under the heading, "Miscellaneous Prose." If a novelist has also written a book of criticism and/or a

biography, these will usually be found under the heading
"Fiction." If he has written considerably in different kinds, as,
to take one obvious example, Mr. J. B. Priestley has done, the
different branches of his work—essays, novels, plays, etc.—
will be found treated separately in the sections devoted to those
subjects.

We have endeavoured to provide for the home reader a guide
which will enable him to read our literature past and present
with pleasure and profit. We have tried to inform the overseas
student of what is traditional in our English genius, and to
show him in what ways Milton and Wordsworth were typically
English. The interest of the overseas student is directed
towards a living people and he asks himself such questions as
this: "What manner of folk are these British, who gave birth
to modern liberty and are its stubborn defenders to-day; who
cower before no aggressor but extend a hand to a beaten foe;
who cleared the seas of slavers and pirates; who used a century
of undoubted supremacy for shielding defenceless races,
peopling empty continents, and augmenting the resources of
nascent nationalities?" We do not undertake to answer this
pregnant question, but we say: "Here and here has Britain
spoken. These are our authentic voices. Hear them." They
are mighty voices, and we do not say that our thoughts and
tones to-day are comparable to theirs of the past. We have
indicated as far as possible those contemporary writers whose
voices ring out with the clear candour and inspiring enthusiasm
characteristic of the great ones of former days. It must never
be forgotten that the great voices are living voices by virtue of
their authority and of the eternal truths in which they dealt.
These things hold us in allegiance to the genuine British
tradition.

It is evident that we, who have, so to speak, taken the chair
before an illustrious tribune of speakers, must make our introduction briefly and make way for those you wish to hear.
Students have been known, in all the civilized parts of the
earth, who have bought a standard manual of this or that, and
have committed to memory names, titles, dates and opinions
with such laborious industry that they have had no time to
read the literature of which that manual was the threshold.

We hope nothing of the kind will occur to our readers. An introduction must be made ; you must have a scheme of reading and a background, but rather than be tedious and diffuse we have practised a ruthless brevity; we have preferred to omit a certain number of books and authors rather than obstruct the reader's access.

This is important both for readers at home and abroad. There are numerous histories of the different branches of our past literature available for the student and the specialist. To them we offer a short, comprehensive survey of the general literature of the past. To the general reader, British or foreign, we have tried to present a compact course of reading so chosen and combined as to justify the widest cultural inferences.

About a century of cardinal books of the past are indicated for the reader's special attention. We have tried to suggest how these works have a definitive value, and we have given them a general background. In the contemporary period choice is bound to be more fluid, and it is easy to substitute one book for another. Copious references are made in the text to works by present-day authors, as it was found impossible to adopt the method used in the earlier part of the book, where, in order to leave room for statements of cultural values, we have adopted from M. Lanson the device of placing in footnotes all dates and biographical particulars. They have been adjusted by the standard of the *Oxford Companion to English Literature*. These footnotes also contain titles of books to extend the reading indicated in the text. They enable the reader whose curiosity is particular, not general, to carry his studies forward in the required direction. We have given titles of books, but only in rare cases have we indicated editions. In view of the fact that at the present time many books are out of print and prices alter frequently we have not thought it advisable to proffer more elaborate and comprehensive suggestions. A typical English private library will contain not only literary works but books of reference and books illustrative of all aspects of British history, scenery, commerce, politics, sport and the rest. Cheap and reliable copies of almost all the older books cited will be found among the volumes constituting "Everyman's Library" and the "World's Classics."

One word more. The great American authors, with the exception of a very few contemporaries, are not included, though they are part of Britain's heritage. We too are heirs of the Declaration of Independence and the Gettysburg Oration, Franklin, Prescott, Irving, Poe, Cooper, Herman Melville, Longfellow, Lowell, Holmes, Whittier, Mark Twain, and yet they are not ours in quite the same way. It would have confused this book to have attempted to do them justice; yet we would not have them forgotten. This also is British: that great independent cultures have arisen in America, Africa and Australasia, to give a new accent and significance to the best English traditions.

For the first two parts of the book (Chapters I–XII) W. J. Entwistle is responsible, for the third (Chapters XIII–XV), Eric Gillett. The authors must express their indebtedness to Miss Margot Heginbothom who compiled the Index and checked many dates and references, to Mrs. Bisson, Miss Mary Chandler and Professor C. J. Sisson who have detected several slips in the manuscript, to Mr. George Sampson, author of the *Cambridge Concise History of English Literature*, whose patience and learning never failed when he was consulted on matters affecting the contemporary authors, and to the Editor of the *Fortnightly Review*, in which a small part of the material appeared.

W. J. E.
E. G.

CONTENTS

THE MAKING OF ENGLISH

By WILLIAM J. ENTWISTLE

PAGE

I. BEFORE CHAUCER 1

The Saxon Foundation (to 1066) . . . 1

The Middle English Period (1066–1385) . . 5

II. CHAUCER AND THE CHAUCERIANS . . . 16

THE ENGLISH CLASSICS

By WILLIAM J. ENTWISTLE

III. DECISIVE STEPS (1475–1625) 28

IV. SPENSER AND SIDNEY 35

V. SHAKESPEARE AND THE DRAMA . . . 42

VI. THE AGE OF MILTON 58

VII. AUGUSTAN VERSE AND DRAMA . . . 72

VIII. AUGUSTAN PROSE 84

IX. THE ROMANTICS 103

X. VICTORIAN VERSE 122

XI. THE GOLDEN AGE OF THE NOVEL . . . 131

XII. VICTORIAN THOUGHT AND ACTION . . 149

CONTEMPORARY LITERATURE TO 1942

By ERIC GILLETT

XIII. POETRY AND THE DRAMA 169

Poetry 169

The Drama 196

PAGE

XIV. PROSE OF ENTERTAINMENT 211

Fiction 211
The Essay 241

XV. PROSE OF INFORMATION 246

Biography 246
Autobiography 251
History 255
Books of Travel and Exploration . . 258
Miscellaneous Prose 265

INDEX 283

THE MAKING OF ENGLISH

I. BEFORE CHAUCER

THE SAXON FOUNDATION (TO 1066)

BRITISH culture is a blend of the two great traditions of modern Europe: the Latin and the Germanic. It is the knot of western civilization. Expressed more often in action than in speculation, it is most completely and subtly reflected in English literature, which combines the discipline and fullness of the classical heritage with the freedom and energy of the North. For the greater part of a millennium these unlike elements were worked and fused together before they reached their new and higher unity in the English of Spenser and the Elizabethans, and for four hundred years they have been moulded and reshaped with striking originality. In this way the variety of British culture is no less remarkable than its unity, nor is its unity less noticeable than the diversity of its origins; it is supremely elastic, adaptable and tenacious.

At first these elements seem to lie side by side. In the Anglo-Saxon tongue we have the heroic poems. *Beowulf*,[1] supported by a number of stirring fragments, links Britain to the peoples of the North Sea coast—to Danes, Saxons and Norsemen—whose hinterland was the area of continental Germany. The use of common Germanic heroic traditions is its most conspicuous feature to such an extent that scholars have declared there is nothing English in it save the language. It is right to make use of the hints it contains, for *Beowulf* is the only full-length specimen of the once widely diffused heroic poetry of northern and central Europe. The lyrico-

---

[1] *Beowulf*. Editions by Klaeber, R. W. Chambers, Sedgefield, etc. The latter gives also *Finnsburh*, *Waldere*, and other fragments. A convenient translation of these epics and of other Anglo-Saxon poems is by R. K. Gordon, *Anglo-Saxon Poetry*. *Beowulf* is preserved in a manuscript of about the year 1000, but its subject-matter goes back to the sixth century. It is touched with Christianity, e.g., in the episode of the bard's song of Creation, and the general tone seems to suit Northumbria in the troubles of the seventh century. We take it as substantially a poem of that period, based on another poem or traditions of greater antiquity.

dramatic pieces in the Norse *Edda* are allusive and elusive, and all other evidence comes from brief fragments or from Latin summaries. What *Beowulf* has to say, therefore, is of unique weight; and that too has been made a source of complaint! The author is censured for dealing with an obscure subject instead of some brilliantly heroic central theme like that of Siegfried and the Rhinegold. The merits of such pieces are, however, like their very existence, a matter of conjecture, but the Old English *Beowulf* is a solid fact.

The sense of lost glories and imminent peril imbues this poem with heroic melancholy. There is light and feasting in the narrow space of Hart Hall, but a toll is taken of the banqueters by dim forces of evil, bestial and supernatural, compounded of bear, watersprite and witch. It is, in fact, the defence of civilization against the destructive malice of moral evil, and the truly English hero Beowulf exerts his reserves of strength and wins through endurance. He is no shining conqueror, for such a figure has seldom touched the English imagination; but he does his duty, returns to his place among his fellows, is modest without shrinking, tolerant, and courteous in a rough heroic fashion. As to style, the *Finnsburh* fragment moves more swiftly in the few lines preserved, and other pieces also have been held to surpass *Beowulf*. Not knowing them as wholes, we cannot judge them against a complete work; *Beowulf* is swift in action but sluggish during the feasts; its athletic, alliterative metre (most effective when read aloud or chanted) covers a well-defined form with an elastic rhythm, while heroic formulas and "kennings"—that is, metaphors used in conventional senses for poetic effect—afford evidence of a matured art.

The *Battle of Maldon* (after 991) represents the same art after the end of the epic period, and is famous for its formula of high courage:

> *Courage be keener, heart be harder,*
> *mood be mightier, as our might faileth.*

The setting is still one of peril and disaster, and this melancholy inspiration flows into a small group of elegies, one of which, *Deor's Lament*, is the nearest Anglo-Saxon approach to the true lyric.

The tradition of Latin Christianity, on the other hand, finds its first great representative in the Venerable Bede,[1] whose Latin style was respected by the Renaissance, and whose authority stood immediately after that of the Fathers during the Middle Ages. His biblical commentaries were then the basis of his fame, but the modern reader is amazed by the refined scholarship, openmindedness, and grave but supple style of the *Ecclesiastical History of the English Nation*. Unique for its lack of compeers, the work is inimitable in its sifting of evidence, comparison of documents, plan of research, firm outline, lucid exposition and pregnant utterance. The conversion of the people was the great achievement of the age, and the *Ecclesiastical History* is the history of the nation in its chief activity. Latin missionaries came from the South with their gift of organization, and Celtic missionaries from the North brought purity of life and language and apostolic zeal. In the background was the smouldering discontent of the Welsh, and the foreground was held by the English rulers, who were not to be swayed by enthusiasm nor made stubborn by prejudice, but weighed the claims of Christ and Woden soberly and impartially before adopting Christianity, as they also compared the rival church disciplines before preferring that of Rome. The welter of petty wars might well have driven a historian to despair, but Bede, with consummate skill, portrays the English people constituting itself from various elements by impartial comparison and sure judgment. The light of poetry flecks his prose in the famous comparison of human life to the fluttering of a swallow through a lighted hall (such a hall as Beowulf defended), and in the calling of Cædmon the poet.

Cædmon's name has been one to conjure with since Bede described his song of the Creation, but there is no extant work that is certainly his. There are two Old English poems on the Creation, and that marked *Genesis B* has an account of the rally of the fallen angels in hell expressed in accents not unworthy of Milton. Certain poems are signed by Cynewulf in an acrostic.

[1] Bede (673–735). Ordained deacon 692, priest 703. Spent his life at Jarrow in the study of the learned languages and the Scriptures. His works are enumerated at the end of the *Historia Ecclesiastica Gentis Anglorum* (731), of which there are various editions and translations.

His interest in themes related to the Holy Cross gives some
encouragement to attribute to him the finest of these Christian
poems, *The Dream of the Rood.*[1] It is the poem least touched
with the martial ardour of the Germanic epics, but in its
brilliant colouring and restrained and stylized passion it calls
to mind a gemmed mosaic in the Byzantine style. The Christ
is not pendent, but supported by the Cross; the scene is not of
shame but of victory. The emotion of triumphant agony is
poignantly rendered by the proudly sorrowful words of the
Rood—of fallen Nature mystically conjoined in the suffering
and triumph of her Redeemer.

In its beginnings, English prose, like the Navy, is linked with
the honoured name of Alfred, who set out steadily to translate
into English the most useful Latin works within his reach.
To do justice to this prose is not easy. Coming late and subject
to Latin Christian influences from the start, this prose was
employed on necessary translations and homilies. The importance of making Bede's history known through the vernacular,
of winning ancient philosophy from Boëthius and history
from Orosius, cannot be gainsaid, but such tasks limited the
scope of originality. Homilies also were tied to their texts,
and moral and religious instruction followed a familiar round.
Chance has preserved an English version of *Apollonius of Tyre*
to make us aware that the novel was not unknown, and it is
probable that the moral stories of the *Gesta Romanorum* were
collected in England. Various writers at various times contributed to the *Anglo-Saxon Chronicle,*[2] a work compiled by the
clergy but written in English. It overstepped the Conquest
and in one version reached down to the year 1154. Opening
with Bede's preface, the *Chronicle* included bare jottings
and miniature sagas, brief poems (including the over-praised

---

[1] *The Dream of the Rood.* Translation by R. K. Gordon, op. cit. Old
English text, ed. Dickins and Ross, in Methuen's Old English Library.
Some phrases are cut in runic characters on the Northumbrian Ruthwell
Cross, which dates from the first half of the eighth century.

[2] Translation into modern English in Everyman's Library. To get the
literary flavour of the *Chronicle* it should be read selectively in passages
dealing with Edward the Martyr, the career of Earl Godwin, the epitaph
of the Conqueror, etc. These embedded sagas have their own unity. A
guide to such reading is C. E. Wright's *The Cultivation of Saga in Anglo-
Saxon England.*

Brunanburh) and rhymed prose. There was probably no dearth of entertaining literature, but in the eleventh century this would be mostly oral, and there was small inducement to put it on paper. What remains of Anglo-Saxon prose is thus a mere detritus, containing so much as seemed valuable for edification or instruction. Even so, it was a considerable achievement. The writers are competent, and their style is singularly direct in the best instances. Its likeness to the oldest Icelandic prose is not fortuitous, since England was then the cross-roads for adventurous Northmen, and Englishmen did much to evangelize the North. The disaster of the Norman invasion cut short the development of prose before it could rise from the miniature saga to the great sagas of Iceland; but the straightforward, affecting language of devotion did not perish utterly; it renewed its life among the medieval mystics and the translators of the Bible.

THE MIDDLE ENGLISH PERIOD (1066–1384)

In the year 1066 England was conquered by William, duke of Normandy. The date was decisive, no less for culture than for politics. The development of the English tradition was severely checked, and a temporary ascendancy was given to French. The area reserved for Latin was increased, and for three hundred years the nation was embarrassed by the weight of three different literatures. England entered the main stream of European thought, and was able to exert a more direct influence on the main issues than she has done at any other time; but she was distracted by a conflict of interests and, though the first of modern nations to develop a vernacular literature, she was late in coming to fruition. What emerged at length was an English type of civilization, not a French one. The history of the period, therefore, is the slow victory of the vanquished over the conqueror.

Already before the conquest a Norman-French faction had gained the ascendancy in the council of the Saxon king, and it is not to be supposed that England would have stood aloof from the sudden burgeoning of French culture in the eleventh and twelfth centuries. Already also the Danish invasions had blotted out the culture of the North, and continual disorders in the South might have led to the withering of literary effort. The Norman conquest was not the sole cause of what happened thereafter; but because of it changes were abrupt and the period of disturbance longer. The ascendancy of French, indeed, was delayed until the second wave of immigrants came in the twelfth century with Henry of Anjou (1154), and it was then that the first important Latin works began to appear. The language of the Plantagenet court and society was French, and their political programme was to advance their continental claims with English support. Religion and history were expressed in Latin; law and romance in French. Devotional treatises were in French or in English, since in this field there was continuity of the English tradition. But all the other ground had to be reconquered.

The English language suffered profound changes, and during the whole period was remarkably fluid. Anglo-Saxon literature had begun to crystallize round the West Saxon dialect, but with the loss of prestige at court, the language tended to dissolve into its component dialects. The opposition between Northern and Southern English, still partly valid, sometimes corresponded to differences of literary schools. The friction of discordant forms led to the loss of the old complicated grammatical system, and the transformation of English into the very simple analytical language we know to-day. Many latinisms and gallicisms lodged in the speech, with the result that it is now three-fifths Romance in its vocabulary, though predominantly Germanic in its colloquial use. So far has it been removed from its Old English form that Anglo-Saxon is in effect, to a modern Englishman, an unfamiliar foreign language. This strangeness is increased by a fundamental change in versification: in place of the old alliterative verse of Germanic type there came into use a verse pattern based on the French system of syllable and rhyme. Present-day English verse is neither French nor Germanic, though more like French; it has, however, more freedom of construction and rhythm than is known in France. There have been critics who, impressed by this sense of difference, refuse to begin the history of English literature before Chaucer or, at any rate, before the conquest; but they have been wrong. What we have to consider is not a new beginning, but the violence of the struggle within the old tradition.

We may follow this struggle in the domain of historical writing. Many of the most vivid passages of the *Anglo-Saxon Chronicle* were written after the conquest, and the last entry is for the year 1154. The use of English in this sphere, therefore, persisted for a century after the disaster. The Latin tradition begins with William of Malmesbury,[1] who wrote his *De gestis regum Anglorum* before 1125, and his *Historia novella* after 1142. Though the language has changed, the interest is profoundly national. The writer takes Bede for his model and the *Chronicle* for his chief source. His literary ambitions and anxiety to tell good stories, coupled with a certain want of organization, make him disappointing to historians, but of more value to students of literary culture. His compilation is indeed a chief source for our knowledge of Old English oral literature. With Matthew Paris,[2] monk of St. Albans, Anglo-Latin history-writing reached its highest point. He was an annalist working in a monastic writing-room, like the compilers of the *Chronicle*, and had an amazing range of information. But he was also an excellent penman, an illuminator, an expert in heraldry and in map-drawing, and his great codex is a combined product of all these arts. A modern reprint gives only a glimpse of the real work, which, being designed for a different sort of publicity, should be judged as it was constituted by the author.

Beside these and other great chronicles in the Latin tongue, there were historical and pseudo-historical works of more

[1] William of Malmesbury (*c*. 1095–*c*. 1143). *De gestis regum Anglorum* and *Historia novella*, ed. Stubbs (Rolls Series), *Gesta Pontificum, Antiquitates ecclesiae Glastonburiae, Vita Dunstani, Liber de miraculis B. V. Mariae.*

[2] Matthew Paris (*c*. 1200–59). Professed in 1217. Continued Roger of Wendover's *Flores Historiarum*, known as the *Chronicle magna (sive majora) S. Albani*, which covered the period from the Creation to 1235. Wrote the *Historia Anglorum (sive ut vulgo dicitur Historia minor)*, covering the period 1067–1253 (ed. Madden, Rolls Series), of which the years 1241–9 are extant in his own handwriting. Other works have been attributed to him, notably *Vitae duae Offarum, Liber de gestis abbatum.*

popular appeal in French, such as Geoffrey Gaimar's *Estorie des Engleis* and the Norman Wace's *Roman de Rou*. These are verse chronicles. But there was no use of English until John of Trèves (or de Trevisa) translated Ranulph Higden's *Polychronicon* in 1387. Higden, who died in 1364, states that in his time even "uplandish men" strove to learn French, English being little in demand; but John of Trèves declares that "now children of the grammar schools know no more French than their left heels" and that "gentlemen have now much left for to teach their children French."

Two other historians writing in Latin were Gerald of Wales and Geoffrey of Monmouth. Gerald was a brilliant journalist, with an acute sense of topical appeal, an endless fund of good stories, of seeming omniscience, of zeal for great causes, and of fundamental instability. He[1] was qualified by his descent from both Norman and Welsh aristocracy to do justice to Wales in Norman eyes by his *Journey* and his *Description*. It is free from the unfriendliness which mars his account of the Irish and veers between candid criticism and passionate eulogy. Although he thought the work of his fellow Welshman, Geoffrey of Monmouth,[2] mendacious enough to shame the devil, he supported Geoffrey's attempt to unite Welsh and French pretensions in contempt of the English. This is Geoffrey of Monmouth's motive for describing the fabulous victories of the Welsh emperor, Arthur, over the Anglo-Saxon invaders. With a great show of historical science, in which a little truth was used to give credit to an ocean of fables, he

[1] Gerald of Barry, or of Wales (Giraldus Cambrensis) (*c.* 1145– *c.* 1220). Born at Manorbier, in Pembroke, and related on his mother's side to Prince Rhys. Archdeacon of Brecknock and twice candidate for the mitre of St. David's. He supported the ecclesiastical policy of Becket, and his advancement was blocked by Henry II. Travelled widely. In 1185 he accompanied Prince John to Ireland, and in 1188 helped Archbishop Baldwin to preach a crusade in Wales. Among his works are: *Itinerarium Kambriae, Descriptio Kambriae, Topographia Hiberniae, Expugnatio Hiberniae, De rebus a se gestis,* etc. The first two are translated in Everyman's Library.

[2] Geoffrey Arthur or Geoffrey of Monmouth (d. 1154). Was at Oxford in 1129, and claimed to base the *Historia regum Britoniae* (*c.* 1135, ed. Acton Griscom, trans. Sebastian Evans) on an ancient British book in the possession of Archdeacon Walter of Oxford. Became Bishop of St. Asaph. The poetical *Vita Merlini* is also attributed to him. He may have been a Briton.

traced the Welsh glories back to Brutus, a grandson of Aeneas, the founder of Rome, and tied up the whole story with the pretensions of his Norman masters by the prophecies of Merlin. His work was one of the most famous in the Middle Ages, and acutely disappointing to a modern reader. The Latin is weak and turgid. As history it ignores even such sources as survive in Wales to this day, having no more substantial basis than a meagre list of names and two well-known works; as fiction, it seems flat. But perhaps improvements would have made the book less successful, since its first appeal may have lain in its barefaced manipulation of certain easily ascertainable classical facts, and its dullness makes it the more like a chronicle. Geoffrey stretched canvases for others to fill in; historians did not tire of repeating the history of Brut, Lud and Lear; political pamphleteers found in Merlin a murky figure of a prophet greatly to their liking; and novelists discovered that any invention would be credited if attached to the court of good King Arthur.

Gaimar's Norman-French rendering of the Brutus history has been lost, but Wace's *Roman de Brut* (1155) introduced it to France and to laymen in England. The circle is completed by the English renderings of Layamon (*Brut, c.* 1205 and *c.* 1250) and Robert of Gloucester. Though denounced by contemporaries, the fiction was too useful to be dropped. Gerald of Barry uses it, and all later historians down to the time of Milton. The later history of Merlin's prophecies belongs to pamphleteering rather than literature. As for King Arthur, later romancers did not share Geoffrey's preference for Gawain and made little use of his episodes, but they used the name as a precipitant for the vast amount of fictional material of a certain kind which then seems to have been available. Some of it was Breton, and represented a French discovery of the fictional resources of the Armorican people. The Breton lay was cultivated with most success by Marie de France, under the patronage of kings of England. In her work marvellous and chivalrous exploits are performed by otherwise unknown heroes. But this sort of fiction gained in bulk and confidence when the protagonists were known as Knights of the Round Table, under such famous names as

B*

Lancelot, Perceval, Galahad, Tristan. The development of the Arthurian cycle was due primarily to the great outburst of romantic story-telling in France, but many of the romancers were subjects of the English king. The Norman Thomas was one such and possibly Robert de Boron. The development of the Grail story is associated by name with the Welshman, Walter Map, another shadowy figure of Geoffrey's circle, whose name also covered a lot of jovial Latin verses; but neither attribution is sound. At long last the Arthurian fiction returned to England with the *Sir Tristram*, *Morte Arthur* (in two forms) and *Lancelot of the Laik* of the fourteenth and fifteenth centuries, until it gave its finest flower out of season in the book of Sir Thomas Malory (see p. 23).

Along with the Arthurian romances there came into England from France a considerable variety of popular works of fiction. Alexander the Great and the Trojan Wars, Breton lays, Byzantine and sentimental stories passed into circulation in the fourteenth and fifteenth centuries, but none were so well received as the series of rough adventures entitled *Guy of Warwick*, *Havelok*, *Bevis of Hampton* and *Horn*. Their course shows the disturbance caused by French ascendancy, for they dealt with English matter, but, being composed in French, they were not accessible to English speakers until about 1300. The first two are novelistic versions of the same event: Athelstan's battle of Brunanburh against Olaf Cuaran and Constantine III of Scots. They transform the affair into terms of romance, but the perversions in *Havelok* represent the standpoint of the Danish-occupied half of England as in the days of Canute the Great, and may once have been used to further the Danish policy. Some kind of settled narrative must have existed for the use of the Norman storytellers who determined the final form for each romance, and who retained the sole use of these legends during the twelfth and thirteenth centuries.

The language of theology was, as we have said, Latin. There were many Englishmen among the great figures of scholasticism, who exerted a mighty influence in their time, though their work has been lost to their countrymen. In the twelfth century there are solitary wandering scholars who accept Spanish benefices in order to translate Arabian books; later there are the schoolmen of Paris and Oxford, Duns Scotus, the critic of Aquinas, and William of Ockham, who revealed the secret contradictions of medieval philosophy. Earlier than these flourished the best latinist and the most humane thinker of them all, John of Salisbury, the author of *Polycraticus*, or "statesman's handbook," which is advancing in esteem to-day. He was a candid and open-eyed traveller, and his witness to Peter Abelard's great struggle for freedom of thought is invaluable.

The languages of devotion were Anglo-Norman and English.[1] In Anglo-Norman were composed metrical renderings of the Scriptures, hymns and prayers, lives of saints, commentaries and prose sermons, by authors of considerable fame and talent. They were addressed to the pious wealthy, who had leisure and resources for the patronage of literature. The English homilies lacked this support, but their fame has been more enduring. They carried on unbroken a tradition of simple, lucid, generous, musical prose from the Anglo-Saxon homilies of Ælfric to the moral works of More and Latimer. The texts upon which they comment are translated with simple dignity, forming a bridge between the noble prose of the Anglo-Saxon Bible and that of George Tyndale and the Authorized Version. The recipients were often pious women. In all lands that sex is the firmest support of the vernacular, and the least patient of pretentious writing. Three sisters in Dorset received the *Ancrene Riwle* (Anchoresses' Rule) in the early years of the thirteenth century, the first satisfying monument of Middle English prose, and a certain Dame Margaret Kirkby was the dedicatee of several of Richard Rolle's treatises. But though the language and treatment are simple, the foundation of these works is sound scholarship and their authors are masters of Latin. This also they have in common with their Old English forebears and their Renaissance followers. Richard

---

[1] For Anglo-Norman literature consult J. Vising, *Anglo-Norman Language and Literature*, Oxford, 1923; and for Anglo-Norman, Anglo-Latin and English see W. H. Schofield, *English Literature from the Norman Conquest to Chaucer*, London, 1906.

Rolle of Hampole stands out as a saintly personality of enormous influence, whose canonization was confidently antici- pated. He wrote (in Latin and English) lyrics, meditations, a rendering of the Psalter, epistles and delightful moral stories. Others who, as writers, have no less merit are still unknown to the general reading public of to-day, though they created masterpieces of English prose like *The Scale of Perfection* and *The Cloud of Unknowing*.[1]

The same moral and religious earnestness inspires certain other works of the fourteenth century which are signs of the coming maturity of Middle English literature. There is a group of poems in the North Midland dialect—*Pearl*, *Purity*, *Patience*, *Sir Gawain and the Green Knight*—which are possibly the work of one author, an inspired anonymous poet. The attraction for him—if we are dealing with one poet, and not with a group— of the old alliterative poetry is evident; as for rhyme, he some- times neglects it, sometimes uses it with virtuosity. His metrical skill is great, and he has a gift for telling phrases. *Sir Gawain* is his most ambitious effort, and in it he freely remodels an Arthurian story so that it will serve as a pattern of virtue, thus anticipating the *Faerie Queene*. In the *Pearl* he writes as a father overcome by sorrow for the loss of his baby daughter, doubtless called Margaret. The habits of the age give him symbols for his thoughts in the form of allegory and biblical paraphrase. No poet can compose without the aid of these or other conventions; but this unnamed singer ranks among the great mourners, not far from the Shelley of the *Adonais*, by virtue of his sincere and poignant expression of changing phases of grief: the stunned sensation changing to wild hope when he sees the beloved vision, then impatience, despair, doctrinal comfort, resignation, and the calm of passion spent.

[1] See R. W. Chambers, *On the Continuity of English Prose from Alfred to More*, Oxford Univ. Press, 1932. Richard Rolle (c. 1300–49). Born probably at Thornton Dale, near Pickering. Studied at Oxford for a time. At the age of nineteen retired to live as a solitary at Hampole. Wrote: *Incendium Amoris*, *Judice me Deus*, *English Psalter*, *Meditations on the Passion*, *The Form fo Living*, etc. A convenient anthology is by Hope Emily Allen, *The English Writings of Richard Rolle*, Oxford Univ. Press. 1931.

The name of William Langland[1] survives to account for the composition of *Piers Plowman*, but we know of him no more than he has chosen to say in this book, which has more than one theme and manner. A medieval "book," owing to the labour of writing and cost of materials, was normally a miscellany; and by compensation, some authors were tempted to give a fictitious unity to heterogeneous compositions. So, for instance, Boccaccio did with the *Decamerone* and Juan Ruiz with his *Libro de buen Amor*. Langland's *Piers Plowman* is one only in its temper and style, like Wordsworth's *Ecclesiastical Sonnets*. We have no right to demand from it any other unity, and shall be disappointed if we do. The author takes up and drops the thread of narrative at will, and one of his charms is the unexpected darting of his mind. He writes an allegory, but the allegory suddenly crystallizes into persons and becomes veracious history. Lady Meed becomes, in all but name, Alice Perrers, King Edward III's mistress; and the Virtues and Vices plead their cause quite regularly at Westminster. A crime at St. Giles's Fair, Oxford, is part of the general indictment of Wrong, the King's officer; and the strengthless, well-meaning King is very like Richard II. Langland slips from allegory into plain sermons, and then we hear of Tom Stowe's troubles with his shrewish wife Felice, of Batt and Betty, Gilbert, Will and Watkin. These may have been the neighbours who complained—not without cause!—that their daily vexations had become immortal verse. But chiefly this flux and reflux of the mind affects his central, but tardily introduced,

---

[1] William Langland (*c.* 1332–*c.* 1400). *Piers Plowman*, ed. Skeat: modernized by A. M. Burrell for Everyman's Library. A chantry priest living in Cornhill, London, with his wife Kit and his daughter Kalot, he lived among Lollards, and says he annoyed his neighbours by including their names in his verses. Was probably of poor but free extraction. He opens his poem with a scene in the Malvern Hills, and he seems to have quarrelled at some time with the Abbot of Abingdon. His poem was used by the rebels of 1381 as formulating some of their grievances against churchmen and lawyers, but there is no evidence that he himself sympathized with any sort of political action. Revision, expansion and correction have given three different texts of this poem, labelled *A*, *B*, *C*. (*A*, 1362; *B*, 1377; *C*, *c.* 1398.) To him has been attributed also another alliterative piece, *Richard the Redeless*, dated September 1399.

figure of Piers Plowman, who is sometimes simply a man standing in the crowd, sometimes an evangelist, and sometimes the Man Christ Jesus. Once we cease to look for formal unity and a logical pattern, we experience a strange fascination in this misty poem, with its abrupt alternation of concrete certainty and dimmest outline.

What we gain from *Piers Plowman* is a singularly full and lively impression of the bustling life of the fourteenth century. Its moral condition is essentially that described by Chaucer and implicit in the teaching of the devotional writers. Langland sees it from beneath; his condemnation is more outspoken than Chaucer's, and yet, in a way, he seems to admit more hope of reformation. He sees hope, as others did, in the honest, godly labourer and his brother, the poor parson; in the world of unseen powers they have Conscience and Reason to their aid; and the words of his Plowman are a veritable gospel. But against them are the lofty oppressors: the robber barons, ravenous tax-gatherers, corrupt clergy, worldly monks, picaresque friars. These are destroyers above the people; but Langland does not spare the wastrels and hypocrites among the proletariat, nor is there any lowborn trick of pride, envy or malice that he does not know by familiar example. Quevedo's *Sueños* do not provide a larger repertoire of typical frauds, nor is Carlyle more convinced of the saving grace of hard work. But with all this, Langland is no satirist or reformer; he has a personal message of regeneration, but no political creed. At times he is inspired by the stubbornest conservatism. He takes no pleasure in wielding the flail, though words of censure are the most usual on his lips. The shortest line through language to his intent makes his style always nervous; he shuns nothing, and his phrases run from the barest prose to lines of piercing loveliness.

Very different was John Wyclif's[1] cast of mind, though his

[1] John Wyclif (*c.* 1320–84). Born at Hipswell. Studied at Oxford and was probably influenced by the teaching of Bradwardine on predestination, Fitzralph on dominion, and Ockham on the duty of priests. Master of Balliol College, 1360. Warden of Canterbury Hall, 1365, but soon ejected owing to doubtful election. On a mission for the government at Bruges, 1374. By 1377 he had developed his views on the authority of the Papacy, and was in conflict with the Church hierarchy,

problems were those of Langland. The secular spirit of the clergy and the abuse of ecclesiastical powers, the need for apostolic poverty and sincerity in religion, the ideal of the poor parson and laborious layman, were common to them both, but in Wyclif they took on a political complexion. He had been employed early as counsel for the Crown in the debate about papal claims; so had many others, but the investigation of the Pope's civil pretensions led him to challenge everything that sets the Bishop of Rome above other bishops. His theory of "dominion" had similar consequences. In itself it was merely an extreme position of a fairly common scholastic doctrine. Mariana and the Jesuits were later to defend tyrannicide, that is the punishment of the ruler who abused his powers. Put positively by Wyclif, "dominion" (possession or authority or enjoyment of any kind) was conditioned by righteousness; "he that standeth in grace is very lord of things." The principle was abstract and ethical, but as formulated in controversy with a Church accused of corrupt living, it seemed to give the nobility the right to revoke the rich donations of the past. So for a time their leaders favoured Wyclif, until it was seen that they also might forfeit their privileges on the same charge of breach of trust. His demand for apostolical poverty was that of St. Francis, Langland and Richard Rolle, but when Wyclif formally denied the Church's right to be wealthy, beyond bare sufficiency, he raised the political issues of disestablishment and disendowment. His advocacy of the Bible in English exceeded what had been accomplished by previous translators, in so far as it claimed for the individual Christian conscience the right of access, without intermediary, to the sources of the faith.

As a literary figure Wyclif has lost greatly in stature. It seems doubtful whether much of the Wyclifite Bible can be

---

especially Bishop Courtenay, but protected by John of Gaunt, Duke of Lancaster, and other nobles. In 1378 the Great Schism occurred. Wyclif's doctrines were condemned on twenty-four points by Bishop Courtenay in the same year. Orthodoxy triumphed at Oxford, and some of Wyclif's associates were affected, but he was living in semi-retirement as vicar of Lutterworth, occupied with his literary work and organizing his " poor priests ". He died unmolested in 1384. *De Dominio Divino*, 1376. Biblical translations, *c*. 1382-4.

referred to him. Its attempt to reproduce the Vulgate word by word makes it curiously gauche and un-English. The rhythms of Tyndale are not those of Wyclif, but of Rolle of Hampole and of the Anglo-Saxon version. It is difficult to distinguish his hand from that of his partisans in the numerous Wyclifite pamphlets; but they commonly lack form and grace, clarity of idiom or of argument. But with all these defects, Wyclif had made one great stride in the development of the English language. He had debated high questions of philosophy and government in the common tongue, and had caused moral issues to emerge from the circle of hermits and their votaries to be an absorbing popular interest. New mental territory had been annexed to the domain of the English mind, never again to be relinquished.

II. CHAUCER AND THE CHAUCERIANS

GEOFFREY CHAUCER,[1] "well of English undefiled" and second only to Dante among the poets of the Middle Ages, is the first author since Bede whose work can be read without allowance for the quaintness of antiquity. In its supreme moments its appeal is universal and timeless. Still the greatest of story-tellers in verse and unrivalled in humour, Chaucer defined by his example the canon of the poetic art. His most gifted contemporaries were attracted by the alliterative system, but

---

[1] Geoffrey Chaucer (c. 1340–1400). His father was a vintner of London in attendance on the court of Edward III, and Geoffrey entered the family of the Duke of Clarence as a page, passing later into attendance on John, Duke of Lancaster. The death of John's duchess was the occasion of his *Book of the Duchess* (1369). In 1372 he left England for Italy on royal business and stayed for about eleven months. From 1374 he occupied various posts in the civil service, especially in the department of Customs, though not without interruptions, and he paid a second visit to Italy. *Boëthius*, 1377–8. *Troilus and Criseyde*, 1379–83. *The House of Fame*, 1383–4. *Legend of Good Women*, 1385–6. *Canterbury Tales* begun in 1386. They include much earlier matter and were continued during the rest of his life. *Treatise on the Astrolabe*, 1391, dedicated to his son Lewis.

Chaucer adhered firmly to the prosody of rhyme and number. Alliteration, not being with him a metric principle, he used as a vehicle of emotion. English syllables are unlike in stress and duration, so that English verse cannot readily follow the strictly numerical plan of the French. Account must be taken of the accents in scansion and different types of feet accepted as equivalent. By his tact Chaucer was able to surmount these formidable difficulties, and to leave English prosody securely founded. The heroic couplet has had no greater master. It is only in language that there is a difficulty in approaching Chaucer without preparation. He keeps final syllables which have since disappeared, and were even then obsolescent in the northern dialects. To scan one must pronounce his "mute" *e*'s as in French verse, but whereas the French are accustomed to do this violence to their normal speech habits, it is for the English an unusual, and now somewhat unwelcome, proceeding. Chaucer's vocabulary contains many terms which have gone out of circulation, especially those which have been replaced by Latin coinages of the Renaissance. Yet these difficulties have to be surmounted. Modernization of Chaucer's language is impossible, for the effect of his verse is calculated to the minutest detail of sound and rhythm, and no other will suffice.

Chaucer's profound originality is, as so often in literature, to be measured by his wider indebtedness. His style was formed by his translation of the opening portion of the *Roman de la Rose*. (Fragment *A* of the English rendering, comprising 1,705 lines, is certainly by Chaucer.) Thereby he learned to handle the octosyllabic couplet (applied later in the *Book of the Duchess* and *The House of Fame*), as well as narrative art, the technique of allegory and the elements of psychology. For his ballades he acknowledges an obligation to "Granson, flower of them that make in France." Dante supplied the suggestion for the *House of Fame*, but little else; the genius of Geoffrey Chaucer was anything but Dantesque. The educative influence of Ovid and Boëthius was more important, but that of Boccaccio was supreme. Chaucer's *Knight's Tale* is from Boccaccio's *Teseide*, his *Clerk's Tale* from Petrarch's rendering of Boccaccio's story of Griseldis, his *Monk's Tale* related to the *De Casibus*, and his *Troilus* to the *Filostrato*. More remarkable than these borrowings was the spiritual affinity of the two writers, each supremely endowed as a storyteller, though their media were distinct, each a humanist before Humanism, each ranging through many varieties of experience. The *Decamerone* and the *Canterbury Tales* are the more closely akin for the want of direct material contacts. Boccaccio's masterpiece is more uniform and finished, but Chaucer has the poet's prerogative of opening new horizons. On the other hand, he derived no inspiration from Petrarch's perfecting of the sonnet, nor saw in Dante more than a graver kind of allegorist. In these matters his taste had been fixed by his French readings, and nothing in his temperament urged him to seek further.

The *Book of the Duchess* attracts attention chiefly for the neatness of its execution and for the happy lines in which the dead lady is remembered. Chaucer proves proficient in the use of conventional resources: the eight-syllabled couplet, the dream motif, and the fable of Ceyx from Ovid. Similar devices give us the *House of Fame*, but with the addition, in the second book, of some typical Chaucerian humour. The short line, however, lacked the flexibility which he found in the decasyllable of all his best poetry. This latter is combined in stanzas of seven lines to make the "rhyme royal," which was Chaucer's peculiar contribution to metrics. The strophe readily blends with others to make a continuous narrative, and has the advantage over *ottava rima* that there is no temptation to be slick in a final couplet. At the same time, the unequal number of the lines and the lacing of the rhymes preserves the identity of the individual stanza. Spenser added a ninth line to the *ottava rima* to make a still nobler metre for continuous verse, but he laid an additional burden on a language which is not rich in rhyme: Chaucer's rhyme royal is more manageable, and it amply satisfied the needs of the best poets that followed him.

It is not only in virtue of this lovely stanza that *Troilus and Criseyde* is the flower of romance. The pathos of the tale is effective in Chaucer's telling amid the elegance and leisure of the genre. He draws his characters like a master, though using the two-dimensional technique which fits this decorative style. His language is supple indeed, and rises without effort to every demand. Nowhere else is he so Spenserian; Spenser has only the additional beauty of notes longer drawn out. For all the subtleties of rhythm, alliteration, pauses and flow from line to line, in this poem Chaucer stands second to none, nor can it be deemed to lack anything but a more copious assurance of real human experience. The *Legend of Good Women*, in couplets, forms a bridge between this poem and the *Canterbury Tales*. Its matter is classical love-tragedy, but the prologue is instinct with realism. It serves as a preliminary study for the sovereign art of the *Canterbury Tales*.

Written at various dates and with various intentions, these *Tales*, whose series is incomplete, are unequal in merit. There are some which have to be excluded in any fair estimate of Chaucer's achievement. Those that remain are remarkable for their variety of texture. In many different styles Chaucer shows the same consummate mastery. The romantic manner is exemplified in his *Knight's Tale* of Palamon and Arcite and in the unfinished *Squire's Tale* of Cambuscan bold, which so fascinated Milton. The *Clerk's Tale* of Griseldis and her constancy bears a moral more operative in the Middle Ages than to-day, but the Wife of Bath's advocacy of the rule of women is sempiternal. Rabelaisian guffaws mark the progress of stories told by the clerical riffraff of that company, but there is conventional propriety in the words of the Monk and Prioress, and evangelical dullness in those of the Poor Parson. The beast epic has never excelled the *Nun's Priest's Tale* of Chantecleer and Pertelote. Goethe's *Reineke Fuchs* is longer, but not more perfect in its kind. But fine as the stories are, they are excelled by their prologues, for it is here that the keenness of Chaucer's perceptions is best displayed. The succession of characters in the general prologue is an epitome of the age. Chaucer deals with types, but the persons he describes have individuality within the type. His estimate of English society is thus easily ascertained, and beneath its humour and sympathy it is desperate enough. The clergy in particular are deeply discredited, as they are in Langland, and vary from the picaresque to the worldly and conventional. Like Langland,

Chaucer sees hope chiefly in the Poor Parson and his brother the Ploughman. Knighthood, rightly understood, both conceive to be a redeeming service, and Chaucer feels the upspringing of hope in the generous enthusiasm of a new generation, typified by his Squire. Yet Langland, in the midst of his denunciations, seems more optimistic than Chaucer, since he sets forth regeneration as a practicable policy. Chaucer seems to accept the world as it was, and is, with a shrug. But in the types as individuals Chaucer discloses more fully his sympathy. His rogues have, at any rate, vitality and resource which would serve better ends. His Monk and Prioress, whatever criticisms may be made against their performance of their vows, have the qualities of a good sportsman and a refined and delightful lady, respectively. The Merchant is short-sighted, selfish, cunning, but venturesome and competent. The Knight and Squire, for all their worthiness, have pleasant foibles. Above all, the Wife of Bath is an amazing embodiment of vitality, surging coarsely, but in triumph, from the nether springs; and though she resembles many another lusty gadabout of the pilgrimages, she is indescribably the one and only Wife of Bath. Two styles of humour are exemplified in these characterizations. If humour arises from some risible disproportion between the thing itself and the way it is said, then the proportions of too much or too little lead to the two methods of exaggeration and understatement. Recent practice has caused us to suppose that the one is "American," the other "English," but "Dan" Chaucer is the unrivalled master of them both. Nor does his humour age. Based on things rather than words, whether sly or broad it requires no commentary and is void of fatigue. He has suffered like other humorists from the charge of superficiality. Doubtless Dante or Shakespeare delves deeper; but Chaucer, like Homer, will reveal profundities to a reflective mind.

Nor should we pass wholly in silence Chaucer's contribution to prose. His *Parson's Tale*, indeed, is a strange relapse from the simple neatness achieved by the mystics of that century, but Chaucer showed in his *Boëthius* that the vernacular could serve as a secondary tool for the philosopher, and his *Astrolabe* is a competent piece of scientific prose. Reginald Pecock was to use English for the study of politics and Sir John Fortescue for law in the next century. These were important steps in the reconquest of the English domain, but Chaucer had taken the essential step before them.

After such brilliant auspices the performance of the English Chaucerians is disappointing: "the moral Gower and philosophical Strode," "Lydgate laureate," Hoccleve and Hawes. They stood too close to Chaucer, and imitated instead of learning. The master was for them a "rose of rhetors all," and they piled on the rhetoric as they lengthened their poems to unmanageable dimensions. The language also was breaking in their hands, and they scarcely knew whether to count or ignore many syllables that no longer had meaning for them. Perhaps only John Gower[1] can still be read with pleasure. He uses the octosyllabic couplet of Chaucer's youth for his *Confessio Amantis*, and it becomes intolerable as it jigs through many thousands of lines; but Gower tells effectively an unvarnished tale, and contemporaries were grateful to him for unfailingly pointing to a moral.

The veritable successors of Chaucer were the Scottish Chaucerians.[2] Captured at the age of three and long a prisoner in the Tower of London, King James I was able to imbibe the prosody and manner and the very dialect of Chaucer. In *The Kingis Quair*[3] his first sight of Lady Joan Beaufort, as she walked in the garden beneath his prison window, is a refreshing variant of the common formula of a vision; the subsequent dream and its allegory are encumbrances. Robert Henryson used the Chaucerian stanza in order to continue the poet's *Troilus and Criseyde*. His *Testament of Criseyde* might claim to be the finest poem in the Scottish language. It is forthright

[1] John Gower (d. 1408). *Works*, ed. G. C. Macaulay. Of a good Kentish family and in easy circumstances; a friend to Chaucer, and an author favoured by John, Duke of Lancaster. It was on behalf of Queen Philippa, the Duke's daughter, that a translation of the *Confessio Amantis* was made into Portuguese: a further translation into Spanish is extant. His *Speculum meditantis* or *Mirour de l'omme* was in French, *Vox clamantis* in Latin, and *Confessio Amantis* in English. These were frequently revised by the author.

[2] The Scottish Chaucerians. See M. M. Gray, *Scottish Poetry from Barbour to James VI*.

[3] James I (1394–1437). His authorship has been disputed, but the poem stands in his name and reveals emotions he alone can have felt.

in the best national manner. Criseyde, abandoned by her seducer, reduced to despair and made horrible by disease, is a tragic figure as familiar in great cities as is the homely fireside which Henryson describes in the opening lines. The pity of it rises to poignant anguish when she, so deformed as to be unrecognizable, meets the still gallant victor, Troilus, whose love she had lightly rejected, and the obscure workings of past tenderness in his mind testify to the poet's extraordinary insight. Chaucer's romance comes to life as something acute, personal and poignantly familiar, but Henryson does not fall into the error of homeliness. On the contrary, he heightens the decorative setting with a council of the gods and the personal intervention of Saturn and Cynthia for the punishment of Criseyde; he obliges the reader to keep his distance, and also makes more credible the catastrophic change in the heroine's condition. His language also has both richness and forthright honesty; to which, in his inimitable *Fables*, he added humour. William Dunbar, following Henryson, proved less inspired. He had not the same gift for large design, and comes before us primarily as a lyric poet. He was more bookish in his choice of themes, and saw less of life. The influence of Lydgate supervened on that of Chaucer and led him into intricate rhyming and the use of the "aureate" phrase. By so much the less has he power to move the heart, yet he is a rich, skilful and entertaining writer, and can speak plainly and well in such pieces as his *London* and *Aberdeen*. His apogee is reached in the *Lament of the Makars* (Poets) which, in its brooding on the mystery of death, is not far behind Villon and Jorge Manrique, while its appreciative catalogue of Scottish poets is proof of a literature in being. Gavin Douglas's translation of the *Aeneid* was made from the original, not unworthily, and was adorned with prologues which are remarkable for their direct observation of nature. His description of Winter, from the prologue to the seventh book, might not have been bettered by Wordsworth. The verse essay on Translation (prologue to Book I) foreshadows a genre which the eighteenth century developed.[1]

[1] Robert Henryson (*c.* 1425–1506), schoolmaster in Dunfermline. *The Testament of Criseyde, Orpheus and Eurydice, Robene and Makyne, Fables.*

William Dunbar (*c.* 1460–*c.* 1530). Apart from the poems cited, his

These authors employed "Inglis" as their language, that is, the Northern or Scottish variant of the English tongue. More homogeneous than Southern English, it possesses a fine store of racy expressions and its own system of associations. These should not be lost to the common weal, and it is the Scottish littérateur's business to transmit his own inherited resources. Such regionalism is not parochial, but is the necessary corrective to undue centralization and loss of innate power. The achievements of the Scottish Chaucerians are the basis and model of all attempts to give a Scottish colour to writing done north of the Tweed, and they head a line which passes through Burns and Scott to Barrie and present-day writers of the Scottish Revival.

In England, on the other hand, an Arthurian masterpiece was born out of its time in *Le Morte d'Arthur*, by Sir Thomas Malory.[1] Completed in 1469, it was printed in a somewhat mutilated form by Caxton in 1483, and the best appreciation of the book is still that of its first printer. All noble lords and ladies, with all other estates (Caxton said) "shall find many joyous and pleasant histories, and noble and renowned acts of humanity, gentleness, and chivalries. For herein may be seen noble chivalry, courtesy, humanity, friendliness, hardiness, love, friendship, cowardice, murder, hate, virtue, and sin. Do after the good and leave the evil, and it shall bring you to good fame and renown. And for to pass the time this book shall be pleasant to read in." The chivalrous ideal had been dead for a hundred years and the age was treacherous and practical; but by a miracle of style Malory recalled its palmiest days, and his Arthur and Lancelot are such as any English gentleman fain would be.

During the whole medieval period the written literature was

---

satires merit attention. He was perhaps the most variously gifted of the Scottish writers.

Gavin Douglas (*c.* 1475–1522).

Sir David Lindsay (1490–1555) was also a satirist, with a direct and mordant style, but his work lacks the liberating grace of poetry.

[1] Sir Thomas Malory or Maleore. Recently identified with a knight of that name, of Newbold Revel, a retainer of Richard Beauchamp, Earl of Warwick, who had seen service in France and, in 1451, was accused and found guilty of various turbulent acts. He may have written his book in prison.

backed by a lively oral or semi-oral tradition. All works were composed to be recited before an audience, the latter being either largely illiterate or at least impatient of reading. In the drama and in certain forms of lyrico-narrative poetry this liveliness led to the formation of large traditional *corpora*, of which fragments have descended to this day. Dramatic performances marked the chief holidays of the calendar, such as Christmas, Corpus Christi, and Easter, and the repertoire of plays was gathered into cycles in such places as York, Chester, Coventry and Wakefield. Performed by artisans, members of guilds, the Miracle plays became a popular summary of the biblical narrative, embroidered with sketches from real life, generally by way of comic interlude. So we have come to know Mac the sheep-stealer and Noah's shrewish wife. A stage in three tiers represented Heaven, middle Earth, and Hell, and simple conventions gave the clues to the personages. Superior to these naïve performances were the Morality plays, which dramatized the story of redemption by means of allegorical figures. *Everyman* is the best of the Moralities, both for its strong dramatic appeal and its wide human sweep. The author's skill appears less in the printed word than when the piece is played on a stage with an austerity like its original setting.

The religious lyrics of the age are numerous, both signed and unsigned, but those which have an abiding place in the English memory are the carols. The word "carol" implied originally a round or chain dance, at first of women only, and then of men and women. A precentor sang the words of a song as the dancers moved round, and they repeated the refrain while making a brief pause. This song, with refrain, was also known as a carol. Carols might be on any theme. Many of the most interesting medieval ones are partisan and political, but in time the practice came to be associated with religious occasions, and especially with the Christmas festival. It is in this sense that carols survive, and carry into the life of the twentieth century the wistful loveliness of medieval sentiment. The number of carols has been swollen by the inclusion of genuine ballads, such as *The Carnal and the Crane*, without reference to the original form.

The carol differs from the ballad not in origin (since the

ballads also seem to arise out of the round dance of the carol), but in transmission, treatment and manner. There was generally written support for the carols, which, with their frequent use of tags from Latin hymns, were more the disport of the clerical class. Ballads remained strictly oral until well into the seventeenth century. We know, consequently, much more of the literary history of carols, but that of the ballads has to be inferred from conjectures. The carol separated text and refrain; the ballads, when they had a refrain, tended to interline the two. It is doubtful whether the English and Scottish ballads were ever danced. Some clearly were shaped for simple recitation, and among ballads in dance form we find many which have migrated from Scandinavia, where, indeed, they were used for this purpose. No dances have survived, but much of the music has been recovered in Britain and America. It is often of haunting charm, and is as traditional as the text. The text, indeed, only yields its full meaning when sung, for the music is its most perfect enunciation.

The apogee of the English and Scottish[1] traditional ballads was in the century from 1450 to 1550. The theme of one ballad, *Sir Aldingar*, we know to have been popular in the songs of the twelfth century, and there is a manuscript of *Judas* from the thirteenth, but, unlike the carols, there is little written testimony to them at an early date. After 1550 a new type developed in England owing to the facilities offered by the press. It was by known authors and more topical and ephemeral. Ballads of this kind continued in large numbers through to the eighteenth century, but the traditional style retreated to Scotland, and in Scotland to Aberdeenshire. Large numbers have been recovered from parts of America, where new ballads of cowboys, negroes, lumberjacks and others have been created. The traditional ballads are English and Scottish, and no firm line can be drawn between the two nations. In general, however, the English ballad is akin to the short verse romances which

---

[1] Ballads. F. J. Child, *English and Scottish Ballads* (there is a reliable one-volume edition edited by Professor G. L. Kittredge). Child gave a few tunes in his fifth volume, but a first impression of ballad tunes is best obtained from J. Goss, *Ballads of Britain*. For their international relations, see W. J. Entwistle's *European Balladry*.
The best collection of English carols is by R. L. Greene.

were the delight of the fourteenth-century populace. The Robin Hood ballads are English and were known to William Langland, and there are political ones on English affairs. The Scottish ballads are those of the Border, those referring to feuds and tragedies in Scotland, and a large body of international songs which have come from Denmark. Thanks to these, the affinity of this corpus with Scandinavia is a distinguishing mark, though there are also attachments between some English songs and French *chansons populaires*.

The ballad charm is indescribable. One must read, or rather sing, *Tam Lin, The Outlandish Knight, The Three Ravens, Chevy Chase, Edward, Child Waters, Clerk Saunders, Fair Annie*, and so many others. It is easier to say what part they have played in literature. They have collected fragments from all the literary types accessible in earlier times (heroic, religious, historical, romantic), and in the process of oral transmission have pruned away all oddities of fashion or form. What remains is quintessential; characters, episodes, language, are universally valid; the whole treatment is discreet and economical, and the phrasing of the best ballads is the perfected conclusion of a myriad preferences. Falling into disuse as a result of the competition of the printed broadsheets, the traditional pieces were rediscovered in the middle of the eighteenth century by Bishop Percy, and gathered into his *Reliques of Ancient English Poetry* (1767). The effect was electrical. The simple nervous eloquence of the ballads made a clean sweep of faded rhetoric not merely in England, but in Germany and all the rest of Europe. Spreading from country to country they called attention to the ballad riches dormant in other lands, while stimulating the production of original lyrics of like style and merit. In this way there came to light, slowly but joyously, the immense oral literature of all Europe, of which the English and Scottish ballads are but a part.

The Middle Ages should not be left without a glance at the *Paston Letters*. They were not intended for publication, and indeed their prose is often flat or involved, but they have the freshness of all spontaneous utterances. The characters of the various members of the Paston family, and especially of Agnes,

Margaret and John, peep through the correspondence, which (covering the years 1434 to 1509) is of unique interest for the private lives of English people during the period of the Wars of the Roses and the Tudor settlement.

THE ENGLISH CLASSICS

III. DECISIVE STEPS (1475–1625)

THREE things, according to Bacon, distinguished his age from all its predecessors: the invention of printing, which has revolutionized literature; the invention of gunpowder, which has revolutionized war; and the discovery of the compass, which has revolutionized geography. We may phrase them differently, but the effect is the same: a complete change in the outlook of civilized man. The invention of printing transferred literature from audiences to readers: easing the strain on memory, it allowed for reperusal and more intimate appreciation, not only by single scholars in monastic libraries, but by a vast new middle class. To them it conveyed the liberating influence of Humanism, and the moral and aesthetic stimulus of the English Bible. The discovery of gunpowder was one of a vast number of scientific observations which increased the content of knowledge far beyond that of the ancients, and rendered anachronistic the blind veneration of Aristotle's works. America was discovered because of an inference made by Columbus from these observations; the discovery enormously augmented material knowledge, and Bacon devised his New Logic, in order to convert observed into systematic Science. Before continuing our history of literature proper, it seems desirable to note these developments as they are linked to certain names, themselves of high literary repute.

William Caxton[1] issued his first English printed books at Bruges, but by September 1474 he was in London, embarked on his bold publishing venture. Though not always faithful to

[1] William Caxton (c. 1422–91). Born of a merchant family, he passed to the Low Countries, where he was for a time acting governor of the Merchants Adventurers. He learned to print at Cologne, probably in 1471, his first book being his own rendering of the *Recuyll of the Historyes of Troye*, 1474. Established at the sign of the Red Pale in Westminster, he issued Lord Rivers's *Dictes and Sayings of the Philosophers* in 1477. He benefited from the patronage of King Edward IV and many noblemen, issued Malory, Chaucer, Gower, and others, up to a total of about ninety-six works and 18,000 pages. He had few helpers, though Wynkyn de Worde and other early printers seem to have been his pupils.

his originals, Caxton was distinguished for his conception of the educational mission of the printer, both in the material content of his publications and in the determination of spelling and idiom, and (though less happily) in the increase of stylistic resources.

Printing powerfully seconded the influence of Humanism which, in England, was perfected in Sir (now Saint) Thomas More.[1] His friends thought him "the sole genius of England," and the Emperor Charles V rated his value as above the best city of his dominions. The first English writer after Bede to win an international reputation, he is the first after Chaucer to stand before us as a fully rounded personality. Chaucer declares himself, but More is known by himself and others. We see him at more intimate moments, walking in his Chelsea garden with Henry VIII's arm round his neck or conversing with "son Roper" or receiving the last passionate, sorrowful kiss from his daughter, Margaret. Roper's *Life* gives us specimens of his table-talk, which was pregnant, witty and graced with apt illustrations. He reproduces More's oration on behalf of the Commons' freedom of debate: a studied discourse, carefully phrased, submissive, yet firm upon principle. A word frequently applied to him is "merry," implying a cheerful serenity which did not desert him on the scaffold. A gentle irony played over his conversation as over his writings, his uprightness made a bad king determined to wring from him a word of approval, and his conciliatory demeanour caused friendly judges to forget that he would never compromise on principle. With those of his circle in London, as with Erasmus, Vives and other friends abroad, private living had become graceful, and with none was this more evident than with More who, in his smilingly serious way, set aside time to "commune with my wife, chat with my children, and talk with my ser-

[1] Sir Thomas More (1478–1535). Brought up in the house and under the patronage of Cardinal Morton. Admitted at Lincoln's Inn, 1496. Lived religiously without vows for four years at the Charterhouse. Friend of Erasmus and Vives. Speaker of the Commons, 1523. Chancellor, 1529. Opposed Henry VIII's divorce and refused to take the oath prescribed by the Act of Supremacy, 1534. Executed, 1535. *Utopia*, 1516. *Richard III* (unfinished). *Dialogue of Comfort against Tribulation*, 1534. Controversial writings against Tyndale. Lives by Roper, Stapledon and Harpsfield.

vants." Such practices were, no doubt, not unprecedented, but
it was Humanism that assigned to them—to man as a private
individual—their worth.

Though we know More so well, we see him only in glimpses,
and in no respect are these so tantalizing as in his writings.
That he was a very great literary figure contemporary fame
attests, but his writings are few and short. We have to draw
large inferences from scanty premises, and these have been
further reduced by the obloquy that fell on his name with his
death. More died because he did not admit that the *raison
d'état* was the paramount law; the State could not (he held)
set aside the law of God, the temporal could not dispose of
the spiritual. Accounts of his martyrdom were circulated by
English Catholics abroad, and became paity documents, but
at home the most favourable lamented "that a man of so
incomparable wit, of so profound knowledge, of so absolute
learning, and of so fine eloquence was yet nevertheless so
blinded, rather with obstinacy than with ignorance, that he
could not, or rather would not, see the shining light of God's
holy truth in certain principal points of Christian religion."
His case was aggravated by his opposition to George Tyndale,
the grounds whereof have been much misunderstood. The
result was that his work was ignored by the succeeding age, and
his character and merits have not been prized until our own.

More's *Utopia*, written in Latin, was ranked by Vives
immediately behind the dialogues of Cicero. Had More
given us the English of it we should not have been offended
by the roughness of Raphe Robinson's Elizabethan version,
for, with no less liveliness and simplicity, he would have
given us elegance. His pleasant irony plays over the story,
as when he describes such a solemn embassy as he had often
taken part in, decked up with chains such as malefactors
might wear and baubles that would delight children. The
description of the ideal commonwealth is not offered as a
practicable ideal, nor with entire seriousness, but poised
between jest and earnest to ask us to reflect. So in the
weighty considerations of the first book (after censuring enclo-
sures, excessive punishments, territorial aggrandizement, and
the extortions of the Exchequer) he describes for light relief, with

Erasmus's own delight, a friar-baiting at Cardinal Morton's table. Morton is agreeably characterized, and he was a principal source of More's *Richard III*. In popular history he has been immortalized in the phrase "Morton's forks," to signify a particularly ingenious extortioner's dilemma, and his whole career has fallen into disfavour. More's history has been deemed a partisan document. He certainly makes his position clear; but he knew Morton better than his readers do, and he lived near enough to Richard III's reign to feel gratitude to the statesmen who ended the English anarchy. We may say of *Richard III* that it closed the age of annalists by opening the age of historians. It is an interpretation of events, selected and marshalled, and based on an estimate of character. Character he brings out in scenes of such dramatic power that Shakespeare took them over integrally to build a great tragedy. More, indeed, recorded one poignant interview which Shakespeare did not venture to use, unless perhaps when penning the appeal of Constance in *King John*. Not only the scenes, but the words, passed from More to Shakespeare with no more than slight changes of rhythm. More's English was supple, and though always distinguished, it passed by swift transitions from vernacular dialogue to passages of stately eloquence. It is astonishing how great diversity he achieves by the most economical means. The *Dialogue of Comfort against Tribulation*, which he wrote in prison while awaiting his death, though less familiar than the other books, has its own graver graciousness. There is the same sunny humour, as in the standing equivocation between the tyrannical Turk (the ostensible persecutor) and the real tyrant Henry VIII. More brushes aside the so-called consolations of philosophy, which would have given a lesser writer many texts supported by a battery of references, and bases his case wholly on those which come from religion and a pure conscience.

More's English is that which George Tyndale[1] used for the

---

[1] George Tyndale (d. 1536). Studied at Oxford and Cambridge. Left for Germany in 1524 and visited Luther at Wittenberg. *New Testament*, 1525–6; *Pentateuch*, 1530. Betrayed, trapped and martyred in 1536. Controversy with More, 1531. For the history of the English Authorized Version of the Scriptures, see H. Wheeler Robinson, *The Bible: Its Ancient and Modern Versions*.

translation of the New Testament. Tyndale decorated the margin of his version with controversial remarks which Henry VIII justly stigmatized as "pestilential glosses." This was the ground of More's complaint against him, though, like most controversialists, More overshot the mark by complaining of the translation itself. Tyndale was as good a scholar in this matter as More himself, and a comparison of his renderings with texts translated by More (for instance, in the *Dialogue of Comfort*) shows virtual identity in wording and, what is more remarkable, in rhythm. It shows that both writers belonged to one tradition of biblical translation, namely that which had come down from Alfred and Ælfric through the medieval devotional writers. But these writers and More dealt with fragments and isolated texts, it was Tyndale—"a man of right good living, studious and well learned in scripture"—who carried their sterling, sturdy English and simple rhythms through the whole New Testament and a crucial portion of the Old. This is the essential English Bible. Its translator hoped to end the currency of "Robin Hood, Bevis of Hampton, Hercules, Hector and Troilus," and such idle tales; and in fact so he did. The Bible in English became the absorbing passion of the age, so that more orthodox translators were compelled to keep it in circulation, though inclining now to Luther, now to the Vulgate, and at last to Geneva. The text of the Psalms is better in the *Book of Common Prayer*, where it is united with collects and litanies in the stateliest prose of worship. After the revisions by Coverdale, Matthew and the English exiles in Geneva came the Authorized Version in 1611.

It is impossible to overprize the influence of this Authorized Version. Its excellence appears in any comparison with its excellent predecessors. No one man's work, it is every man's English; the turns of its phrases are on every Englishman's tongue. The plain style finds there an imperishable model, and by its standard no insincerity of the rhetoricians escapes detection. Bunyan in the novel and Bright in oratory are but two who owe their whole art to poring over its sentences, and its indirect influence is universally pervasive. Not only has it reached the rarest perfection of idiom, but it has imposed its own language, despite the dimming of age, so that Englishmen are moved far more than they understand. More modern renderings have been devised for the understanding of scripture, but only the Authorized Version (men allow) reveals the dignity, the beauty, the divine inspiration of the original.

The effect of the great ocean voyages and of the struggle with the Invincible Armada was to convert Britain from an off-shore island into the centre of a maritime empire. The first sign in literature of this sea-change was the appearance of Richard Hakluyt's *Principal Navigations, Voyages, Traffiques and Discoveries of the English Nation.*[1] Here is the honest prose of men who have done deeds by land and ocean, the tarry savour of old sea terms, and the strange sights of outlandish parts, together with sailing directions of the utmost exactitude, and patriotic enthusiasm for great adventures. Some of Hakluyt's material was translated from Spanish and other sources, and only the Iberian nations possessed in that age a more copious literature of adventure. The English series has never been interrupted, but in the nineteenth century rose again to a peak with the travels of African, Asiatic and American explorers. The scholarly side of Hakluyt's work has been continued in the long and splendid series of Hakluyt Society translations. The English geographical literature, first and last, is thus the richest in the history of man.

Advances made in geography, botany, zoology, and similar disciplines were paralleled by Gilbert's studies of magnetism, by mathematical activity, and by signs of progress in chemistry. The content of science was rapidly expanding, and the dogmas of the Schoolmen could not be sustained in the realm of natural philosophy. But, in Francis Bacon's opinion, systematic knowledge had not kept pace with discovery for lack of an adequate

---

[1] Richard Hakluyt (*c.* 1553–1616). Born in London, of Welsh extraction. Began lecturing at Oxford in geography shortly after taking his M.A. degree in 1577. *A Particular Discourse concerning Western Discoveries*, 1584; *De orbo novo Petri Martyris*, 1587; *The Principal Navigations*, 1598–1600.

Samuel Purchas (1575?–1626) published some of Hakluyt's manuscripts in *Hakluytus Posthumus*, 1625, as well as his own *Pilgrimage*, 1613, and *Pilgrim*, 1619.

method.[1] This was what he offered in his *Novum Organum*. The Baconian manner is revealed in the earlier editions of his *Essays*, which would now have to be termed (for loss of the meaning of his title) "assays." The essays are brief examinations of such themes as "Studies," "Gardens," "Truth," with the object of sifting and defining. Very lucidly, but in the most laconic fashion, they criticize their subject by means of comparison, antithesis, distinction and rejection. For lack of flesh they now seem rather the skeletons than the bodies of essays, and their proceeding according to predetermined plan is what Englishmen would consider characteristic of the French style. The more sinuous and insinuating glancing manner of Montaigne is now more current in England. *The Advancement of Learning* is an essay on an ampler theme, in which the author takes stock of the whole field of learning, examines its ramifications and criticizes its deficiencies. This work becomes, in more condensed form, the introduction to the main theme of the *Novum Organum*, namely, the announcement of the new inductive method.

Bacon's method did not come from the void. His insistence on experiment and his attacks on the Schoolmen had been made before by the Humanist Juan Luis Vives in works that Bacon may have read. He himself admits the existence of a "vulgar induction" by repetition of instances, which he distinguishes from his own method of restriction and rejection. Bacon seems to have failed to grasp the importance of specialist scientific work done in his own time, and his account of the humanities is inadequate. In this respect he is partly guilty of the schism between science and the rest of knowledge, which still embarrasses English thinking. He rejected the syllogism too absolutely, and probably did not allow enough scope to the natural, as apart from the controlled, movements of the human mind. But these things being admitted, one is amazed by the profundity and imperishability of his thought. His bold claim for

[1] Francis Bacon, Baron Verulam and Viscount St. Albans (1561–1626), son of Sir Nicholas Bacon. Educated at Trinity College, Cambridge, and later entered at Gray's Inn. Entered Parliament, 1584. *Essays*, 1597, 1612, 1625. *The Advancement of Learning*, 1605 (in Latin and augmented, 1623). Lord Chancellor, 1616. *Novum Organum*, 1620; *Henry VII*, 1622; *Apophthegms*, 1624; *New Atlantis*, 1626.

the scientific examination of all natural things, without regard to theological presuppositions, his conception of proximate causes as the proper study of the scientist, and his acute analysis of the possible types of experimental error, though announced before any of the great systematic advances, could not be bettered by the wisest of modern researchers instructing a group of young graduates. The whole is expressed with lucidity and condensed into pithy phrases made memorable by the gravity which the Latin language allows. The English equivalent of the same weighty and elegant style can be found in the *Advancement of Learning* which, laying aside the informality of the *Essays*, is a fitting instrument for a Lawgiver of the Sciences.

IV. SPENSER AND SIDNEY

THE "sage and serious" Spenser[1] was the immediate successor of Chaucer—the Chaucer of *Troilus and Criseyde*. Great minds have the quality of great peaks; they call to each other over immense distances. Spenser recognized, even better than Henryson, the richness of the Chaucerian legacy. He explored the vocabulary for words old and new; he drew out the music

[1] Edmund Spenser (*c*. 1552–99). Born in London and educated at the Merchant Taylors' School and at Cambridge, where he became friendly with Gabriel Harvey, the scholar and critic. Acquired proficiency in Latin, Greek (especially the philosophy), and also Italian and French. Resident in Lancashire, 1576, where he courted the "Rosalind" (Rose Dinely) of the *Shepherd's Calendar*, 1579. This work he dedicated to Sir Philip Sidney, whose temper and ideals were similar to his own, and whose friendship was probably the most important personal influence in his life. Sidney is remembered in the *Astrophel* and *Ruines of Time*, as the brave courtier of *Mother Hubberd's Tale*, and by some fine conceptions of the *Faerie Queene*. Spenser visited Ireland in 1577, and resided there 1580–9. Sir Walter Raleigh visited him there in 1589, and among his other distinguished friends was Sidney's sister, the Countess of Pembroke. He married Elizabeth Boyle, for whom he wrote the *Amoretti* and *Epithalamion*, 1595. *Four Hymns* and *Prothalamion*, 1596. *Faerie Queene*, I–III, 1590: IV–VI, 1595. His prose *View of the Present State of Ireland* was issued posthumously.

of rhyme royal into the sinuous harmony of his own stanza; he too embroidered an antique tale, but gave it immediate moral significance. As Chaucer had fascinated the poets of the fifteenth century, so Spenser became "the poets' poet," whose influence is not yet exhausted, despite the new lessons taught by Shelley.

Spenser's *Shepherd's Calendar* was recognized by several sensitive critics as the beginning of a new hope for poetry, though at first sight it might seem to be reactionary. There were already some important achievements in what was to be the Renaissance style of English verse. Sir Thomas Wyatt and Henry, Earl of Surrey,[1] had acclimatized the sonnet and (less successfully) blank verse, making direct use of Petrarch. Despite some false quantities and strained accents Wyatt had achieved smoothness and elegance, together with a more sensuous conception of beauty. Thomas Sackville's *Induction*, though perhaps more backward-looking in its use of vision and allegory, had been distinguished both for high purpose and exquisite finish.[2] Spenser, however, in the *Calendar* made a cult of rusticity, limiting his thoughts, laming his rhythms, and combining raw dialect with an artificial archaism. It is an experimental set of essays in verse, and those critics were discriminating who saw whither his genius led. The harshness of some pieces emphasized the sweetness of others. Spenser had much to unlearn about diction, but he was on his way to forming his own unique poetic dialect. He was exploring the roots of the language. His themes were personal and dramatic, moral, religious, courtly and satirical, and his verses were of many patterns. Though not a triumph in itself, the *Shepherd's Calendar* contains the hint of all Spenser's triumphs.

The poet's progress was not easy. His vein was more exquisite than Chaucer's but less versatile; his first discovery had to be of himself. To escape from English parochialism he had to absorb the lessons of Petrarch, Ariosto, Marot and

[1] Sir Thomas Wyatt (1503?–42) and Henry Howard, Earl of Surrey (1517?–47), poems published in Tottel's *Miscellany*, 1557.
[2] Thomas Sackville, Lord Buckhurst and Earl of Dorset (1536–1608) wrote *Gorboduc* (a tragedy, with Thomas Norton), 1562; the *Induction* and *Complaint of the Duke of Buckingham* in the *Mirror for Magistrates*, 1563.

Du Bellay, and yet to preserve his English savour. Well-meaning and classically minded friends offered him traps, which he had to avoid. Among his lesser works there are several which are disappointing, coming from so great a poet. The sonnet sequence of the *Amoretti* is only technically a success. In them he perfected the English type of sonnet formed of three quatrains and a couplet, which always tends to break up into separate verses. In rhythm, language and fluency there is nothing wanting, but the spiritual record is not deep and the expression is conventional. It is otherwise when his courtship of Elizabeth Boyle passed into marriage. The quiet content-ment and pensive passion of *Epithalamion* make it a poem unique in literature. Spenser is almost alone among English-men in having mastered the art of the canzone. He had rhymes enough to employ the difficult scheme without embarrassment. (It is a very different matter to write a canzone in English than in Italian or Spanish, in which languages rhymes are abundant, and many can be obtained from the verbal conjugation.) His full, flowing style of expression fills the succession of verses of "linkèd sweetness long drawn out," so that each answers to each and all are parts of the whole. *Prothalamion* is shorter, and its charm more immediately seized. The poet had in mind two of the loveliest English scenes for comparison: a quiet reach of the Thames with two white swans, and two young ladies in their bridal white. There is no personal emotion involved other than the poet's delight in sheer beauty, but that is purely and consummately expressed in the most liquid lines of the language. This creed of beauty is formulated in his noble *Four Hymns*.

But it is the *Faerie Queene* which is Spenser's claim on our worship. Planned on a vast scale, this work was to display the metrical and narrative skill of *Orlando Furioso*, the national enthusiasm of the Arthurian romance, and the moral signi-ficance of the English Reformation. Twelve books, each of twelve cantos, would set forth twelve cardinal virtues embodied in separate knights, and all these virtues would be consum-mated in a Prince Arthur, the chivalrous lover and courtier of Gloriana, the Fairy Queen. Gloriana was Queen Elizabeth, viewed in a more kindly light than now strikes upon her, and the various knights were to have been recognizable among her courtiers, though idealized. The poem as a whole would teach Englishmen of how much excellence they were morally capable. It was left half-finished; and better so. There was an inevitable sameness in the adventures of Spenser's heroes, which not even his amazing resourcefulness can disguise. They come from the unknown and proceed to an appointed goal, which swallows them into anonymity. Each book is an epic in itself, and the first book especially is an epic without a flaw; most poets would have been content to labour a whole lifetime upon one great epic, but Spenser had enough confidence in his powers to project twelve in the one series!

The *Faerie Queene* cannot be a popular book. Its author's view of reality is too rarefied to be generally shared, for he had not Shakespeare's advantage of daily contact with the crowd. Sidney, Raleigh and the great and polished wits of the age were equal to such a book, but not the average mind, either then or since. There is so little to be grasped and retained. The Knight of Truth, no doubt, exemplifies the struggle which the man of upright mind still must make to speak absolute truth. But this is not very clearly set forward in the figure of a knight who runs tilts against his enemies, however are these labelled. Further, on comparison with Bunyan's Christian we see how far this is removed from ordinary experience, since neither do we habitually cultivate one virtue at a time, nor are the temptations of vice always to be resisted in the same manner. To read the *Faerie Queene* therefore requires a power of abstraction which will never be found in the majority of readers, and to that extent it fell short of being, as the author intended, the national heroic poem.

But to the more finely attempered mind the *Faerie Queene* is of inexhaustible suggestiveness. The verbal and musical resources of the poet seem never to fail; his motions are always novel and his superb stanza is always fuller than the amplest expectation. The pensive mind is stirred to new reflections, and there is a suffused light of beauty, in colour, music and form, not to be equalled even by those who, with Keats, have made beauty their cult and programme. This sensation is not lessened, but rather increased, by Spenser's puritanism, which makes him rate virtue above beauty. His Knight of Temperance destroys the enchantment of Acrasia's Bower (II, xii), amid scenes of bliss and felicity on sea and land, with the result that the beauty which might have remained annexed to the soil is liberated into the ideal. Just as Dante's vision ends on the brink of ineffable truth, so Spenser stops short of a beauty more exquisite than the human soul can bear.

There is more mastery of life to be found in Spenser's friend and patron, Sir Philip Sidney.[1] Wit, scholar, courtier, soldier, the idol of his age as Garcilaso had been of the court of the Emperor Charles V, Sidney "slipped into the title of a poet," and one's imagination cannot help wondering how great a poet he might have been had he had more leisure or length of days. As it is, we have no more than glimpses of his mind. Apart from the pastoral *Arcadia*, he achieved a rank next to Shakespeare's by his sonnet-sequence of *Astrophel and Stella*, which is indeed the finest set of pure love sonnets in English. Those addressed to Sleep and the Moon might have been by Shelley; indeed, the first line of the latter is unmistakably Shelleian in thought and rhythm. Might he who gave so sound an exposition of Euripides' *Hecuba*, and who had Sackville's *Gorboduc* and Buchanan's *Jephthes* before his eyes, have implanted Euripidean tragedy in Elizabethan England and so short-circuited Racine? Almost anything might have come from his pen, for he clearly knew men and cities as well as books, and was abreast of both modern and ancient learning. With what consummate ease he bypasses opposition in his *Defence of Poesie* by approaching expert poetry through horsemastership—an art rarely commanded by the devotees or opponents of poetry! Yet it is with complete lack of affectation and perfect urbanity that he sets forth the claims of his poetic art to excel both philosophy and history as an aid to

[1] Sir Philip Sidney (1554–86). Son of a Lord Deputy of Ireland who became Lord President of Wales, nephew of the great Earl of Leicester, he studied at Christ Church, Oxford, where he became friendly with Richard Hakluyt and the antiquarian Camden. In 1574 he spent several months in Venice, and sat to Veronese for a portrait. Had many important commissions. His works were written between 1580 and 1585, but published posthumously: *Arcadia*, 1590; *Astrophel and Stella*, 1591; *Defence of Poesie*, 1596. Memory of his death at Zutphen is enshrined in a gracious anecdote.

virtue, because it excels them in delight. He gives due praise to Chaucer (it is the *Troilus* once again that counts), Sackville, Surrey and Spenser, offers some counsel, but tactfully avoids the more wearisome details. These are to be found in George Puttenham's *Art of English Poesie*, where the desire to dictate rules leads to undue notice of the trivial and finical. Yet, in general, Puttenham[1] gives the same genealogy of Poesie as Sidney does, and he even makes a remarkable effort to acquire for English use the bejewelled manner of the Timurid sultans. Like all Elizabethans he never fails to be entertaining in his digressions.

Members of Sidney's circle read classical and foreign authors in their own languages, but the general reader was introduced to the greater world of letters by the unique series of "Elizabethan" translations. Lord Berners gave them Froissart and the mannerist Guevara; North translated Guevara and Plutarch; Painter's *Palace of Pleasure* presented Bandello and Shelton englished the first part of *Don Quixote* before the second had appeared in Spain; Chapman's version of Homer is still the most forcible. Philemon Holland and Fanshawe (the translator of Guarini, Antonio de Mendoza and Camoens) carry the line to the middle of next century. Some of these are significant because Shakespeare read them and so became, despite his "little Latin and less Greek," in effect a classical scholar; they all played their part in keeping English literature in touch with the best that Europe could offer, precisely when English minds were best able to use and transform such suggestions. They aimed collectively at spirited equivalents of their originals. Living genius they represent, if somewhat inaccurately as to detail, by lively versions, which are still to be read with pleasure not unmixed with astonished admiration.

Through Berners's Guevara it is probable that John Lyly[2] felt that dissatisfaction with the plain style which is the leading

---

[1] George Puttenham (1529–90). *The Art of English Poesie*, 1589. Also attributed to his brother Richard (1520?–1601?).

[2] John Lyly (*c.* 1553–1606). At Magdalen College, Oxford, he began to earn his reputation as "a noted wit." Attached to Lord Burleigh. *Euphues*, 1579; *Euphues and his England*, 1580; and plays written between 1580 and 1600; *Alexander and Campaspe*, 1584; *Endimion*, 1591; *The Woman in the Moon*, 1597; etc.

characteristic of his *Euphues*. He wrote, not novels, but peregrinations with a commentary on men and opinions. Though he did not succeed in persuading playwrights to use prose, the "new English" of his *Euphues* threatened radically to change English style. The plain manner in unskilful hands becomes bald, and in any case does not offer pleasures of fancy which Lyly deemed to be within the power and province of prose style. He cultivated the glancing classical allusion, unexpected vernacularity amid refined "conceits," and romantic natural history, to give point to his prose and attract attention, even if at the cost of logic. A reaction of displeasure has overwhelmed the memory of his "Euphuism," which represented a natural revulsion of an artist from dullness and one of the extremes within which prose may oscillate.

The dramatist Marlowe left unfinished at his death the fine classical romance of *Hero and Leander* and Shakespeare issued at about the same time his *Venus and Adonis* and *Rape of Lucrece*. These three pieces serve very well to mark the state of narrative poetry at the close of the sixteenth century. They are on classical subjects, and in those years all the poets of Europe were beginning to challenge comparison in the modern styles with the best the ancients could afford. Marlowe used his decasyllabic couplets with the freedom of a Chaucer, and Shakespeare used Chaucer's stanza for his *Lucrece*, but the sextine of the *Shepherd's Calendar* for his *Venus and Adonis*. How Marlowe would have finished we cannot know; but the fragment he left is full of noble oratory. Shakespeare's narrative poems are Euphuism in verse. With forty plays to his credit he is relatively unproductive. (Calderón and the Greeks composed nearly three times as many, and Lope de Vega wrote whole acts before breakfast!) As if to show that this limitation of output was not due to any limitation of fancies, Shakespeare poured them in a flood into a mould of his *Venus and Adonis*, with a prodigality which would seem astonishing even on the shores of the Mediterranean. It is rich, to the point of lushness; and his *Lucrece* is as rich, but graver. But his principal gift to English literature, apart from his plays, is the much more sober and moving vein of his *Sonnets*. They are wrapped in personal mystery. Who was the "Mr. W. H." to

c*

whom they were sent? and why by "T. T." rather than by their author? and who is the "dark lady of the Sonnets"? and what is it all about? These are matters for wild conjecture or cautious inference, and hardly a year passes without some proffered solution; but the certainty eludes us. We can only feel that there were deep and passionate experiences of "the ever-living poet" which found their discharge in this the greatest sonnet-sequence of the language. Their theme is love, but they owe so little to Petrarch. We do not know the personal reasons for them, but their universality is only the more apparent. Brooding upon affinity and love, friendship, ambition, injury, decay, mutability, and "the wide world dreaming on things to come," Shakespeare's verses enlarge, without enlightening, our experience, and from casuistry the sonnet is converted to philosophy. Here, as in *Hamlet*, we meet the enigmatic Shakespeare who does not "abide our question."

V. SHAKESPEARE AND THE DRAMA

THE great periods in dramatic history are customarily brief; they seldom surpass a century. The reason is perhaps that too many favouring circumstances are required at one and the same time. There must, of course, be genius. Genius is doubtless adaptable, and in non-dramatic ages it may find its outlet elsewhere. The secondary causes thus mount to the first rank. It seems that there must be a large public, such as only the capital of a state can offer; it must also be vividly interested in the theatre, and of substantially one mind as to the entertainment it expects. The art of representation must be sufficiently developed, and the actors expert without arrogance. When the great actor seeks to enslave the play to his own personality it is not good for the health of drama. The actors must rather be a team under the intimate direction of the poet, and the poet in consequence must be, in knowledge if not in practice, an actor.

Now, in the second half of the sixteenth century, interest in the stage set in as a full current throughout all the countries of Western Europe; in England, France, Spain, Italy, and even Germany. In some of these countries there was a schism of critical opinion, which divided the "judicious" spectators from the vulgar mob. The "judicious" ones cited Greek and Latin examples and praised only their modern imitators, but the crowd wished to be amused, and not bored by rule. In France and Italy this schism nullified the advantages gained by medieval and early humanistic drama, so that the stage did not come to its fruition until much later. Civil discord and disputes among petty states were doubtless also discouraging features. It was only in England and Spain that the drama took great strides at the end of the sixteenth century and gave its finest gifts in the early seventeenth.

The parallelism between English and Spanish drama is curiously exact, and the more significant because there is no direct contact between them. In each case it was after the year 1560 that promising experiments began to appear, and for the next thirty years in each case the chief problem was to assign a place to the claims of classical art. About 1590 the norms were fixed by a great poet: in England by Marlowe, in Spain by Lope de Vega. Lope de Vega lived many years and carried his type of drama to its highest perfection; but Marlowe died young, and it was for Shakespeare to complete his work. Great names clustered round these protagonists. They were succeeded by a later generation who used the same technique with more emphasis, giving the Websters and Fords of the English drama, and rising to the after-glory of Calderón in Spain.

A main cause of progress in either country was that the plays were practical successes. Drama must be spoken and to an audience; the drama of the closet is something quite different. But here there is a difference between England and Spain. In Spain the collaboration between public and author was exceptionally close. Lope de Vega was a writer exquisitely sensitive to popular applause; he divined what his public wanted, and gave it without regard to the "rules." In this way he came to establish early a convenient formula for successful play-making; within it he worked, and from it his pupils selected such aspects as suited their individual genius. This apparent concentration on immediate effect was summed up in a famous formula which may be paraphrased thus:

> *For since the public pays, we must*
> *be fools and please it—that is just.*

It is not true; the Spanish dramatists were great poets and they often pleased themselves by writing fine scenes or deep thoughts to which the public did not fail to respond. But the notion that drama was an ephemeral matter, that it was less than art, did conduce to indolence and neglect; while the too slick formula made for box-office successes at the expense of the poet's veritable intention.

In England drama by recipe came only with Beaumont and Fletcher, thirty years later than in Spain; and those thirty years were the most glorious. Not only were the plays of Marlowe, Shakespeare and Ben Jonson practical successes, but they were expressions of the powerful individuality of these authors, and indeed of the changes of their mental states. The temperament of the individual artist counted for more than in Spain, and each work was a new experiment. Though the plays they wrote are vastly fewer, they represent more types than in Spain. There is little repetition of stock persons and plots, of a common poetical idiom and a common dramatic formula, in which depth is sacrificed to superficial polish; theirs is a variety of moods, each thoroughly and convincingly explored.

The first thirty years of Queen Elizabeth's reign saw many indeterminate experiments. They represent much the same tendencies as were to be encountered on the continent of Europe; several of these were considerably developed, and all have the interest of unfulfilled promise. The high classical line was generally taken by "judicious" persons, such as Sir Philip Sidney; and it might have given interesting results had Euripides indeed been established as a model. England might have had her Vondel. In practice, however, the classicists came to recommend the rhetorical manner of the tragedies attributed to Seneca, and in comedy Plautus was set up for imitation. The *miles gloriosus* found a modern counterpart in Nicolas Udall's[1]

---

[1] Nicholas Udall (1506–56). *Ralph Roister Doister, c.* 1553.

Ralph Roister Doister, and stiff declamation was to be enjoyed copiously in Sackville and Norton's *Gorboduc*, its theme of fratricide recalling the Senecan *Thebaïs*. Such work was at home in the school or the study; but at the court a gayer tone was preferred. John Lyly[1] supplied the need by making classicism decorative and modern in his *Endimion*, *Campaspe*, *Mother Bombie*, etc. He used prose, in all but one of his plays, with the brilliance and insubstantiality of an Oscar Wilde. It was the necessary antidote to the stiff respectability of *Gorboduc*, and it had its effect on Shakespeare's early work; but these were trifles too airy to serve as the basis for a national drama. Writers found, doubtless by box-office experience, that verse served their turn better than prose, and Lyly's precedent was not followed until Ben Jonson came to write his realistic studies of London life. Encouragement to use verse would have been found in the mellifluous work of George Peele,[2] who, neglecting the fundamentals of the theatrical art, polished his lines and showed that spoken poetry could in itself be successful. Working on different lines, Robert Greene[3] explored the possibilities of the heroic play and of satirical comedy. A ranting vein was opened by Thomas Kyd.[4] For most of these writers their university education counted for much. Though they had not devised any great play, they had made notable strides. They had educated the public and raised it to a high pitch of expectancy. The Elizabethans were now accustomed to declamation and the plain colloquial, to smooth verse and witty prose, to robustious rant and discretion, to kings in their purple and to commoners, to girls disguised as boys, brazen heads and magic, exotic or topical allusions, realistic farces, decorative classicism, allegory, and all the rest of the ingredients of great drama. Only genius was lacking; and genius came abundantly.

First, there came the astonishing personality of Christopher

[1] Sackville and Lyly. See pp. 36 and 40 respectively.
[2] George Peele (1558?–97?). *The Arraignment of Paris, c.* 1581; *The Old Wives' Tale*, 1595; *David and Bethsabe*, 1599.
[3] Robert Greene (1560?–92). *Friar Bacon and Friar Bungay*, 1594; *Alphonsus*; *James IV*.
[4] Thomas Kyd (1557?–95?). *The Spanish Tragedy*, 1594.

Marlowe.[1] Within the space of seven or eight years he revolutionized English playwriting, endowed the theatre with masterpieces, and set all other poets, including Shakespeare, on the road for greatness. His turbulent spirit and high-flying genius found a fit echo in the rhetoric of the stage expended on grandiose themes. Power fascinated Marlowe: imperial power in *Tamburlaine*, the power that knowledge gives in *Doctor Faustus*, moneyed power in *The Jew of Malta*, the loss of power in *Edward II*, and even its insolence incarnated in the figure of Gaveston. Squandering all his resources on these themes he heaped up incidents on a cumulative plot carried forward on his potent and passionate rhetoric. "Marlowe's mighty line," thunderous but beautiful, was a revelation to his age and is still unsurpassed. These lines he combined into blank verse to form paragraphs held together by expectancy and climax rather than by any subtler modulation. They would be monotonous but for the inexhaustible resources of the mind that fashioned them, and they prove admirably adapted to his purpose, viz., the construction of monologues. Dialogue, as an exchange of speech on equal terms, does not exist in Marlowe; what we remember are Tamburlaine's jeers at his captive kings, Faust's impassioned apostrophe of Helen, Edward II's deposition of greatness, and the long quasi-soliloquies in which the Jew of Malta voices his pride and hate. The ranting tone is sometimes heard, especially in *Tamburlaine*, and it was not unwelcome to his contemporaries. The response of an Elizabethan public to such things was more naïve than ours. Thomas Kyd outranted Marlowe, and the *Spanish Tragedy* was a stock piece for twenty years. In Marlowe, however, there is usually passion enough to justify the use of the most swelling words, and he has his own subtlety. The figure of the Maltese Jew embodies on a grand scale the intolerable, unpardonable wrongs which Christians have inflicted on Jews, and the peculiar ruthlessness of the Jewish revenge. In the first two acts he is a living,

[1] Christopher Marlowe (1564–93). B.A., Cambridge, 1583. Translated parts of Ovid and Lucan. May have served in the Low Countries. *Tamburlaine*, before 1587, published 1590; *Dr. Faustus*; *The Jew of Malta*; *Edward II*, 1594; *The Massacre of Paris*; *Dido*. Narrative verse; *Hero and Leander*, 1598. Lyric: *Come live with me and be my love*. Died in a brawl at the age of thirty.

suffering creature, contrastedly associated with his daughter Abigail as with a shallower nature, incapable of equal extremes. But the accumulation of crimes by the Jew forfeits our sympathy and even our belief in his possible existence. This cumulative method is applied to *Doctor Faustus* with more success. Though its scenes are rather successive than related, this play is a more direct consequence of Marlowe's temperament, since Faust longs for the poet's desires: superiority of mind and the possessive enjoyment of beauty.

As there is no give-and-take of dialogue in Marlowe, but only harangues and inferior replies, so there is no relief. All is tragically intense, without sufficient normality to afford a measure of the tragedy. His fine classical training may have contributed to this end, since the ancients did not mix tragedy with comedy. From the same source came his preference for five acts and his use of the English verse most like the Greek iambic trimeter, though he did not attempt to dress up Euripides as an Elizabethan. Without sacrificing the modern note, Marlowe made the greatest possible use of hints from the classics, and so set the peculiar law of the English stage. He familiarized the public with classical allusions, brilliance of fancy and effect, and solid grandeur. He enhanced the dignity of the chronicle play, and taught Shakespeare how to plan his great series, and he revealed the sublimity of human ambition, the vastness of human tragedy. What could be accomplished by blank verse—how much sonority and variety lay in that undeveloped medium—was patent to all the world after Marlowe had swept victoriously through the London theatres.

Shakespeare[1] was Marlowe's equal in age, and had not given

---

[1] William Shakespeare (1564–1616). Born at Stratford-on-Avon, the son of a farmer-trader in prosperous circumstances. Married Ann Hathaway in his nineteenth year, and went to London at some date and for reasons unknown. His first literary commissions were probably to refurbish old plays for representation. *The True Tragedy of Richard Duke of York*, attributed to Marlowe and Greene and possibly Shakespeare, was remodelled as *Henry VI* by Shakespeare. Hence arose an accusation by Greene of plagiarism, in 1592, in a context which implies that Shakespeare's success was already apparent. The dates and the canon of Shakespeare's plays are not entirely certain, but the following scheme will suffice:

EARLY WORK (1591–4). *Love's Labour's Lost, Two Gentlemen of Verona,* any convincing proof of genius when Marlowe perished in a brawl. A mind so complex was slow to mature; the experience he drew upon was gradually gathered. Most authors find it profitable and easy to continue work in any one style that has proved successful, but almost every piece by Shakespeare represents a new manner, and every one is packed full of new thoughts. Yet he would seem to have written rather to meet a practical demand for means of entertainment than by such a temperamental urge as Marlowe's, and at a relatively early age he was content to withdraw from playwriting, after a successful career as a partner in a theatrical company. But his mind was wide open to all sorts of suggestions, and he never ceased to adopt new ones, transmuting them by subtle alchemy into his own rich thought.

Because of his supereminence, Shakespeare has become, like Dante and Cervantes, a literature in himself. His name has attracted every trained and untrained pen, and echoes to the war-cries of battling professors and to the squeaks and jibbers of laborious cranks. He did not preside over the publication of his plays, and the more the problems of date, text and canon are studied, the more causes arise for dispute. Archival studies, planned to elucidate his life, have chiefly brought to light the personalities of others. We are aware that his plays are the results of deep experience, but their biographical causes are beyond our knowledge. The brilliance of the early period, the serenity of the second, the abrupt change to bitterness in the third, and the apparent reconciliation at last, doubtless have their significance in the history of his mind. He seems to have

---

Comedy of Errors, Henry VI, Richard III, Richard II, Titus Andronicus, Romeo and Juliet, and the poems Venus and Adonis, Lucrece.

HISTORIES AND COMEDIES (1594–1601). King John, Merchant of Venice, Midsummer Night's Dream, Taming of the Shrew, Henry IV, Henry V, Merry Wives of Windsor, All's Well that Ends Well, Much Ado about Nothing, As You Like It, Twelfth Night, Julius Caesar.

TRAGEDIES (1602–8). Hamlet, Troilus and Cressida, Measure for Measure, Othello, Macbeth, Lear, Timon of Athens, Coriolanus, Antony and Cleopatra, and the Sonnets.

FINAL WORK (1608–13). Pericles, Tempest, Cymbeline, Winter's Tale, Henry VIII. He may have contributed also to Cardenio, Two Noble Kinsmen, Sir Thomas More. Three pages in the manuscript of this last piece have been claimed as Shakespearean autographs. Otherwise only half a dozen signatures, usually abbreviated, survive from his hand.

lost faith for a time in woman, but it is a flimsy matter to connect this with the legacy to his wife of his "second-best bed"! An interesting point established has been that Elizabethan playwrights were constantly in attendance at the law courts, often in the character of defendants, and that they prided themselves on the technical accuracy of their legal terms. The trial scene in *The Merchant of Venice*, therefore, cannot serve as proof of Shakespeare's legal training, but only as evidence of his amateur interest. Indeed, it is a strange trial in which the parties wrangle without judicial control; in which a lawyer addresses, not the judge, but the public; and where the counsel for the defence is invited to pronounce a sentence on the plaintiff: in fact, it is a purely theatrical trial. Similarly, with the knowledge of horses or of medicine, Shakespeare knows that which is useful for his strictly artistic purposes, and we must not press him further. He conceals his own person. We should like to know what was his creed in that age of religious strife, but he offers us with regard to ghosts the Catholic orthodoxy of Old Hamlet, the scepticism of Horatio, and the Lutheran mistrust of Hamlet himself, leaving no certainty about the Shakespearean view. It was not likely to have been negative, but he had no wish to expose it for public inspection. When he lays bare part of his soul in the *Sonnets*, the effect is profoundly moving, but scarcely less enigmatic. As a playwright his function was not to reveal himself, but to seize upon everything that would give life and interest to his puppets.

Were it established for certain that part of *Sir Thomas More* survives in his handwriting, the fact would give editors confidence in revising his texts. They have rested for long on the faith of the First Folio edition (1623), but in recent times the authority of the Quartos has been resurrected. The Quartos are divided into "good" and "bad"; but the terms are relative. There is some sort of authority inherent in most of them, and the task is to define and delimit. We must remember that Shakespeare himself published none of his work. At best, the editions we have rest either on his manuscript (and then mistakes might be due to peculiarities of his handwriting), or to prompt copies, which may have been somewhat altered for performance on the stage. "Bad" quartos may be wholly the work of memorizers, or they may rest partly on the testimony of some actor, who reproduced pretty accurately his own speeches and scenes. In this way we have gained more information about the true text of Shakespeare than could be found in the Folio alone.

Equally valuable is the line of approach through the customs of the age and the practice of the theatre. To look through the eyes of an Elizabethan spectator is impossible in the absolute sense, but it is necessary to know "what happens in *Hamlet*" (or other works) before we can judge the poet's accomplishment. The Elizabethan conception of statecraft, for instance, is so unlike our own that we might fail to recognize a dramatization of it. There is a permanent truth to experience in Shakespeare no less than in Homer, but there was an even intenser contemporary vitality which in Homer's case is irrecoverable, but in Shakespeare's just eludes us. These conceptions his art was charged to put upon a certain stage. Actor-managers are now less loath to take the advice of scholars about Shakespearean production, and scholars are less satisfied with criticism which does not take into account scenic effect. The details of Elizabethan production are closely studied, and imitated in miniature models or in experimental performances. There have been at least two gains from this: we no longer oppose Shakespeare "the dramatist" to Shakespeare "the playwright," alleging the insufficiency of the latter to carry out the grand ideas of the former; nor do we leave out of account in our criticism the fact that all Shakespeare's ideas and effects conform to the need for representation in public. As a consummate playwright, he is wrongfully mutilated by the modern producer who supposes his arrangement ineffective—though not all his effects may have modern counterparts. As a writer for the theatre his business was not to represent things and persons as they are, but as they would plausibly appear on a stage. His boys, for instance, are more boyish than in fact; love is a more instant emotion; villainy is more tortuously evil and virtue more translucent. There is grease-paint here, but the effect is convincingly natural under the given conditions.

The topical intention of his plays is another field of controversy, enlivened by occasional flashes of enlightenment; and yet another is that of his relationship—his "indebtedness," as the unlucky phrase goes—to his fellow-workers. Begging the question of indebtedness, this consideration is at least helpful for the comparative assessment of his plays, with their varying humours and interests. Shakespeare's mind lay open to every seminal suggestion, but it germinated in its own unique fashion. The earliest plays show him still one of the group of Lyly, Peele, Greene and Marlowe. Though not a university graduate, he was, by adoption, a "university wit." Peele's sweetness and the arabesques of Lyly's wit go to make up *Love's Labour's Lost*, which does not stand out wholly from the mass of such work; yet Don Adriano de Armado and the schoolmaster Holofernes, in the comic solemnities of their entourage, foretell the antics of Bottom in *A Midsummer Night's Dream*, Sir Toby Belch in *Twelfth Night*, and even Falstaff in *Henry IV*. Shakespeare was already entering into his own monarchy of the absurd. He may have begun his work on the chronicle-play under the tuition of Marlowe and Greene, and in *Richard III* he accumulates horrors in the old manner. Yet he works with economy, thanks partly to the sound dramatic guidance given by Sir Thomas More's history. In *Richard II* Shakespeare has not only reduced and humanized the tragical effect of Marlowe's *Edward II*, but he has introduced the new principle of relief—pathetic and tender relief—which Marlowe did not know.

He draws away more distinctly from his peers in *Romeo and Juliet*, the supreme example of romantic tragedy in English. Without deep reflection as yet, Shakespeare is passionate and beautiful and reckless in the persons of his two young lovers, with only a hint at their futility in his Mercutio. The *Merchant of Venice* gives us a Jew to place beside that one which Marlowe discovered in Malta. Shylock is not more tragic nor more humanely conceived than Barabas, and Abigail is worthier than Jessica. The plot is composed of a naïve anecdote followed by a quibble; yet Shakespeare has made it probable by his convincing humanity. Nor does he fail to add to his self-centred, romantic ladies and gentlemen, and the tragic Jew, the absurdities of the younger and elder Gobbo, only one degree less rib-tickling than those of Dogberry in *Much Ado About Nothing*.

Peele or Lyly might have had a thought worthy of the *Midsummer Night's Dream*, but they could not have given us its ethereal poetry. The passion, the pathos and the humour of another plane of being, delightfully parodying this one for the better, makes the comedy *sui generis*. For the most part, in the plays of this period Shakespeare entered serenely into the world of ordinary human affairs, both in his histories and his comedies. In the former he may have owed something to Ben Jonson's effective simplification of character for stage purposes. Jonson observed real people, but gathered their qualities behind some dominant and interesting characteristic. His Captain Bobadilla is roystering, mendacious and cowardly, like the Falstaff of *Henry IV*, both being *milites gloriosi*; but he has nothing of the genial amplitude of Shakespeare's creature, a lord of misrule and sublimation of witty knavery. In *Henry V* Shakespeare expressed what is very rare in English literature: the glories of a conqueror. It is a consummate document of patriotism, and yet perhaps he more truly divined his country-men's thoughts when uttering their love of their island in Lancaster's speech in *Richard II* and their resolute resistance in that of Faulconbridge in *King John*. As for the great comedies —especially *As You Like It* and *Twelfth Night*—they have added Arden and Illyria (as later Bohemia) to the map of the mind as lands endowed with a salubrious, delicate, delightful and amusing air.

The plunge into tragedy was all his own. The outward sorrows of a Marlowe were unlike the probing of the innermost heart in *Hamlet*, *Macbeth*, *Lear*, *Othello*. There is nothing like them in all literature. Aeschylus in the *Agamemnon*, Sophocles in the *Oedipus*, and Euripides in the *Medea*, alone approach him; but either their problems are more abstract or, in the *Medea*, the probing is less thorough. Shakespeare lays bare the secretest possibilities of ambition, ingratitude and jealousy, exploring the mind on the narrow margin between despair and madness. In *Hamlet* the complexity of the human problem seems even to escape this greatest of humans. The "melancholy Dane" is somehow Shakespeare himself, though he is also a puppet pulled by strings. No one approaches the play without glimpsing some transcendent "meaning" behind

Hamlet's hesitations, yet no one divines that meaning. It has often been put into words; but the words dissolve under our sense of their inadequacy. Hamlet puts off action, and yet he is a swift actor; he is ambiguously mad and very crafty; he is gross and divine; he is ineffective and (we have recently been told) a consummate Machiavellian—and so the tale of explanations goes on. That Shakespeare saw more in Hamlet than any of his critics is certain; but it is not certain that even he saw in him anything more than an enigma—an enigma created by his own brain, but none the less baffling.

Shakespeare's *Julius Caesar*, derived wholly from North's Plutarch, is an instructive contrast to Ben Jonson's *Sejanus*, derived from the original authorities. How much more Roman are Shakespeare's Romans, who speak so much less Latin! But it is in *Antony and Cleopatra* that he gives us the final revelation of an imperial Rome far more sumptuous in its dazzling pomp and headlong overthrow than the spiritless capital of the first Caesars.

In the end Shakespeare elected to pass from us with a smile of reconciliation. The Prospero of *The Tempest* may have been a Shakespeare who had not solved but survived the febrile brooding of Hamlet; or it may have been that the poet caught at a new and entertaining suggestion by Beaumont and Fletcher. Do not analyse too much; do not construct too methodically; enjoy the genial appearance of things, and tie loose ends as occasion offers! Whether of his own motion or by the suasion of others, it is certain that Shakespeare's last period is one of careless mastery. The plot of *Cymbeline* or *A Winter's Tale* preoccupies him little; and if that of the *Tempest* is more integral, it is conventional and slight. A person catches his eye here and there—a Prospero, Miranda, Imogen or Autolycus—and he pours out his old magic; but he will not condemn an Iachimo as once he did Iago, and he will have no one end the play unhappily. With these genial works closing a reign of twenty years, being but forty-eight, Shakespeare ceased from creative work. We do not know precisely what he did, but fancy pictures him as retired to his property at Stratford and passing the last years of his life as a well-to-do, *average* provincial gentleman.

Shakespeare (it is said on the best authority) does not "abide our question," though he is for ever interrogated. Ben Jonson[1] has answers cut and dried, but he is rarely questioned. He is the "great unread" of English literature. There is no want of skill in his writings and their historical importance is undeniable. He enjoyed the maximum of respect from his younger contemporaries, the "tribe of Ben." A friend of Shakespeare, he could, despite that overpowering presence, stand forth as the protagonist of a type of drama quite un-Shakespearean; a type which enjoyed success in its time and contained many of the elements which have constituted the most modern manner. Some light on this paradox is perhaps found in Coleridge's remark that the very earnestness with which Jonson avowed himself a great poet placed him in the second rank. He protests too much, is too heavy-handed. Even his lyrics smell a little too much of the lamp; they are not quite spontaneous. His remarkable discoveries as to construction and characterization are also too laboured; the moral lectures which his Knowells and Wellborns read are so remorselessly complete that they suggest the immoral, and his observations of type so thorough-going that the type staggers under their burden.

It seems to have been Shakespeare himself who recognized the merits and originality of the epoch-making *Everyman in his Humour*. He took a part in the performance, and as leading shareholder in the company he bore the greatest financial risk. The play was a great success. Jonson revealed that "no country's mirth is better than our own," especially in the revised version, in which the persons bear English, not Italian, names. Ordinary London scenes and characters (he proved) were the

[1] Ben Jonson (1572–1637). Of Scottish descent, born in Westminster, and educated at Westminster School under Camden and at Cambridge. Served as a bricklayer and soldier before settling in London in 1597 to marry and write for the stage. Suffered a term of imprisonment for the death of an actor, 1598; converted to Catholicism and remained a Catholic for a dozen years. *Everyman in his Humour*, 1598; *Everyman out of his Humour*, 1599; *Cynthia's Revels*, 1600; *The Poetaster*, 1601; *Sejanus*, 1603; *Volpone*, 1606; *Epicene*, 1609; *The Alchemist*, 1610; *Catiline*, 1611; *Bartholomew Fair*, 1614; etc. Court masques. *Timber, or Discoveries upon Men and Matter*, is his commonplace book. William Drummond of Hawthornden published his *Conversations with Ben Jonson*, 1619.

proper objects of English wit, and prose the fitting medium, except when verse brought out the gravity or bombast of a scene. The technique of "humours" enabled him to make these types practical dramatic models. A single quality was emphasized, to preside over all others, and the interplay of these "humours" constituted the action. A formal plot was of less importance, and Jonson's are slight. In *Everyman in his Humour* the plot relates how an old gentleman learned that his son was less studious than he imagined, and how the young man eloped with his friend's sister. But this plot is not the play; it is merely the motion given to the characters who connect together so many recognizable scenes from London life, complete with their actors such as a downright squire, a braggart, town and country fops, a suspicious old man and a jealous one, and a testy magistrate. Testy old gentlemen are Jonson's forte. The final scene—in which reconciliation is effected by a cranky old judge in the name of wit and general goodwill—is worthy of Dickens, of whom Jonson is a perpetual reminder. Jonson and Dickens are sentimental, ethical, crotchety, perspicacious, racy, vernacular and urban; but there is more genial warmth in Dickens, whose medium, the novel, is better suited to this purpose.

In *Cynthia's Revels* and *The Poetaster* Jonson reintroduced the personal satire of the Greek Old Comedy, but the details of literary rivalry no longer interest. *Volpone* and *Epicene* are plays in which the plot is more prominently asserted; and the former is an instance of the impossibility of maintaining interest in a play wherein no character has a redeeming grace. It is, none the less, an effective stage play of manners, which bears representation. But with *The Alchemist* we reach a truer effusion of his genius; it depicts roguery, justified by its very completeness, among persons for whom Dickens coined the term "artful dodgers." This live-and-let-live policy and sympathy for amusing rascals reminds one of the best picaresque effects of Spain. The height of his skill, however, is reached in *Bartholomew Fair*. The trickle of plot and the fugitive appearances of characters are natural in the encounters and separations of a fairground; but it is the Fair itself, the bustling good-humour of the Cockneys of London, which is the "hero" of his comedy. This collective miracle did not occur again before the *Pickwick Papers*.

Jonson's many masques lie outside this survey, and his later comedies lack the appeal of the earlier ones; but his two tragedies, *Sejanus* and *Catiline*, witness to his powerful originality. The care with which he ransacked authorities to present an authentic picture of Sejanus anticipates the methods of Sienkiewicz, Flaubert or Ebert. There is concentration on the theme to the exclusion of all trivial matter, giving a unity of treatment otherwise unknown in European drama before Racine. The language is full of gravity; it bears the weight of the world-wide dominion sustained by its speakers. The ambitious favourite is nobly conceived, and his fortunes massively presented. But the labour lacks just that felicity which Shakespeare could not fail to impart; the documentation is too intrusive, and the attempt to dramatize Tacitean epigrams merely shows that they are not dramatic. For *Catiline* he had (alas!) even more rigid preconceptions.

Jonson laboured too much, and Beaumont and Fletcher[1] too little. Their long and successful collaboration was based on the acceptance of the fashions of the moment, without criticism or interpretation, as the ready-made ingredients of playmaking. The ruff and doublet of the early Jacobean are never out of sight, so as to let us call any of their work universal and permanent. They make use of the standard conventions about love and honour, embodied in standard exaggerations; and, in fact, they reduce drama to formula. Their slick efficiency and up-to-dateness was a new thing in English drama, and gave them twice as much popularity as Shakespeare during the next fifty years. In their use of conventions and theatrical devices they strongly resemble their contemporaries of the school of Lope de Vega; nor are they uninfluenced by Spanish literature

---

[1] Francis Beaumont (1584–1616), educated at Oxford and buried in Westminster Abbey, and John Fletcher (1579–1625), educated at Cambridge. Jointly they produced *The Knight of the Burning Pestle*, 1609 (printed 1613); *The Maid's Tragedy*, 1611; *A King and No King*, 1611; *Philaster*, 1611 (all printed in 1620). Fletcher composed *The Faithful Shepherdess*, 1609?; *Rule a Wife and Have a Wife*, 1624; *Bonduca*, 1614; *A Wife for a Month*, 1624; *The Wild-goose Chase* 1621; etc.

and fashions. The latter set the model for the Europe of King James's day, and the two clever young graduates were well in the fashion. The indebtedness of *The Knight of the Burning Pestle* to *Don Quixote* is as obvious as it may be misleading; for the remarkable feature of that play is its innovation of the doubly interrupted plot. The players are supposed to have a comedy about a runaway marriage, into which the quixotic antics of Ralph are grafted by the demands of the personified audience. The latter, Citizen George and his Wife, are extraordinarily vivid, especially the Wife; and they give an excellent rendering of the lively, intelligent, practical and disturbing criticism which emanated from the Jacobean public. In such a piece as *The Wild-goose Chase* we see how Fletcher bridges the gap between the Elizabethan comedy and Restoration "amoral" drama. His versification is negligent, and supposes a very colloquial utterance, almost all the bonds of verse being lax and in danger of dissolution into prose.

There are many other names in Elizabethan drama, but nothing new emerged. Old conventions persisted with a more outrageous emphasis. John Webster, Philip Massinger, John Ford and James Shirley[1] stand out, the last for a single famous address to Death, the third and second for the plaudits of Lamb and Coleridge respectively, and Webster because his *Duchess of Malfi* is still actable. It marks the extreme of tragic horror, and by so doing topples over the verge into ridicule. As intrigue succeeds intrigue, crime follows crime, and the pile of corpses—elaborately staged—mounts before the spectators' eyes, the tragic tension snaps into a titter, and melodrama falls to a barnstormer's anticlimax. Its immediate audience responded, no doubt, with less sophistication, and had attention to spare for the original characterization, skill of management and full-blown rhetoric of this tragedy.

---

[1] John Webster (1580?–1625?). *The White Devil, c.* 1608; *The Duchess of Malfi, c.* 1614.
　　Philip Massinger (1583–1640). *A New Way to Pay Old Debts,* 1633.
　　John Ford (fl. 1639). *Love's Sacrifice,* 1633; *Perkin Warbeck,* 1634; etc.
　　James Shirley (1596–1666). *The Contention of Ajax and Ulysses* (1659) has the famous dirge, "The glories of our blood and state are shadows, not substantial things."

VI. THE AGE OF MILTON

BETWEEN Spenser and his spiritual heir, John Milton, there
intervened certain important developments in English song,
prose and thought. Milton is in one sense the last of the
Elizabethans; in another, the product of a more factious age;
and in a third, the prophet of a new poetry throughout Europe.

Apart from the ode, sonnet, and forms borrowed from Italy,
the English lyric is based upon song. It had been so during
the Middle Ages. Chaucer's authority did not suffice to
popularize the art-forms of the medieval French lyric, but there
was much good in unpremeditated hymns and songful ejaculations. In the age of Henry VIII and Elizabeth a splendid
efflorescence of chamber music provided a demand for texts,
such as Shakespeare and many others were skilled to supply.
Their stock-in-trade consisted of simple notions, unforced
expression, tunefulness and often some elementary parallelism;
but no such integration as to commingle an intellectual interest
with the emotional response. In this style the songs the great
poet has strewn among his dramas remain unmatched. They
imposed the law of brevity on the English lyric, which is its
distinguishing quality when compared with those of Latin lands.

Without ceasing to be brief, and being generally satisfied with
two or three stanzas, Ben Jonson and Thomas Campion[1]
imposed structure on the song. They conformed to a design
and had the beginning, middle and end required by classical
precept. Horace was their model in this respect, as well as in
the care they expend on the choice of words; yet they are more
singable than Horace. Poets of the next generation reckoned
their forefathers "from Homer down to Ben," but the magis-
tral importance of the latter they perhaps exaggerated. His
model, Horace, was accessible to others, and yet it is clear that
only Marvell, among them, gave a Horatian allure to his verses.
In rounding off his pieces, Jonson made use of ingenious

---

[1] Thomas Campion (d. 1619). *Poemata*, 1595; *Observations in the Art
of English Poesie*, 1602; *Books of Aires*, 1610–12, containing lyrics set to
music by himself.

transpositions which were the delight of the young courtier-poets who proclaimed his sovereignty.

Ingenuity was carried much further in the work of John Donne,[1] the most enigmatic figure of that age. His lines are essentially unsingable. Their enunciation depends on their meaning; and though this reveals harmonies unknown to the Elizabethans before him, Donne is not slow to force an accent nor forward to make an appeal to the senses. According to Milton's famous definition, poetry should be "simple, sensuous and impassioned." Donne is neither the first nor the second (though he is often sensual); and as for his passion, though sometimes raised to a white heat, it is predominantly intellectual. These qualities extend from his short lyrics and sonnets to long compositions. The *Second Anniversary* (of a lady's death) is one of the great poems of the language, though it twists the tongue and teases the brain. He revealed in it similitudes more apt and suggestive than the trivial round of Elizabethan comparisons, and he was a doughty champion of sincerely English thinking as against their superinduced classicism. The great series of his religious sonnets (though they cannot be ranked as formal masterpieces) showed how closely this type could be moulded to the actual movements of a perplexed mind; and his satires (even in their roughness) afford a penetrating analysis of the spiritual alternatives of the age.

Donne's English wit delighted his age; its daring transitions were imitated by the young Cavaliers, but confined within the neat framework devised by Jonson and Campion. A common but inappropriate denominator has been found for these writers in Samuel Johnson's word "metaphysical." He meant

---

[1] John Donne (1572–1631). Dean of St. Paul's. He was born of Catholic parentage and probably destined for the priesthood. His early career is obscure. An imprudently early marriage terminated his career as a wit acceptable in great families, and his choice of the Church as a medium was not entirely to his taste. It was also with dispeace that he subscribed to Anglican doctrine. He was the first pulpit orator in the grand manner, and became Dean of St. Paul's, but his poems reveal a mind under incessant strain, paradoxical, ingenious and divided. Their strong neo-scholastic bias and method is due to his Catholic training. A certain affinity between his style and that of the younger poets of to-day has led to a strong revival of interest in him.

simply that they give one to think, but not that there is profundity in the thought. The term is now obligatory, though it obscures essential differences. Among the "metaphysical" poets we may distinguish the group of Cavaliers[1]—Suckling, Carew, Lovelace—marked by their elegance, gay wit, and hint of unhappiness; poets who have blended in the popular mind with a traditional antithesis between the Cavaliers and the grim, virtuous, victorious and unlovely Roundheads. Herrick was not one of them, being a clergyman, though a Royalist; but his *Hesperides* does represent the best that was in them. His lyrics, just a few words at a time, are dainty, finished, light and musical, not without touches of pathos and deeper things. At times he draws the whole effect from a single word, such as the word "liquefaction" in *Whenas in silks*; not even Tennyson has excelled him in this inevitability of perfection.

As the composer of *Noble Numbers*, Herrick introduces us to the other group of "metaphysical" poets, namely, the religious lyrists. Yet their qualities were unlike, having only in common the power of arresting attention by interesting transitions of ideas. The poems included in Herbert's *Temple* are in remarkable opposition to those of Donne; for, though Herbert did not surrender worldly ambitions without a struggle, his poetical acquiescence in his creed is complete and the range of his ideas far from audacious. Quietness, decency, order and a glow (not a blaze) of religious fervour are his

---

[1] These poets are best studied in anthologies. They appear in all, but Sir H. J. C. Grierson's *Metaphysical Lyrics and Poems of the Seventeenth Century* is especially helpful. Herrick is not included in that work.

Sir John Suckling (1609–42).

Thomas Carew (1598?–1639?).

Richard Lovelace (1618–58), who gives the best expression of the union of Cavalier love and loyalty in *To Althea from Prison*.

Robert Herrick (1591–1674). Educated at Cambridge, incumbent of Dean Prior in "dull Devonshire" from 1629; *Hesperides and Noble Numbers*, 1648.

George Herbert (1593–1633). Public Orator at Cambridge, then rector of Bemerton. *The Temple*, 1633.

Richard Crashaw (*c*. 1612–49).

Henry Vaughan (1622–95).

Andrew Marvell (1621–78). A Puritan with Royalist leanings, joint Secretary of State with Milton, and his friend in later life; Member of Parliament for Hull under the Restoration. His *Poems* were published posthumously, 1681, 1689.

characterizing marks. There is more of ecstasy in the verses of Crashaw, who found in conversion to Catholicism an opportunity for the outpouring of emotion. Vaughan, in the same group, combines the eye and sentiments of a nature poet with a high degree of mystical insight, and his rhapsodies foretell Shelley.

The greatest of all these singers was, no doubt, Milton's friend, Andrew Marvell. Marvell wrote what is perhaps the only convincing imitation of Horace in the English language, the *Ode upon Cromwell's Return from Ireland*, and his few occasional poems are remarkable for their variety of type and mastery, for a felicity of expression surpassing mere wit, and for the echoes of a mightier eloquence born of moral persuasion. The age had split so that grace and invention went to the one side, but fervour and worth to the other. Marvell's personality does not make a complete synthesis, for which a greater than he was reserved.

This was John Milton.[1] Milton's life took a new direction with the outbreak of the Civil War, and the collected edition of his early poems in 1645 puts a period not only to a phase of his activity, but also to an aspect of his character. A sweet reasonableness arises from the balance between serious purpose and outward grace, between scholarship and accomplishments

---

[1] John Milton (1608–74). His father had been disinherited on his embracing the Protestant creed, and had removed to London, where he proved an able man of business. He destined his son for the Church and sent him to Cambridge. There Milton's great powers and fine Latin scholarship attracted keen sympathies, but he felt unable to accept the Anglican position and retired to his father's house to pursue an elaborate programme of study. On the outbreak of the Civil War his leanings were towards the Presbyterians, and on their behalf he made his attacks on prelacy. But being convinced that "new presbyter is but old priest writ large," he transferred his sympathies to the Independents, finally reaching an isolated and heretical theology which he expounded in his *De Doctrina Christiana* (unpublished until 1825). His visit to Italy in 1637–9 introduced him to J. B. Manso, Dati, Deodati and others, and was the ground of his European reputation as a Latinist. Married unhappily in 1642, this infelicity giving cause for his works on divorce. Latin Secretary of State, 1649; dismissed, 1660. *Ode to the Nativity*, 1629; *L'Allegro* and *Il Penseroso*, 1632; *Comus*, 1634; *Lycidas*, 1637; *Reason of Church Government*, 1641; *Apology for Smectymnuus*, 1642; *Education*, 1644; *Areopagitica*, 1644; *Doctrine of Divorce*, 1644; *Poems*, 1645; *Way to Establish a Free Commonwealth*, 1660; many other prose works; *Paradise Lost*, 1667; *Paradise Regained*, 1671; *Samson Agonistes*, 1671; *De Doctrina Christiana*, 1825.

evenly poised. His instinct for superior merit associated his mind with "my" Shakespeare and "the sage and serious" Spenser, passing over the heads of the poets of his own age. Yet he shared with them the liking for ingenuity, though it took a more architectonic turn. His *Nativity Ode* combined Spenserian puritanism and elegance with a deeper Miltonic note, and it already reveals his peculiar skill in extracting the utmost effect from the combination of classical and Hebrew mythology. The alternation of study and recreation whereby he governed his days is described in the first Latin Elegy (to Carlo Deodati), and then perfected in the companion pieces *L'Allegro* and *Il Penseroso*. Courtliness is united to moral purpose in the masques of *Arcades* and *Comus*, and it is only in the elegy *Lycidas*, on the death of Edward King, that the shadow of contention lies. The equilibrium of poetry and puritanism had been restored in the person of John Milton, half a century after Spenser, and it would have been good for England could that conjunction have endured. Had it lasted, however, a temporary felicity would have cost the world one of its greatest spiritual experiences. The path to Milton's supreme master-pieces lay through the dust of prosy controversy, and it is now appropriate to consider both the developments effected by English prose and the evolution of the puritan conscience.

The same years witnessed a notable advance of English prose. It acquired rhythms and dignity hitherto unknown, and its themes were of far-reaching significance. The grand style was introduced by Hooker and has never surpassed the height attained in Milton's *Areopagitica*. Its first great document was an assertion of the principle of law in matters of religion, and it closed (one might almost say) with the firmest demand made in England for complete political freedom. Liberty and law are the poles of a great debate which occupied the energies of the nation, and gave at length that ordered liberty which is the pride of Britain and her Empire, and the Americas.

Richard Hooker's[1] *Laws of Ecclesiastical Polity* is the classi-

---

[1] Richard Hooker (1554?–1600). Educated at Corpus Christi College, Oxford. (Cartwright was of Cambridge.) Master of the Temple and later rector of Boscombe in Wiltshire, and of Bishopsbourne in Kent. *Of the Laws of Ecclesiastical Polity*, books I–IV, 1593; V, 1597; VI, 1648; VIII, 1651. Book VII first appeared in 1662.

cal statement of the *via media* adopted by the Anglican Church. It is less than a complete theology, since the author's special purpose was to confute the radical reformers who, with Thomas Cartwright at their head, demanded thoroughgoing changes on Calvinistic lines. This was the period in which the Presbyterian Church of England arose to challenge the Episcopal Church, offering an alternative method of government and a plan of speedier reform. More impatient innovators, under the name of Brownists or Independents, advocated a complete break with the official Church and the setting up of Scripture, interpreted by the individual conscience, as the sole religious authority. The word "puritan" came to be identified at last with these extremists, but it is of wider and vaguer application. The Church of England came into being by virtue of the agelong quarrel of kings and popes. The authority of the latter over English Christians (whether clerical or lay) had frequently been debated in the Middle Ages, and the stronger monarchs had taken steps to retrench the papal prerogative. Henry VIII, naming himself Head of the Church, intended no doctrinal change. But the Lutheran and Calvinistic examples, the remains of the Wyclifite protest, and the tradition of a simple evangelical faith and practice in England, supported by the many editions of the Bible, led to a demand for simpler forms of cult and the elimination of certain intrusive dogmas. These things, together with a higher moral code in private life, constituted puritanism as Spenser and Sidney knew it. But the restoration of Catholicism by Queen Mary had led to a dispersal of the more zealous Puritans, some of whom remained content with the episcopacy and the Prayer Books, while others were moved to champion the Protestant discipline of Geneva. These latter returned home to demand the removal of all things not justified by direct scriptural warrant, the dethronement of bishops, and the setting up of presbyterial committees of ministers and elders, the latter elected by the votes of the congregations. This was Hooker's problem. He was little embarrassed by the arguments of Catholics of the Roman persuasion on the conservative side, and as for the radicals, the Brownists served him as examples of the ecclesiastical anarchy towards which his opponents seemed to be heading.

Least of all had he to deal with atheists or agnostics. It was common ground that England should be Christian, and should be deemed one single community, comparable to those ancient churches of Rome, Ephesus, etc., which the Bible represented as major local divisions of the whole body of Christians.

Hooker's theme, therefore, is the inevitability of law in human affairs, its oneness in essentials and its kinds. The absolute authority of Scripture does not exclude (he argues) the operation of physical and prudential laws not verbally formulated in the Bible. Among the latter are those by which human communities, such as the Church, are regulated. Here custom and experience count, and the abilities of certain out-standing individuals are recognized both by Scripture and by common practice as conferring authority. In this way he justifies episcopacy, the aristocratic principle, against the popularly constituted presbyteries. To his opponents he makes all the concessions that a fair-minded debater should; he is patient under disagreement and tolerant yet firm in his con-clusions; and as a vehicle for his great argument he fashioned a stately prose of Ciceronian cut, somewhat lacking in colour and vernacular idiom (there are sermons by Hooker which show a more trenchant style), but lucidly reasonable and gravely persuasive.[1]

The grand or periodic style was used by Sir Walter Raleigh for his world history and by Donne for his sermons. It is most exquisite in Sir Thomas Browne's[2] *Religio Medici*. By Browne

[1] The principal document left by the Presbyterian faction was the *Westminster Shorter Catechism*, presented to the English Parliament in 1647. On the failure of the English movement, this catechism continued to be the mainstay of religious instruction in Scotland. It is hardly to be accounted a literary document, but its effect on Scottish mentality has been profound. Children who have memorized the 107 questions and answers "with the reasons annexed" not only possess a firm theology (not common in England), but develop a faculty for logic and disputa-tion. Educationists, who have since shown that this plunge into the abstrusest questions of theology and metaphysics is not suited to the development of the child's mind, have probably overlooked the use of the nimble childish memory to store up certain doctrines which become intelligible years afterwards. With the disappearance of the *Shorter Catechism* from Scottish education there will come a loss of the characteristic quality of the older Scottish mind.

[2] Sir Thomas Browne (1605–82). *Religio Medici*, 1643; *Hydriotaphia, or Urn Burial*, 1658; etc.

the common idiom is reserved to give surprise; the stuff of his discourse is a delicately calculated latinity. The long sentences roll in polysyllables through smooth swelling rhythms, so that his prose has the brocaded elegance of a cavalier by Van Dyck. His work is a prolonged meditation on first and last things rather than an exposition, and his thoughts are copious, though not profound. His character is that of an average, though aesthetically gifted, Englishman who, in the exercise of his individual judgment, has adopted the faith most widely established, without animus against any who may think otherwise. Tolerance, social cohesion and individual liberty are three ingredients of the British temperament better exemplified in Browne than in greater men. In his *Urn Burial, Garden of Cyrus* and other writings he is equally entertaining, but less significant. He and Robert Burton,[1] the author of the *Anatomy of Melancholy*, are masters of the elegant use of the Latin quotation. Their vast and irregular learning enables them to let the latinized sentence overflow into the Latin quotation, the latter buttressed with a reference for the sake of elegance rather than verification. The simple, unquestioningly orthodox piety of Izaak Walton's[2] *Compleat Angler* is yet another instance of the unconstrained acquiescence by most Englishmen in the established religion, and is part of the book's singular charm. This first and best classic of outdoor sport combined with the half-serious technicalities of anglers the attractions of a piscatory eclogue, views of English country life, field naturalism, meditation and literary reminiscence. The biographer of Hooker, Donne, Wotton and Herbert could offer rich literary feeding.

The great voice among the Puritans was John Bunyan's.[3] His spiritual history is contained in *Grace Abounding to the Chief of Sinners*, a work to be set beside the *Confessions* of

---

[1] Robert Burton (1577–1640). *The Anatomy of Melancholy*, 1621.

[2] Izaak Walton (1593–1683). *Donne*, 1640; *Wotton*, 1651; *The Compleat Angler*, 1653; *Hooker*, 1665; *George Herbert*, 1670; *Bishop Sanderson*, 1678.

[3] John Bunyan (1628–88). Born at Elstow, near Bedford, the son of a tinker. Served in the Civil War. Baptist preacher, 1657. Imprisoned at Bedford for various periods between 1660 and 1672 for unlicensed preaching. *Grace Abounding*, 1666; *Pilgrim's Progress*, 1678; *The Life and Death of Mr. Badman*, 1680; *The Holy War*, 1682.

St. Augustine and the *Life* of St. Theresa. In it he reveals a mind exceptionally sensitive in religious matters, a "wounded conscience" which forced him to face and overcome much despair and many perplexities. The son of a tinker, without a regular education (though his father had had him instructed in reading and writing), Bunyan had to fight his way through many doubts which are removed for other people by a better schooling; but in doing so he acquired a singular knowledge of the trials and difficulties of humble folk. His wholehearted conviction would have moved him to speak " of God's love and his mercy to me even to the very crows that sat upon the ploughed lands before me." His language consisted of texts from the Authorized Version and of expressions which barely disguise such texts; Bunyan is the first of English authors to be wholly biblical in his eloquence. His honest and racy style, his unquestioned sincerity, his insight into ordinary human problems, his vivid and homely pictures, made Bunyan the greatest preacher of his day; but the State demanded production of a licence to preach, and Bunyan, whose licence was only from God and his heart, spent many years in prison. His books are simply extensions of this preaching activity from speech to print. Their great literary merits were a minor consideration to their author, and were overlooked in his day. Not criticism (though critics have applauded since Johnson praised him) but unceasing popular support has placed Bunyan firmly in English letters.

Memories of medieval pilgrimages to Our Lady of Walsingham were probably not remote in the Bedford of Bunyan's youth. They had once served to give a religious pretext for the pleasures of travel, and now, when discontinued, they gave to a story of travel religious profundity. There was this to distinguish the movements of Christian in the *Pilgrim's Progress* from any common journey, without at all restricting Bunyan's freedom to include characters and scenes that everyone would recognize on the road between Elstow and Bedford. The bewilderment of the simple countrymen in a great city gave him his Vanity Fair. His own interrogation before narrowminded judges gave the great trial scene, and his memories of the Civil Wars produced Mr. Greatheart. The work has the most vivid actuality, and yet it has a vent of escape into romance. Its giants and mountains and dungeons belong to the woodcuts which illustrated chapbooks of chivalry. Bunyan did not know them except by using the same broadcloth imagination as was to be found among all his comrades at Bedford. They also are, in their special way, real, since they belonged to normal imaginative experience. The Christian path traced for one soul in the First Part is followed by a family in the Second; the allegory therefore lacks no kind of completeness in our experience as individuals or members of social groups. Many of the incidents are implicit in the metaphors used in *Grace Abounding*; the metaphors become adventures because it was Bunyan's manner to think in concrete instances. The march of the narrative is swift; the language strong, racy and biblical. There is an organic flow throughout the work which was not foreseen in all its details. Character is thus gradually revealed in action and developed by events, and the latter have some of the waywardness of current experience. Above all, *Pilgrim's Progress*, with *Robinson Crusoe* and *Gulliver's Travels*, is a book which captures the imagination of British children in their freshest youth, even before they can read. They pore over the illustrations after their parents have read some of the text, very likely on a Sunday and immediately after morning prayers. This practice, added to the vivid honesty of the narrative, has given to *Pilgrim's Progress* its unique air of veracity; and has made it a most powerful educator of English youth. The account of an English lawcourt in it was a fair picture of contemporary usage; if it now seems a travesty of justice, the improvement is due very largely to this book. No other work has done so much to establish a good conscience, without respect of gain, as the rule of life.

In the political sphere the debate between law and liberty lay between absolutism and republicanism. English common sense embraced neither extreme, but both have notable exponents in literature. The absolutist extreme is represented by Thomas Hobbes's[1] *Leviathan*. Hobbes is a bold and independent

---

[1] Thomas Hobbes (1588–1679). Graduated at Oxford, and served several distinguished persons in the capacity of tutor, being mathematical teacher to Charles II. His mathematical studies brought him into controversy with Descartes. *Leviathan*, 1651.

thinker, a critic of the Aristotelianism of the schools (as befitted Bacon's most intelligent secretary), affected by the advances in mathematics, optics, chemistry and mechanics registered in his time, but an un-Baconian dogmatist. He essays a rigorous materialism based on the single principle of motion, and this leads him to an unsatisfactory account of Reason as no more than an addition and subtraction of words duly defined to correspond to concepts. There is a gap in this sort of reasoning and there is crudeness in Hobbes's picture of the human body as composed of the equivalents of springs, wheels and strings. He cleared away many theological prejudices from his theme, but his manner is that of a lay dogmatist; his arguments are chains soldered by dogmas. As for the State, Hobbes professed to know the terms of the Social Contract, and to be able to assert that the rights of the individual have been totally and irrevocably surrendered to the State or "Artificial Man." The motive he alleged was mutual fear; though we may doubt whether fear could cement any society. The Social Contract postulated by Hobbes is questionable both as psychology and as history; its absolute application cannot be inferred from the terms as he gives them, and by denying all redress it makes its own conservation impossible. Yet *Leviathan* is the first grandiose attempt to grapple with the problems of political science in English, and is the first classic in its series. The style is lumpish, and the thought often more lucid than exact.

When Milton informed Dryden that his master was Spenser he was not referring either to his prose or to the intellectual content of his greatest verses. His youthful work, though not unrelated to the style of his age, was indeed linked to Spenser by affiliation of genius. But his prose has for dominant note civil and ecclesiastical liberty. He had been educated to serve the Church, but had not been willing to subscribe to its articles. On the first stirrings of the Civil War he cut short his grand tour of Italy, omitting to visit Greece. "I thought it base [he wrote] to be travelling for amusement abroad while my fellow-citizens were fighting for liberty at home. . . . I saw that a way was opening for the establishment of real liberty." He devoted his pen to the service of religious, domestic and civil freedom.

This was to be based on right education, for virtue is "the only genuine source of political and individual liberty." His plan of studies, in his dissertation *Of Education*, was nobly utilitarian.

Its classical bias was due to the fact that Latin was still the language of science and theology as well as of the ancient literature which supports the literatures of modern Europe. Italian, he suggests, could be learned at any odd hour. It is noticeable that his plan for sports serves to form good cavalry officers; Milton did not make the mistake of later demagogues who have believed that the free man is not called upon to defend his freedom. In the matter of religious liberty (*Of Reformation in England* and *Apology for Smectymnuus*) he may have thought at first that it would suffice to abolish prelacy, as the chief hindrance to a reform of doctrine and morals, but he later transferred his sympathies from the Presbyterian to the Independent wing of the Puritans, seeing that "new presbyter is but old priest writ large." His *Doctrine of Divorce* is his chief contribution to individual liberty. That his arguments served to some extent his own ends as a sufferer from the too peremptory obligations of marriage has caused him to be unworthily traduced. The subject is a vital one for human happiness, and Milton refused to bury it under taboos and conventions. "Marriage [he represented] is not a mere carnal coition but a human society. Where that cannot reasonably be had, there is no true matrimony." With the Parliamentary triumph there seemed little need to champion civil liberty. It had been apparently won. Milton merely defended the action of the English people in bringing to justice the king who had [in his view] violated by tyranny the Social Compact of the kingdom. Law governed all men, including, and chiefly, the king. But when Cromwell died Milton was left as the sole great figure in the Commonwealth, and his *Ready and Easy Way to Establish a Free Commonwealth* is the boldest republican pronouncement in the English language. He foresaw and described in advance those corruptions of Restoration society which Macaulay has so vividly portrayed in retrospect; he was unwilling to bow his haughty neck or to lose the two parts of freedom, viz., "liberty of conscience, which above all other things ought to be to all men dearest and most precious," and "that other part of freedom, which consists of the civil rights and advancement of every person according to his merits."

It is in the *Areopagitica* that the poet's exalted spirit soars above his theme, and his argument is "more philosophical than philosophy." The immediate occasion was a proposal to institute a licensing board for books. Milton declares that the plan would be un-English, unwarranted by the practice of any illustrious state, and ineffective to curb evil writings. On the contrary, the mind must make a free choice of good over evil, and it must not be prevented by prejudice from creating some great and novel good. But then he transcends this argument to treat of liberty as an essential part of the mind itself, to acclaim the invincibility of Truth, to view London as "a city of refuge, the mansion house of liberty," the head of a nation "as an eagle mewing her mighty youth, and kindling her undazzled eyes at the full midday beam; purging and unscaling her long-abused sight at the fountain itself of heavenly radiance." For God reveals Himself, "as His manner is, first to his English-men." In this book Milton's prose soars above all other prose in the English language. The long sentences thunder through their manifold clauses, but the clauses are short and pithy; impassioned poetry ennobles the prose, which is none the less flexible and full of business. Elsewhere there are times when his eloquence fails. The paragraphs become untidy, and the phrases creep; the argument may be harsh and unfeeling, the jests in bad taste, and the sarcasms blustering. Milton did not hesitate to summon on occasion "the invincible warrior, Zeal, shaking loosely the slack reins, to drive over the heads of scarlet prelates and such as are insolent to maintain traditions, bruising their stiff necks under his flaming wheels." His vehemence was often excessive, but in the *Areopagitica*, where all the strands of liberty were gathered to be knotted or cut at once, no zeal could be too much.

So for fifteen or twenty years this great poet was diverted from the pursuit of poetry to mingle in the battlefield of ideas, "not without dust and heat." He lost some of the charm and freshness of the young Milton; he emerged with narrowed sympathies, a censorious mind, and a style embattled. Was this experience of polemics a total loss when, in his old age, the blind poet came to pen *Paradise Lost*? Who can say? The heroic poem may be written with speed, but it rarely lives without deep experience. Milton could have written one or several epics in the lost years, but he could not have been the poet of Conscience if he had not obeyed it, nor of Liberty if he had not fought in its defence. He might, of course, have kept his subject better within bounds, narrowing it. *Paradise Lost* unquestionably fails to "justify the ways of God to man," unlike Vondel's *Lucifer*, which makes its point. Satan rouses himself in his ruin, as in the Anglo-Saxon *Genesis*, with his proud cry "better to reign in hell than serve in heaven." He shows "a mind not to be changed by time or place," seeking "what reinforcement we may gain from hope; if not, what resolution from despair." So the villain becomes the hero, and by a glorious failure the poem surpasses its plan. When the Tempter himself uses superior force (of guile, in his case) upon Eve and Adam, he forfeits sympathy, which is transferred to his human victims. Their fall, though foreknown, is none the less full of dramatic suspense, and the workings of conscience, heralded by the first sullen drops of the coming tempest, are poignantly felt. The blank verse is derived and refashioned after the best in Shakespeare, and depends for its effect on just such paragraphs as Milton had evolved in *Areopagitica*; like Spenser he has created his own language out of words new and old, and he is a supreme artist in fashioning clangorous sequences of names. Heaven gives him dazzling light, hell gives murky flame and black frost, and his earthbound scenes vary from the idyllic to the tempestuous. His theme allows him to exploit all natural and supernatural effects; it is cosmic yet terrestrial, local but without limits, familiar and sublime. The old Hebraic sublimity of the vast and mysterious finds its most glorious exponent in Milton.

The quieter beauty of *Paradise Regained* attracts fewer readers, but in *Samson Agonistes* Milton restates his main theme, with the hero rightly cast. Old, blind, mocked by his enemies and stung by self-reproach, Samson gathers strength for one last defiant effort, though it ends in his own slaughter. Samson's tragedy, like Satan's and Adam's (and also Christ's triumph in *Paradise Regained*), lies within. Milton anticipates Klopstock by transferring the heroic theme from externals to the heart of man, or rather overleaps Klopstock and anticipates Goethe. His choice of subject and his technique, on the other hand, recall the best epic methods of the Renaissance. His genius belonged to the past and the future, but it was strange to the men of his own date.

VII. AUGUSTAN VERSE AND DRAMA

THE Age of Dryden and the Age of Pope are two phases of the self-criticism through which England passed in the century and a half which constitutes the Augustan Age. In prose and in verse she examined her religious and philosophical beliefs, her political foundations, her society and manners, her aesthetic principles and the texture of her speech, and though some measure of naïvety returned with the Romantics, she could never again display the fresh charm or undisciplined weakness of the Elizabethans. The last of these, John Milton, had still to pen his greatest works when the current had already set in another direction. The man of the age was John Dryden,[1] who was not unheralded or unique, but was supremely representative. The first in the second rank of authors, Dryden earns his place in history by virtue of more permanent contributions than have been made by more gifted writers: the heroic couplet, poetical diction, the heroic play, everyday prose, literary criticism, satire and meditative verse.

Dryden's unique talent for constructing an argument was joined to inability to abide by its conclusions. He was fitted

[1] John Dryden (1631–1700). *Heroic Stanzas on the Death of Cromwell*, 1658; *Astraea Redux*, 1660; *The Wild Gallant*, 1663; *The Rival Ladies*, 1664; *The Indian Emperor*, 1665; *Annus Mirabilis*, 1667; *Essay of Dramatic Poetry*, 1668; *The Conquest of Granada*, 1670; *Of Heroic Plays*, 1672; *Aurungzebe*, 1676; *All for Love*, 1678; *Absalom and Achitophel*, 1681; *Religio Laici*, 1682; *The Hind and the Panther*, 1687; translations, 1693–7; *Alexander's Feast*, 1697; *Fables, Ancient and Modern*, 1700.

to appreciate and state a case, but not to use the verdict against other parties. Fair-minded, acute, trenchant, he followed his argument as easily in verse as in prose. The quotable sentence is frequent with him, and is the more effective when modulated by rhythm and tipped with rhyme. Among his firstfruits are verses which show him able to appreciate both the strong rule of Cromwell and the cessation of faction with the return of the Monarchy. In his *Essay of Dramatic Cricitism* he appreciated in turn the merits of classical tragedy, the manner of Corneille and the Elizabethan drama; having expressed his preference for the last, he reached his highest point in the comparative estimates of Shakespeare, Jonson and Fletcher. Dryden gave the law to British criticism when he averred that its business was not to censure but to recognize the merits of writers; and he did so, not unduly influenced by prejudices acquired through theory. He sums up the religious debate in *Religio Laici* and *The Hind and the Panther*, concluding once in favour of the Anglican settlement, but later for Rome. The latter is the better poem, for the decision was imposed at length not by reasoning but by sentiment, and there are some deeply felt lines devoted to the "unspotted hind" of Rome. In *Absalom and Achitophel*, Dryden achieved the greatest personal satire in the English language. His attack on Shaftesbury and the Whigs—the sponsors of a bad and stupid cause—was devastating, but that alone would have been of transitory interest. The poem's permanent appeal is through Dryden's Tacitean craft of character-building in epigram, which has pilloried his Achitophel and Zimri for as long as the language endures.

For the creation of the heroic play and the comedy of society Dryden has not been much thanked. Both were Spanish inventions, but the best Spanish work was unknown in England. It had been mirrored at a distance by Beaumont and Fletcher, and Corneille had subjected Spanish models to neoclassical rules in his best plays. Satisfaction with contemporary standards of life and thought is an element in all this work, and gives it a superficiality intolerable to countrymen of Shakespeare. Dryden sought to "heighten" tragedy by concentrating the passion and raising the tone of the language. For this purpose his heroic couplet was well enough adapted; and yet

D*

his common sense told him that Shakespeare was still more
lofty. In *All for Love* he admits that his merits come from his
predecessor, though he strives to write in the new idiom; and
if we can shut our minds to the searing comparison with *Antony
and Cleopatra* we may enjoy a drama on the stilted level of the
younger Racine. The heroic tragedy failed. Thomas Otway's[1]
Venice Preserved was the most successful piece of the age.
After a vigorous first act, this tragedy dissolves into blood in
the tedious late Elizabethan manner. Fielding's *Tom Thumb*
covered with ridicule the heroic play.

The new comedy arose from the fact that, according to
Dryden, gentlemen had acquired a taste for laughing at each
other. The great Elizabethans had their roots in the country,
but in the days of Charles II the court and the aristocracy were
urbanized. The jest was often the same one, crude at bottom,
but it conformed to a polite pattern; in place of the guffaw,
there arose the snigger. It was not for Dryden to excel in such
work, which suited better the wit of Wycherley,[2] Etheredge and
Farquhar. William Congreve was not salacious, like the first
of these, and his wit was abundant; but the amoral pose is
fatiguing, and one too rarely encounters the man beneath the
"gentleman."

It remains to mention Dryden's services to prose style. His
prose is clear, direct and full of business, and conforms to the
requirements of scientific accuracy formulated by the Royal
Society, founded in his time; but it is also balanced and dignified. Capable of oratory, it did not aspire to the effects of
poetry, and its purview extended over the whole field of communication of thought. His was the first prose-of-all-work; the
first instance of what was to be the singular glory of the
Augustan Age. From verse Dryden cleared away (not without
acknowledging a debt to Waller) the inopportune wit of the
"metaphysicals" and their careless utterance. He disciplined

---

[1] Thomas Otway (1652–85). *Venice Preserved*, 1682.
[2] William Wycherley (1640–1715). *The Plain-dealer*, 1674.
George Etheredge (1634?–91?). *The Comical Revenge, or Love in a
Tub*, 1664.
George Farquhar (1678–1707). *The Beaux' Stratagem*, 1707.
William Congreve (1670–1729). *The Double Dealer*, 1694; *Love for
Love*, 1695; *The Way of the World*, 1700.

the ten-syllable couplet so that each line and half-line for-
warded the author's intention and left a definite mark on the
reader's mind. Besides the metre, he brought the language
under rhetorical control, devising a heightened diction, not (like
Spenser's and Milton's) for his private use, but as the general
language of elevated speech. This substitution of rhetoric for
imagination has been condemned, yet its educative value was
real, and the flexibility of Dryden's creation is evident when we
find within its limits such highly contrasted styles as those of
Pope, Goldsmith, Johnson and Crabbe.

A man of good sense and taste, having read Alexander
Pope's[1] early *Pastorals*, advised him that no poet had yet
arisen in Britain who was at once great and correct, and
exhorted him to aim at accuracy and elegance. These qualities
he achieved in a superlative degree, and so carried to its peak
the Augustan movement towards urbanity in verse; but he
incurred a doubt not merely whether he was a great poet, but
whether he was a poet at all. There is no question that he did
his work well; the dispute is whether such work should be
undertaken by a poet. Wordsworth quoted from Gray samples
of Popean diction as evidence of what poetry should *not* be. In
the Romantic "Return to Nature," Pope was pilloried as the
protagonist of artifice; the Romantic poets and critics reached
out hands to the Elizabethans, caring only for the Augustan
Age when, as sometimes in Dryden, there was an old aroma,
or, in Collins and Gray, some foretaste of the new. Between
their hammer and the Elizabethan anvil, Pope's reputation was
shattered, and it is even now hard to do him justice. The
difficulty lies in sharing his intentions, and allowing as legitimate his plan for poesy.

It was Pope who, long before the Romantics, said "First
follow Nature." His "Nature" was not theirs and, for all their
authority, we must allow them no monopoly. In *Windsor
Forest*, written at the age of sixteen, his praise is for a majestic

---

[1] Alexander Pope (1688–1744). Educated privately. Greatly admired
Dryden's verse, but merely saw him once. *Windsor Forest*, 1704
(revised, 1713); *Essay of Criticism*, 1711; *Rape of the Lock*, 1712; *Iliad*,
1715–20; *Eloisa to Abelard*, 1717; *Odyssey*, 1723–5; *Dunciad*, 1728;
Essay on Man, 1733–4; *Moral Essays*, 1732–5; *To Arbuthnot*, 1735.

parkland of hills and dales, woods and plains harmoniously confused, "where order in variety we see." Of Skiddaw and Duddon, Chamounix and Xanadu, not a word! Untended Nature was the Romantic's passion, but the normal Englishman nourishes his love of the country and open air in landscapes that have been disposed by art and culture, and chiefly by the foresight and skill of men of the eighteenth century. It is scarcely natural to exclude the works of man from Nature, nor to exclude man himself. For Pope "the proper study of mankind is Man," without excepting the poet; and he did not hesitate to take men and women at their most urbane. Their actual life and interests were those of his poetry, and he kept intact a social coherence that the Romantics were destined to sever. By and after them poetry was excluded more and more from urban experience unless for burlesque and comic effect. Pope cultivated the urban burlesque in *The Rape of the Lock*, but with an exquisite lightness, grace and polish which have never again been equalled. Here his accuracy and elegance have their full value; not a word, not an accent is misplaced or wrongly weighed. He bound himself within the heroic couplet for all but epigrams and an occasional lyric, and he construed that couplet more precisely than Dryden had done. He accepted limits as narrow as those of Ovid's elegiacs; but his consummate virtuosity gave him perfect freedom within them. The metre that served for airy badinage in the *Rape of the Lock* is a vehicle of intense, though highly stylized, passion in the epistle of *Eloisa to Abelard*. Between the two extremes we find the mean of his moral essays and imitations of Horace: the *Essay on Man*, *To Arbuthnot*, *Moral Essays*, *On Criticism*. In these he shows a unique capacity for clear statement in verse; from them exquisitely phrased lines have passed into everyday speech in numbers only less than from Shakespeare and the Bible. The thesis of the *Essay on Man* may be superficial, and the observations in the *Essay on Criticism* are often unessential, but the expression is perfect for grace, liveliness and precision. What no sympathy can save is Pope's *Dunciad*, which raised a furore in its time. The wretched objects of his satire are neither typically nor personally significant, and its manner and method move to loathing.

We cannot, however, avoid seeing the eighteenth century through the double focus we have inherited from Romantic criticism. We are forced to divide the poets and say that Prior, Gay, Swift, Johnson, Goldsmith and Crabbe[1] are among those who did not feel the "tyranny of Pope" or the "dominance of the heroic couplet" oppressive, but found ways of using the accepted mode for their very diverse tempers and purposes. Prior and Gay had the lyrical gift denied to Pope. The former is exquisite in society verse, and the latter gives entertaining counsel in his *Fables*. Gay's *Beggar's Opera* begins in wit, as a parody of the inflated Italian mode of the day; but it ends in an unexpected revelation of gold in base alloy. Swift's octosyllables are a more pointed prose, but Johnson meditated more deeply than Pope in his *London* and *Vanity of Human Wishes*. The verse is heavier and the language latinized, but his pessimism never lacks corroboration in the experience of any age. His massive contrasts of grandeur and ruin owe to poetry their sculpturesque finality. In Goldsmith's *Deserted Village* the same antithesis is mellowed by sympathy; decay is enveloped with a tenderness that prosperity could not command, and the verse itself moves on tiptoe. No doubt there was sentimentalism in this, and Crabbe discards both sentiment and generalized rhetoric, aiming at presenting in his *Village* an unrelieved picture of things as they are. It is a grim poem in uncompromising metre. The reader is always in doubt whether this is poetry at all; and yet he finds his imagination fettered not merely by the truth of the portrayal, but by a convincing sincerity in the verse.

Nor was there anything in Pope's rule which prevented a great part of the century's Parnassus from lying beneath the twin stars of Milton and Spenser. John Philips[2] proved, somewhat naughtily, in *The Splendid Shilling* that even the mighty Miltonic paragraph could be lightly applied. Of course, so

---

[1] Matthew Prior (1664–1721).
  John Gay (1685–1732). *Trivia*, 1716; *Fables*, 1727; *Beggar's Opera*, 1728; *Polly*, 1729.
  Swift, Johnson, Goldsmith. See pp. 88, 94, 96.
  George Crabbe (1754–1832). *The Village*, 1783; *The Parish Register*, 1807; *The Borough*, 1810.
[2] John Philips (1676–1709). *The Splendid Shilling*, 1705.

applied it was not quite the same paragraph, nor when employed as a medium for aesthetic reflections in Akenside's[1] *Pleasures of Imagination*. Edward Young[2] had to thank Milton for portentous seriousness, a habit of expostulation, and his metre, when composing *The Complaint, or Night-Thoughts*, a poem of amazing Continental vogue. Those nine nights were more than a nine-days' wonder in a Europe avid for gloom, charnel-houses, rhetorical melancholy and moral improvement; but perhaps Young was more influential when unread. He set the fashion for the graveyard school, and so his name was on the lips of so enlightened a Spaniard as Cadalso. That was enough; perhaps few Continentals troubled to suffer his wooden prosody, his interminable "O thou's," or his affectation of misery without evident cause. There was cause enough for the melancholy of Cowper[3] in the menacing approach of his madness, and yet it has no such outlet in his *Task*. "I sing the sofa" was his exordium; and his task was to use the Miltonic line for a homely theme, feeling through sincerity for the chord of our common humanity. But blank verse cannot lay aside its splendours without sinking to prose, and for a sofa it had been better to use the unheroic couplet of Pope. Cowper is remembered for a handful of hymns, for *The Diverting History of John Gilpin* (one of the most Pickwickian things before *Pickwick*), and for half a dozen felicitously simple lyrics. His *To Mary* and *The Castaway* disguise the tragedy of the approach of madness under no artifice of words, and are almost unbearably pathetic.

Both Milton and Spenser influenced James Thomson,[4] upon whom nineteenth-century criticism looked with favour as the first to "raise the standard of revolt" against "the poetry of the Town." His *Seasons* enshrines first-hand descriptions of Nature in a diction sometimes sincere, sometimes conventional. Avoiding the rugged in Nature, he yet does not require her to

---

[1] Mark Akenside (1721–70). *The Pleasures of the Imagination*, 1744.

[2] Edward Young (1683–1765). *Night Thoughts*, 1742–5.

[3] William Cowper (1731–1800). *Olney Hymns* (with John Newton), 1779; *Table-Talk*, 1782; *Conversation*, etc.; *The Task, John Gilpin*, 1785; translation of Homer, 1791; Letters.

[4] James Thomson (1700–48). *The Seasons*, 1726–30; *Sophonisba*, 1730; *The Castle of Indolence*, 1748.

be landscaped. His blank verse moves smoothly, if without depth, and his pen is guided by the master hand which wrote the *Georgics*. An allegorical poem entitled *The Castle of Indolence* represents his vain effort to recapture in the eighteenth century the magic of the Bower of Bliss as described in the *Faerie Queene*. The Spenserian stanza and quaintness are there, used with considerable charm but not with the Spenserian magic.

With him we may associate the lyrical poets, Collins and Gray.[1] By addressing odes to the passions and to Highland superstitions, Collins showed that England, like France, was weary of the Age of Reason. His *Ode to Evening* is in Marvell's stanza and in the manner of Horace. The classics, as Lessing later saw, could be used to correct the neoclassics, and it is in this sense that Gray, a scholar deeply versed in the ancient humanities, represents a break with the more gallican tradition of Dryden and Pope. Simplicity of form, lucid thought, planned progress, and thrice chosen language mark Gray's odes, together with his own brand of scholastic melancholy. The gulf between teacher and pupil has not often yawned so widely as in his *Ode on a Distant Prospect of Eton College*, nor have the illiterate yokel and the pensive scholar been so separated as in his famous *Elegy Written in a Country Church-yard*, and yet both poems are marked by as much sympathy and truth as our discordant human nature allows. The scholar's *Ode to Spring* and *Hymn to Adversity* are utterly unlike those of the farmer or the outcast; yet they have their place in the scheme of things. His Pindaric odes on *The Progress of Poesy* and *The Bard* show his mind open to suggestions, whether from the ancient Greek or from as much of the Welsh as he could know, and in less successful verses he comes under the influence of the newly recovered Norse mythology. Every line by Gray is memorable, and no volume so slender has left so clear a mark on English thought.

A different symptom of restlessness is the appearance of two remarkable mystifications in the middle of the century. The

[1] William Collins, (1721–59). *Odes*, 1747.
Thomas Gray (1716–71). *Eton College*, 1742; *Elegy*, 1750; *Progress of Poesy*, 1754; *The Bard*, 1757; Letters.

more excusable was Thomas Chatterton's[1] *Rowley Poems*, though exposure and obloquy drove the poor boy to suicide. His feeling for the felicity of old ballads already announces Coleridge's *Ancient Mariner*, and many older and younger "discoveries" like his have been deemed legitimate devices in the craft of letters. Chatterton's purpose was not to make money by the sale of false antiques, but to give utterance to his liking for the scorned "Gothic"; but the age was not ready for him, and he died. James Macpherson's[2] Ossianic poems are less commendable, for they are turgid, incoherent false and impudent. Yet his *Ossian* was a universal triumph, and partisans to the debate offer us the dilemma that Macpherson must have been either a plagiary or a genius. He was not either, but a good deal of both. Genuine Ossianic poems have existed in Scotland and Ireland demonstrably since the fifteenth and eleventh centuries respectively, and some such lay before Macpherson. He knew others indifferently well, and among them may have been some now lost. So much was genuine; but he amplified, combined, reshaped, faked without scruple, and poured the whole into a prose half rhythmical (with a too insistent ballad rhythm), half flat. This seemed convincing to his contemporaries, and later to the Germans, who placed *Ossian* beside Homer, and to Scottish Highlanders, who were pleased to find themselves for the first time important in the eyes of Europe, without knowing quite on what grounds. Some of his own feeling for shrouded landscape Macpherson

[1] Thomas Chatterton (1752–70). *The Rowley Poems*, 1765–8. They purported to be the work of a fifteenth century monk, Thomas Rowley, of Bristol, and temporarily deceived so good a judge as Horace Walpole.

[2] James Macpherson (1736–96). Born in the Badenoch district of the Highlands, and as a boy a spectator of the collapse of the Highland revolt in 1745. *Fragments of Ancient Poetry*, 1760; *Fingal*, 1762; *Temora*, 1763. These are the Ossianic poems, being ascribed to an authentic Irish hero, Oisin, celebrated in the *Book of the Dean of Lismore*, and are conveniently entitled *Ossian*. The unwelcome enthusiasm of believers forced Macpherson to busy himself with the "Gaelic text" and one was issued at last in 1807, being a not very competent translation of the English. The ballads circulating in oral tradition were collected by J. F. Campbell in his *Leabhar na Feinne*, 1872 (untranslated). Campbell's pieces and those gathered by Sir James Macgregor, Dean of Lismore in Argyll, four hundred years ago (edited and translated by N. Ross, *Heroic Poetry from the Book of the Dean of Lismore*, Edinburgh, 1939), are evidence for the antiquity of this literature in Scotland.

mingled with current sentimentalism and idealization of the "noble savage"; and his readers, encountering the expected, believed. There were, of course, English unbelievers like Johnson and inquirers like Gray, but no direct rendering of the Ossianic ballads would have seemed authentic to the general reader—they have, in fact, none of the Romanticism for which readers of the late eighteenth century yearned, but are incoherent and often in the style of a catalogue. It was Macpherson, with his refurbished Celts, who thawed one of the fountain-heads of European Romanticism.

The eighteenth century was also an age very rich in song. Elizabethan music is set for conditions so different from those of the present that its recovery and interpretation is a matter for scholarship. Englishmen are only beginning to appreciate the glories of this art from Byrd to Purcell. Handel and the Italian opera submerged this native tradition in more ambitious works, and at the close of the century the music of the great Germans was alone considered high art. But the domain of song remained a national preserve, and there emerged such pieces as *Sally in our Alley*, *Black-eyed Susan*, *The Miller of Dee* and *Tom Bowling*. The nineteenth century displayed a less happy vein, but Sullivan used native melodies as suggestions for the music to Gilbert's operas, and song-writers of the twentieth century are exploiting the inborn sense of melody of the English. There was a parallel development in sacred song. The hymns of Isaac Watts, William Cowper, Charles Wesley and Augustus Toplady are phrases in every English mouth. Wesley, in particular, was a new St. Ambrose for the direct felicity of his verses and their basis in a firm theology. Their music is now generally of the nineteenth century. That age, moreover, under the influence of the Tractarian movement added Newman's superb hymns and J. M. Neale's translations from the Latin of the earlier Church. In the twentieth century hymnologists have gathered suggestions from the Celtic Church of Ireland, from European sources and from modern English poets such as Chesterton and Kipling. Special attention has been given to the recovery of fine tunes buried beneath the prejudices of the nineteenth century. Such a collection as the Presbyterian *Church Hymnary* is a fine anthology of the psalmody of all Christendom focused upon the needs of the present age; and it keeps alive the connection between lyric and music which poetry forgets only at its peril. *Hymns Ancient and Modern* is doubtless more familiar to most Englishmen, but it is more conservative and monotonous.

One can hardly praise Scotland for her devotion to the *Metrical Psalms*, though a few are fine and many tunes are most impressive, but one can rejoice in her double tradition of authentic popular songs: those of the Highlands and of the Lowlands. The haunting strains of the Highland music have become generally known only in the twentieth century and that chiefly by the zeal of Mrs. Kennedy-Fraser; but the direct accents of the Lowlands found their finest expression in the eighteenth century. They constituted the poetry of Robert Burns,[1] the inspired peasant. So true is his touch in pieces like *Green grow the Rashes*, *John Anderson*, *Comin' through the Rye*, *Ye Banks and Braes* and *My Love is like a Red, Red Rose* that one does not know where tradition ends and creation begins. His verses came to his mind on the wings of traditional tunes like "Peggy Ramsay" and "Graham's Strathspey," and are scanned not by syllables but by notes. The faithfulness of this Lowland dialect survives even in his ambitious poems, despite his admiration for the Popeans and a certain contagion of their diction. It is prudent, with Burns, to proceed from the small to the big, so as to take him at his most informal. His verses *To a Mouse* and *To a Daisy* are perfect examples of his poignant sincerity and economy of words; his verse epistles show, at times, virtuous indignation, at others, social ease; and there is rollicking recklessness of humour in his cantata, *The Jolly Beggars*. *Holy Willie's Prayer* is a fair sample of his scornful contempt for hypocrisy and *The Cottar's Saturday Night* is the finest eulogy of simple piety. As for his skill in narrative and his broad humour, they reach their apogee in *Tam o' Shanter*.

---

[1] Robert Burns (1759–96). Son of an Ayrshire farmer, took the farm of Mossgiel in 1783 with his brother Gilbert. Poems published at Kilmarnock and Edinburgh, and visit to Edinburgh, 1786. Appointed to a post in the Excise and married Jean Armour, 1788. Removed to Dumfries, 1791.

His contemporary in England was William Blake,[1] artist, poet and seer. The accident of date places him at the end of the eighteenth century, though his genius is not one to enter into chronology with others. His style is isolated by its visionary honesty. It commingles two arts, since the verses are often incomplete without the drawings, and the author engraved them both together. He contrived an elaborate and solitary symbolism to reveal his deeper meaning, and the key is not to be found. For the scholar and literary epicure Blake is rich feeding; the generality are bound to read him without commentary, context or illustration, and they remember him by a dozen brief and thrilling lyrics drawn from *Songs of Innocence* and *Songs of Experience*. By virtue of these, Blake is a children's poet, which is as much as to say a poet for the humbler among the wise. He is unlike the Augustans before him or the Romantics after him, though he has much in common with them both; and in his loneliness he is discerned by the modern symbolist, seeking through the extreme of candour some clue to the eternal riddle.

Of the drama there is little more to add. No tragedies have survived on the stage or in the study, and few comedies. After Congreve's plays in the opening decade of the century, it is a long wait till we reach Oliver Goldsmith's *Good-natured Man* and *She Stoops to Conquer* in 1768 and 1773. Bright humour and skilful characterization mark his work for the stage as for the novel. Sheridan's[2] brilliantly witty comedies completed

---

[1] William Blake (1757–1827). After an unsuccessful attempt to illustrate Young's *Night Thoughts*, his reputation as an artist was not restored until his work on Blair's *Grave* in 1808. Illustrations of *Job* and the *Divine Comedy*. His drawings can be seen in the Tate Gallery, in London. They are remarkable for their spiritual power, expressed in long, pure lines and highly imaginative composition. *Poetical Sketches*, 1783; *Songs of Innocence*, 1789; *Songs of Experience*, 1794; *Milton*, 1804; *Jerusalem*, 1804; etc.

[2] Richard Brinsley Sheridan (1751–1816). Born in Dublin, the son of an actor and of a playwriter and novelist, he was educated at Harrow. Bought Garrick's share at the Drury Lane Theatre, 1776. Member of Parliament for Stafford; took a prominent share in the prosecution of Warren Hastings and in opposing the war with Revolutionary France. In 1809 Drury Lane Theatre was burnt down, and in 1812 he lost his seat in Parliament. Died in debt. *The Rivals*, 1775; *St. Patrick's Day*, 1775; *The Duenna*, 1775; *The School for Scandal*, 1777; *The Critic*, 1779; *Pizarro*, 1799.

the work of Congreve by producing examples of wit acceptable to both taste and morality. The "cape and sword" intrigue is still the mainstay of *The Rivals*, but Sheridan was spared Congreve's obligation to cultivate a cynical pose. At the same time he made his comedy more apt by basing it on real, not imagined, foibles of the day, such as recur ever under new guises. The sentimental novel-devouring young miss, the Byronic young man, the peremptory ancient and the lady who "cannot open her mouth without putting her foot in it," the impetuous yokel and the genial swaggerer are faithfully recorded types of his day, and yet belong to all time. There is a deeper note in *The School for Scandal*—the wrath of the jester against the hypocrite—but there is the same brilliant impressionism in character-drawing. *The Critic*, though less suitable for revival, is distinguished for one unique personality, revealed in the first act, while the second and third are devoted to the impasse in which tragedy was floundering. During the course of the century the star of Shakespeare had risen. Fielding had demolished Dryden, Otway and Addison. Johnson mentioned Ben Jonson beside him, but without pressing the comparison. The Shakespearean model had imposed itself on people who were unacquainted with the Shakespearean stage and traditions and the laughable ineptness of plays made by confounding a good recipe is the theme of *The Critic*.

VIII. AUGUSTAN PROSE

TOWARDS the end of the eighteenth century, Edward Gibbon, the historian, "after the completion of an arduous and successful work," could not "reflect without pleasure on the bounty of Nature, which cast my birth in a free and civilized country, in an age of science and philosophy, in a family of honourable rank, and decently endowed with the gifts of fortune." Had the latter conditions been absent, he might have recorded the gross and murky beginnings of the revolutions at its close, but the eighteenth century, taken at its own valuation, has a commendable record of achievements. The poets and dramatists, even, knew their minds and achieved success. Later criticism has cast doubts on the value of such success which (it has been held) is not worthily the aim of poetry and the drama. No such doubt can rest on Augustan prose which established itself not less for works of erudition than of entertainment. It has the unity and decorum of the age's domestic architecture, itself another symbol of an agreed standard of taste. At that time learning was polite, and wit instructive; wealth and rank were allied to taste; and the distressing schisms of our own day unknown or unrevealed.

The beginning of this state of things can be seen in the cultured negligence of Dryden's verse and prose. It has been noted already; to it we have now to add other evidence of the new precision and intimacy of literature in the later seventeenth century. The Royal Society for Improving Natural Knowledge, so highly favoured by Charles II, "exacted from all its members a close, naked, natural way of speaking; positive expressions, bringing all things as near the mathematical plainness as they can." All "amplifications, digressions and swellings of style" avoided, writers were expected to "deliver so many things in almost an equal number of words." The great periods of Browne and Milton were eclipsed, and Hobbes, with his dogmatism, was anachronistic; but the pithy and experimental Bacon and the judicious Hooker rose to a new esteem. Controversy against the strange and arbitrary speculations of the schools gave to some passages of the new writing a whimsical and extravagant air, which is no part of their essential thought. Thus Robert Boyle,[1] in *The Sceptical Chymist*, has to direct his argument against the four elements of the Aristotelians and the three principles of the Paracelsans, in order to free chemistry from the magical conception of the world which impeded its further advance. The reader's mind strays to this curious lore and takes for granted (since it is now commonplace) the true

[1] Robert Boyle (1627–91). Formulator of Boyle's law in physics. Educated at Eton and on the Continent. Worked at Oxford and took part in founding the Royal Society. *The Sceptical Chymist*, 1691. Wrote on a variety of physical and chemical subjects, and also on religion.

originality of Boyle's thought: the insistence on experiment in the quest for the chemical elements. His style is clear and decorous, though at times prolix.

The intervention of John Locke,[1] who introduced the philosophical debate of the age, was yet more decisive. His themes had a wider appeal, since they dealt with the nature of knowledge and the function of government. A perspicuous, sure-footed style, select in phrase and more natural than fluent, added conviction to his argument; a conviction increased by his assumption of a prudent ignorance concerning the unknowable, and the practicable limits he gave to his conclusions. Locke's *Essay Concerning Human Understanding* was designed to clear the new experimental science from the trammels of preconceived opinions. The reigning theory of "innate ideas" saw in the results of experiment only the recognition of truths innate and latent in the mind. It stultified new truths by representing them as old and forcing them to take their stand in old, unsuitable contexts. Locke's polemic had force to change the connotation of the word "idea" in all the languages of Europe, making it mean "the object of thinking." Ideas (he argued) derived from experience through the senses or from the "internal sense" of reflection. The difficulty of accounting for abstract ideas under this theory led to the philosophic debate of the eighteenth century; but Locke's fundamental position remained unchallenged, and science was free to experiment. In the first of his two essays *Of Civil Government*, Locke refuted the theory of Divine Right, not as expounded by Hobbes, but by the more fashionable and superficial Filmer. The negative was needed in its time, but serves now only as a historical preface to the doctrine of the Second Essay: that political power exists "only for the public good." There is an implicit contract between the ruled and the ruler, and its terms are readily

---

[1] John Locke (1632–1704). Educated at Winchester and Oxford. Lecturer in Greek at Oxford. Physician to the Earl of Shaftesbury, 1667. Member of the Royal Society. During the reign of James II lived in France and Holland, returning with William III in 1689. *Epistola de Tolerantia*, 1689; *Second and Third Letters concerning Toleration*, 1690, 1692; *Essay concerning the Human Understanding*, 1690 ff; *Two Treatises on Government*, 1690; *The Reasonableness of Christianity*, 1695; *The Whole History of Navigation*, 1704.

applicable against either insubordination or tyranny. The natural state of man is "perfect freedom," and only conditionally is this freedom yielded to a society which prevents the annoyance that would come from unlimited mutual interference. Locke's doctrine suited the Whig state of the eighteenth century, and fitted still better the written constitution of the United States of America. His *Letters on Toleration* complete a circle of ideas which has made modern England so unlike the England of the Tudors; yet of all Locke's reasonableness one principal source is the Elizabethan Hooker. Locke advanced English thought; he did not sever its thread.

The personal and private note had been sounded in the lyrics of the Cavaliers, who were sufficiently assured of their social status to air their private feelings. Walton's *Compleat Angler*, though executed under the Commonwealth, and his later *Lives* show the same tendency, which reaches a peak in Pepys's *Diary*. Kept in code and for his sole private entertainment, this diary has been justly famed as the most revealing of human documents. No inhibitions restrict the writer; he appears as a lovable mixture of shrewdness and foibles, amid the scarcely less distinct portraits of his wife and friends. We should not presume too far, as some readers have done, and extend patronage to Mr. Pepys. His love of informality and self-revealing frankness actually conceal the fact that he was one of the best civil servants Britain has ever had, one of the founders of the Royal Navy. Evelyn's *Diary* also is a revelation of an alert and interesting mind.[1]

Defoe's[2] *History of the Plague in London* brings the matter before our eyes with the vividness of an eyewitness. Herein lay his great strength. His style and outlook was that of a

---

[1] Samuel Pepys (1633–1703). The *Diary* (published 1825) extends from 1660 to 1669.

John Evelyn (1620–1706). The *Diary* (published long after his death) covers 1641–97. His other writings deal with gardening, trees, engraving, medals, etc.

[2] Daniel Defoe (1660?–1731). Whig pamphleteer. Joined Monmouth's army in 1685, and William III in 1688. Glass Duty Office, 1695–9. *Essay on Projects*, 1694–5 (published, 1698); *The Shortest Way with Dissenters*, 1702; *Robinson Crusoe*, 1719–20; *Captain Singleton*, 1720; *Moll Flanders, Journal of the Plague*, 1722; *Tour Through Great Britain*, 1724–7; etc.

newspaperman, both in his strong sense of topical interest and
in the liveliness of his presentation. Character, unless in the
figure of the heroine of *Moll Flanders*, he does not aim to
create, and by so much he falls short of the veritable novel.
But he always holds attention in relating events, and the chief
episodes of *Robinson Crusoe* are naturally translated into the
coloured pictures of nursery books. The book is the British
child's gateway to romance, and it takes its place in the mind
long before one can conceive of literary or historical values.
The permanence of its hold is due to another source of strength.
Neither Crusoe nor Man Friday can be said to make a philosophical discovery of the world; comparisons with the celebrated *Philosophus Autodidactus* are therefore misleading.
Defoe's business is with the adventure of civilization. Crusoe is
thrown on a desert island, but with a sufficiency of provisions
and tools; after good-humoured attention to Friday's naïve
views of the universe, Crusoe makes him a member of the
English Church. What we have to admire is a plausible picture
of successful colonization; the creation of new values by adding
labour to land (as Locke would put it), and the reclamation of
the savage.

In Dean Swift's[1] *Gulliver's Travels* the topical instinct is
strong; the presentation is less realistic, but the criticism of life
bites deeper; and the narrative is borne upon a style which,
though unadorned, secures the maximum of effect by the
arrangement of words for emphasis. The phrase marches
urbanely until it is overthrown by some devastating innuendo
at the close. It is the same with the narrative. The British boy
of twelve follows the adventures of Gulliver as a romance, and
is only from time to time pleasantly aware of an incongruous
relationship with his own world. It is the child's introduction
to social criticism; but only a considerable historical reading
serves to bring out the range and corrosive nature of the Dean's
satire. This is an advantage which *Gulliver's Travels* enjoys
over the *Tale of a Tub*, the *Battle of the Books*, the *Modest*

[1] Jonathan Swift (1667–1745). Dryden's cousin. Secretary to Sir
William Temple after 1689. Ordained, 1694. Dean of St. Patrick's,
Dublin, 1713. *Battle of the Books, A Tale of a Tub*, 1704; *Bickerstaff
Papers*, 1708–9; *Meditation upon a Broomstick*, 1710; *Drapier Letters*,
1724–5, 1735; *Gulliver's Travels*, 1726: *Poetical Works*, 1736; *Journal
to Stella*, 1710–13, published 1766, 1768.

Proposal or the *Bickerstaff Papers*, which cannot be read save as satires. In them he is supreme among English writers for his sardonic wit; but their themes grow old, and the modern reader is more attracted by the tenderness of the *Journal to Stella*, a document never meant for more eyes than hers.

Defoe's and Swift's works are important steps towards two of the great achievements of the eighteenth century: the creation of the novel and the essay. The essay received its definitive mould in Steele and Addison's[1] *Spectator*, which also, by devising the figure of Sir Roger de Coverley, contributed an element still wanting to romance. In the *Spectator* the word "essay" lost its Baconian and etymological sense. Its object was no longer to make tests of truth, but to insinuate good taste and good morality by the way of entertainment. In imitation of Defoe and Swift, the authors evaded personal implications by referring their papers to a club, manned by fictitious persons; but this is a device which is often left transparent. Steele was the more inventive, but Addison perfected their combined style. The phrasing is lucid, fluent and carefully avoids emphasis. The writer glides obliquely into his theme, without warning of his purpose. The essays are sometimes light and descriptive, sometimes educative or philosophical; but no reader draws back from the threshold through fear of triviality or depth. This indirect approach has come to be characteristic of the English essay, and is an apparent negation of the Buffonian preconceived plan which rules in France. Despite the avoidance of emphasis, Addison conducted an effective, if philistine, campaign against the Italian opera; brought Milton's *Paradise Lost* into the company of the classics; and placed before the general reader lay thoughts on the religious calendar and the philosophical background of life.

This fund of criticism and observation contributed towards the work of the mid-century: the creation of the English novel. To the legacy of Defoe, Addison and Swift we must add the fund of excellent letters and journals which are a leading feature of the epoch. They can be no more than mentioned.

---

[1] Sir Richard Steele (1672–1729). *The Christian Hero*, 1701; *Grief à la Mode*, 1702; *The Conscious Lovers*, 1722; *Tatler*, 1709 (under the pseudonym "Isaac Bickerstaff"); *Spectator*, 1711–12 (with Addison).

Joseph Addison (1672–1719). *The Campaign* (a poem), 1704; *Cato* (a tragedy), 1713; *Tatler* and *Spectator* essays; Whig pamphlets.

The universal employment of a serviceable prose style—a condition unknown before or after—gives grace and decorum to their informality. An elegant negligence is encountered in all, though with clear marks of personal idiosyncrasy. Lord Chesterfield's[1] letters to his son and godson are, perhaps, more formal than the essays of the *Spectator*. Their author devotes each to an exposition of some particular requirement of good breeding, speaking as a man of the world, a senior companion of youth. The fundamentals of education and religion are not his affair; doubtless he took it for granted that these were supplied by tutors and parsons. His object is to take the gauche mind and polish it to shine in society. Chesterfield is indifferent to the complaint of social injustice and inequality; he assumes it is valid for the youth he wishes to form. This preoccupation with veneer and want of interest in fundamentals has raised against the author a clamour of immorality. To maintain an amoral attitude over so many letters is a feat rarely accomplished by a moral mind, yet there is no actual justification for the reproach. There is some for a reproach of mental tyranny. There is a barely concealed suggestion of compulsion in Chesterfield's counsels to his son, which probably explains his practical failure as an educator. The boy became pliant and obliging, but not distinguished. The epistolary form was used by Gilbert White[2] in his *Natural History of Selborne* as a cover for such observations of nature as Walton placed in his dialogues and Evelyn in his diary. His dissertations cover the twelve months of the year, and make him the prince of birdwatchers. Horace Walpole's[3] letters also are not far removed from the essay. He regards their form with a critical eye and

---

[1] Philip Stanhope, Earl of Chesterfield (1694–1773). Member of Parliament for Lostwithiel, 1722; Ambassador at The Hague, 1728–32. Contributor to *Fox's Journal, Common Sense, Old England, The World*. Lord-Lieutenant of Ireland, 1744. *Letters to his Son*, 1744; *To his Godson*, 1817.

[2] Gilbert White (1720–93). Fellow of Oriel College, Oxford. Born and died at Selborne (Hampshire). *The Natural History of Selborne*, 1789; *A Naturalist's Calendar*, 1795.

[3] Horace Walpole, Earl of Orford (1717–97). Youngest son of Sir Robert Walpole, the Prime Minister. Educated at Eton and King's College, Cambridge, to which he followed Gray. *Private Correspondence*, 1820; *Anecdotes of Painting in England*, 1762–80; *The Castle of Otranto, a story*, 1764; *Description of the Villa of H.W. at Strawberry Hill*, 1774.

causes each letter to develop its proper theme; but the subjects
are of all sorts, with a special knowledge of polite society and
writings in the Whig interest. Some foibles and malice add a
personal savour. The letters of Gray and Cowper[1] were for the
unique delectation of their correspondents, and have the multi-
fariousness of informal letter-writing. The former, in the calm
of his Cambridge retreat, deals chiefly with literature and
scholarship; the latter enlivens the daily round of country life
with humour and observation, being more successful in the
lively prose of the letters than in the prosy verse of *The Task*.
The reader has a choice of sweets among these letter-writers;
but there are many who would choose for reperusal Cowper,
with "the charm and ease of his style, his domestic wit, his
serene good sense, his winning playfulness."

Among the journals, that of John Wesley,[2] founder of the
Methodist movement, stands out as a document of high importance for the religious history of the age, touching depths
below the gay surface of its success. An attractive and sprightly
picture of the Court on its domestic side is to be found in
Fanny Burney's[3] *Diary*, in which diary and letters combine.
The achievements of two great sailors, Anson and Cook,[4] are
written in a clear prose which reveals the competent mind.
Anson's journal forms a rounded narrative, since it deals with
the one voyage of 1740, when he circumnavigated the world.
It is in the form of an extensive report. Cook's voyages took
him round the world in 1771, towards Antarctica in 1772–5,
and along the western side of North America in 1776–80. The
account given is strictly businesslike; it possesses (if we may
borrow a term from architectural criticism) functional beauty.
The competence of the seaman, the magnanimity of the man

---

[1] Thomas Gray and William Cowper. See pp. 79 and 78.
[2] John Wesley (1703–91). *Psalms and Hymns*, 1738; *Hymns*, 1748
(both with Charles Wesley, 1707–88); *An Account of the People called
Methodists*, 1749; *Journal*.
[3] Fanny Burney, Mme d'Arblay (1752–1840). *Evelina*, 1778; *Diary*,
1842, 1904–5 (giving the original text for 1778–1840).
[4] George, Lord Anson (1697–1762). *A Voyage Round the World*
(1740–4), 1748 by R. Waters.
Captain James Cook (1728–79). Explorations in Oceania, the
Antarctic, Western America, Australia and New Zealand. Accounts of
his voyages issued 1773, 1777, 1784.

and the solid worth of his explorations place Captain Cook's
Voyages of Discovery in the forefront of the literature of
travel.

There being thus in the eighteenth century an art of privacy
and of correspondence, it was not surprising that a Mr.
Richardson,[1] a publisher, should have been commissioned to
write a manual of polite letter-writing for young ladies. To
increase its interest he caused the letters to follow a simple plot;
his scheme had also the worthy intention of showing virtue
rewarded. It was from this unlikely cause that the true novel
began to emerge in English letters. *Pamela, or Virtue Rewarded*
banished from ladies' boudoirs the improbable romances of
Clelia, Astraea, Cassandra and the *Grand Cyrus*. It was revealed
that readers could find sighs, languishing and palpitations as
easily below or above the stairs of an English home as in the
remotest Persia. What is more, by some curious divination of
feminine psychology, Richardson was able to follow the succession of emotions in his heroine far more intimately than had
ever been done; perhaps in more subtle detail than anyone
since has achieved. His manner was perfected in the vast
Clarissa, also in letters; but he failed to create a corresponding
masculine character in his *Sir Charles Grandison*. Here he
encountered one of the limits of his creative range. Another is
his confinement within four walls, so that there is a wealth of
sentiment with but little real life in his writing; and yet a third
defect is the circumstance that those who are formed to display
examples of morality under temptation frequently fall into
equivocal situations. There is a conventional, calculating
element in Pamela's too conspicuous virtue that offended the
spirit of a far greater writer, Henry Fielding.

Fielding[2] saved the nascent novel from degenerating into a
new kind of sentimental romance. His indignation against

[1] Samuel Richardson (1689–1761). Coming to London at the age of
seventeen, he entered the printing trade, and in time purchased a moiety
of the patent of King's Printer. *Pamela*, 1740–1; *Clarissa*, 1747–8;
Sir Charles Grandison, 1753–4.

[2] Henry Fielding (1707–54). Born in Somersetshire. *Love in Several
Masques*, 1728, a play. Wrote twenty plays (farces, burlesques, comedies), including *Tom Thumb the Great*, 1730, a parody of heroic drama in
Dryden's manner; *Joseph Andrews*, 1742; *Tom Jones*, 1749; *Amelia*,
1751; *Journal of a Voyage to Lisbon*, 1755. Died at Lisbon.

Richardson's unctuousness caused him to commence *Joseph Andrews* in a spirit of parody, which, however, passed away in the interest of creation. The first of the four "books" passes before the true line of march is entered; and it must be admitted that the plot, which ends in a highly improbable double recognition, is not to be commended. But with the second book Fielding comes under the powerful leadership of Cervantes, whose *Don Quixote* (first part) affords guidance as to its development, incidents, characters, handling, irony and style. Fielding proclaimed this influence on his title-page, and it is significant because his "imitation" is fundamentally indepen-dent. His Parson Adams is a kind of Quixote, but is entirely English; and his Parson Trulliber is a figure of amazing vitality who owes nothing to Cervantes. While he describes his homeland as seen on the roads, just as Cervantes described Spain, this is no hispanized England. Fielding often appeals to Hogarth's pencil as visualizing his descriptions. This novel, as we have remarked, suffers from a divided mind in the author, and is thus inferior to *Tom Jones*, which Coleridge sup-posed to possess the finest plot in our language, and which Gibbon prophesied would outlast the Escorial and the eagles of Austria. It is, as he said, "an exquisite picture of human manners." In it Fielding put a final end to the reign of senti-mental romance, and romance, when reintroduced, had to conform to some kind of reality on pain of being denounced for a sham. Human nature was his theme and his model, neither idealized nor debased; and into *Tom Jones* he poured a multi-tude of lively figures who have each their relevance to the action. The technique and irony of Cervantes have, in this work, become absorbed into the author's brand of sympathetic wit and representational skill; and if his plot does not raise some of the unsatisfied questionings of *Don Quixote*, it is much better constructed and more veracious. Homer as his other master—the source of many excellent mock-heroic similes—perhaps helped him to keep so close to human verities.

For the next hundred years the English novel was either Richardson or Fielding, that is, either psychological with a minimum of happenings, or primarily representational. The two currents do not unite before George Eliot. Neither Smollett nor Sterne[1] attain to their stature, and the work of the former may even seem retrograde. Smollett was attracted by Lesage into the outworn picaresque manner, thus surrendering the more generous humanism of Cervantes and Fielding. Like his hero, *Roderick Random*, he was pugnacious and assertive rather than sympathetically understanding, there is more of incident and less of character in his presentation, the style contains fewer subtleties; but the reader has to thank him for a very generous slice of real life, seen in the raw. This we owe to the strong autobiographical element in his writing. In his last work, *Humphrey Clinker*, the tone is mellower. As for Sterne, in *Tristram Shandy* and *A Sentimental Journey*, he is a past-master of whimsical narrative. Both the style and the course of narrative are made to obey his wayward whims, and to afford openings for his humour and sentimentalism, the former both Rabelaisian and prurient, and the latter both pathetic and mawkish. Episodes are his principal care and there is no plot in *Tristram Shandy*; but it offers us a group of the most entertaining and likeable characters in any novel.

To pass from the history of a style of writing to that of a group of friends is doubtless illogical, but it obeys the facts of literary history. Samuel Johnson's[2] circle is gathered into an incomparable book: Boswell's *Life of Johnson*, to which Boswell's *Journal of a Tour to the Hebrides with Samuel Johnson* is a kind of preamble. Macaulay amused himself with the paradox that Boswell wrote the greatest of all biographies

[1] Tobias George Smollett (1721–71). Ship's surgeon, present at the battle of Cartagena, 1741. *Roderick Random*, 1748; *Peregrine Pickle*, 1751; *Sir Lancelot Greaves*, 1762; *Adventures of an Atom*, 1769; *Humphrey Clinker*, 1771.

Laurence Sterne (1713–68). *Tristram Shandy*, 1759–67; *Sermons of Yorick*, 1760; *Sentimental Journey through France and Italy*, 1768; *Letters to Eliza*, 1775.

[2] Samuel Johnson (1709–84). Born at Lichfield, son of a bookseller. Pembroke College, Oxford. Left without a degree, owing to poverty. Taught for a while in a school. Removed to London in 1737, and lived precariously on the earnings of journalism and literature. Met Boswell 1763, when he was in easier circumstances. *London*, 1738; *Irene, Vanity of Human Wishes*, 1749; *Rambler*, 1750–2; *Idler*, 1758–60: *Dictionary of the English Language*, 1755; *Rasselas*, 1759; *Journey to the Western Isles of Scotland*, 1775; *Lives of the Poets*, 1779–81 (*Life of Savage*, 1744).

James Boswell (1740–95). *Account of Corsica*, 1768; *Journal of a Tour to the Hebrides*, 1785; *Life of Dr. Johnson*, 1791.

because he had the shallowest of minds; he could do no other than reflect his hero. The critic's sophistry lies naked when one considers the artistic superiority of Boswell to Johnson, and the circumstance that, in a measure, Boswell created Johnson. It is only by virtue of the *Life* that the ponderous doctor becomes the literary and moral arbiter of the eighteenth century. Boswell induces him to utter phrases more significant than he ever wrote, setting them against the foil of the biographer's assumed foppishness and against the contrasted characters of Goldsmith and other friends. It is a biographer's business to keep away from the spotlight, and this Boswell did at the expense of his reputation. His artistic serious-ness and personal intelligence can be otherwise assessed, or they can be esteemed for the book itself and not for the evidence so unfairly used by Macaulay. The conditions of this perfect biography are, indeed, such as are never likely to be repeated: the biographer's complete intimacy with his model, his chances of provoking the reactions he wanted, his long-sighted choice of theme and assiduous persistence, Johnson's habit of living in public with his friends, his essential greatness, and the art of conversation then most exquisitely perfected. All this conspires with Boswell's skill to give a revelation of one human being such as has never been made before or since. Johnson's contribution was his char-acter. It gave him a certain pre-eminence in his circle, joined to his faculty of monumental phrase and realistic vision. These qualities are somewhat obscured in his own works, where there is a lack of the relief given by the biographer and some disturb-ing influences of indolence and erudite convention. The power to hew phrases may be seen in Johnson's *Dictionary of the English Language*, a monumental achievement for a lonely scholar and famous for its, at times, surprisingly felicitous and trenchant definitions. As a novelist Johnson's *Rasselas* placed him in an out-of-date class of moral romancers. The quality appears most clearly if the book is read along with Voltaire's *Candide*; for though both adopt the same convention, the Frenchman is as contemporary and sprightly as the Englishman is remote and doctrinaire. The Addisonian essay was culti-vated by Johnson in the pages of the *Idler* and the *Rambler*, names singularly unfit for his serious morality and weighty speech. Johnson, indeed, hardly does himself justice in any writing save one or two of the *Lives of the English Poets*. Many of these merited no more than a brief notice; his sympathies did not extend to some forms of greatness. Yet there is an honesty in his reactions to such a one as Milton, and trenchant judgments that raise him to the front rank of critics. English eighteenth-century criticism (including Warburton and the Wartons) has the merit of direct knowledge of the thing judged, and freedom from the vices of mystical theorizing and arbitrary labelling which have since been imported to its hurt. The best of Johnson's *Lives*, however, is that of his friend, Savage, in which, with bitter personal experience, he arraigns the system of literary patronage then normal. In refusing to submit to that which wasted Savage's genius, Johnson achieved his finest work for literature: the emancipation of the man of letters.

As society was small in London in those days, the most interesting literary and artistic figures were to be met in the vicinity of Dr. Johnson. Mrs. Thrale (or Piozzi) preserved anecdotes and some letters, and Oliver Goldsmith[1] portrayed the company in his good-humoured *Retaliation*. Goldsmith was treated with some condescension, since it was "generally circulated and believed that he was a mere fool in conversation," and that was the ground of his *Retaliation*. The literary historian is embarrassed by Goldsmith, whose success seems in no way dependent on the fashion of his times. He used the current modes, but with a strange felicity, "touching nothing he did not adorn." This lack of ambition seems to conflict with the regular sequence of his successes, since success is not to be obtained without a struggle. Yet in the *Vicar of Wakefield*, Goldsmith, without innovating, but telling a very simple story, is more memorable than greater novelists. The reflective and the humorous poem he handled deftly, and composed two

---

[1] Oliver Goldsmith (1730–74). Spent years on the Continent supported by no more than his flute, and tried many shifts at a livelihood in England, including school teaching. *The Bee*, 1759; *Citizen of the World*, 1762; *The Traveller*, 1764; *Vicar of Wakefield*, 1766; *Deserted Village*, 1770; *The Good-natured Man*, 1768; *She Stoops to Conquer*, 1773; *Retaliation*, 1774; Various histories.

of the still living comedies of that age. He contributed largely to periodical literature, and himself issued *The Bee* and *The Citizen of the World* (the latter on the model of Montesquieu's *Lettres persanes*). His gaiety and light-hearted versatility make it hard to give to him the epithet "important"; yet his work is more permanent than that of more "important" writers. He lived by his pen without patronage no less than Johnson did, but without troubling to raise a question of principle. The actor, David Garrick, was another member of the circle, and Sir Joshua Reynolds,[1] the painter and first President of the Royal Academy, added another art. Garrick had a neat hand in verse, and contributed powerfully to the rising fame of Shakespeare. Reynolds not only defined the grand style of painting in his fifteen discourses, but at the same time founded higher art education in this country. His style, less studied than Johnson's, is dignified and balanced as well as plain and lucid. Edmund Burke's *Essay on the Sublime and Beautiful* is a work of the same school.[2]

This later Augustan prose did not differ from the earlier in the fundamental insistence on a classic orderliness of thought and language. Yet it has travelled a long distance from the elegant negligence of the earlier epoch. It requires its words to have not merely fitness, but also weight. The plain structure of the sentence is altered by insistence on balance, leading to the rhythms and cadences of the orator. The clause has lengthened. Thought is no longer merely rational, but dappled with senti- ment, sometimes extravagant or lachrymose. English prose was moving in the direction which French literature took from the purism of Racine to the open or concealed emotionalism of Rousseau and Voltaire. But the classic façade of eighteenth- century art was rarely broken, and the signs of literary unrest at this time need not hold our attention. There was a "Gothic" craze as exemplified in Horace Walpole's[3] *Castle of Otranto*, soon to be eclipsed by the more genuine medievalism of Sir Walter Scott; an "oriental" extravagance pervades the

[1] Sir Joshua Reynolds, P.R.A. (1723–92). *Discourses*, 1769–90.
[2] Burke. See p. 101.
[3] Horace Walpole. See p. 90.

E

conduct of Beckford[1] and his romance *Vathek*. These and other signs might be taken to announce the coming of Romanticism, and contributed in themselves to the variety of their age; but they are not masterpieces nor do they constitute an achievement.

Locke had defended the reasonableness of Christianity, but others had developed his principles to support deism, ignoring the Christian revelation as such. The argument, however, by-passed many of the mysteries and difficulties which had made the acceptance of revelation unpalatable, and in his famous *Analogy of Religion* Bishop Butler[2] put to an acid test proofs that had been offered as to the immortality of the soul and the moral government of the world. He showed that religious conviction stands not upon proof, but upon faith. But, in exchange, without making use of the teachings of revelation or of the deductions which have principally been made therefrom, he undertook to show that there is an analogy between these things and the facts of the natural order. By analogy we arrive at the probability of a moral order and, in practical experience, men act with assurance whenever there is a balance of prob-ability to favour one line of conduct. Butler's *Analogy* is the *Summa contra gentiles* of Anglicanism in its avoidance of arguments held valid by Christians as such, but the bishop expects much lower profits from demonstration.

The philosophic problem of the eighteenth century was pro-pounded by another bishop, George Berkeley.[3] His approach

---

[1] William Beckford (1759–1844). Born at Fonthill and privately educated. *Vathek* was written in French. Henley's English translation was published in 1784 and appeared under the disguise of a translation from the Arabic. Beckford, annoyed, published the French text in 1787. He bought Gibbon's library at Lausanne, and returned to live in literary and artistic extravagance in his fantastic palace at Fonthill.

[2] Joseph Butler (1692–1752). Educated at Tewkesbury by Samuel Jones, and at Oxford. Corresponded with Dr. Clarke on the subject of his Boyle Lectures, 1704–5. Bishop of Bristol, 1738; of Durham, 1750. *Fifteen Sermons preached at the Rolls Chapel*, 1726; *The Analogy of Religion, Natural and Revealed, to the Constitution and Course of Nature*, 1736; *Six Sermons*, 1739–48; *Charge to the Clergy of Durham*, 1751.

[3] George Berkeley (1685–1753). Born near Kilkenny, Ireland. Student and Fellow of Trinity College, Dublin. Dean of Derry, 1724. In America, 1728–31; Bishop of Cloyne, 1734. *A New Theory of Vision*, 1709; *Principles of Human Knowledge*, 1710 ff.; *Three Dialogues*, 1713; *Alciphron*, 1732; *Theory of Vision*, 1733; *Siris*, 1744.

to the matter lay through studies of the science of optics, which had been opened up by Sir Isaac Newton, a name portentous in the history of thought, though not of literature. In these studies, Berkeley had to deal with the evidence of the senses, and so was led to the theory of knowledge expounded in his *Principles* and *Three Dialogues*. From Locke he took over the view that all knowledge comes from experience, and is transferred through the senses to become our ideas. But these ideas, he pointed out, are the only things we know, and apart from what goes on in our own minds there is nothing of which we have any knowledge. We cannot know anything except by the process of knowing. This one principle, which seemed of crystal clarity to Berkeley, he repeated again and again in the face of every possible argument, and in a style so purely fluent (unlike Butler's) as to leave no lurking-place for doubt. Yet to his contemporaries he seemed to speak a dark paradox, in making the reality of things depend on our knowing them. Johnson refuted him by stubbing his toe against a stone; but philosophers found refutation more difficult; and since Berkeley modern philosophy, like that of the ancients after Zeno the Eleatic, has never been entirely sane. The reality of things being due to a knowing mind, Berkeley found therein a proof of the existence of God, the Mind which by knowing all makes all reality. David Hume,[1] a Scotsman, took over the problem from Locke and Berkeley in his *Treatise of Human Nature*. The first part is devoted to "An Enquiry concerning Human Understanding." The second deals with the "Principles of Morals." From these he passed through his *Essays* and *Political Discourses* to his *History of England* (*1603–88*) and *History of the House of Tudor*. His final studies were of Natural Religion. Thus Hume is the builder of an entire system, unlike Berkeley who is the expositor of a single thought. He indulged in a measure of agnosticism or scepticism so long as he felt the

[1] David Hume (1711–76). Judge-Advocate to General St. Clair, 1747. Keeper of the Advocates' Library, Edinburgh, 1752. Paris, 1765. Retired to Edinburgh, 1769. *Treatise of Human Nature*, 1739–40. *Essays*, 1741–2; *Human Understanding*, 1748; *Principles of Morals*, 1751; *Political Discourses*, 1752; *History of England*, 1754–61; *Natural History of Religion*, 1757; *Essays and Treatises*, 1770; *My Own Life*, 1777; *Natural Religion*, 1779.

general trend of his thoughts to be sound. He distinguished between sense impressions and ideas, so that the latter became to some extent criticisms of the sensual data; and in the ideas he found relations of likeness, contiguity in time or place, cause and effect, which form mental complexes that constantly recur and are our guarantee of objective reality. He agrees with Berkeley that all our ideas are particular, but he argues that some particular ideas come to have a representative quality which makes them general. So he believed he had saved the external reality of things. His dealings with "the sceptical philosophy," especially in the items of the immortality of the soul and of personal identity, aroused considerable alarm.

Apropos of the name of Hume it is convenient to note the brusque rise in the amount and value of the Scottish contribution to English literature. There was much for them to learn about the southern idiom, and Hume acknowledges the corrections of a friend; but they were the products of a better educational system, and hard reasoning was acclimatized among them. Edinburgh was still far enough withdrawn from London not to yield its mental life under the enticements of the English court. So, in this second half of the eighteenth century and during the first third of the nineteenth, Scotland was able to influence in a marked and characteristic way the general trend of English culture. The Lowland dialects served as a Doric in the songs of Allan Ramsay, Lady Nairn and Burns; Smollett brought Scottish realism into the novel; and Hume and Robertson[1] founded a new school of historical writing. It was rooted in "human nature," and obtained therefrom both the means of criticizing evidence of things past and reasons for combining the facts into new and instructive syntheses. The ground they occupied has been traversed by others; but the work of an English historian, an admirer of Hume and admired by him—Edward Gibbon,[2]—remains intact as a masterpiece of

[1] William Robertson (1721–93). *History of Scotland*, 1759; *Charles V*, 1769; *America*, 1777.

[2] Edward Gibbon (1737–94). Left Oxford on conversion to Roman Catholicism, but was later reconverted at Lausanne. Served with the Hampshire militia, 1760–3. Visit to Italy, 1764. Member of Parliament. Retired to Lausanne. *Decline and Fall of the Roman Empire*, 1776–88; *Memoirs of my Life and Writings*, 1796.

the philosophic manner in historical writing. His theme is of importance to all Western civilization, and Gibbon forged a stately prose, not unlike Johnson's, which proved equal to the matter. The whole is governed by the thought embodied in the title, *The Decline and Fall of the Roman Empire*, extending from the felicitious age of the Antonines to the extinction of the Empire in the East. It may be said that he exalts the Antonines too much and gives too little credit to the Byzantines; that he is overindulgent to the Saracens and too sceptical in his dealings with Christianity; but his vast and multifarious erudition is preserved by a certain skill in avoiding perishable details of fact; his progress is grand and general, and no advance in knowledge can prevent his work remaining one cardinal interpretation of fourteen centuries of human experience. His *Memoirs* and letters are subservient to this design, and the former as blandly balk the reader's curiosity in personal matters as they are revealing in the realm of mind.

Parallel with the great historians, we encounter great orators in this age. They have in common the settled tradition of eighteenth-century prose, upon which they graft their personal idiosyncrasies. In the elder Pitt (Lord Chatham) the indignant torrent of eloquence is supreme; in the younger[1] we admire chiefly the consummate parliamentarian; in Sheridan, wit; in Fox,[2] generous and eloquent sentiments. The crown for written oratory (though in the spoken field things went differently) belongs to the eloquent Irishman, Edmund Burke,[3] since, apart from the fullness and rhythm of his words, his more laboured discourses announce some of the leading propositions of British statecraft. This is notably so in his *Speeches on American Affairs*, which condemn the attempt to govern a colony by the criterion of the motherland's interest or by any legalistic procedure. His orations and pamphlets on the French Revolution are not less eloquent, but are more liable to fall into

[1] William Pitt (1759–1806). Orations on the French War, 1793–1801.
[2] Charles James Fox (1749–1806). Speeches on the French War, 1792–1800.
[3] Edmund Burke (1729–97). *On the Sublime and Beautiful*, 1756; *Thoughts on the Present Discontents*, 1770; *Speeches on American Affairs*, 1774–7; *Reflections on the Revolution in France*, 1790; *Letters on a Regicide Peace*, 1795–7.

sophistries through excess of passion; and the statesmanlike arguments against France must be sought in Pitt's discourses, while those on behalf of peace and understanding belong to Fox and Sheridan.

These mighty contenders were alike in birth and education, in style and background, and in their approach to uniform types of problem. Their constitutionalism acknowledged as one of its sources a Bill of Rights, from which could be intelligibly deduced such general principles as were written into the American Constitution. But the language and ideas of Thomas Paine's[1] *Rights of Man* were outside their range, since Paine claimed natural rights over which no constitution was supreme. Acute, but sometimes crude, Paine's work was adapted for the widest circulation, propelled by the enthusiasm of the French revolutionaries. On the other hand, the merely political issues of the century were about to be complicated by the economic problems arising out of the Industrial Revolution. The economics of the mercantilist age, with its unwarrantable intrusions of the state, had become unsuitable, and in France Turgot and the Physiocrats had leaped to the too easy assumption that all wealth comes from the soil and can be subjected to a single tax. A Scottish professor, Adam Smith,[2] who owed a good deal to the Physiocrats, came to the forum of debate with his famous *Wealth of Nations*, to deal with the new conditions in a spirit of luminous sanity. Though Smith did not either found or complete the science of political economy (as some partial judges have held), his treatment is the oldest still to retain its full value, and from his two principles of self-interest and natural liberty has flowed the greater part of the deductions of a later age. Price, rent, wages and labour, capital, the commercial system, commerce and revenue are themes he is the oldest to develop in terms still instructive. As the other half

---

[1] Thomas Paine (1737–1809). Went to America and served in the American Army, 1774 ff. Returned to live chiefly in France, 1787. Returned to America, 1802. *The Rights of Man*, 1791–2; *The Age of Reason*, 1793.

[2] Adam Smith (1723–90). Born at Kirkcaldy, to which he retired in 1767. Professor of Moral Philosophy in the University of Glasgow, 1752. Visit to France, 1764. *The Wealth of Nations*, 1776. Rector of Glasgow University, 1787.

of his professorial work led him to consider man as a moral
being, he was far from supposing self-interest the only motive
or from erecting the gaunt figure of "economic man." In this
sense he added a new science to the encyclopaedia, and the
beginnings of another are to be found in Malthus's essay on
the *Principles of Population*, with its grimly realistic appraisal of
the pressure of an increasing people on a stationary food
supply.[1] The events of the next hundred years eluded his
argument, since the world's stock was increased in various
ways; but there is now no sight of another Golden West, and
the pressure of population is becoming more insistent. After
influencing biological thought in the nineteenth century, the
grim Malthusian doctrine bears once more upon human
society.

IX. THE ROMANTICS

THE emergence of five great poets and one great novelist within
the period 1798–1832 constitutes the English Romantic school.
The word "romantic" had been in favour for half a century,
being used of young ladies, scenery, disordered speech, etc.
To use a capital letter and to speak of a "school" is evidence
of the word's reflux from the Continent, where labels and
abstractions are more in vogue than in Britain; but with
"Romanticism" fairly established in our language, much ink
has been shed in the attempt to assign to it a constant meaning.
The opposition to the previous age and especially to Pope is
sufficiently clear (except in Byron) to warrant the antithesis to
"Classicism." The early eighteenth century was "classical"
inasmuch as it believed in the perfectibility of literary effort;
the prototype of such perfection it saw, as all preceding ages
had done, in the literary circle which surrounded Augustus in
the height of Roman glory, for which reason the eighteenth
century was also called "Augustan." The principal charac-

[1] Thomas Robert Malthus (1766–1834). *An Essay on the Principle of
Population*, 1798; *Rent*, 1815; *Principles of Political Economy*, 1820.

teristic of the age, as we have seen, was its urbanity. To urbanity pertains interest in man, chiefly as living in civilized society; in domesticated nature; in usefulness and the moral way; in the whole more than the part; in construction and rule; in doctrine, in logic, wit and polish. Solitary man, wild nature, revolt, imagination, passion, defiance of rule, tolerance of episode—these ingredients, together or separately, help to make up the Romantic manner.

Within the common features of date and difference from their predecessors the great Romantics are marked by the most strenuous individualism. Coleridge and Wordsworth combined in the *Lyrical Ballads*, but only to show that true poetry flows from two quite distinct principles: the rationalizing of the bizarre by fancy, and the imaginative enriching of the ordinary. Byron denounced them both as unintelligible, and enthroned Milton, Dryden and Pope as the trinity of English verse. The European continent acclaimed Byron as the great Romantic by virtue of his defiant pose, so unlike the quietness of Wordsworth amid his lakes. Wordsworth, Coleridge and Southey were fired by the enthusiasm of the early stages of the French Revolution, seeing in it a hope for the equality of all men, but they reacted against its later violence and became intransigent; Byron and Shelley continued to denounce "tyrants"; but Sir Walter Scott treasured up every old tradition and superstition. He had (according to Hazlitt) a dim perception of the present and none at all of the future; but Shelley's whole genius was in an imagined future and Byron was bounded by the present. Keats was concerned with none of these things, but with a search for beauty of form; Coleridge's flights had no certain trajectory. So we could continue to pile up distinctions, amounting to six irreconcilable techniques; and we should still have failed to mention Miss Austen who, as great in her way as any of the others, has nothing whatever of the Romantic in her!

It is clear, then, that the notion of a "school" is unhelpful to the reader, for whom the significant fact is the uprush of creative inspiration within the third of a century. To this inspiration we owe the finest lyrics and rhapsodies of the language, the rebirth of romance in the novel, a more subtly

appreciative criticism, the enrichment of prose with rhythm.
There were losses: weakness in handling the larger traditional
moulds, loss of urbanity and of common form, defect of wit
(except in Lamb and Byron), and abundance of tomboy
pleasantries. Coleridge denied that poetry and prose were
dissimilar, but only both opposed to science. A fissure opened
here which we have not noticed in the eighteenth century, since
science ("the acquirement, or communication, of truth") was
now not encouraged to attempt also "the communication of
immediate pleasure." The urbane prose of the eighteenth
century was as much at the disposal of the educator as of the
novelist, but not so the "animated prose" of the Romantic
which tended, along with the verses of the poet, to produce a
"pleasurable emotion, a peculiar state and degree of excitement" in both author and reader. It is not that good informative writing ceased—far from it—but a standard had been
removed, and erudition had licence to be slovenly. The return
to Nature, also, was achieved at the expense of man, who, with
his works, is not really less natural than a mountain or river.
There was on the one side an expansion of the domain of
poetry, on the other a contraction, since the withdrawal of
social topics left a gap between poetry and the normal urban
realities of the age. The eighteenth century could sing of tea
and a sofa, but the nineteenth was dumb before the railway
train.

The Romantic period is opened by Wordsworth and
Coleridge's[1] *Lyrical Ballads* in 1798. The latter's share was
"to interest the affections by the dramatic truth of such
emotions as would naturally accompany" supernatural incidents and agents, supposing them real; and this he carried out
to perfection in *The Rime of the Ancient Mariner*. In it the poet
evokes an emotion of mysterious horror, starting from a commonplace opening, such as only the most magical ballads (*Tam
Lin*, for instance) could inspire. In its quaint marginalia and

[1] Samuel Taylor Coleridge (1772–1834). Educated at Christ's Hospital (with Lamb) and Cambridge. Met Wordsworth, 1795. Tour with
Wordsworth in Germany, 1798. *Lyrical Ballads*, 1798; contributions
to the *Morning Post*; *Christabel*, 1816 (written 1797, 1800). Resided
at Highgate. *Biographia Literaria*, 1817; *Aids to Reflection*, 1825;
Essays and Lectures; *Works*, 1828, 1834.

E*

spelling the *Ancient Mariner* might have been one of Chatterton's *Rowley* ballads. It is significant that Coleridge wrote a monody on Chatterton, and his imitations of Ossian prepare us for the ejaculatory manner of his *Ode to France* and *Hymn to Mont Blanc*. The character of the *vates*—the bard plenarily possessed by the daemon, as Plato had described him in *Ion*— is nowhere so well upheld as in *Kubla Khan*. The story of its composition is essential to the poem. Coleridge states that he fell into a doze over a passage from *Marco Polo* copied by Purchas, and in this state his mind composed two or three hundred lines, which he began to pour without stop on paper when he wakened. But an interrupter came when only fifty-four lines were written, and the inspiration could not be recaptured. The lines are luxuriously magical; the rhythms vary, ebb and swell, and the topics change abruptly; the reader's excitement is tightly wound up to expect an ineffable revelation, and then the break cuts all short. A fortunate break! It is true we have lost some hundred lines of superb poetry, but the unspoken music is sweeter, the unfinished chords more echoing. The unfinished *Christabel* is some proof of this assertion. The first part was written in 1797, and the second (incomplete) three years later. The wizardry of metre and language is not less potent throughout than in *Kubla Khan*, and yet its length takes away some of the poignancy, while still the thought defies conclusion. Indolence was Coleridge's besetting vice. His verses are mostly fragments and jottings, and he added nothing of interest after 1802; but the felicity of his few great moments is indescribable.

Wordsworth's[1] share in the *Lyrical Ballads* was to deal with subjects chosen from ordinary life, "such as will be found in every village where there is a meditative and feeling mind to seek after them." His contribution to the first edition was not

---

[1] William Wordsworth (1770–1850). *Lyrical Ballads*, 1798 (with Preface, 1800). Early travels in France and later in Germany, with residence near Coleridge during the composition of their joint work. Settled at Grasmere, 1799, removing to Rydal Mount, 1813. Poet Laureate, 1843. *Poems*, 1807, 1815, 1845; *Excursion*, 1814; *Waggoner, Peter Bell*, 1819; *Sonnets on the River Duddon*, 1820; *Memorials of a Tour on the Continent*, 1822; *Ecclesiastical Sonnets*, 1822; *Prelude* (written 1799–1805), 1850.

noteworthy, but in the second there appeared his Preface which, with an Appendix and an Essay on Poetry, are among the most important documents of the new poetry. Wordsworth was that rare phenomenon in English literature, a poet with a programme. Criticizing the work of his immediate predecessors, he condemned their trust in metre and poetic diction, accusing them of creating a hubbub of words. The language of poetry (he held) differs in no essential from that of good prose. The poet "is a man speaking to men: a man, it is true, endowed with more lively sensibility, more enthusiasm and tenderness, who has a greater knowledge of human nature, and a more comprehensive soul." "I have said [he continued] that poetry is the spontaneous overflow of powerful feelings: it takes its origin from emotion recollected in tranquillity." The distinction between Fancy, which ornaments the surface of things, and Imagination, which gives them a deeper significance, is of great importance for Wordsworth's practice; still more influential was his celebrated "return to Nature."

From the considerable bulk of his writings it is necessary to make large deductions. Had Time been so gentle with Wordsworth as with the Greek tragedians, by withdrawing from memory the most perishable part of his work, his glory would reach its meridian. Nearly all his later pieces would be forgotten: those which earned for him from Browning the title of "the lost leader." They were written in his retreat at Rydal Mount, where he lacked the stimulus of contact with the wide world, hemmed in by loneliness and poverty. Thus he descended to parochialism; but the events of his earlier life—travels in France in the revolutionary age, contact with the mind of Coleridge, the Napoleonic peril, the first views of the Lake District and of parts of Scotland, the visit to Germany—these things provided the fund of powerful feelings which were for him the external condition necessary to the birth of poetry. His poetic soul was not self-moved; but once stirred, its utterance in controlled calm is more moving than the splutterings of a rhetorical passion. In breaking down the division between prose and poetry Wordsworth lost the support given by technical processes. He proved incapable of the larger moulds, which, in the *Excursion* and the *Prelude*, become wearisome,

apart from those moments when his imagination is truly afire.
His greatest success was achieved precisely where he submitted
to the strictest discipline, in the *Sonnets*. He is the third great
master of the English sonnet, the peer of Shakespeare and
Milton. There is volcanic energy in Milton's political sonnets;
in those of Wordsworth there is incandescent passion. He
gives a deeper meaning to patriotism, making the love of
country one with the love of freedom, truth and honour.
Shakespeare takes us into the depths, but they are more
troubled. In the sonnets to the Duddon we find that powerful
emotion may be aroused by the simplest natural scenes and
by day-to-day experiences. The seeing eye and the feeling
heart draw sermons from stones. This familiar magic is at
work in many of his travel lyrics, such as *The Highland Girl of
Inversneyde*, *The Reaper*, *Ruth*, etc., or again in his view of
simple objects, such as *The Skylark*, *The Cuckoo*, *The Daffodils*,
Yarrow Visited, *The Daisy*. In them he revealed a new world
of pleasure for the imagination. The accuracy of his view of
nature was not less than the intensity of his sympathy.

The *Lines Composed above Tintern Abbey*, written on the
18th July 1798, are the quintessence of Wordsworth. They
may be contrasted with the set pieces of the preceding century
or centuries, such as Pope's *Windsor Park*, to show that
Wordsworth's vision, though not less exact as to outward
detail, involves both eye and mind, sense and emotion, sight
and thought. When set beside Coleridge's *Hymn to Mont Blanc*,
they show his inspiration to be independent of the spectacular
and his thought free from the temptation to slip into a too
convenient vague deism. The "inward eye" carries with it the
impression of loveliness from the Wye Valley to purify the
mind in hours of weariness, amid the hubbub of cities, to
lighten "the heavy and the weary weight of all this unintelligible world." Crabbe observed detail as closely in his *Village*,
but his sight was purely external. Gray, like Wordsworth,
remembered the scenes of childhood with emotion, but in the
Ode on the Intimations of Immortality these recollections are
transmuted into an impassioned exultation as loftily intellectual as the highest flights of Plato. This is the Nature to
which Wordsworth caused poetry to "return," in a fashion so
little like the consequences of Pope's advice "First follow

Nature." It is a highly sophisticated mood, for which the long previous centuries were a preparation. Man as a theme for the poet has the disadvantage of his individualism. Though Shakespeare shows a unique sympathy with Hamlet, yet Hamlet is Hamlet at last, and Shakespeare's mind is not fully revealed. The landscapists had pursued the objective study of Nature, as the object which, informing the senses, stimulated man's ideas; but the thing and the minds remained apart. It was Wordsworth who found that the impersonality of Nature was fit to symbolize the succession of emotions within the poet's own soul, free from every dramatic and pictorial impediment. He became the Berkeley of poetry, since the reality of things was dependent on the operations of his own mind. It was likewise with his prosody and diction. Their simplicity, their "naturalness," are deceptive. The previous age had chosen words with a view to elegance and propriety, but Wordsworth's choice was no less arduous in his search for propriety and spontaneity. The peril of the eighteenth century had lain in the fading of eloquence, but Wordsworth's risk of falling into the prosaic was yet more insidious. He is a victim frequently enough in the *Prelude* and the *Excursion*. When no movement of spirit is there, there is certainly no artifice of words to beguile the tedium; but when the poet's mind kindles, the exquisite sincerity of the verse, the sense of measure and choice no less than the sense of immediacy, give the emotion the most adequate outlet. These passages are not separate from their context, since the quickening of the pulse occurs without forewarning. We scan the panorama of the poet's mind, revealed by natural symbols, as its humdrum continuity flashes every now and then into revealing vividness.

Of Robert Southey,[1] the unequal third of this triumvirate, it is not necessary to say much. His industry was unflagging, his poems vast, his fortune small. A few brief ballads, such as *After Blenheim*, are his most enduring memorials, apart from his admirable prose. His *Life of Nelson* might claim to be the best short biography in the English language. Southey's

---

[1] Robert Southey (1774–1843). Associated with Coleridge in the Utopian dream of Pantisocracy. Removed to Keswick, 1803, having shed his revolutionary views. Poet Laureate, 1813. *Thalaba*, 1801; *Madoc*, 1805; *Curse of Kehama*, 1810; *History of Brazil*, 1810; *Life of Nelson*, 1813; *Roderick*, 1814; *Vision of Judgment*, 1821.

name, however, has its place assured by the scornful wrath of Byron, who lashed him more savagely than any other of the Lake poets.

Byron dedicated his *Don Juan* to Southey in "good, simple, savage verse," and crushed him with his own *Vision of Judgment*. From Coleridge ("to turgid ode and tumid stanza dear") he demanded an explanation of his metaphysical explanation, and he considered Wordsworth "unintelligible," except in so far as he proved by precept and example that "prose is verse and verse is mainly prose." Milton, Dryden and Pope were the somewhat ill-assorted models which he proposed, and Scott, Moore and Campbell[1] were ranged as his allies. As for Scott, his verse is naturally associated with his prose and will be noticed later. Moore's *Irish Melodies* are supremely singable, exploiting artistically a notable expansion of Anglo-Irish balladry in the eighteenth century, and they have their parallels in the *Hebrew Melodies* of Lord Byron. Campbell's place among poets of the second class is firmly assured by his *Lord Ullin's Daughter*, *Hohenlinden*, *Ye Mariners of England*, *The Battle of the Baltic*, and other pieces which enter all anthologies. His verse is stirring and full of sound, though not liberating the spirit. Byron scored similar effects in the famous Waterloo verses beginning "There was a sound of revelry by night."

Goethe advised Eckermann to learn English in order to read Byron,[2] and he merited from Lamartine the address

[1] Thomas Moore (1779–1832). *Poetical Works*, 1801; *Irish Melodies*, 1807–35; *Lalla Rookh*, 1817.
Thomas Campbell (1777–1844). *The Pleasures of Hope*, 1799, 1803. Played an important part in the foundation of London University.
[2] George Gordon, Lord Byron (1788–1824). Inherited the title at the age of ten. The Calvinism of his Scottish upbringing produced in him a kind of apologetic rebelliousness, defying conventions which he knew were too firm to be upset. This mental schism marks all his life, which is both defiant and remorseful. The "Byronic pose," copied by so many abroad and at home, was a protective shield over his own wounds. Travelled abroad as far as Greece and recorded the adventure in *Child Harold*, 1812. Married 1815, but was at once left by his wife, and in the ensuing scandal he left England for ever in 1816. Switzerland and Italy, 1816–23, making Shelley's acquaintance. Died of fever at Missolonghi, fighting for Greek independence. *Hours of Idleness*, 1807; *English Bards and Scotch Reviewers*, 1809; *Corsair, Lara, Giaour, Bride of Abydos*, 1813; *Childe Harold*, 1812–18; *Hebrew Melodies*, 1815; *Manfred*, 1817; *Beppo*, 1818; *Mazeppa*, 1819; *Don Juan*, 1818–24; *Vision of Judgment*, 1822.

"L'Homme." He was the first poet in English to win a contemporary fame in Europe, heightened, perhaps, by some sense
of partisanship in the matter of his misfortunes. His reputation
stood equal to Wordsworth's until the days of Matthew Arnold.
The subsequent collapse is the more ungrateful. Extracts from
Childe Harold maintain their place in the curriculum for semi-
philistine reasons; the rhythm is obvious enough and the travel
motif sufficiently informative to arrest the attention of children
of a certain age, not yet ripe for the subtleties of poetry. But
does anybody read Byron for refreshment? His ego is too
insistent, and leaves the less leisure to esteem his literary worth.
His ostracism by society reveals the paradox of an age as
prudish as it was dissolute. It is a matter for wonder, but does
not advance the appreciation of his verses. Manfred and Lara
excite no consolatory longings in any virgin breast, and the
secret hope of being "misunderstood" has descended to quite
junior schoolboys. The complaint of aesthetic insensitiveness
is made against Byron. He who would not "understand"
Wordsworth risks losing the rank and title of poet. The balance
can hardly be redressed in his favour without greater efforts of
sympathy than have recently been attempted. We are, however, beginning to realize that Wordsworth may have misrepresented Pope, through not allowing for his intentions in poetry,
and therefore that Byron may have had just cause of complaint
against Wordsworth. The Romantic Revival, beneficent as it
was, was accomplished not without loss: loss of those things
particularly dear to Byron.

Byron's hatred of all mystifications, flummery and sham
made him intolerant of mystery and subtlety. His character
had a core of moral and intellectual honesty which was outraged by what he took for the sycophancy of the Lake poets
in their later years, and it was this that brought down on
Southey's head the terrible retribution of the *Vision of Judgment*; this also, rather than any sight of future good, that
joined his denunciations of tyrants to those of Shelley. When
indignation dictated verses, Byron lashed his blows without
discretion, maiming friends as well as foes. His gift of mordant phrase ran away with him. The animation of his style
not only makes him supreme in satire but supreme also in

appraisement; but it lies under a suspicion of rhetoric since it is concerned with externals. His apostrophe to Ocean ("Roll on, thou deep and dark blue Ocean, roll!") is as fine an evocation of the thing itself as it is wholly without sympathetic identification of poet and subject. The attitudinizing of Manfred and Lara is evidence of recklessness due to a fundamental morality outraged by ruling convention. It is honesty itself that makes Byron suspect the sincerity of his own warmer appreciations, which he qualifies in *Don Juan* with some satirical diminution. The flippancy is superficial, disguising a deeper seriousness; yet it chills the response of reader to poet. As a storyteller in verse, Byron had no peer in his age; his strokes are so sure, vivid, essential. The verses rush with the fleetness of *Mazeppa*'s steed; no one fails to be thrilled by the swoop of the swift syllables in "The Assyrian came down like a wolf on the fold." Chaucer alone is his peer in narrative verse, and Dryden alone in satire. He is swifter than Chaucer, more bitingly indignant than Dryden; but he lacks the reasonable argument of the one, the tenderness of the other.

One might well ask what Keats[1] was doing in this galley, since he was not united to the first three by special sympathy, nor was he Byron's ally in the fray. Only Wordsworth's *Laodamia* could serve to announce the wholehearted cult of classical beauty to which he devoted the few years of his life. He was not, like Coleridge, a Greek scholar. His enthusiasm for the Greek ideal, though fed on Lemprière's Dictionary and Chapman's *Homer*, was purely intuitive, and yet perfectly realized in the *Ode on a Grecian Urn*. His classicism is either that of the freshest age of Greece (*Endymion, Hyperion, Lamia*) or of the eager early Italian Renaissance (*Isabella, Eve of St. Agnes*), a period which seems to Englishmen to share most of the Greek spirit. The Ode became his sovereign domain (*To a Nightingale, To Autumn*), with an equal balance of form and passion; and he could treat the appropriate themes in the lighter as well as in the graver style (*To Fancy, The Mermaid Tavern*). By way of preamble to his longer poems Keats had declared that "a thing of beauty is a joy for ever." It is the assurance of his immortality and the limitation of his audience.

[1] John Keats (1795–1821). *Poems*, 1817; *Endymion*, 1818; *Lamia, Isabella, Eve of St. Agnes, Hyperion*, etc., 1820.

The poet and the connoisseur go back to Keats with whetted appetites; his "loveliness increases"; the magic of phrase and form "will never pass into nothingness." His poems are a school for poets, next only to Spenser's. But the more general reader, like the Roman Horace, wants to mingle profit with sweetness (however dimly the profit be perceived), and he finds that experience is none the richer for Keats. His poetry is in another dimension from ordinary human striving; but it rewards the chosen ones who enter.

Shelley[1] mourned for the death of Keats in one of the finest elegies in the language, *Adonais*, with its flux and reflux of sorrow and consolation, indignation and apotheosis. He shared his Greek enthusiasm, but with a better foundation of Greek scholarship; his passionate love of beauty was as intense. But Shelley is as unmistakably romantic as Keats is classical, and though a friend of Byron his genius is closer to that of Coleridge. To Matthew Arnold Shelley seemed a "beautiful and ineffectual angel," but Shelley counted himself among the "unacknowledged legislators of mankind." Arnold's criticism loosed upon his own head vials of wrath which—incidentally—swept away the reputation of Byron, for whom he was entering a special plea. It was grounded on too short a view of the poet's mission. The thoughts of Shelley have not the practical applications of the statesman or preacher, though he made his forays into the realms of politics and morals. They are incoherent, impracticable, but wingèd. It is their power to stimulate, ennoble and transmute that gives them their dominion over experience. There have been other protests against seemingly omnipotent tyranny than those in *Prometheus Unbound*, but Shelley gives a new dimension to liberty when he says

> to be
> *good, great and joyous, beautiful and free;*
> *this is alone Life, Joy, Empire and Victory.*

[1] Percy Bysshe Shelley (1792–1822). Expelled from Oxford for his pamphlet on *The Necessity of Atheism*, 1811. His monument in University College is now a goal of pilgrimage. Left England for Italy, 1818. Drowned. *Queen Mab*, 1813; *Alastor*, 1816; *Revolt of Islam*, 1818; *Lines written among the Euganaean Hills*, 1818; *Cenci*, 1819; *Prometheus Unbound*, 1820; *Adonais*, 1821; *Hellas*, 1822; *Julian and Maddalo*, *Witch of Atlas*, posthumous poems, 1824.

Such freedom is not in protocols, but makes the law luminous. The insatiate thirst for the beauty of knowledge revealed in *Alastor*, though it leads to disappointment and an early grave, stirs our sympathies like a *sursum corda*; as the poet says, it is "not barren of instruction to actual men"—the sort of instruction that a poet should give.   So it is when the poet sings of the vanity of empire in the sonnet to "Ozymandias, king of kings."   So also in the mood of despondency revealed in the *Lines Written among the Euganaean Hills.*

Apart from the thought-suggestiveness of his ecstatic verses, there is the educative interest of their form. Shelley was rarely able to carry through a big design: his genius surged upward in enraptured flights, but was liable to falter in a long traverse. His formal lesson is not as to wholes, nor as to surface and texture (as in Keats), but as to freedom of utterance. He is the master-worker of every kind of accent-shift and substitution of feet, till the thought flows in living rhythms, ever varied without loss of pattern. The astonishing flexibility he conferred on English verse was a field for poets' exploration during almost a century, and even so was not exhausted. Browning was his scholar, if Tennyson was Keats's: Swinburne also was his disciple. If it was only with Mr. Eliot in the twentieth century that English poets sought to drink from the Continental Hippocrene, it was because with Shelley they already enjoyed an unexhausted variety of music and range of symbols.

Critical pronouncements by Wordsworth and Shelley are of singular importance for the making of poetry; those by Coleridge have the double basis of his poetry and his philosophy. The eighteenth century had looked to the critic for judgments, but with the Romantics appreciation acquired prior rights. Coleridge performed the service to Shakespeare of "putting the sun in heaven"; he was able to give some adequate impression of the nature and extent of the Shakespearean miracle. A like service he performed for Cervantes and Dante, interpreting not merely as a poet, but questing among the deeper philosophical prerequisites of creative work. Hazlitt[1]

[1] William Hazlitt (1778–1830). *Characters of Shakespeare's Plays*, 1817–18; *Lectures on the English Poets*, 1818–19; *On the English Comic Writers*, 1819; *On Dramatic Literature of the Age of Elizabeth*, 1820; *Political Essays*, 1819; *Table Talk*, 1821–2.

also served Shakespeare well. His vision was acute and his word full of force. His prejudices and arrogance, which are strong, give spice to his judgments; an honest partiality is often more revealing than characterless esteem. His essay on Scott, for instance, declares the full value of Scott's antiquarianism by the violence of Hazlitt's revulsion from it, no less than his direct eulogy reveals Scott's mastery of character. Lamb[1] and, to a lesser degree, Leigh Hunt,[2] have a genius for revealing unexpected beauties; they haunt the less spectacular ways of the literary world or explore the bypaths of high genius. In their *Tales from Shakespeare* Charles and Mary Lamb brought criticism into the nursery, giving children an idea of the worth of the plays as stories and groups of characters.

These critical writings form but part of the wider demand for essays made by periodical literature. The demand was for entertainment, not for instruction. The planned essay was at a discount, and that which seemed a chance part of a conversation was in high favour. This essay style was not commended by the lucidity which characterized the eighteenth century, but by some other quality, such as whimsicality or richly imaginative writing. Hazlitt and Leigh Hunt were eminent practitioners, with a wide range of topics, but Lamb and De Quincey share the prize. Lamb's *Essays of Elia* endear themselves by their quaint unexpectedness, their sly humour and warm friendliness; they entice by their indirect approach and unforeseen turns. Those on George Dyer, on dream-children, and on roast pig are household favourites. In his *Letters* we find the same inimitable Lamb, not untouched by sorrow and fortitude. De Quincey,[3] in *Confessions of an English Opium-Eater* and *Murder as One of the Fine Arts*, anticipates *Les Fleurs du Mal* in the cult of the decadent. The texture of the prose is as of rich velvet, the rhythms of a somewhat sickly sweetness, full of vague imaginative evocations. Elegance of a more formal kind distin-

---

[1] Charles Lamb (1775–1834). Educated at Christ's Hospital, with Coleridge. *Tales from Shakespeare*, 1807; *Specimens from the Dramatic Poets*, 1808; *Essays of Elia* and *Last Essays of Elia*, 1822–4, 1833.

[2] James Henry Leigh Hunt (1784–1859).

[3] Thomas de Quincey (1785–1859). *Confessions of an English Opium-Eater*, 1822; *Murder as one of the Fine Arts*, 1827; *Autobiographical Sketches*, 1834–53.

guished the Lucianesque *Imaginary Conversations* of Walter Savage Landor,[1] in which the great dead reveal contrasted standpoints rather than their characters.

At such a time and in such company it is disconcerting to encounter so forthright a realist as William Cobbett,[2] the compiler of the *Weekly Political Register* for over thirty years and of the celebrated *Rural Rides*. One who looks among Englishmen for a typical John Bull might well decide that the character was wholly unrepresentative, unless his eye should light upon Cobbett. His passions were strongly partisan, but honest; full of pugnacity he needed only a worthy opponent to knock down; and he used for the purpose the direct colloquial punch of Bunyan and Defoe. The son of a farmer, his interest was in the use of the land as he rode through it, and his alert intelligence, ranging over all topics from potatoes to grammar, gives rise to some of the most forceful and vivid descriptive writing in English.

The clearest white light falls on one little corner of this England in the novels of Jane Austen.[3] Nothing could be more free from romanticism. This curious anomaly is partly to be explained by the fact that they are usually much older than their year of publication. *Sense and Sensibility* was written under the title of *Elinor and Marianne* about 1792 and remodelled in 1797–8 from its epistolary form. *Pride and Prejudice* was also extant earlier under the title of *First Impressions*. But they owe much more to the author's self-knowing mind, which determined her manner entirely without reference to any "school." Her initial impulse, however, was a fastidious aversion from the habits of other lady novelists; from the sentimentality which Sheridan incarnated in Lydia Languish, and from the hobgoblinery of *The Mysteries of Udolpho*. There is thus an element of parody in *Sense and*

[1] Walter Savage Landor (1775–1864). *Imaginary Conversations*, 1824–9.

[2] William Cobbett (1763–1835). *Weekly Political Register*, from 1802; *Cottage Economy*, 1822; *History of the Reformation in England*, 1824; *Rural Rides*, 1830; *Advice to Young Men*, 1829.

[3] Jane Austen (1775–1817). *Sense and Sensibility*, 1811; *Pride and Prejudice*, 1813; *Mansfield Park*, 1814; *Emma*, 1815; *Northanger Abbey*, 1818; *Persuasion*, 1818.

Sensibility and *Northanger Abbey*. "I can feel no sentiment of approbation (said Mrs. John Dashwood) inferior to love," and as her daughter Marianne shared this view, she passed through many causeless flutterings before pairing with the unromantic Colonel Brandon; but her sister Elinor Dashwood handled real difficulties with sense and discretion. The "horrid mysteries" of the *Udolpho* school are demolished by the polished irony of *Northanger Abbey*. But while this first movement, as so often, was inspired by books, the inimitable charm of Jane Austen is her interest in life. There was no great variety thereof coming under the eyes of a clergyman's daughter who lived in unbroken quiet in the south and west of England, but her clear eyes took in the minutest movements and set them down in lucid, cool, sub-ironical prose. Richardson was her favourite author, and at first inclined her to use the epistolary form. He gave her, perhaps, her unconvincing patterns of men, but he also showed what could be done with the minute, yet significant, psychology of women in everyday middle-class settings. "Jane," however, is not prolix like Richardson. There is a deft economy in her technique which allows the fullest effects from each device, together with a quiet resourcefulness which for ever springs surprises. The playful irony which discounts the romantic emotion slowly reveals evidence of more abiding worth; the sublime mediocrity of her manner shifts ever so slightly from gentle innuendo to quiet seriousness, steering clear of farce or tragedy, so that her course is perfectly, if unadventurously, run. To one who would select an outstanding book from her list to be read as a sample there is only one piece of advice: read them all! There is no loss of touch in the later novels, *Emma*, *Mansfield Park* and *Persuasion*, and every one of the six has champions who assert its primacy. And the tribe of the "Janeites" deems the pleasure of communing with her pages to be above all earthly bliss.

With the name of Sir Walter Scott[1] we re-enter the great

---

[1] Sir Walter Scott (1771–1832). As a boy he would recite ballads from Percy's *Reliques* to his schoolfellows, and in early manhood he made regular "raids" into the Lowlands in search of authentic oral versions. *Minstrelsy of the Scottish Border*, 1802–3; *Ballads from the German*, 1796; Translation of Goethe's *Götz von Berlichingen*, 1798; *Lay of the Last Minstrel*, 1805; *Ballads and Lyrical Pieces*, 1806;

world; he is titanic and universal. Those who divide romanticism into the revolutionary and the antiquarian branches
place Scott at the head of conservatives. Hazlitt grumbled that
"he is just half of what the human intellect is capable of being:
if you take the universe, and divide it into two parts, he knows
all that it *has been*; all that it *is to be* is nothing to him," but he
admitted that Scott was the most popular writer of the age, and
"lord of the ascendant" for the time being. His business was
to restore romance by showing that nothing is so romantic as
the truth. The eighteenth-century inquiries concerning human
nature had not revealed to the searching philosophers that
human nature is its own contrast. Even the historian Gibbon,
sifting and registering the records of past ages, had not thought
that Roman emperors should be judged otherwise than
eighteenth-century statesmen. This was revealed to Scott, that
ardent hunter of old ballads and collector of scraps of superstition. He knew the past down to its minutest details of costume
and environment, and he peopled it with real human beings,
not an abstract human nature. Hazlitt's essay becomes a
breathless catalogue of persons that we actually know—know
intimately, though separated by hundreds of years and of
miles—because we have met them in Scott's pages. All Europe
set about writing historical romances in his manner; the trick
of remoteness in time was so easy, but the consequences so
flaccid, that a weary reader cries out against the whole convention. But it is not this trick of local and temporary colour that
constitutes the Scott we know; it is the convincing nearness
of his persons, though their circumstances are not ours nor

Marmion, 1808; *Lady of the Lake*, 1810; *Vision of Don Roderick*, 1811.
Settled at Abbotsford, 1812. WAVERLEY NOVELS, 1814–32. *Harold*,
1817; *Lives of the Novelists*, 1821–4; *Life of Napoleon*, 1827; *Tales of a
Grandfather*, 1828–30. In 1826 Scott was involved in the bankruptcy
of Constable & Ballantyne and, though not legally liable, accepted the
burden of £117,000 debt. He paid off £63,000 by unremitting literary
labour, but perished under the strain. The WAVERLEY NOVELS deal
with Scottish history (*Waverley, Old Mortality, Monastery, Fair Maid
of Perth*, etc.) or private life in historical times (*Heart of Midlothian,
Bride of Lammermoor, Rob Roy, Black Dwarf*, etc.); with English
history (*Ivanhoe, Talisman, Kenilworth, Fortunes of Nigel, Woodstock*,
etc.); and with Continental history (*Quentin Durward, Anne of Geierstein,
Count Robert of Paris*).

their motives quite those of this day. We understand and sympathize, and the difference of the attending circumstances helps to expand our knowledge of the adjustment of men to environment. The imaginative perception of past ages as lively wholes passed into the baggage of the historian, shaming him out of his philosophic abstraction.

Bishop Percy had discovered old ballads in manuscripts, but Scott encountered them in circulation among the crofters of the Border country. He had the additional incentive that one of the great Border heroes, Willie Scott of Buccleugh, had a place in his own pedigree. In his "raids" into southern Scotland, Scott was not affected by prejudices in favour of antiquity or of authentic texts, since the critical school of ballad-hunters had not yet arisen. He gathered old and new, and he prized above all the spirit and vigour of the poems. They took him into past environments and forgotten minds; and conversation with all sorts and classes of informants combined with his movements across country to store his memory with Scottish scenes and characters. He became, says Hazlitt, "only the amanuensis of truth and history"; "he conversed with the living and the dead and let them tell their own story in their own way." The firstfruits of these "raids" were the highly plausible ballads of *Glenfinlas*, *Cadyow Castle*, etc., but he soon found he needed a more ample canvas. The old ballad-mongers had no need of atmosphere, since they sang of the things they lived among; but Scott needed space for re-creation. So he turned to the lay; *The Lay of the Last Minstrel*, *Marmion*, *The Lady of the Lake*. In paragraphs of swifting-moving octo-syllabic couplets he carries the reader with him through unfamiliar scenes and times in the wake of characters who engage sympathy by their nobility and misfortunes; but the reader draws no special advantage from the verse. It is adequate, but negligent and unremembered; the writer acknowledged as much when he read Byron's tales in verse. He abandoned the lay, and took to the novel.

The project of writing romances seems to have been an old one. Scott says it was inspired by reading *Don Quixote*, and that the first plan was to describe the adventures of a Jacobite Quixote. Between this primitive impulse and *Waverley* (1814) there was much development, so that what emerged was a completely new genre. The success of this work was immediate and immense, not only in Britain but throughout the Continent. Readers were on tiptoe for each new volume as it was announced, and advance sheets were rushed abroad so that the translations could appear on the same day as the originals. By an innocent ruse Scott concealed his authorship of these works, though this was never a matter of doubt for his friends, nor other than an open secret for the intelligent among his readers. The author's fertility was equal to the demand. He had gone through a long period of preparation, and his encyclopedic memory never lost hold of a fact. His mind was fully stored, and only required space to expand. He wrote swiftly, somewhat negligently, but with assurance, of life; characters, scenes, landscapes, atmosphere—all were ready to spring into being. Their merits, indeed, are unequal, and those composed too hurriedly after the crash of 1826 are the worse for the strain. With the passing of years it is the Scottish novels which gain in stature, and especially those which depend more on character than on history. The mental tragedy of Jeanie Deans in *The Heart of Midlothian* owes to its date and place only the attendant circumstances necessary to any narrative. In *Rob Roy* and *The Fair Maid of Perth* interest is excited by the emplacement upon the dividing line of Highlands and Lowlands, the meeting-place of two races with incompatible histories. *Ivanhoe* and *The Talisman* carry the mind back to the Middle Ages with a richly circumstantial embroidery that has dazzled the imaginations of men; but they groan beneath much dead weight of description and "tushery." *Quentin Durward* also reaches back to the Middle Ages, and is the prototype of those books—chiefly for boys—which employ the movements of an unimportant hero in order to bring before us the enigmatic great. *Kenilworth, The Fortunes of Nigel* and *Woodstock* are second only to Shakespeare's "histories" in fixing our conception of English history.

One of the best of Scott's novels was his life. He recorded some of it in an autobiography, but his heroic stature is revealed fully in Lockhart's *Life of Scott*,[1] by common consent the second among English biographies. Boswell makes his hero speak his own history; Lockhart is descriptive, but is inexhaustible when illustrating the ideas, prejudices, feats, habits, daily routine, generosity and courage of a greater than Johnson. We see Scott's genius gradually clearing itself, and exercised with herculean energy. He becomes famed and fêted in all Europe, and *facile princeps* among his Scottish countrymen. Then, when the disaster of bankruptcy falls on him, he is not stunned like other men, but rises to a new height of sublime generosity as he devotes every ounce of his mighty energy to sparing his creditors all loss and clearing his own good name.

Beside the vast figure of Walter Scott, James Morier[2] may appear an insubstantial laughter-maker, and his use of the Persian convention a sort of throwback to Goldsmith and Montesquieu. There is something of this mustiness in his *Hajji Baba in England*, though the book is sprightly enough; but his original *Adventures of Hajji Baba of Ispahan* is a perennial spring of the outlandishly comic that will outlive many a graver work. Real and detailed knowledge of eastern life and manners is blended with suggestions both exotic and picaresque and the sentiments and events graze and start away from our western experience so as to be half fanciful, half a phantasmagoria, but wholly unique.

[1] John Gibson Lockhart (1794–1854). *Spanish Ballads*, 1823; *Life of Burns*, 1828; *Napoleon*, 1829; *Life of Scott*, 1838.

[2] James Justinian Morier (1780?–1849). *A Journey through Persia to Constantinople in 1808–9*, 1812; *A Second Journey between 1810 and 1816*, 1818; *Hajji Baba of Ispahan*, 1824; *Hajji Baba in England*, 1828.

X. VICTORIAN VERSE

TEN years lie between the death of Shelley and Tennyson's[1] first verses, and another ten between Scott's last novel and the definitive establishment of Tennyson as a poet. Within these narrow limits a new age had been introduced, though there was no sign of revolt. Keats and Tennyson, Shelley and Browning, Wordsworth and Matthew Arnold are related as masters to pupils; but while those experiment, these prefer to polish, vary or perfect. The generations are divided also by a temporary bar. The Romantics have passed to their account, and their place in the history of letters is undisputed and undisturbed; but the Victorians are only emerging from an abyss of censure through a vale of mockery to the lower slopes of Elysium where they may be expected to dwell. The scornful indifference of the caricaturist distorts the judgment of the honest critic, and their reputations must still be deemed fluid.

In the forefront of the age stand undoubtedly the complementary figures of Tennyson and Browning. Their general likeness provokes an antithesis, such as that which one of Browning's editors sought to establish between form and substance, between the mere artist and the thinker. Browning's thought was for long the delight of ladies' literary clubs, though it has since been charged with facile optimism; a sole appreciation of Tennyson's workmanship obscures his mind's grapple with great problems. It was characteristic of them both to accept unchallenged the basic assumptions of the society about them, and to show continuity in their artistic methods. Arnold's restlessness forms a point of transition to the aesthetic abstraction of the Pre-Raphaelites and the revolutionary radicalism of Swinburne. The end of the century saw the Victorian serenity at the point of dissolution into the pessimistic indecision of the present age.

[1] Alfred Tennyson (1809–92). Educated at Cambridge. Poet Laureate, 1850. Baron, 1884. *Timbuctoo*, 1829; *Poems, chiefly Lyrical*, 1830; *Poems*, 1833; *Poems*, 1842; *The Princess*, 1847; *In Memoriam*, 1850; *Maud*, 1855; *Idylls of the King* (first series), 1859; *Lucretius*, 1868; *Queen Mary*; *Harold*; and other plays.

A prize poem on *Timbuctoo* introduced Tennyson to the poetical career. He soon appealed to the public as a lyrical poet. His verses appeared at intervals between 1830 and 1842, and at the end of those ten years his stature had been taken. They showed a passion for artistry taken over from Keats, and more minutely exercised. Tennyson worked with words like a jeweller, weighing them against each other, testing their lustre, placing them in their foil; yet they are mostly current coinage. His thought touched the basic emotion as it were at a tangent, so that the individual experience passed into the general. *Claribel* is a sample of this new lyrical manner, and *Mariana* is yet more perfect. It was natural for the poet to seek persons outside his own personality, and partially to dramatize his emotion. A lifelong fondness for the Arthurian legend gave him the right to use this medium for *The Lady of Shalott* and *Sir Galahad*. Still better adapted to his use were classical reminiscences, such as those embodied in *Oenone*, *Ulysses* and the late *Lucretius*, which is one of the noblest and saddest of poems. He was following the way beaten by Wordsworth's *Laodamia* even more than Keats's *Endymion*, but he infused his poems with a new dramatic urgency. The deserted and faded Oenone, Ulysses impatient for the last adventure, and the great mind of Lucretius cracking under the burden of truth, are not only classical examples but modern parables; and their medium is a highly wrought blank verse which is entirely new. *The Dream of Fair Women* is perhaps the characteristic achievement of the Tennysonian art; it is impeccable in diction and rhythm, highly burnished, and of twice-distilled, but still vibrant, passion. He is rather less successful when he brings his focus nearer, as in *Locksley Hall* and *The Queen of the May*, for he found difficulty in coping with the insistent present. The bardic tone seemed out of place; when, however, he was pleased to drop it, he could write such excellent ballads as *The Charge of the Light Brigade* and *The Revenge*.

In Memoriam is neither a long poem nor a collection of short lyrics, but something not quite successfully pitched between the two. The death of his friend Hallam in September 1833 affected the poet deeply, and after a period of numbness he began to seek relief in meditative songs. The personal tragedy widened into the universal tragedy, as the poet's mind swung from individual sorrow to its typical significance. Tennyson wrote nothing finer than "Thou comest, much wept for" and "The Danube to the Severn gave," where personal grief is eternized. Frequent and slovenly quotation has cheapened such phrases as " 'Tis better to have loved and lost than never to have loved at all," but they are not cheap in their setting, since there we see at what cost of doubt and despair they were forged. They gain from their context; yet there are also passages written without the god, and suggesting a complaisant spirit. But there is no complaisance in the great opening hymn, "Strong Son of God," though it leans for support upon the righteousness of the universe. The many planes of composition found in *In Memoriam* become one only in *Maud*, where Tennyson more conveniently deals with tragedy in an imagined character.

The Princess has dated badly. It is remembered for a few bejewelled lyrics, and for Gilbert's parody, *Princess Ida*, which, however, itself is losing ground because of the difficulty of calling to mind the original. The Tennysonian blank verse proved to be an unsuitable medium for the Arthuriad entitled *The Idylls of the King*. That which should have been a moral criticism of the age, breaks into unrelated episodes; the verse also is too highly polished to last. It is essentially lyrical or episodic, but when so read, as in the magnificent *Morte d'Arthur*, it is replete with noble sound.

The urge to dramatize was still more marked in Browning's[1] case. The source was probably different. Tennyson, being averse from uttering "wild and wandering cries," sought to put his emotion upon another; Browning had no personal joy or sorrow to communicate, but was genuinely interested in the varieties known to others. It is an experimental interest, for it is less than what is required to make a character live on the

---

[1] Robert Browning (1812–89). *Pauline*, 1833; *Paracelsus, Strafford, Sordello, Pippa Passes*, 1835–46. Married Elizabeth Barrett, 1846, and went to live in Italy. *Men and Women*, 1855; *Dramatis Personae*, 1864; *The Ring and the Book*, 1869; *Balaustion's Adventure*, 1871; *Dramatic Idylls*, 1879, 1880; *Parleyings with Certain People*, 1887; *Asolando*, 1889.
Elizabeth Barrett Browning (1806–61). *Sonnets from the Portuguese*, 1850; *Casa Guidi Windows*, 1851; *Aurora Leigh*, 1857.

stage. The case for the worldly bishop is brilliantly stated in
Bishop Blougram's Apology, and that for the conscienceless
Renaissance rascal in *My Last Duchess*. *Caliban upon Setebos*
is a brilliantly imaginative presentation of the obscure grop-
ings of a savage mind among the evidences of superhuman
power.

These pieces represent Browning in the larger manner.
When the scale is increased beyond a thousand lines, the
dramatic analysis too greatly disturbs the exposition. *Sordello*,
for instance, is not really obscure, but the story is hinted at and
never developed; the style also takes so many short cuts that
it is the longest way to its purpose. For these reasons it seems
hard to agree that *The Ring and the Book*, Browning's largest
and most typical work, can be reckoned his best. He is better,
one thinks, when working within the thousand lines. Here we
find such monologues as the marvellous *Abt Vogler*, where
Browning makes effective use of his often excessive scholarship,
Rabbi ben Ezra and *The Grammarian's Funeral*. Here too is
the famous Epilogue to *Asolando*, courageously penned in the
maw of death. The *Dramatic Lyrics* include pure song (in the
cavalier convention) and experiments in sound, such as *How
They Brought the Good News from Ghent to Aix*. How much
of Browning's most effective work is due to experiments in
rhythm is ignored by those who would have us regard him
as primarily a thinker. The rhythms are not vulgar, but twisted
and wrought so as to fit the sense; when the sense is grasped,
the rhythm reveals its subtle craftsmanship. But such filigree-
work is for lyrics and short poems; and in the very long ones
the pattern is lost.

We cannot forget, concerning Matthew Arnold,[1] that he was
a critic, and a product of his father's reform of the English
public schools. His inhibitions and his dogmatism betray
him. It is true that he demanded an "undogmatic Christianity," but this hardly amounts to more than admitting he dared

[1] Matthew Arnold (1822–88). Son of Dr. Arnold, of Rugby. Edu-
cated at Winchester, Rugby and Oxford. *The Strayed Reveller and Other
Poems*, 1849; *Empedocles on Etna and other Poems*, 1852; *Poems*, 1853;
(with Preface), 1855; *New Poems*, 1867; *Essays in Criticism*, 1865, 1888;
On Translating Homer, 1861; *On the Study of Celtic Literature*, 1867;
Discourses on America, 1885, etc.

not press his intellectual dissatisfaction so far as a rupture. The "undogmatic" creed would still have had its dogmas. These are reduced, in his critical writings, sometimes to single words. Tennyson is "distilled" and Homer "natural," the words being repeated and worried until they become almost sophistries. A Mr. Newman did wrong to translate Homer into the ballad style, because the ballads and Mr. Newman were eminently "ignoble," but Homer always noble. With a slight expansion of the phrase we hear of "the grand style," "high seriousness," "a criticism of life." These things are very well said in themselves; it is their iteration that makes them dangerous, as when the last led Arnold into a wrong-headed attack on Shelley. In fact, they tend to get into the critic's way, and no less prevent his enjoyment of some of the best things than they give exaggerated importance to some that are not so good. This gift of phrase led him to evoke a strange wraith of the "Celtic imagination" (upon a quite insufficient knowledge of any Celtic literature) to confuse the critical vocabulary of Europe. His services to English criticism are, however, unmistakable. The Romantics had been masters of delicate appreciation, but in weaker hands this became haphazard. Arnold recalled critics to the need for principle, and even for label (in the French manner). He worried at insular self-gratulation, though he shared most of our prejudices. The checks and weights of his meticulously balanced phrases were a reminder that there is a formal craft of prose, made to a nation that has ceased to study rhetoric.

In like manner his verse has its charms and inhibitions. It is elegantly wrought, but short in the wind. His pessimism prevents his embarking on bold creations, and even of finishing what he has begun. His grace is classical, but cold. The *Scholar Gipsy* and *Thyrsis* (the latter a monody on the death of his friend, A. H. Clough) are the pieces which reveal most of his mind; and both are eminently academic. For the rest he takes refuge in other-personalizing his ideas, and generally he sets them at a farther remove than Tennyson and Browning: on the shores of the Caspian in the sombre *Sohrab and Rustum* or among the ancient Norse in *Baldur Dead* and *The Forsaken Merman*.

Edward Fitzgerald[1] has a place among the greater poets of that age by virtue of one translation: the *Rubaiyat* of Omar Khayyam. Persian scholars have estimated the distance which separates Fitzgerald's version from Omar's original. The uncemented apophthegms of the Persian, selected and ordered by the translator, form a loosely connected monologue on the uncertainty of life and the unprofitableness of effort; the thought is sensual and fatalistic; and the stanza with one unechoed line is both voluptuous and melancholy.

Two painter-poets who gave colour and outline to English verse during the later years of the nineteenth century were D. G. Rossetti and Morris.[2] It is the pictorial quality of *The Blessed Damozel* which first catches the eye, and at all points Rossetti's paintings and drawings are the best commentary on his poems. From the Italian primitives he learned mysticism and fastidiousness, and this was confirmed in his exquisite translations from the early Tuscan poets, especially Dante's *The New Life*. Dante was, indeed, his chief poetical inspiration, and his discipleship is made perfect in the fine *Dante at Verona*. The ballads fascinated Rossetti, who made use of their device of refrains in *Lilith* and *Eden Bower* and the more moving *Sister Helen*. But he treats the ballad in the style of an illuminator. His sister, Christina, has a more limited talent, yet of great purity within its limits. Her language was crystalline, and her religious songs are devoutly sensuous and simple. There was not the same fastidiousness in Morris, who is often (normally,

[1] Edward Fitzgerald (1809–83). Translations of Aeschylus, Sophocles and Calderon, 1853; *Rubaiyat*, 1859.
[2] Dante Gabriel Rossetti (1828–82). Son of Gabriel Rossetti, an Italian exile. Joined the Pre-Raphaelite brotherhood with J. E. Millais, Holman Hunt, etc. Made the acquaintance of Morris in connection with the *Oxford and Cambridge Magazine*. "Ecce ancilla Domini" (painting), exhibited 1850. Arthurian drawings, "The Blue Closet," "The Bridge," "Beata Beatrix," etc. Verses contributed to *The Germ*, 1850; *Early Italian Poets with Dante's Vita Nuova*, 1861; *Poems*, 1870; *Ballads and Sonnets*, 1881. Various editions by his brother, W. M. Rossetti.
Christina Rossetti (1830–94). *Goblin Market*, 1862; *The Prince's Progress*, 1866.
William Morris (1834–96). Exeter College, Oxford. Founded the *Oxford and Cambridge Magazine*, 1856; *Defence of Guenevere*, 1858; *Life and Death of Jason*, 1867; *Earthly Paradise*, 1868–70. Settled at Kelmscott. *Sigurd the Volsung*, 1876; *Chants for Socialists*, 1883; *News from Nowhere*, 1891. The Kelmscott Chaucer, 1896.

indeed) prolix, but there was even more creative energy. The painter in him contributed the sense of grouping in the scenes of the epics and the richly suggestive colouring; but the outline is less pure than in Rossetti. His vocabulary was simple and select, full of languorous iambic rhythm, but his speech was not plain. For lack of plain speech Morris proved incapable of tragedy. In the last book of *The Life and Death of Jason* he covers the same ground as Euripides in the *Medea*. It is astonishing to see how much more "modern" the Greek is; more modern simply because more veracious. The motives and words used by Morris are all incredible, in fact, when compared with the violent revulsions of Medea's feelings. But the comparison is undoubtedly an unfair one. It serves merely to show how completely Morris was rooted in literature, not life. *Sigurd the Volsung* shows the same two-dimensional tapestry effect. Probably nothing better represents Morris than *The Defence of Guenevere*, his first important work. Its new rhythmical suggestions, though not at once appreciated, combine with the author's artistic aloofness to make it highly characteristic, and the length of the piece is not so great as to lead to languor.

The Victorian age was brought to a close by the brilliantly disruptive work of Swinburne.[1] He was, above all things, a melodist. The effect of first encountering his verse is overwhelming; the reader's mind becomes incandescent with the speed and the passion of it. Alliteration and echoes increase the power of the spell, which is exercised through stanzas of novel construction. It is necessary, indeed, to halt the mind; to go back over the lines and verify what has been established. Swinburne's pace often exceeds the reader's thought, and sometimes the poet's also. That is his chief weakness: genuine thought is too often absent, having been lost in some alliterative or rhythmic suggestion. His was

[1] Algernon Charles Swinburne (1837–1909). Educated at Eton and Oxford, where he studied Greek Literature with avidity and made the acquaintance of French and Italian. *The Queen Mother, Rosamund,* 1860; *Atalanta in Calydon,* 1856; *Poems and Ballads,* 1866, 1878; *Songs before Sunrise,* 1871; *Erechtheus,* 1876; *Mary Stuart,* 1881; *Tristram of Lyonesse,* 1882, etc.; *The Study of Shakespeare,* 1879; *The Age of Shakespeare,* 1909.

a spirit in revolt: in revolt against kings and priests, established religion and ordered society. These left much to be complained of, and their smug self-satisfaction exasperated the poet. No one can be more torrential in denunciation than Swinburne. When his hate is aroused, whether in verse or in critical prose, he delivers an overwhelming attack; and he is almost as effective in praise of what he likes, though often one-sided. Among poets he admired (after Shakespeare) the great rebellious spirits of Marlowe and Shelley; and it is the last implications of Shelley's technique that he reveals in his own style. After almost a century of indifference, Swinburne was the first English poet to take cognizance of the new developments that had occurred on the Continent. He took Victor Hugo for a master and hero: Victor Hugo, who had been regarded askance by Victorian England as impious and not respectable. From Baudelaire he learned much, and old Villon was also fitted to be a Swinburnian hero.

In *Atalanta in Calydon* and *Erechtheus* Swinburne solved a problem which had remained open during the whole century. With unwearied industry the great poets had fashioned dramas in verse, and there was no reluctance among actors to perform them. But they had not succeeded. The drama requires the assent of the audience, and this was withheld, for intelligible reasons. In his lyrical tragedies Swinburne largely dispensed with this support, since they were conceived as parts of a literary tradition. He gave a new flexibility to the heroic couplet in his *Tristram*, but it is chiefly for his lyrics that he lives. These are grouped in the various series of his *Poems and Ballads* and in *Songs before Sunrise*. The former contain evidence of his various enthusiasms: for Sappho and the Greeks, for Hugo and Baudelaire, for tragic ballads. The sensuality, sometimes as gross as animalism, which pervades his work, is found unabashed in the first series of the *Poems and Ballads*. Swinburne drew exquisitely decadent pleasure from despair (*Laus Veneris*), sin (*Phaedra*), and cruel lust (*Anactoria*), while in the *Hymn to Proserpine* he exalted the ancient Apollinean paganism. There is decadence in such thoughts. A surfeit of peace and material prosperity had exhausted normal pleasures, and led to an aberrant exquisiteness. This was,

F

indeed, disruptive. In the brilliance of his execution Swinburne revealed the hollowness of much Victorian work. He toppled down the old values with a resounding crash; but he established no firm new ones. He concluded one age and announced a new one; a new age of much confusion, manifold striving, and no certain accomplishment.

Among the minor poetry of the Victorian Age we should not forget the mass of good humorous verse, for which the pages of *Punch* and other comic papers afforded an outlet. It was in the pages of *Punch*, in 1843, that there appeared Hood's *Song of the Shirt*, to prove how searing can be the wrath of a jester, when indignation makes him turn aside from the manufacture of puns. The three types of humour—nonsense, broad parody and subtle suggestion—had worthy exponents. The cream of nonsense is to be found in Edward Lear's *Book of Nonsense*, which Ruskin placed first in a list of a hundred delectable volumes. The broader parodic effects were sought by W. S. Gilbert[1] in the libretti of his famous Savoy operas. They are ingenious in rhyme, convincing in logic, and topsy-turvy in their inferences. The verse is not clothed with the beauty of an Aristophanes—whose plays are their nearest analogues— but Sullivan's music gives them this higher grace. It is not only the perfection of light and humorous music, but is a revival of genuine English melody-making. The sheer delight of the songs and the opportunities for imaginative settings now supplant the interest once felt in Gilbert's satire, since this is no longer topical nor yet historically interesting. C. S. Calverley[2] is the master of subtle parody and ingenious surprises both in English and Latin verse. He has had many followers in parody, but his impressions of Tennyson, Browning, Rossetti and Tupper are peculiarly fresh, and will last as long as their

[1] Edward Lear (1812–88). *Book of Nonsense*, 1846.
Sir William Schwenck Gilbert (1836–1911). *Bab Ballads*, 1869–73; *The Happy Land*, 1873; *Trial by Jury*, 1875; *The Sorcerer*, 1877; *Pinafore*, 1878; *Pirates of Penzance*, 1879–80; *Patience*, 1881; *Iolanthe*, 1882; *Princess Ida*, 1884; *Mikado*, 1885; *Ruddigore*, 1887; *Yeomen of the Guard*, 1888; *Gondoliers*, 1889; *Utopia Limited*, 1893; *Grand Duke*. 1896.
Thomas Hood (1799–1845).
[2] Charles Stuart Calverley (1831–84). *Verses and Translations*, 1862; *Fly Leaves*, 1866.

sou.ces. He places the incongruous thought or epithet in his light verse with a skill begotten by Horace.

XI. THE GOLDEN AGE OF THE NOVEL

THE reign of Queen Victoria was the Golden Age of the English Novel. Several writers were qualified to put forward claims to supremacy in the art on the basis of their separate and distinct merits. There are backers for each, since between a reader and his novelist there is a personal relation of sympathy which forbids our attempting any absolute order of merit. Just as everybody is in some sort an artist in speech, by virtue of the choices we habitually make between words and clauses, so everyone has some practice in narrative and, as the saying goes, "has one good novel in him." It follows that everyone has a characteristic outlook on experience and will instinctively prefer one novelist's approach to another's. It is less artistry that inclines us to Thackeray rather than Dickens (or the reverse) than some private motive arising from experience or a longing for escape. It is possible to like both, but scarcely possible to do so in equal measure. Trollope's worship of Thackeray involved censure of Dickens, and Charlotte Brontë's was at the expense of Fielding. Within this period, however, Thackeray,[1] Dickens, the Brontës, George Eliot and Hardy have each supporters who would acknowledge no other supreme name. Taken together they testify to a miraculous outpouring of genius.

[1] William Makepeace Thackeray (1811–63). Born at Calcutta, educated at Cambridge. Contributor to *Fraser's Magazine* and to *Punch*, and first editor of the *Cornhill*, 1859–62. *Yellowplush Correspondence*, 1837; *Paris Sketch Book*, 1840; *Great Hoggarty Diamond*, 1841; *Barry Lyndon*, 1844; *Jeames's Diary*, 1845; *Book of Snobs*, 1847; *Vanity Fair*, 1846–8; *Pendennis*, 1848–50; *Esmond*, 1852; *Newcomes*, 1853–5; *English Humourists of the Eighteenth Century*, 1851, published 1853; *The Four Georges*, 1855–6, published 1860; *Virginians*, 1857–9; *Lovel the Widower*, 1860; *Adventures of Philip*, 1861–2; ballads and rhymes.

The art flourished under the signs of Richardson and Fielding, and during the earlier years these names marked styles which did not commingle. Fielding's warmest admirer and most direct successor was Thackeray. "They say he is like Fielding (Charlotte Brontë wrote); they talk of his wit, humour, comic powers. He resembles Fielding as an eagle does a vulture: Fielding would stoop on carrion, but Thackeray never does." There is no doubt that Fielding's Tom Jones does some pretty disreputable things. It was no part of his maker's purpose to portray him as spotless, nor to gloze over his backslidings. His realism is quite unsentimental. But Thackeray is, after the Victorian manner, secretive of real evil. It happens somewhere in the background, but the pages of the novel bear only the unhappy consequences, together with the entrances and exits of certain unpleasant characters. The device is not merely selective, but also sentimental. Thackeray is an optimist about goodness, and will not see it finally wronged. His writing in its defence is surcharged with emotion, and he is thereby more moving and affecting than Fielding. Tragedy lies outside his orbit, but he is a master of pathos, of which one of the finest instances in all literature is the account of good Colonel Newcome's end. He establishes a bond of sympathy between the reader and even the reprehensible Becky Sharp, though he energetically reprobates the virago, Widow Mackenzie. In fact, we must love or hate his heroes and heroines, but we must not merely observe them. This occurs despite the fact that he borrowed from Fielding the device of the cynical reflection. His chapters frequently open with reflections delivered in a worldly-wise tone, which some readers have resented, and others felt to be somewhat tedious. They lack the negligent ease of Fielding's remarks, perhaps because the old unity of understanding between all cultured persons was no longer there. Thackeray talks at his reader, rather than with him. This language of unsentimental analysis had been Fielding's shield against the charge of cant, for under its cover he could reveal his love of the better way. It serves Thackeray in the same way; but Thackeray was at bottom a sentimentalist.

The great mass of Thackeray's writings boils down to five novels of permanent consequence: *Vanity Fair*, *Esmond* and

The Virginians, *Pendennis* and *The Newcomes*. Two pairs are associated by family ties. *Vanity Fair* is the first of the great series, and has claims to be considered the best. It has an unusually ample range of human nature, and the character of Becky Sharp is truly remarkable. She is an adventuress and is brought to the bar of poetic justice for her intrigues. They are dexterous and vain. But they arose from the nature of things—from the incompatibility between her meagre opportunities and her superior talents. The reader censures, not without sympathy and regret. It is characteristic of Thackeray that Becky presents no problem. He does not ask why a woman should have no reasonable outlet for unusual abilities nor why society is so constructed as to waste the greater part of its human resources. The day for the interrogation-mark had not yet arrived, and Thackeray was still at the stage of observing and recording the facts. It is on a woman also that interest centres in *Esmond* and *The Virginians*, namely on the beautiful and imperious Beatrix Esmond. She is young and headstrong in *Esmond* and in *The Virginians* is old and sardonic. The sequel is less interesting than its first part, since upon *Esmond* Thackeray lavished his unexampled knowledge of English literature and life in the times of Marlborough and Addison. The impression of Queen Anne's England is vivid and complete. It must be allowed also that Henry Esmond is a less colourless sample of goodness than George Warrington, his grandson. Harry Warrington's rake's progress is a duplicate of Arthur Pendennis's. *The Newcomes* is also concerned with matrimonial tangles and addresses wrongly delivered, but it develops into a notable duel between the vulgarian Mrs. Mackenzie and patient self-tortured Colonel Newcome. The nobleness of his soul burns the more clearly as misfortune purges away the dross of his misunderstanding. He atones for his errors by patience and courage, and by accepting a poor man's end without repining.

The lectures on the *Four Georges* and on *English Humourists* belong to the background of these great novels. The former show how Thackeray built up the view of the Hanoverian era for his *Esmond, Virginians* and *Vanity Fair*. The latter are an examination of humorous styles by a great humorist. It throws light on his own original contributions to wit. The *Yellowplush Correspondence* and *Jeames's Diary* are still readable, though their jests have staled. It is necessary to believe more firmly in caste than we now do, if we are to find fun in the revelation of a flunkey's soul. There is more life left to Thackeray's excellent ballads and rhymes, such as *The Mahogany Tree* and *Little Billee*.

To Anthony Trollope[1] we might assign the rank of Thackeray's lieutenant. His admiration for his contemporary was very high, and he shared the same affiliation with the naturalistic manner of Fielding. But his formation had been different and his style was more workmanlike. Trollope carried into literature the methods of a good civil servant, working with regularity, neatness, plain desire to please, and silence before critics. In the *Autobiography* he is so frank as to reveal the financial gains that accrued to him from authorship, setting before young writers his own experience of the art and craft, without ignoring its economic aspects. This candour has done him harm, for the public likes to make a mystery of letters, to believe in inspiration rather than craftsmanship, and an urge to write rather than an expectation of profit. Yet the urge was no less powerful with Trollope than with a more reticent man, and the practical details afford true guidance. He was indeed a notable artist, and a creator of one county in the England of the mind. This is Barsetshire, which had its centre in the cathedral and close of Barchester. *The Warden* brought this place into being, complete with bishop, dean, archdeacon and chapter, and later novels added the scandalous Duke of Omnium, the spendthrift Sowerby, the hard-driven Crawley family, and other members of a complete society. It had two limitations. It was composed almost wholly of the clergy and the leisured classes, lacking deep popular roots. The method of portrayal was also somewhat photographic.

[1] Anthony Trollope (1815–82). Entered the General Post Office, 1834. Spent many years in Ireland and then did useful service as an organizer in England. A keen hunter. His mother, Frances Trollope (1780–1863), was also a talented novelist. His first novels were written to exploit his special knowledge of the Irish, but he attained success only when he began the "Barchester series": *The Warden*, 1855; *Barchester Towers*, 1857; *Dr. Thorne*, 1858; *Framley Parsonage*, 1861; *The Small House at Allington*, 1864; *Last Chronicle of Barset*, 1867; *Autobiography*, 1863.

Though the characters arose in Trollope's mind to embody the situations that he wished to work out, they looked so life-like that he was constantly asked to identify their originals. There were no such originals, and yet the question would hardly have arisen if theirs had been a life more than ordinarily intense. The plots are conducted with speed, neatness and interest, with a modicum of social satire and little Thackerayan sermonizing; but they also contained deeper implications that may be overlooked. The Reverend Septimus Harding's crisis of conscience about an ecclesiastical sinecure in *The Warden*, the too easy preferment of the Reverend Mark Robarts in *Framley Parsonage*, and the too severe poverty of the Reverend Josiah Crawley's perpetual curacy in *The Last Chronicle of Barset*, reveal three different faults in the organization of the national Church. All that is lacking to Trollope, who has such remarkable representational skill, is a certain luminosity, whereby he might have transfigured his naturalism.

Such transfiguration is a mighty resource of Dickens.[1] Dickens and Thackeray form the great "either . . . or" of modern English literature, to such an extent that the ardent Dickensian is almost interdicted the use of his rival. They were personal friends, if we discount one unlucky misunderstanding; both humorists, both sentimentalists, both reformers, both middle-class. But Thackeray's humour was nearer to wit, and Dickens's to farce; Thackeray's sentiment was curbed by his "cynicism," while that of Dickens was made to gush; Thackeray used irony against the evil thing, but Dickens grew hoarse with clamour; Thackeray put his acquaintance into books, but Dickens discovered the Cockney. The crux of the matter is the "Dickens character." Because it relies wholly on "character" and has no real plot, *The Pickwick Papers* is the most typical and revealing of his books. In others our

---

[1] Charles John Huffam Dickens (1812–70). Born in London. Read widely among eighteenth-century novelists, notably Smollett. *Sketches by Boz*, 1836; *Pickwick Papers*, 1837; *Oliver Twist*, 1838; *Nicholas Nickleby*, 1839; *The Old Curiosity Shop, Barnaby Rudge*, 1840–1; *American Notes*, 1842; *Martin Chuzzlewit*, 1843–4; *Christmas Books*, 1843–8; *Dombey and Son*, 1846–8; *David Copperfield*, 1849–50; *Bleak House*, 1852–3; *Hard Times*, 1854; *Little Dorrit*, 1855–7; *Tale of Two Cities*, 1859; *Great Expectations*, 1861; *Our Mutual Friend*, 1864–5; *Edwin Drood* (unfinished).

judgment is distracted by considerations of plot or purpose, but in this first of his successes we have only the *dramatis personae* and the scenes and settings which give them scope. Here, then, are Mr. Pickwick and Mr. Winkle, the Wellers, the Fat Boy, Mr. Jingle and the rest; here also are the Eatanswill Election, Mr. Winkle on the ice, and the case of Bardell *v.* Pickwick. We may extend either list indefinitely by adding to the one Micawber, Mrs. Gamp, Pecksniff, Uriah Heep, Fagin, etc., and to the other Sidney Carton on the scaffold, Scrooge at the Christmas party, the treacle ration at Dotheboys school, etc. The scenes, however, are less memorable than the characters; they are often strained, and tolerable only for the latter. It is easy to find fault with Dickens, to censure his style as jerky and his pathos as melodramatic. He is not a model to be set before a young author; but what an inspiration!

"The primary object of a novelist (wrote Trollope) is to please; and this man's novels have been found more pleasant than those of any other. . . . I do acknowledge that Mrs. Gamp, Micawber, Pecksniff and others have become household words in every house, as though they were human beings; but to my judgment they are not human beings, nor are any of the characters human which Dickens has portrayed. It has been the peculiarity and the marvel of this man's power, that he has invested his puppets with a charm that has enabled him to dispense with human nature." It is well said, even if unfavourably. To compare Trollope with Dickens (that we may avoid the usual, but more complex, comparison with Thackeray), we find that the Warden is a "human being" whom we are convinced we have met. This conviction troubled its author, who was forced to asseverate that the character had arisen wholly out of his own invention; its merit of persuasiveness, however, consists in the way it melts into a background of real persons known to us. We have never met a Pickwick or a Micawber; cross-examined, we should be bound to admit they do not exist, and yet we should react violently against that admission. We do not compare them with our acquaintance, but our acquaintance with them. Thus they are the more vivid realities, and we are fragments and reflections of them. We identify a

Micawber instantly because he resembles, perhaps momentarily, *the* Micawber, and not because he belongs to a class of Micawbers, as the Warden belongs to a class of honest clergymen brought suddenly up against the demands of conscience. The old Jonsonian formula of the "humour" is perfected in Dickens.

A second characteristic, derived from Smollett, is his unexpected milieu. Dickens's readers were of the same class as Thackeray's, though more numerous, but he does not introduce them to persons they expect to meet. On the contrary, they find themselves in a thieves' kitchen in *Oliver Twist* or in a stingily conducted school in *Nicholas Nickleby*. Here are vices of an unusual order, somewhat stagy but effective; and here are quite unexpected points of goodness. You cannot foretell which of the persons will grip your interest. It is as likely to be Tom Pinch as Martin Chuzzlewit, though the latter gives his name to the novel; but you also eye with fascinated horror the villainies of Pecksniff, though his ultimate castigation rather eases our resentment than engages our approval. The autobiographical *David Copperfield* has a first-personal pronoun in half the titles of chapters, but our attention is held by the Heeps, Micawbers and Peggottys—and by the extraordinary fact that Peggotty lived under an upturned boat. In *A Tale of Two Cities* Dickens took a piece of social refuse—worthless and inclined to maudlin self-pity—and redeemed Sidney Carton by the performance of one heroic act—a self-pitying and declamatory one—the one act of which his nature was capable. At the same time, he put a new construction on the historical novel, since a past epoch was necessary to his plot and yet its appeal was not to the past but to permanent character.

Nor should we omit to enter to Dickens's credit the secondary considerations that won him so many readers. His vehement onslaught on pettifogging lawyers in *Great Expectations*, the open scandal of Fagin's thieves' kitchen, the monstrousness of the usurer Heep, the oppressive rule of schoolmasters and beadles—all this social doctrine excited the readers of his time and misses the mark in ours. Yet the removal of such scandals owes much to Dickens's crusades, and the vehemence of his hates and loves remains incandescent in his style. His cult of Christmas, too, in the *Christmas Books* has

F*

proved a sweetener of life, even though it has been lowered to a commonplace.

There was no one like Dickens, but perhaps the nearest in spirit were Wilkie Collins and Charles Reade.[1] The former was a craftsman, without the touch of genius, but he included memorable characters in his *Woman in White*, and *The Moonstone* has been called "the first, the longest, and the best of modern English detective novels." Charles Reade made his bow with *Peg Woffington*, when he was nearly forty, and followed it with the powerful social document called *It is Never Too Late to Mend* and the historical *Cloister and the Hearth*, which brings Erasmus's *Colloquies* bodily to life. Charles Kingsley[2] cultivated both the historical and the social fields. In the historical he made a successful appeal to ingrained prejudices in his *Westward Ho!*, with gallant Elizabethan sea-dogs and sinister Spanish dons as per formula. There is no halt in his narrative, no lack of superficial liveliness and of the energetic virtues. *Hereward the Wake* is another such extract from John Bull's history of England, and in *Hypatia* he cleverly exploits the contrast between decadent Rome and the savage but inquiring Goths. *Yeast* and *Alton Locke* represent his social doctrine; *The Water-Babies* and *The Heroes* are his classics for children. His brother, Henry, is remembered for *Ravenshoe*. Bulwer-Lytton,[3] belonging to an older generation than these, exploited the historical novel in a more ponderous fashion, and is most enjoyed when briefest, in *The Last Days of Pompeii*. The great name of Disraeli[4] has to be included among

[1] William Wilkie Collins (1824–89). *The Woman in White*, 1860; *The Moonstone*, 1868.
  Charles Reade (1814–84). *Peg Woffington*, 1853; *It is Never too Late to Mend*, 1853; *The Cloister and the Hearth*, 1861.
[2] Charles Kingsley (1819–75). Professor of Modern History at Cambridge; Chaplain to the Queen. *Alton Locke*, 1850; *Yeast*, 1850; *Hypatia*, 1853; *Westward Ho!*, 1855; *The Heroes*, 1856; *The Water-Babies*, 1863; *Hereward the Wake*, 1865.
  Henry Kingsley (1830–76). *Ravenshoe*, 1862.
[3] Baron Edward George Earle Lytton (Bulwer-Lytton, 1803–73). *Pelham*, 1828; *The Last Days of Pompeii*, 1834; *The Last of the Barons*, 1843; *Harold*, 1848.
[4] Benjamin Disraeli (1804–81). Earl of Beaconsfield, and Prime Minister. Son of Isaac d'Israeli (1766–1848), author of *Curiosities of Literature*, 1791. Privately educated. *Vivian Grey*, 1826; *Coningsby*, 1844; *Sybil*, 1845; *Tancred*, 1847; *Lothair*, 1870; *Endymion*, 1880.

the lesser lights of literature, since he could only give it intermittent attention. Brilliance, cleverness and the political themes keep his novels alive.

Because his style was too easily parodied, Charles Lever's[1] reputation suffered a temporary eclipse. His rollicking pictures of carefree, hard-drinking Irish society cannot remain in limbo, though probably his readers will not often go beyond the *Confessions of Harry Lorrequer*. Lorrequer and his associates are "typical" Irishmen, and there is just enough truth in their portraiture to confirm the English tourist in his preconceptions and form part of the mirage which surrounds him in a tour of Southern Ireland. They beget in him a degree of affability not always reciprocated by a humourless, unforgiving nation.

The line of George Borrow[2] is traced back to Defoe. Like Defoe he confounds observation and invention in a style so natural that he defies the labeller. One doubts whether he is a novelist, an autobiographer, or a traveller, and yet his style and matter is always constant. No good story loses by his telling, but he is not a writer of fiction. He invents no character, possibly no episode; yet the episodes are those of a biographical romance, and in dialogue and character-sketches Borrow is equal to the best masters of the novelist's art. He had an immense though unsystematic knowledge of languages, and an unlimited interest in all kinds and classes of persons. His friendship for horse-dealing gipsies gave him an insight into a Britain unknown to the English, and it served him also in Spain. A comparison of the *Bible in Spain* with the original

[1] Charles James Lever (1806–72). Educated for the medical profession at Trinity College, Dublin. His early work appeared in the *Dublin University Magazine*, and included *Harry Lorrequer*, republished in 1839; *Charles O'Malley*, 1841; *Jack Hinton*, 1843; *Tom Burke of Ours*, 1844; etc. Later settled abroad at Florence and Spezzia, and contributed novels to *Blackwood's Magazine* and the *Cornhill*.

[2] George Henry Borrow (1803–81). Born at East Dereham, in Norfolk, son of a recruiting officer. Engaged in desultory linguistic studies. Employed as a hack writer by Sir Richard Phillips, whom he left after severe privations. Became a travelling hedge-smith and obtained an intimate acquaintance with gipsy horse-dealers. Agent for the British and Foreign Bible Society in Russia, 1833–5, and Spain, 1835–9. *Romantic Ballads* (from the Danish), 1826; *Embéo e Majaró Lucas* (St. Luke in Spanish Romany), 1837; *The Zincali* (Gipsies of Spain), 1841; *Bible in Spain*, 1843; *Lavengro*, 1851; *Romany Rye*, 1857; *Wild Wales*, 1862; *Romano Lavo-Lil*, 1874.

reports sent by Borrow to the Bible Society gives some idea of the touches which transformed events into the vivid experiences of his prose. He is sparing in the static parts of narrative, such as scene-painting, but copious in dialogue; ignoring formal recipes for style, he employs a language that never flags in interest; and by the wayside of his narrative there continue to spring up figures that are instantly recognizable as alive. The *Bible in Spain* and *Zincali* are connected with his Spanish mission; *Lavengro* and *Romany Rye* are an autobiography novelized. Though generally reckoned as romances, they are hardly more so than the two books previously named, and as a portrayal of English gipsy conditions they have become prime documents of a "fancy" or hobby among learned philologists and folklorists. In *Wild Wales* there is no loss of vivacity, but the writer overdramatizes himself.

The novel is that branch of literature in which women have attained the same stature as men. Nineteenth-century England was prolific in women novelists, some of whom made contributions of cardinal importance to the art. It is not only that the change of sex brings a change of focus, and that a woman sees clearly that half of experience which is blurred for men, but the Brontës with their revelation of passion, and "George Eliot" with her psychological insight, introduced into the craft two new factors, which have continued to be dominant.

The Brontë sisters,[1] Charlotte, Emily and Anne, form a close group in their inspiration and style. Their leader was Charlotte, the most productive and skilful member of the group. Emily was the author of a work of strange and unequal genius, but Anne was rather a talented than a great writer. Charlotte Brontë's *Jane Eyre* traces the growth of a selfless love against a loveless background, showing it triumphing over the rudest shocks. Some of these were, in that age, considered to be

[1] Charlotte Brontë (1816–55), Emily (1818–48), Anne (1820–49). After an unhappy schooling at the Clergy Daughters' School, Cowan Bridge, Charlotte and Emily studied for a while in Brussels. Returned to Haworth, 1844. The lives of the sisters were made distressing by the vices of their brother, Bramwell Brontë, who died in 1848. Charlotte married the Rev. A. B. Nicholls in 1854, but died soon after. Charlotte wrote *Jane Eyre*, 1847; *Shirley*, 1849; *Villette*, 1857. Emily wrote *Wuthering Heights*, 1847. Anne wrote *Agnes Grey*, 1847; *The Tenant of Wildfell Hall*, 1848.

scandalous, since they involved an attempt at a bigamous marriage. Apart from the fact, however, that the bigamy was not of Jane Eyre's making and from the circumstance that a more modern taste does not require the novelist to shut his eyes to kinds of events that actually do happen, there is the fuller realization of the novel's deeper meaning. We must discount everything but the heroine. The story is "poetically" conceived, as its author insisted novels should be, and it takes place in the heroine's soul, in the fibres of her being. A passion of devotion is aroused in her; passion is healthy and purifying when it is true, but debasing and devastating when it is false. The ancient objection of moralists to works of fiction, that their love-scenes are incitements to lasciviousness, is thus answered, since selfless passion cleanses and ennobles. This inwardness is an extension of Richardson's psychological method into regions which Jane Austen had deliberately avoided. In the outward or objective aspect of the novel there are evident defects. The male characters are out of drawing, and Jane's childhood is both tedious and unconvincing, though it is based on autobiography. The blurred focus, however, serves to pick out more distinctly the spiritual veracity of the heroine in the history of her love. The fault has been corrected in *Shirley* and *Villette*, which are the products of Charlotte Brontë's matured pen. In *Shirley* we find offset genuine passion and its self-regarding simulacrum, embodied in a group of well-conceived characters set against a solid Yorkshire background; but just because they are many, the book has not the Rembrandtesque effect of *Jane Eyre*. Emily Brontë's *Wuthering Heights* is a strange rugged book, perverse and elemental. She displays warped and explosive passions, moroseness and caprice. The Yorkshire background is savager; the narrative is interrupted by awkward transitions from relation to action. There is an attempt to exploit the motif of mysterious horror, and to set up a Byronic character of a man. These injure the book formally, but it lives by the strange imaginative intensity of its author's insight into abnormal temperaments. Anne Brontë, with *The Tenant of Wildfell Hall* and *Agnes Grey*, is manifestly of the same school, though not of the same rank of genius.

Mrs. Gaskell[1] is associated with the sisters by her *Life of Charlotte Brontë*, and also by the Northern tang of her writing. The Brontës were of Yorkshire, Mrs. Gaskell was of Lancashire, and specifically of Manchester. The background of industrial unrest which we find in *Shirley* becomes the main subject of Mrs. Gaskell's *Mary Barton*. In *North and South* she contrasts conditions in the two halves of England, and in *Sylvia's Lovers* she carries the struggle of classes backwards by a story of the press gang. In all these works she shows great talent in the portrayal of classes and communities under the revealing stresses of the Industrial Revolution, but her plots are not remarkable, nor does she develop arresting characters. In character-drawing she has rather the eye of an observer, more sympathetic and less shrewd than Jane Austen, and her gifts get full play in the idyllic *Cranford*, recollections of the Knutsford of her own youth. It is a community she can bring to life by her own special art. Its faded little ladies shyly reveal their sterling worth, and the cunningly negligent style, which seems at first (as befits such a village) to be mere gossip, floats the reader into the story long before he realizes his progress.

Charles Reade enthusiastically greeted George Eliot's[2] *Adam Bede* as "the finest thing since Shakespeare." Such an unapproachable superiority is not claimed for her even by those who would give her the crown of her art, and yet there is a Shakespearean quality in this woman's achievement. She solved the problem which had baffled Cervantes—the problem of how to tell a long story without irrelevance and without tedium. Cervantes gave it up; he smuggled extraneous episodes even into the second part of *Don Quixote*, and in his

[1] Elizabeth Cleghorn Gaskell, *née* Stevenson (1810–65). Brought up by an aunt at Knutsford, Cheshire, and married William Gaskell, minister of Cross Street Unitarian Chapel, Manchester, 1832. On the death of her only boy she began to write novels in 1844. *Mary Barton*, 1848; *Cranford*, 1853; *North and South*, 1855; *Life of Charlotte Brontë*, 1857; *Sylvia's Lovers*, 1863–4; *Wives and Daughters*, 1866.

[2] "George Eliot," Mary Ann Evans, later Mrs. J. W. Cross (1819–80). Wrote under encouragement from her friend, G. H. Lewes. *Scenes of Clerical Life*, 1858; *Adam Bede*, 1859; *Mill on the Floss*, 1860; *Silas Marner*, 1861; *Romola*, 1863; *Felix Holt*, 1866; *Middlemarch*, 1872; *Daniel Deronda*, 1876.

last work plunged into a sea of stories. The framework of a novel was, with him, the incidents of a journey; with the chivalresque and picaresque authors it was the events of a life. There is a lax and profuse quality in the plots of all English novelists before George Eliot, who carried out George Sand's programme of true situations, true and even actual characters, grouped round a type destined to bear the principal message of the book. Relevance and coherence become essential features of construction with George Eliot. She works outward from character. She has the keenest eye for discerning the almost imperceptible swerve, as of the points of a railway-line, due to egoism or indulgence; but all that follows is continuous and cumulative. The crucial moments are fixed by incidents, often of small weight in themselves, which are seen to be vitally important in the retrospect, both as to action and character. Moreover, this tightening of the novel's structure brought the tragic within its reach. The older, manifold art was rather tragi-comic. It is the legacy of Cervantes that the storyteller, even when dealing in great truths, should unwind the coils of his taut imaginings by humorous disclaimers. Sometimes the novelist felt bound to break the tragic sequence by some anticlimax. Thus Fielding and Thackeray maintain their cool mundane poses; and those who do not fear to lose their balance, such as Dickens or Emily Brontë, are wont to fall into the melodramatic. But Hetty Sorel's pitiful little life and the disruption of Arthur Donnithorne's career are pure tragedy. There is something Shakespearean also in her objectivity. She shows more partisanship in *Silas Marner* than in *Adam Bede*, perhaps because the former is a more direct statement of her positivist creed; in *Middlemarch* there is not the old glow. But she does not abandon herself to her creature, as Charlotte Brontë or even Thackeray do on occasion; the same cool intelligence watches all her puppets. It is characteristic of her that her portraits of the men and women do not show sexual bias. She wrote under a pseudonym, and there was no clue in her character-drawing to her sex. The veracity of the persons was often guaranteed by their place in her biography. Adam Bede was her father, Mrs. Poyser her mother, and Dinah Morris an aunt. So it is also with *The Mill on the Floss*; yet there is no less certainty in the strokes when the characters are remote and historical, as in *Romola*. A specifically feminine touch in her work, however, is her portrayal of women with a mission. Such is the sweet Dinah Morris of *Adam Bede*, whose vocation to comfort the sick poor and preach in the Methodist connection was historically fulfilled. In *Middlemarch*, however, the problem arises bristling with strictly contemporary difficulties. In this work Dorothea has the vocation of a Saint Theresa, to spend herself for some great object; but as to what or how, her status as a woman leaves her without guidance. She mistakes pedantry for learning in the person of the Reverend Edward Casaubon, without fully realizing the greater error of having mistaken a stick for a man. Her efforts end in frustration, mitigated in some dim way by the highmindedness of the effort itself. Society, and perhaps nature, condemns these fine-touched female spirits to obscurity and a trivial round, but their hidden lives are (says George Eliot) "incalculably diffusive." *Middlemarch* also is autobiography.

Immediately before the rise and recognition of Thomas Hardy, George Meredith[1] enjoyed the principate of the novel. Like Hardy he made little impression on the bulk of readers, not because he had a doctrine too hard for them, but because of the preciosity of his style and method. The words "brilliant" and "fantasy" impose themselves with Meredith from the date of the *Shaving of Shagpat*, a brilliant Oriental fantasy. His style becomes increasingly tricky as one proceeds from *The Ordeal of Richard Feverel*, through *The Egoist* to *Diana of the Crossways*. Some of the apostrophes, personifications, transitions and quotations from unwritten books smack of Carlyle, though Meredith is a wholly urbane writer. The appeal of his

---

[1] George Meredith (1828–1909). *Shaving of Shagpat*, 1856; *Ordeal of Richard Feverel*, 1859; *Evan Harrington*, 1861; *Modern Love* (poems), 1862; *Emilia in England*, 1864 (later renamed *Sandra Belloni*); *Rhoda Fleming*, 1865; *Vittoria*, 1866; *Harry Richmond*, 1870–1; *Beauchamp's Career*, 1876; *Essay on Comedy*, 1877; *The Egoist*, 1879; *The Tragic Comedians*, 1880; *Diana of the Crossways*, 1885; *Poems and Lyrics*, 1883; *Ballads and Poems*, 1887; *A Reading of Earth* (poems), 1888; *One of Our Conquerors*, 1891; *Lord Ormont and his Aminta*, 1894; *The Amazing Marriage*, 1895.

verse is wrecked by this ingenuity, by which it loses the needful sensuousness. The clue to Meredith's manner is to be found in his *Essay on Comedy and the Uses of the Comic Spirit*. An English reader is surprised that his country's comedy should be identified with Congreve; a French reader might be gratified to find Alceste and Tartufe recognized as the supreme comic creations, though he would be baffled by Meredith's reasons. Comedy, with Meredith, has little to do with fun, farce, humour, satire, irony or ridicule. It is Mind hovering above events; clearsightedness which sees both real and ostensible motive simultaneously, and knows us for what we are and what we would like to appear. This clear-sightedness, according to Meredith, is found among women rather than among men; it refers to the present and not to the future; and it is eminently social. This highly rarefied conception of comedy—"impersonal and of unrivalled politeness, often no more than a smile"—is exemplified in the novels. The age-old theme of fathers and sons gives the matter for *The Ordeal of Richard Feverel*, a book which, as the first of Meredith's developed manner and yet free from excessive ingenuity, is by some critics rated as his best. Sir Austin Feverel has, like Chesterfield, a passion for moulding youth. He educates his son admirably up to the crucial point of a choice of wife, and then by clever persistence his system leads to a tragic collapse. This is sad matter, but it supports Puck's remark "what fools these mortals be," and is therefore part of the human comedy. The method is fully developed in *The Egoist*. It does not allow for criticism of the presuppositions of society, since this is taken as the frame needed for the situation. Situation and character are conceived with penetration and psychological subtlety, but statically. Sir Willoughby Patterne is always the same egoist; we have no play of cause and effect as in the egoists of George Eliot, nor do we have the revelations of many-sidedness given by the older novelists; we merely see more and more surely into the mental cancer of the patient. Diana Merion, from *Diana of the Crossways*, is a character more attractive and more suited to common conceptions of comedy, but she is equally fixed as the same attractive, high-spirited Irish girl throughout the novel.

Thomas Hardy's[1] public, like Meredith's, must always be a select circle, but for a different reason. The deterrent in Hardy is not verbal or cerebral; it is the acrid flavour of his thought, too keen for the majority who seek chiefly entertainment. To call it pessimism would perhaps be unfair in view of his own statement that the artist's business is representational: "a novel is an impression, not an argument." In so far as pessimism is a philosophy, it lay outside his duty as a writer; as such his business was to see life, and to transfer to paper what he saw. But this vision was uniformly sombre. Hardy saw a blemished planet, society at discord with nature, domestic division, and the seeds of death and ruin germinating in the hearts of men. So much, indeed, was not unprecedented, but with a burst of sentiment or emotion other writers have softened these asperities for their readers. "Facit indignatio versum," the Roman poet had said, and he eased his spirit thereby. But this relief is just what Hardy will not allow; he will neither sentimentalize nor be indignant, and we must gaze fixedly even while we wince. The result is a subtle and somewhat cruel view of human conduct, particularly as it is disturbed by sex, set forth in a tone of unimpassioned curiosity. Thus in *The Woodlanders* he treats of matrimonial schism, not on the narrow ground of a broken contract, but on the broader basis of promoting as much happiness as may be during "the brief transit through this sorry world." In *Jude the Obscure* matrimonial dispeace became an entanglement that seems to have affrighted the author himself. He refuses to solve his problem, but only to state it. Such an "attempt to give artistic form to a true sequence of things" passed beyond the social limits of Meredithian comedy. In *Tess of the d'Urbervilles* he develops his critique of society. The subtitle, "A Pure Woman," seemed to him justified as a summary impression

---

[1] Thomas Hardy (1840–1928). As an ecclesiastical architect in Dorchester (Dorset) he became familiar with the "Wessex" of his novels. *Under the Greenwood Tree*, 1872; *A Pair of Blue Eyes*, 1873; *Far from the Madding Crowd*, 1874; *The Return of the Native*, 1876; *The Mayor of Casterbridge*, 1886; *The Woodlanders*, 1887; *Tess of the d'Urbervilles*, 1891; *Jude the Obscure*, 1896; *Wessex Poems*, 1898; *The Dynasts*, 1904–8.

when the work had ended, and his readers will not deny this title to Tess. Yet cruel chance and outrageous persecution inflict on his morally guiltless heroine the grossest stigmas. The woman pays (as the saying is), not for her own deeds, but for the brutal assaults and revulsions of others. Hardy's sole comment is to put the word "justice" into italics as either questionable or a misnomer, and yet one sees that it is in the constituted state of things that Tess should suffer. Against "the merely vocal formulæ of society," which most people think to be true morality, he sets the authority of Nature and tacit agreement among men; but he does not judge or take sides. The root of the trouble lies deeper than our conventions. The character of Eustacia Vye, in *The Return of the Native*, contains the seeds of death and disgrace for all around her. This is the darkest of his novels.

A second great service by Hardy to English letters was his creation of Wessex. Trollope had created the model of an English cathedral town in his "Barchester," complete with families, buildings and interrelations; but Hardy built his Wessex from the ground up. It is chiefly Dorset, with some outlying points in the neighbouring counties; but its most important characteristics are that it is as much of England as the mind can grasp and it is far enough from the metropolis to be eternal. The soil of this Wessex is a part of the fortunes of its people; the people are indigenes, with their own folklore, superstitions and racy turns of speech. In Tess, for instance, the slope of the ground, the lie of the watershed, and the nature of the soil condition her various mischances. A powerful vivification (not a description merely) of Egdon Heath at the opening of *The Return of the Native* is a prelude to the interference of that savage waste in all the crises of the story. Men and earth are so bound that they seem both enslaved by the same resistless determinism, the more so as Hardy has allowed a place to chance in human affairs. He seems to recreate the Greek dogmas of retribution and divine ill-will as they appear in the titanic musings of Aeschylus; but the material grounds thereof are indisputably English.

To Robert Louis Stevenson[1] we go for style rather than thought. The natives of Samoa, among whom he spent his last years, called him "Tusitala" (teller of tales). Theirs was a right instinct, for Stevenson has spun the most marvellous yarns. His prose is fluid and engaging, carefully jointed and somewhat lacking in vigour. The reader is not held up by a knotty sentence or a rugged thought. He begins to speak and casts a spell. This was already evident in the elegant fantasy of the *New Arabian Nights*, and is perfected in *Treasure Island*. This swiftly moving yarn was submitted to the criticism of a child, and is wholly without tedium or false sentiment. The pace is maintained, the surprises are well timed, and the characters clear and distinct. In *Dr Jekyll and Mr. Hyde* he added a new compound noun to the English language, and made all men familiar with the notion of schizophrenia. Medieval English material went to the making of the splendid boys' story of *The Black Arrow*; *Kidnapped* and *Catriona* with *The Master of Ballantrae* are Scottish. They challenge comparison with Sir Walter Scott, and in so doing are discovered to be slighter in erudition, characterization and national significance; but they are more effective as stories. *The Wrecker* was written in collaboration, and is in another vein. We owe to Stevenson also two entertaining travel books and some of the best children's verses.

The mention of Stevenson is a reminder not to overlook the *opera minora* of the Victorian age which were addressed to children. In some instances, such as Mrs. Ewing's *Jackanapes* and Anna Sewell's *Black Beauty*, we encounter nursery classics as idiomatically perfect as they are unpretentious.[2] Hughes's *Tom Brown's School Days* and Dean Farrar's *Eric* (now some-

[1] Robert Louis Stevenson (1850–94). Born at Edinburgh. *An Inland Voyage*, 1878; *Travels with a Donkey in the Cevennes*, 1879; *Virginibus Puerisque*, 1881; *New Arabian Nights*, 1882; *Treasure Island*, 1883; *Child's Garden of Verses*, 1885; *Dr. Jekyll and Mr. Hyde*, 1886; *The Black Arrow*, 1888; *Kidnapped*, 1886, and its sequel, *Catriona*, 1893; *Master of Ballantrae*, 1888. Visited Father Damien in 1890, and then settled at Vailima (Samoa) for his health's sake. *The Wrecker*, 1892; *Vailima Letters*, 1895; *Weir of Hermiston* (unfinished), 1896.

[2] Mrs. Ewing, *née* Juliana Horatia Gatty (1841–85). *Lob-lie-by-the-fire*, 1873; *Jackanapes*, 1884.

Anna Sewell (1820–78). *Black Beauty*, 1877, the "autobiography" of a horse.

what in disfavour for its priggishness) are boys' school favourites which bear reading afterwards. The motif of adventure is
seen in Marryat's *Masterman Ready*, Kingston's *Peter the
Whaler*, or Ballantyne's *Coral Island*.[1] Boys demand up-to-
dateness in their adventures, and the books of one generation
will not serve another; yet these cited are only the most
permanent of a vast mass of innocently entertaining fiction.
More complex reasons for survival are found in "Lewis
Carroll's" *Alice in Wonderland* and *Through the Looking-Glass*.[2]
They are, in the first place, excellent and surprising tales told
to a little girl, but as interesting for boys or adults. The plots
follow the courses of a card game and a game of chess respectively. The pattern of the games can be recognized, though
strangely transformed by the novelist's fancy. They rely also
on nonsense, but it is a calculated nonsense which just eludes
our comprehension. Their creator was not so successful in
other works in this vein, apart from the riotous absurdities of
The Hunting of the Snark.

XII. VICTORIAN THOUGHT AND ACTION

THE early years of Queen Victoria's reign witnessed a second
great reform movement within the English Church. The first,
that of John Wesley, had been evangelical; this second reform
was doctrinal and sacramental. The first had led to the

[1] Thomas Hughes (1822–96). *Tom Brown's Schooldays*, 1857 (Dr.
Arnold's Rugby); *Tom Brown at Oxford*, 1861.
   Frederic William Farrar (1831–1903). *Eric, or Little by Little*, 1858;
and many theological works.
   Frederick Marryat (1792–1848). Captain R.N. *Peter Simple*, 1834;
Jacob Faithful, 1834; *Midshipman Easy*, 1836; *Masterman Ready*, 1841.
   Robert Michael Ballantyne (1825–94). *The Fur-traders*, 1856; *Coral
Island*, 1857; *Ungava*, 1857; *The Dog Crusoe*, 1860; *The Gorilla Hunters*,
1862.
[2] "Lewis Carroll," Charles Lutwidge Dodgson (1832–98). Mathe-
matical Lecturer at Oxford. *Alice's Adventures in Wonderland*, 1865;
Through the Looking-glass, 1872; *Hunting of the Snark*, 1876; *Sylvie
and Bruno*, 1889.

departure of the Wesleyans or Methodists from the national communion. The second has split that communion into two discordant parties, the one Catholic, the other Protestant. The theme of the age was the conflict between rationalism and faith, taking these terms in a lay sense as well as a religious, and in this light the Tractarian Movement may be regarded as an affirmation of faith. Sweet reasonableness had been enthroned in the Church's councils by the eighteenth century, but the Tractarians demanded definition and authority. They repudiated the word "Protestant," holding that Anglo-Catholic faith and practice depended on the unbroken authority of apostolical and episcopal succession. It differed from the Roman Catholic, they held, by its greater fidelity to the way of the primitive Church, as being free from the "popular errors" due to later corruption. The movement did, in fact, restore to the Church authority, dogmatic precision (among those who have accepted these views), catholicity, reverence for the sacraments, and a certain type of saintliness.

The hymns in John Keble's *Christian Year* are one of the fruits of this movement, but its most remarkable literary consequence was Newman's[1] *Apologia pro Vita Sua*. The immediate purpose of this work was to refute some improper allegations by Charles Kingsley, by showing that the process of Newman's conversion originated in his own thought and consciousness. The obvious sincerity and spirituality of the apologia vindicated him in the eyes of all fair-minded readers; but these qualities alone would not have sufficed to raise the work so high among the great confessions of Christendom. The workings of a strange and subtle mind and of a conscience

[1] John Henry Newman (1801–90). Fellow of Oriel College, Oxford. Vicar of St. Mary's, to which was attached the living of Littlemore, After a European tour in 1832, he returned to initiate the Oxford or Tractarian Movement, that is, a movement centred at Oxford and working through tracts. The *Tracts for the Times* were by various writers, who sought to secure for the Church of England a definite basis of discipline and doctrine. *Tract XC*, an examination of the Thirty-nine Articles, by Newman, appeared in 1841. It placed on the Articles, indeterminate in themselves, a consistently Catholic interpretation. This raised a storm of protest, and the *Tracts* were discontinued. Newman was received into the Roman Church in 1845. Cardinal, 1879. *Tracts, 1833–41*; *On the Scope and Nature of University Education*, 1859; *Apologia pro Vita Sua*, 1864; *Grammar of Assent*, 1870.

tender where most are indifferent gives it a peculiar *cachet*. Newman was a sceptic avid for dogma. His analysis of the history and content of dogma was corrosive, but was compensated by a passionate submission to authority. He was impressed by Bishop Butler's argument that, though the supreme truths cannot be known by exact demonstration yet their probability serves for certainty as a basis for action. Newman endeavoured to square the circle by affirming that this probability could give rise also to mental certainty. He affirmed that there was an Anglican dogma before he inquired into its texts, and was surprised when his Catholic interpretation of the Thirty-nine Articles was emphatically repudiated by the majority of his fellow-churchmen. To settle this doubt he clung more and more to the authority of tradition, and his historical examination of primitive heresies convinced him that this tradition was embodied in the Roman Church. As he puts it, he was unable to overcome a "doubt" in favour of the Roman position in his Anglican days; the "doubt" grew and became preponderant; and conversion was complete when he had extinguished a "doubt" still attaching him to Anglicanism. This was a curiously negative procedure. With conversion he found the infallible authority he desired, but there is no evidence in the *Apologia* that he had overcome the doubts inspired by certain practices, notably the cult of the Virgin and the saints.

Within the Roman communion Newman ranked as a "Liberal Catholic." He disliked the notion of papal infallibility, and in his *Scope and Nature of University Education* (lectures pronounced in the Catholic University in Dublin) he sought to guard against obscurantism in education. Arguing that religion and science cannot come into conflict, except in so far as one or the other is misrepresented or misunderstood, he called for the greatest freedom of teaching and thought, but so co-ordinated through the university as to be "safe from the excesses and vagaries of individuals, embodied in institutions which have stood the trial and received the sanction of ages, and administered by men who are supported by their consistency with their predecessors and with each other."

This view, while it may be permanently true, was somewhat optimistic at that time. The conflict between new knowledge and received opinion filled the Victorian Age with the hubbub of debate. Travellers extended our knowledge of the world objectively considered; scientific theorists examined its inner structure; political economists and moralists deduced conclusions which scandalized the average man. Behind all this, the growth of wealth and material power favoured a materialistic interpretation of experience, tacitly accepted in most departments even by the orthodox. For this materialism the authority of science was wrongly claimed, since scientists rightly halted within the physical limits imposed by their premises. The growth of idealistic philosophy at the close of the period was one symptom of the reaction provoked by such views, but there was more contemporary efficacy in the discordant protests of such men as Carlyle and Ruskin, who refused to accept "self-interest" or "utility" as sufficient explanations of human conduct.

It was an age of rapid advance in geographical knowledge. The preceding centuries had revealed the shape of continents by charting their coasts, but Africa, America, Australia and much of Asia were still blanks on the maps. Mungo Park[1] opened this new age of landward exploration by tracing the course of the River Niger, and distinguishing it finally from the Nile. The German, Alexander von Humboldt, proved to be the most famous of travellers in South America, but there were important consequences from the visits of the Englishmen Waterton, Bates and Darwin.[2] The first was an enthusiast for the Guianas. Bates ascended the Amazon in search of zoological specimens. He explored 1,400 miles of the river and collected 8,000 entomological specimens new to science, and he is second only to Humboldt for descriptions of a tropical forest. Darwin's *Voyage of the Beagle* is of double interest; as a narrative of the surveying voyage carried out in 1831–6 it contained important additions to geological and zoological knowledge, but it was also the basis of his later superstructure of the *Origin of Species*. Thus biological research proved to

[1] Mungo Park (1771–1806). *Travels in the Interior of Africa*, 1799.
[2] Charles Waterton (1782–1865). *Wanderings in South America*, 1825. Henry Walter Bates (1825–1865). *Naturalist on the Amazons*, 1863.
Charles Robert Darwin (1809–81). *Voyage of the Beagle*, 1845 (and various reports, 1839–46); *Origin of Species*, 1859.

be the strongest incentive for travel in Spanish America, but the revolt of the colonists and the career of Bolivar were also followed with interest in Great Britain, and some of the leading adventurers left memoirs.

In Africa the geographical puzzle of the age was to discover the sources of the Nile (since Park had distinguished the Niger) and the Mountains of the Moon. This question was solved by Speke and Grant on the 28th July 1862. The full account of their expedition is given in Speke's[1] *Journal of the Discovery of the Source of the Nile*; it is full, frank and attractively written. Speke was introduced to African exploration by Burton,[2] the discoverer of Lake Tanganyika, and it was Burton who, in consequence of a quarrel, chiefly opposed his revelations. A greater fact than the Nile had been discovered, viz., the Great Rift Valley, which determines the position of the African lakes and is the connecting link between several phenomena observed in isolation by the explorers. Burton was the most active of all travellers as well as a linguist of the first rank. He published rapidly, too rapidly to give permanence to his writings, and his style and character were harsh. His first studies were of the Indus valley and Goa, and these were followed by his sensational *Pilgrimage to Al-Medinah and Mecca*. This book combines the interest of sound documentation from Arabian authors with an intensely personal record by the author. Next he transferred his attention to Tanganyika, publishing the results in his *First Footsteps in East Africa*. In West Africa he knew Dahomey and Abeokuta; he visited the uplands of Brazil and the battlefields of Paraguay; Syria and the Sinaitic peninsula were other scenes of his travels. His version of the *Arabian Nights* is remarkable for its encyclopedic knowledge of Moslem life, and in his life of Camoens and translation of the *Lusiads* he could draw on an unrivalled knowledge of the sites

[1] John Hanning Speke (1827–64). *Journal of the Discovery of the Source of the Nile*, 1863.
[2] Sir Richard Francis Burton (1821–90). *Scinde*, 1851; *Falconry in the Valley of the Indus*, 1852; *Pilgrimage to Al-Medinah and Mecca*, 1855; *First Footsteps in East Africa*, 1856; *Lake Region of Central Africa*, 1860; *Wanderings in West Africa*, 1863; *Letters from the Battlefields of Paraguay*, 1870; *Land of Midian*, 1879; *Thousand Nights and a Night*, 1885–8; *Lusiads* and *Life of Camoens*, 1880–1.

known to the poet. Lane[1] had preceded him as a translator of
the *Arabian Nights*, and in *Modern Egyptians* had produced an
unexcelled picture of life in the Near East. David Livingstone[2]
completed the African travels of his predecessors by discovering
the Victoria Falls on the Zambesi, Lakes Ngami and Nyasa
and the whole system of waters centring on Tanganyika.

In Australia the explorer's problem was like that posed by
Africa, but with more dangers and no proportionate rewards.
The emptiness of the land, however, made an exceptional
demand on white immigration, and as a protest against haphazard methods Wakefield[3] wrote his *Letters from Sydney*,
developing his full theory of state-aided and controlled
colonization in an appendix to his anonymous *England and
America*. He took a prominent part in the settlement of
Canterbury in New Zealand, and part of his correspondence
on the subject was published after his death by his son. At the
other end of the century, when contact was at last effected with
the native mind, there came into being Spencer and Gillen's[4]
classical accounts of the Central Australians, which have been
ever since a primary document of anthropological science.
Polar exploration was also a passion of the age, and gave such
classics as Franklin's *Journey to the Polar Sea*.[5] He died in the
far north of Canada, having discovered the secret of the North-
west Passage, which had been a principal object of English
mariners since the days of Queen Elizabeth. The search for
Franklin was continued for over forty years, and itself is the
subject of a large literature. Akin to Arctic travel is vertical
adventure among the high peaks. Edward Whymper,[6] con-

[1] Edward William Lane (1801–76). *Modern Egyptians*, 1836; *Arabian Nights*, 1838–41.
[2] David Livingstone (1813–73). *Missionary Travels in South Africa*, 1857; *Narrative of an Expedition to the Zambesi*, 1865; *Last Journals*. 1874.
Sir Henry Morton Stanley (1840–1904). *How I Found Livingstone*, 1872
[3] Edward Gibbon Wakefield (1796–1862). *Letters from Sydney*, 1829; *England and America*, 1833; *The Art of Colonization*, 1833; *Founders of Canterbury* (correspondence, edited by his son), 1868.
[4] Sir Walter Baldwin Spencer (1860–1929), and F. J. Gillen. *Native Tribes*, 1889; and *Northern Tribes of Central Australia*, 1904.
[5] Sir John Franklin (1786–1847). *Journey to the Polar Sea*, 1823, 1828.
[6] Edward Whymper (1840–1911). *Scrambles among the Alps*, 1871; *Travels among the Great Andes*, 1892.

queror of the Matterhorn, Chimborazo and Cotopaxi, recorded his experiences in two great books.

These works are no more than excerpts from a great and fascinating literature of travel which is one of the prime merits of the Victorian Age and of our own. The reader cannot go wrong among such books; whichever comes to his hand will have interest. The choice made depends chiefly on the subject-matter, since that work will give most pleasure which is nearest to the reader's special experience. Absorption in the interest of the adventure generally makes the style lucid and lively; the matter speaks for itself. When travel is not so remote, however, more is required from the author, who compensates by the interest of personality for want of newness of scene. George Borrow is the great master of self-display. As we have seen, his work may be classified as novel based on autobiography or as romanticized travel. Richard Ford[1] was more objective in his *Gatherings from Spain*, which he enlivened by his own marked idiosyncrasies and prejudices. The best work in this kind, however, was Kinglake's[2] *Eothen*, a book which has eclipsed the vast bulk of its author's *History of the Crimean War*. His subject was the Near East, and he dipped his brush in strong colour. It is witty and sensitive, and the author had the fortune to encounter in Syria the eccentric and colourful Lady Hester Stanhope. She had kept house for her uncle, William Pitt, when that statesman was measuring his civil genius against the military ascendancy of Napoleon; and after his death she achieved a new authority among the Druses of Lebanon so firm that Ibrahim Pasha had to be assured of her neutrality in his invasion of Syria.

The Victorian period was one of intense activity in commerce, finance and industry. Various circumstances were especially favourable to British efforts. The Industrial Revolution had given her a lead over Continental rivals, since the most necessary materials were within her shores. Political stability confirmed this lead. As effort was not prevented from meeting

---

[1] Richard Ford (1796–1858). *Handbook for Travellers in Spain*, 1845; *Gatherings from Spain*, 1846; *Letters*, 1905.
[2] Alexander William Kinglake (1809–91). *Eothen*, 1844; *History of the Crimean War*, 1863–87.

with success, the process seemed to conform to law, and the science (if such it be) of political economy made great strides in this its classic age, from Ricardo's *Principles*[1] to J. S. Mill. Self-interest was postulated as the leading, but not the only, motive. It was called "enlightened self-interest" when there was need to distinguish it from shortsighted greed, and in so far as a man acted under its influence he could be deemed "economic man." But from economic man the minds of moralists recoiled with horror. Carlyle and Ruskin were especially loud in their protests against the "dismal science," and their attacks served to break down its rigidity. "Economic man" was no longer a figure in Marshall's[2] *Principles of Economics*, in which the force of this criticism was allowed. By the end of the century the range of the science had been increased through an alliance with history, in such works as Vinogradoff's[3] *Growth of the Manor* and Maitland's[4] Domesday studies; but there was still no sign of the political interference which has, in the twentieth century, subordinated economic "laws" to policy. Closely associated with the classical economics was the growth of the English utilitarian philosophy, founded by Bentham and James Mill. These precursors watched over the education of the latter's son, John Stuart Mill,[5] who expounded the doctrine in his essay on *Utilitarianism*. Mill's style was one of great superficial lucidity, attractive and reasonable. It veiled unresolved contradictions of thought, which, though they diminish the value of his doctrine, are due to a keener sympathy and openness of mind than that of his

---

[1] David Ricardo (1772–1823). *Principles of Political Economy and Taxation*, 1817.

[2] Alfred Marshall (1842–1924). *Principles of Economics*, 1890.

[3] Sir Paul Gavrilovitch Vinogradoff (1854–1925). *Villainage in England*, 1892; *Growth of the Manor*, 1905.

[4] Frederic William Maitland (1850–1906). *Domesday Book and Beyond*, 1897; *Township and Borough*, 1898; *Canon Law in England*, 1898; *English Law and the Renaissance*, 1901; *Life of Leslie Stephen*, 1906; *History of English Law* (with Sir F. Pollock), 1895.

[5] John Stuart Mill (1806–73). *Logic*, 1843; *Principles of Political Economy*, 1848; *Enfranchisement of Women*, 1853; *On Liberty*, 1859; *On Representative Government*, 1861; *Utilitarianism*, 1863; *Examination of Sir W. Hamilton's Philosophy*, 1865; *Auguste Comte and Positivism*, 1865; *Subjection of Women*, 1869; *Autobiography*, 1873; *Three Essays on Religion*, 1874.

predecessors. Thus, the greatest happiness principle (or the principle of the greatest happiness of the greatest number) does not establish itself in his writings, nor does he even ensure acceptance of the *summum bonum* of happiness however defined; but it does serve as a point of departure for the study of happiness as it affects human conduct. The author completed his system by treatises on *Logic* and *Political Economy*, both important in their time, but he attains his full stature in the essay *On Liberty*, to which his *Subjection of Women* is a special annex. It is curious to contrast the second chapter of Mill's *Liberty* with Milton's *Areopagitica*. Both writers contend for the most absolute liberty of thought and discussion, and the Victorian is free from the sectarian reservations of his predecessor. He seeks out and meets, more successfully than Milton does, the arguments for repression. One feels the steady glow of his humane purpose. Yet it is to Milton that the mind returns for the defence of liberty, for Milton's style is embattled; the torrent and clangour of his indignation stirs the heart to defend freedom, and does not merely move the reason (as with Mill) to approve.

At the same time, mental exploration among the sciences was proceeding rapidly, with important consequences for British thought. There were striking advances in chemistry and physics, but the most revolutionary steps occurred in the domains of geology and biology. Through the study of extinct kinds of shells Sir Charles Lyell[1] determined important ages in the formation of the earth's crust, setting up a geological time-frame into which he fitted the human species. He played a notable part in persuading Darwin[2] to give to the world that abstract of his researches into the origin of species which embodied the results of twenty years of close observation. Darwin had drawn up statements of his views in 1842 and 1844, but he preferred to carry on his investigations towards a *magnum opus*. In June 1858 he was surprised to receive from an unknown correspondent, a field naturalist named Alfred Russel Wallace, a communication outlining the theory he had

[1] Sir Charles Lyell (1797–1875). *Principles of Geology*, 1830–2: *Elements of Geology*, 1838; *Antiquity of Man*, 1863.
[2] Charles Robert Darwin. See p. 152.

in mind, and even taking the same *Essay on Population* by Malthus as a starting-point for his biological theory of the survival of the fittest. Referring the matter to Lyell, the latter suggested that two papers should be read to the Linnæan Society in July 1858, and that Darwin should publish the heads of his researches as soon as possible. Thus the *Origin of Species* appeared in November 1859. It is not an easy book to read, and yet it is a model of scientific address to the intelligent reader. The matter is admirably marshalled, and lucid, straight-forward, significant prose converts evidence into conviction. The logic of the argument is, as Huxley remarks, the perfection of scientific logic. It is both inductive and deductive. Certain evidence suggested to Darwin the probability of certain laws; assuming these laws to be valid, he deduced certain conse-quences which were duly confirmed by experiment. The diffi-culty of the book is due to the close attention which the writer demands from the reader. The generalizations are worked out in particular statements, whose universal validity it is for the reader to recognize without further explanation. These state-ments are the conclusions of intricate observations and long experiments for which there is no place in this book. They thus appear, at first sight, arbitrary, whereas they are really demon-strated to the full. They constitute an imperishable element of the *Origin of Species*, which far excelled all previous treatises, and has never since been surpassed as a collection of all the observations relevant to the problem of species. Darwin took over evolution from previous writers, but he gave it convincing evidence; and in some form or other, evolution has become a cardinal principle not only of biological explanations, but also of the humane branches of learning. The notion of a struggle for existence came from Malthus together with that of natural selection. These and other terms belong to the Darwinian theory, which has been contested and modified. Much mis-understanding would have been avoided, however, if critics had noted that Darwin defined natural selection as "the main, but not the exclusive, means of modification." There is nothing in his work to exclude emendations of his theory. The centre of the most violent controversy of its age, it is not at all controversial.

The combative spirit was that of Huxley.[1] He had the dangerous gift of incisive speech, and was not slow to chastise those who would prop up the "cosmogony of the semibarbarous Hebrew" to oppose "the justice of scientific conclusions." "Extinguished theologians (he wrote) lie about the cradle of every science as the strangled snakes beside that of Hercules, and history records that whenever science and dogmatism have been fairly opposed, the latter has been forced to retire from the lists, bleeding and crushed, if not annihilated; scotched, if not slain." At about this time Newman had been assuring an audience in Dublin that there could be no conflict between religion and science rightly conceived, and Huxley, indeed, did not say otherwise. The dogmatism he attacked was an unwarranted intrusion of ignorance into the scientific domain under cloak of religion. Conversely, no one was more scrupulous in keeping scientific statements within the range of their own postulates. It is the business of physical science to examine the materials out of which the world is made, and its affirmations will therefore be material; but those are misguided who have acclaimed Huxley's authority for philosophic materialism. The philosophic consequences of the advance in the sciences were developed by Herbert Spencer.[2] He announced a doctrine of *Progress*. Progress he found to be a movement from the simple to the complex, involving increasing differentiation of function. In this way the solar system has evolved from an indiscriminate nebular matter, the earth has been covered with more and more layers, animal species have multiplied, society has distributed its powers and services, language and the arts have become more complex. Progress is thus a natural law at work everywhere, and in our own experience. The argument, however, covers some misstatements and still more misunderstandings. The term could not be applied in the same sense in all cases, or, conversely, it would have to be so vague as to cease to give a direction to

---

[1] Thomas Henry Huxley (1825–95). Assistant surgeon on H.M.S. *Rattlesnake*, 1846–50. President of the Royal Society, 1883. Retired, 1885. *Collected Essays*, 1893.

[2] Herbert Spencer (1820–1903). *System of Synthetic Philosophy*, 1862–96 (including *Psychology*, 1855, and *Sociology*, 1876–96); *Progress, its Law and Cause*, 1852; *On Education*, 1861; *Autobiography*, 1904.

thinking. The evidence for retrogression is ignored; the continual improvement of the species is too easily assumed. Still, the Spencerian philosophy is a notable attempt to bring together coherently the new knowledge, and it is the last wholly English creation. In the second half of the century the Oxford school attached philosophical thought to the study of the Greek classics, with Plato predominant, and to the commentary of the German idealists, Kant and Hegel. The lifeline with Locke was slipped; the topics were more and more removed from experience; the place allotted to historical exposition was greatly increased. Spencer thus brought a great tradition to an end, and he opened up some subsidiary sciences. His essays on *Education* made a plea for the study of science as most conducive to the wellbeing and entertainment of men of our day. The facts of society have, as he wished, lodged the exact sciences firmly in the curriculum, but they have not removed the humanities which he wrongly reprehended. His arguments lodged education itself as a subject for intelligent discussion in universities and the public forum. He protested against history as a meaningless catalogue of names and dates, and advocated in its place the science of sociology. Sociology—everything relating to men as social beings—has proved too wide a title to cover any single science; but history has broadened its borders to include, as it did in Ibn Khaldun's day, the social record, and anthropology has arisen to perfect that record where the dates history requires are lacking.

Hugh Miller's[1] *Old Red Sandstone* brought geology within the reach of the average reader who, if he lived in Scotland, could find in him an entertaining and instructive guide, making well-known spots full of novel instruction. His style was based on Bacon and Addison, and his knowledge began at the practical level of a journeyman stonemason. The tradition of White of Selborne was carried forward by Richard Jefferies,[2] author of *Wild Life in a Southern County*, and other collections of essays in natural history.

[1] Hugh Miller (1802–56). Stonemason of Cromarty. *Old Red Sandstone*, 1841; *My Schools and Schoolmasters*, 1854; *Testimony of the Rocks*, 1857.
[2] Richard Jefferies (1848–87). *The Gamekeeper at Home*, 1878; *Wild Life in a Southern County*, 1879; *The Story of My Heart*, 1883.

The voices of two essayists, or rather three, were loud in protest against the teachings of the economists, utilitarians and materialists. The third was Matthew Arnold, whose particular enemy was the "philistine," the moneyed boor who despises culture. There is moral indignation in his writing, but, as it is closely allied to his poetry, we have noticed it in another place. The other two were Carlyle and Ruskin; two prophets vehement in denouncing their age, upon whom posterity has taken the ironical revenge of regarding them as typical Victorians and making them too the subjects of expostulation. This has been particularly true of Ruskin.[1] The cult of the sham Gothic in architecture has been laid to his charge, and his name is anathema to those who proclaim the beauty of functional building. For this there is some justification. Ruskin spoke with authority about the arts in England, and yet he has little artistic criticism. In the *Seven Lamps of Architecture*, for instance, he drops the modern reader at the threshold of the book, by proclaiming that walls and roof are "building," but needless additions are "architecture." A clue to his meaning is given later, when he insists that a moulding, for instance, should be continued with equal care where it passes out of the spectator's sight, not that by so doing there is an aesthetic gain, but as a test of honesty. He is, in fact, a moralist, and the qualities he finds in great architecture are ethical, not aesthetic. The lecture on books entitled *Sesame* provides, probably, the most satisfactory introduction to Ruskin. It is short, and so avoids repetition and the ampler meanders of his thought. The subject, too, is more within everyone's experience. Books afford intercourse with the mighty dead, who teach not merely truth, but righteousness. Had his audience frequented them (he thundered) they would not have proved despisers of literature, science, art, nature and compassion. There is but little leaven of righteousness in the national lump. This tone of moral indignation was, perhaps, the only one that could gain a hearing for art-criticism at a time when aesthetic appreciation

[1] John Ruskin (1819–1900). *Modern Painters*, 1843–60; *Seven Lamps of Architecture*, 1849; *Stones of Venice*, 1851–53; *Unto this Las t*, 1862; *Sesame and Lilies*, 1865; *Ethics of the Dust*, 1866; *Crown of Wild Olive*, 1866; *Fors Clavigera*, 1871–84; *Munera Pulveris*, 1872; etc.

G

would have been brushed aside as trivial. It did assign a degree of importance to art and the artist in the days when Spencer supposed that art was merely a replica of some better thing existing in nature, upon which the scientist was best fitted to judge by his superior knowledge of natural objects. Cultivating an opposite obtuseness to Spencer's, Ruskin would not be at peace with political economists or applied scientists in such matters as trains and tunnels.

The other apocalyptic figure, Thomas Carlyle,[1] was more extravagant and more subtle than Ruskin. It is less easy to shake him off. He commenced writing as one like unto Southey and his whimsicality resembles Lamb, if facetiousness may take the place of playfulness. In *Sartor Resartus* he came out with a new style: facetious, rugged, clamant, ejaculatory. He was determined to call attention to moral issues at all cost. In the supposed memoirs and lucubrations of the German Teufels-dröckh, the philosopher of clothes, he found a means of amusing and exasperating his readers, as he vociferated his doctrine of silence and work. He attacked utilitarians and economists, and proclaimed, in the teeth of science, the reality of miracle. He opposed to evolution and progress the notion of the cataclysmic in history, and to democracy he opposed his *Heroes and Hero-Worship*. He renewed respect for a great Englishman in *Oliver Cromwell's Letters and Speeches*, and he too readily palliated the crimes of Frederick II of Prussia in his *History of Frederick the Great*. His *French Revolution* gave him ample opportunity to ride the whirlwind, amid striking personalities and fantastic catastrophes. Its conclusions are open to unlimited revision, but the book cannot be replaced. It is a triumph of style. The writhing, twisted sentences defy all rules of composition and rise to be a more telling rhetoric. The ejaculations and rapid transitions keep the whole whirling scene vividly present to the imagination, facetiousness, edged with grim desperation, becomes more tragic than tragedy, which

[1] Thomas Carlyle (1795–1881). *Life of Schiller*, 1825; *Sartor Resartus* (in *Fraser's Magazine*, 1833–4), 1838; *Essays*, 1839–57; *Chartism*, 1840; *French Revolution*, 1837–9; *Heroes and Hero-Worship*, 1841; *Past and Present*, 1843; *Oliver Cromwell's Letters and Speeches*, 1845; *Latter-Day Pamphlets*, 1850; *Life of Sterling*, 1851; *History of Frederick the Great*, 1858–65.

has its reserves and decencies. There can be nothing to equal Carlyle's narrative of the taking of the Bastille and the deaths of Marat and Robespierre, and his account must stand, for its breath-catching actuality, beside whatever other account may be framed on the same or a different interpretation of the facts.

In Carlyle history was united to prophecy, but there were other and more peaceable historians who made this period one of the great ages of British historical writing. Only a rough notion can be given of this wealth by the mention of some outstanding names. Unlike our contemporaries, they treated history as an art; but the art felt more and more the pressure of science and in the end capitulated to the demand for documents. When our period opened this was one branch of the art of politics. The Liberalism no less than the learning of Grote[1] informed his masterly *History of Greece*. Macaulay[2] was supreme in this manner. Never has Clio had so dazzlingly versatile a suitor. His memory was phenomenal. He read by paragraphs, and had at his command the minutest details of memoirs, relations and letters, which he could combine at will to give scenes of unequalled liveliness. The great canvas of Charles II's deathbed, inserted in the *History of England*, is justly celebrated. Macaulay was happy to be complimented on writing something as exciting as a novel. Not only are the main facts there in clear array, but the words, gestures, movements and positions of a crowd of figures are studied in their due perspective and all thoroughly authenticated. The period he chose to illustrate was the "Glorious Revolution," that is, the deposition of James II and the establishment of constitutional monarchy by the great Whig clans. It was an event of great moment for the history of British liberty, and Macaulay summoned up all his astonishing resources to do it justice. He had no divided belief. The Whigs were right and the Tories wrong; the Whigs brought liberty and the Tories advocated tyranny. So thorough was his partisanship that he scarcely needed to advocate his faction's cause, and this was the easier since the actual course of events was shaped by the Whigs, who

[1] George Grote (1794–1871). *History of Greece*, 1846–56.
[2] Thomas Babington Macaulay (1800–59). *Lays of Ancient Rome*, 1842; *Essays*, 1843; *History*, 1848–55.

thus receive the approbation that history awards to the successful. Of another interpretation of the same facts there is no
suspicion in Macaulay's brilliant, confident prose. Yet the
facts are as he has established them, and their arrangement
cannot be more lively. More judicious writers merely fail to
gain the ear of their readers, since they seem to cavil rather than
to correct. One simply cannot remember a word of what they
say! What Macaulay intends is engraved on the mind by his
short, stabbing clauses which combine into sentences long and
short, according as they serve to stir the emotions or drive
home a conclusion. A subtle management of the nouns almost
does away with the need for grammatical particles between
sentences, and the use of proper names both enlivens the text
and converts all abstracts into concretes. A gay and dashing
use of encyclopedic learning—which Macaulay attributed to
his famous schoolboy—is convincing advocacy and a stiff
rampart against opposition. It appears in the *Essays* applied
not only to political, but also to literary themes. Among the
essays there are many fine and many presumptuous things.
His *Milton* is a magnificent appraisement, and his attack on
Montgomery a demolition without parallel. His weakness and
strength both appear in his *tour de force* upon Boswell's
Johnson. Too good a man of letters not to appreciate at its full
value Boswell's achievement, and too rigid a Whig to sympathize with minds so unlike his own, he devised the explanation that Boswell's biography is so great precisely because its
writer was so petty: an explanation clearly untenable, but
argued with amazing cogency. Macaulay devised for India a
code of laws which was an ingenious reduction of the English
common law. He made a plan for Indian education which was
intended to be "an application of sound Liberal principles."
The intention was generous, but it took no account of the quite
different aspirations of the Indian peoples; it was another
example of Macaulay's self-assurance. As well as this insensitiveness to values outside his code, we find in him a certain
incapacity for poetry. His *Lays of Ancient Rome* and his
Armada are things known to every schoolboy for their vigorous
rhetoric and prosodical skill, but they in no way enrich the
imagination.

Dean Milman,[1] the historian of the Jews and of Latin Christianity, and Finlay,[2] the historian of Byzantine Greece, hold their places rather better than Freeman,[3] the apostle of the unity of history. He proposed to demonstrate this unity in the *History of Sicily*, since many races and cultures played their parts in that one island. But the tale is disjointed; he did better with the more limited theme of the *Norman Conquest*. Though he did not ascend so far as manuscript sources, Freeman performed an essential service by insisting on the use of the best authorities. Not so Buckle,[4] whose *History of Civilization* is remarkable for its wide sweep and bold thesis. The great contemporary generalizations of biologists tempted him to propound general laws for progress and retrogression in human societies. He held that society, like other living things, might be variable in the particular but subjected to strict law in the mass; differences of climate, soil, food and natural aspects he believed were bound to produce a cumulative effect on the several peoples, and to these he added the effects of a constant advance of mental activity. Froude[5] recognized the stimulating quality of this work as well as its inconclusiveness in a celebrated lecture on *The Science of History*. To Froude, history offered, not a scientific thesis, nor even political lessons. It was a drama of persons and events, as undidactic as Homer or Shakespeare, but like them capable of yielding manifold lessons according to the perceptiveness of the reader. Hence his style is supremely colourful and dramatic, as were also the subjects which he preferred to describe. The age of the Refor-

---

[1] Henry Hart Milman (1791–1868). *History of the Jews*, 1830; *History of Christianity to the Abolition of Paganism*, 1840; *History of Latin Christianity*, 1855.

[2] George Finlay (1799–1875). *Greece under the Romans*, 1844; *History of the Byzantine and Greek Empires*, 1854; *Greece under the Ottoman and Venetian Domination*, 1856; *History of the Greek Revolution*, 1861.

[3] Edward Augustus Freeman (1823–92). *Norman Conquest*, 1867–79; *William Rufus*, 1882; *History of Sicily*, 1891–4. Professor of Modern History at Oxford.

[4] Henry Thomas Buckle (1821–62). *History of Civilization*, 1857–61.

[5] James Anthony Froude (1818–94). Professor of Modern History at Oxford, 1892. *History of England*, 1856–70; *Short Studies on Great Subjects*, 1867–83; *The Spanish Story of the Armada*, 1892; *English Seamen*, 1895; *Lectures on the Council of Trent*, 1896. Also writings on Caesar, Luther, Carlyle, Bunyan.

mation and the Tudors was marked by striking characters and dramatic contrasts, and Froude (after a brief profession of impartiality) plunges gaily into the fray on behalf of those he favours. Thus he is on Luther's side against Erasmus, and on behalf of both of them against the Papacy, in his *Times of Erasmus and Luther* (*Short Studies on Great Studies*), and the contrast he allows himself to draw between the saintliness of the thirteenth-century Catholic Church and the corruptions of the fifteenth is as vivid and effective as it is illfounded in fact. His style made him a consummate historical lecturer. He is most adequate when dealing with men of his own dashing type, as in *English Seamen in the Sixteenth Century*. There is partisanship also and a strong sense of the dramatic in John Richard Green's[1] *Short History of the English People*, exercised on behalf not of picturesque persons, but of the growth of liberty in the commonweal.

These sturdy and varied prejudices cause Victorian historical writing to be very much alive. One feels the thrust and parry of partisan feelings not unlike those which went to the making of the real events. But in the end, the impartial analysts were destined to triumph in the work of S. R. Gardiner.[2] Nothing has so divided Englishmen as the topic of the Puritan revolution, which has left separate churches, opposition of castes, and the memories of a civil war and a dethronement. Gardiner proved that it could be treated dispassionately by the many volumes of his *History of England*, covering the years from 1603 to 1660. They are exhaustive and philosophical, grounded on the minutest research, fair and shrewd, but cold. With him there stands, at the close of one epoch of historical writing and the opening of a new, the imposing figure of Bishop Stubbs.[3] His great work was the *Constitutional History of England*, supported by his *Select Charters*; but fully as important are

[1] John Richard Green (1837–83). *Short History of the English People*, 1874; *History of the English People*, 1877–80.

[2] Samuel Rawson Gardiner (1829–1902). *History of England from the Accession of James I to the Outbreak of the Civil War*; *History of the Great Civil War: History of the Commonwealth and the Protectorate*.

[3] William Stubbs (1825–1901). *Lectures on Medieval and Modern History: Registrum Sacrum Anglicanum*, 1857; *Constitutional History of England*, 1874–8; *Select Charters*, 1870. Editions of Roger of Hoveden, William of Malmesbury, etc. Bishop of Chester, 1884; of Oxford, 1889.

the nineteen volumes which he edited for the Rolls Series of "Chronicles and Memorials." In these the clearing of the foundations for history proves more important than the structure itself. History had become a science, not as revealing natural "laws," but as a system of scrupulously tested statements. Less legitimately, it had become a science by a certain falling off in literary art.

The works of Vinogradoff and Maitland, mentioned above, founded economic history. Dean Stanley's[1] *Memorials of Canterbury* are a singularly attractive contribution to local history, where this has a national significance. Symonds and Pater concerned themselves with aesthetics and the Italian Renaissance, and Maine[2] with Ancient Law. Justin M'Carthy's *History of Our Own Times* was a brilliant and delightful account of Victoria's reign.[3] From Bagehot's *English Constitution* the historical element was carefully excluded. It was his object to describe that organism as he found it actually operating in the years 1865–6, at which time it had no democratic parallels outside the United States. Bagehot[4] was careful not to confuse actual power with established forms, he avoided doctrinaire speculations on, for instance, the supposed checks and balances of the different organs of government. Penetrating to the reality behind the form, he found that the English constitution was grounded in the Cabinet system, with its definite but not incompatible party cleavages and co-operative relations to the legislature. The function of the Crown he supposed to be

[1] Arthur Penrhyn Stanley (1815–81). Dean of Westminster. *Life of Arnold*, 1844; *Sermons and Essays on the Apostolic Age*, 1847; *Sinai and Palestine*, 1856; *Lectures on the Eastern Church*, 1861; *Memorials of Canterbury*, 1854; *Memorials of Westminster Abbey*, 1868; *History of the Jewish Church*, 1863–5, 1876.

[2] John Addington Symonds (1840–93). *Study of Dante*, 1872; *Studies of the Greek Poets*, 1873–6; *Renaissance in Italy*, 1875–86.

Walter Horatio Pater (1839–94). *Studies in the History of the Renaissance*, 1873; *Marius the Epicurean*, 1885; *Imaginary Portraits*, 1887; *Appreciations*, 1889; *Plato and Platonism*, 1893.

Sir Henry James Sumner Maine (1822–88). *Ancient Law*, 1861; *Village Communities*, 1871; etc.

[3] Justin M'Carthy (1830–1912). *Dear Lady Disdain*, 1875; *Donna Quixote*, 1879; *History of Our Own Times*, 1879–97; *History of the Four Georges*, 1884–1901.

[4] Walter Bagehot (1826–77). *English Constitution*, 1867; *Literary Studies*, 1879; *Economic Studies*, 1880.

dignified only in effect, whereby it served as a magnet for popular support of the system, and in the Second Chamber he saw the beneficent workings of delay and revision. His thought is bold and stimulating, and his exposition lucid. If some of his views may be questioned and all are subject to the mutability of the political organism itself, his broad, sane appraisement of the constitution at a significant moment does not run the risk of losing its documentary value.

Lastly, it is to be recorded that the Victorian period was the Silver Age of British oratory. There was still sufficient unity in politics and religion to give pattern to rhetoric, though there was less homogeneity than in the eighteenth century. Keble's assize sermon on *National Apostasy*, preached at Oxford, had mighty repercussions. Dean Stanley attained to the perfection of cathedral oratory, and the Nonconformist, C. H. Spurgeon, revived the raciness of Latimer's prose. There was a profusion of set debates in Parliament, and the questions at issue were political and ethical rather than technical. There was also substantial agreement as to style; it was only at the end of the century that the grand manner was shed under the hail of blows from Joseph Chamberlain's more incisive style. Not all famous speeches survive in print, and those of the Victorian Age must be studied in anthology. They are then found to be both homogeneous and varied. Gladstone excelled all orators in the moral earnestness he infused into his sometimes dis-ingenuous policies; his rival, Disraeli, concealed statesmanlike intention behind a battery of flouts and jeers. Wit and passion mingled in Daniel O'Connell's appeal for Catholic Emancipation; Macaulay's speech on Copyright was a *tour de force* based on his amazing memory for literature; John Bright, battling against the declaration of war in 1853, combined the purity of Biblical English with Miltonic sonorities.[1]

---

[1] A useful conspectus of British political oratory from Burke to Gladstone is given in the anthology of *Selected English Speeches*, edited by E. R. Jones, in "The World's Classics" (Oxford University Press).

XIII. POETRY AND THE DRAMA

POETRY

THE last years of the nineteenth century resounded to varied and sometimes striking melodies. The languid harmonies of the decadents were drowned by the clangour of Rudyard Kipling's excessively military band. George Meredith, Thomas Hardy, Robert Bridges and A. E. Housman competed for a hearing, and although the new music had not the rich assurance which glowed through the works of the Victorian poets, there was no doubt that the poets of the 'nineties, following their separate paths, were pressing onward, and that they were not content to repeat as they went the old songs that had inspired and cheered their fathers.

With one or two exceptions the new writers did not possess the stamina of their literary ancestors. They were more hardly beset by doubt and fears. Of course, it must not be supposed that a new order of poets suddenly sprang up with brand-new equipment at the end of the nineteenth century and that no more poetry was written in the old tradition. Of the later nineteenth-century poets, Browning and Swinburne, in particular, had their disciples. The brusquerie of the one and the magnificent harmonies of the other were palely reproduced by numerous minor adherents in the 'nineties and later.

In 1892 the first *Book of the Rhymers' Club* was published. Two years later a second followed it. Among the contributors were four poets whose work has come to be associated almost exclusively with this period. They were Lionel Johnson (1867–1902), Ernest Dowson (1867–1900), Arthur Symons (b. 1865) and Richard le Gallienne (b. 1866). Alike melancholy, decorative and mannered, though the last-named was given to a kind of airy trifling not often successful, these poets, with Oscar Wilde, whose only important poem is the *Ballad of Reading*

G* 169

Gaol (1898), wrote what has come to be known as the poetry of the Decadence.

It would not be unfair to say that these writers were subject more to the influences of literature than of life. Dowson's *Cynara* has been heavily anthologized. His little play, *The Pierrot of the Minute*, is graceful and charmingly done. Symons' translations from the French represent the crown of his poetical achievement. Johnson was the most thoughtful and sincere of the group, whose literary reputation was at its height in their lifetime. Two poets who wrote with a strongly Catholic strain are Coventry Patmore (1823–96) and Francis Thompson (1859–1907). Patmore is an interesting and uneven writer, who chose to sing the pleasures of a happy domestic life. His *Angel in the House* (1854–6), a novel in verse, is his greatest popular success, but *Unknown Eros,* a series of odes, shows him at his best. Francis Thompson, drawing freely on the liturgy of the Church for his imagery, is now best known for his posthumously published *The Hound of Heaven,* which clearly shows his debt to Crashaw and other seventeenth-century poets. It shows, too, their tendency to drop suddenly into bathos. The romantic circumstances of his life added to the appeal which his poems made. His essay on Shelley is a striking piece of literary appreciation. Two other religious poets, protégés of Robert Bridges, were Richard Watson Dixon (1833–1900), also known as a church historian, and Digby Mackworth Dolben (1848–67). Dixon was at his best in the short lyric. Dolben was too young when he died to have realized the marked promise which his verses show.

As a poet Thomas Hardy was a strong individualist. It is probable that he was influenced by Browning's *Dramatic Monologues*, but in his poems he concerned himself again and again with the ironies and satirical aspects of life. He wrote hundreds of poems, which might, in no disrespectful spirit, be called anecdotal. The reader may find Hardy's poetry angular and repellent at first but love for it grows with reading, and it is shot through with a lyrical strain which sometimes emerges in full and unalloyed beauty. Neither in form nor theme was he sentimental and this perhaps explains the increasing attention which has been paid to his poetry in the present unsentimental age.

Greatest of his works and the greatest poetical achievement of the century is his epic drama, *The Dynasts* (1904–8). This remarkable combination of poem and historical drama, with beautifully written stage directions, was not intended for performance. The conception and presentation are entirely Hardy's own. It may be said at once that *The Dynasts* lacks grace, since Hardy was never a graceful writer, but it has perspective, present throughout its hundred and thirty scenes, a most vivid depiction of Europe during the Napoleonic wars, and an unrivalled portrayal of England and the English, urban and rural, under the stress of a great conflict. He knew his countrymen and women and he had thoroughly assimilated a vast mass of historical material, which is digested and inserted unobtrusively into place, as the tremendous drama is unfolded without haste and without the slightest unnecessary digression. Hardy had not been an architect in his youth for nothing. The seemly proportions of *The Dynasts* form one of its outstanding merits.

A commentary on the human scene is furnished by the "over-world," the Spirits of the Years, the Pities, the Spirits Sinister and Ironical. The author claims for these that they are "contrivances of the fancy merely." Their comments, in verse, are not always among the author's happiest poetic inventions.

In his stark, unillusioned view of life, Hardy resembled the great Greek writers. He is still too near to us for his work to be judged in proper perspective, but it is certain that it has appeared to grow in stature and significance with the passing of the years.

There is some similarity between *The Dynasts* and two of the poetic dramas of C. M. Doughty, the author of the great *Arabia Deserta*. For Doughty, literature had ceased with the work of Spenser, whose influence, with that of the Authorized Version, is perceptible in his gnarled and difficult verse style.

In *The Cliffs*, "a drama of the time" (1909), Britain is invaded by the Persanians. Men land from a balloon and kill a Crimean veteran. *The Clouds* (1912) shows England with the Eastlanders part masters of the country. "Air-wolves" are prevalent. England's rulers are unprepared. This is a tragic picture which has the stuff of prophecy in it. If Doughty's style was not so forbidding he would have many readers now.

Robert Bridges (1844–1930) was always a scholar, but he never forgot that he was first of all a man. A tireless experimenter in the theory and use of metre, in reformed spelling, pronunciation, and "pure English," by a strange irony he roused the ire of the popular press some time after his appointment as Poet Laureate in 1913, because he did not write commemorative odes on state occasions. Actuated always by a strong sense of what was fitting and dignified, on a visit to the United States he refused to talk to the reporters and he did not fail to appreciate the subsequent headlines in the New York newspapers, "King's Canary Refuses to Chirp." He could afford to laugh, since few English poets have sung as beautifully and melodiously as he has done in his *Shorter Poems*, lyrics which are firmly set in the crown of our literature. It is by these, above all, that he will continue to be known and appreciated. He had an acute eye and a relevant pen for natural manifestations. His last great work, *The Testament of Beauty* (1929), is convincingly named, as Bridges was a lover and poetical chronicler of beauty all his life, but it is not to be compared in literary importance with many of Bridges's other poems. Its wide popularity, on publication, when many editions were sold, was due almost entirely to the author's eminence and to the fact that he was eighty-five when it appeared. The British public has always applauded Grand Old Men, whether they excel in sport, politics, literature or in anything else which brings them into prominence, and for this reason, and because the public wanted a long, generous poetical work, *The Testament of Beauty* was received almost hysterically, not so much for what it was but for what it might have been. Old age and sincerity had done the trick, and even the popular press made amends for their earlier ill manners.

It has been said that much of this fine poem is not suitable for poetical treatment. Here is a long philosophical poem, written out of a ripe experience of life and learning, in which the author pledged himself to define the place of beauty in his religion. As he develops his thesis, many other subsidiary questions are asked. They are not always fully answered. Bridges was sometimes handicapped by his medium, "loose Alexandrines," "neo-Miltonic syllabics," and by his material, which was often better suited to a scholar-philosopher's commonplace book. Many pages of the poem are really brilliant talk, loosely versified. No one could have better expressed these thoughts in admirable prose than their author, whose excellence as a prose writer is undeniable, as such masterpieces as his *Memoir* of Dolben, his *Three Friends* and his essay on the poetry of Keats clearly show.

Bridges is a poet in the great English tradition, stern, sincere, gifted with genius. His code and standards were high. He experimented tirelessly and sometimes mistakenly, always in pursuit of the best. Now he has his place and it is among the great writers of the lyric. His best work is to be found in the five books of *Shorter Poems* and in *New Poems*.

Evidence of a change of method in the work of William Butler Yeats (1865–1939) is shown by the fact that Yeats, who published his first book of verse in 1886, and won acclaim with the *Wanderings of Oisin* in 1889, earned the esteem of the very young poets before his death in 1939. In the meantime, he became the leading figure of the Irish literary revival, surpassing Synge, whose plays had at first received more attention. Synge was pre-eminently a dramatist. Yeats was always primarily a poet, even in his work for the stage.

In his youth he got to know the peasantry of Sligo and was fascinated by their tales and legends. This early contact stimulated his desire to explore Irish history and myth, and the results of his researches, blended with a knowledge of eastern theology and philosophy, were magically transmuted into the cool and radiant melodies of his poems. These are always individual. He read widely among the French poets, but whatever learning he acquired he moulded and shaped to suit his own purpose. He was always master of his material. He accepted or rejected with a sure confidence in his own powers as a poet, and although he tended, as he grew older, to work on themes which were increasingly remote from human experience, he could always compel attention and affection by sheer poetical accomplishment. The appeal of his work is so wide that it belongs not merely to Ireland but to poetry itself. Beginning with an element that was predominantly decorative and melodious—*The Lake Isle of Innisfree* is the outstanding example of what he could do in this kind—he came gradually to reject all ornament and embellishment until he made a new music which satisfied his needs by substituting austerer, graver harmonies, fashioned from the wealth of beliefs and images which his mind contained, and expressed with a simplicity and a reliance upon words in everyday use that prove him to be, in the fullest and finest sense of the term, a poet. His pursuit of beauty was as unswerving and determined as that of Bridges, though he was not sustained by a religion from which he never deviated. He was the eternal seeker to whom beauty presented itself at different periods of his life in varying phases, which were inspired by the lore or philosophy in which he was steeping himself at the time. They never affected the patina of his verse. He knew exactly what he wanted to do as a poet and almost always was able to do it. In *The Rose* (1893) and *The Wind Among the Reeds* (1899) will be found the best examples of his earlier style. *The Wild Swans at Coole* (1919), *Michael Robartes and the Dancer* (1921), *The Tower* (1928), and *The Winding Stair and Other Poems* (1933) show his later method. An admirable summary of Yeats's work has been given by Frank Swinnerton in *The Georgian Literary Scene*. It was written before the poet died: "But though the subjects vary, the voice is ever the same, a singing voice, the voice of one who listens for faery horns and sometimes thinks that he hears them, or that if they are not the horns of faery they may almost equally well be the voice of the spirit or a message from the stars, so long as it is agreed that they come from another world than ours. To all these possibilities he would offer his mind, at once credulous and sceptical; for he is a man of logical imagination, and not of illogical dogma, and will submit his intellect to anything finer than intellect, so long as he may after his investigation of its properties turn away to something else."

Among his numerous prose works mention must be made of

the *Collected Essays* (1924), and of the autobiographical *Reveries over Childhood and Youth* (1915) and *The Trembling of the Veil* (1922).

It is convenient to mention here Yeats's contemporary, George William Russell (1867–1935), who, as "Æ" wrote some good lyrics. A man of varied gifts, as a poet he showed obvious general excellence but did not write any poem which became current coin. James Stephens (b. 1882), another Irishman, began with two books of slight and delightful poems, showing distinct individuality and promise of greatness, but he wrote little afterwards and nothing comparable to them in merit.

Before returning to the main stream of English poetry it is necessary to turn to other poets who lived about the end of the nineteenth century and whose work deserves notice. James Thomson (1834–82) is best known by a long, despairing poem, *The City of Dreadful Night* (1874), which reads as though it had been hammered out with difficulty and is almost forgotten now. In happier moments he was capable of better writing, as in "Weddah and Om-el-Bonain" and "The Naked Goddess."

William Ernest Henley (1849–1903) was also a London poet who was well known as a journalist and editor and as the collaborator with R. L. Stevenson in three plays. His verses are bright and ringing, full of movement and colour. In *In Hospital* he turned his own experience to use and presented a number of portraits in verse. It was a new mode, but much of it is more nearly allied to journalism than to poetry. *London Voluntaries*, more consciously poetical, is less successful. His best work, the unambitious and altogether charming *Arabian Nights' Entertainment*, is a delightful reconstruction of his boyish pleasure in that great chronicle of oriental magic. It is curious that Rudyard Kipling's debt to Henley has not been more widely recognized. John Davidson (1859–1909), a strange curious blend of poet-publicist, who wrote some good ballads, was also a London poet. His best work is his *Fleet Street Eclogues* (1893–6).

The great obstacle to the popularity of T. E. Brown's (1830–97) verses is his free use of the Manx dialect. Brown was interested in nature, in simple folk, and in expressing himself honestly and individually. He had a mystic strain in him. The merits of his verse are considerable, but he lacked a sense of proportion. The *Fo'c'sle Yarns*, *Epistola ad Dakyns*, and some of the short lyrics are fairly representative of his large output.

Wilfred Scawen Blunt (1840–1922) was a man who craved adventure. Writing poetry and breeding Arab horses were only two of his many interests. Like Landor, who also possessed a fiery temperament, Blunt could write lyrics beautifully conceived and shaped. He could also write poetry which bears the stamp of his own unruly moods. The *Love Songs of Proteus* (1880) owe something to Byron. *Esther* (1892), a story told in a sonnet sequence, has speed and humour strangely mingled with its beauty.

Lord Alfred Douglas (b. 1870) has written some good sonnets and lyrics which do not linger in the mind because they lack the memorable line and are sometimes inspired by art rather than by life and experience. His *Collected Poems* (1919) are impressive. They reveal a sensitive poet with marked technical ability.

Three writers of polite and urbane verse, Austin Dobson (1840–1921), Andrew Lang (1844–1912) and Sir Edmund Gosse (1849–1928), all worked within clearly defined limits, and within these limits Dobson achieved great success. The eighteenth century fascinated him and he absorbed its atmosphere in art and books so fully that in the ballade and other contemporary verse forms he was entirely at home. For this reason his work is read and appreciated now.

The swift, pictorial, journalistic approach which Henley used in some of his verses is seen much more highly and skilfully developed in the verse of Rudyard Kipling (1865–1936). He always spoke of his "verse" and there is no doubt that the greater part of his output should come under that heading. His verses are terse, muscular, slangy and vibrant with strong feeling. He had great enthusiasms—the Empire, India and Sussex among them. He was keenly interested in machines and the men who tended them. He loved the sea and wrote magnificently about it. He was a visionary whose mind pierced far into the future and who seemed to be in constant communication with the dim and distant past, which came alive for him at his almost casual evocation. He was a born writer, whose child-hood and early life in India seem to have made life for him all blazing light or inky darkness. It is the sunshine rather than the colour of the East that strikes the reader of his verse and stories, and he wrote always at a full pitch of intensity peculiar to him-self and not achieved by any other English writer. He was a fear-less writer who chose his subjects because they came naturally to him, and although he became weary and more mannered as he grew older, there are five books of verse which cannot be ignored. These are *Barrack-Room Ballads* (1892), *The Seven Seas* (1896), *The Five Nations* (1903), *Songs from Books* (1912) and *The Years Between* (1919). The fighting soldier, the engineer, India, the peaceful English countryside, the tre-mendous trust which had devolved upon the British people—these are only some of the matters which occupied his pen. He has often been accused of jingoism, but supporters and accusers alike are more to be blamed for this than Kipling should have been. His love of country and Empire was not uncritical, but it is true that he thought that his own people were best fitted to administer the countries and races which were as yet unable to fend for themselves in the hurly-burly of an industrial age.

His verse, at its best, is purified by the intensity of the flame within it until it burns with the steady white glow of authentic poetry. This occurs in the eerie ballad of "Danny Deever," "Mandalay," "McAndrew's Hymn," "The *Mary Gloster*," "Sussex," "My New Cut Ashlar" and a number of other poems.

The position of Kipling as a poet is likely to be disputed for many years, but it cannot be denied that he did exactly what he set out to do, and there are few writers of whom that can be said.

One of the most widely read and quoted poets of our time is A. E. Housman (1859–1936). An eminent Latin scholar, who cherished the pagan ideal, Housman wrote brief lyrics, beauti-fully shaped, which sing the praises of courage and lament the passing of all too brief human strength and beauty. In three short books, *A Shropshire Lad* (1896), *Last Poems* (1922) and

More Poems (1936), Housman commemorated the charm and the tragedies of a single county, but he made his appeal so skilfully that it is universal, and within its small compass, perfectly expressed. His scholarship made him severely critical of his own writings. He passed nothing that did not satisfy his peculiarly high standaids, with the result that the critics have been content to applaud his achievement, to comment occasionally with disfavour on his pessimism, and to ignore altogether the fact that he had little to say. The mood of his poems was congenial to numerous poetry lovers in the 'nineties. It seems equally sympathetic to the youthful pessimists of to-day. His perfection as a writer of the miniature lyric assures him of a place among the poets, and the subtle modulations and harmonies that he introduced into his verses are completely satisfactory to the most critical ear. The secret of his popularity lies in the fact that his poems are immediately and clearly understood, that they never insult the intelligence, and that overlying the profoundly tragic content there is a happily familiar landscape where the cherry blossom is for ever in bloom and the friendly hills stand out against the sunlit white and blue of the sky. Housman was a romantic who expressed himself with the admirable economy of the contributors to the Greek anthology.

Sir Henry John Newbolt (1862–1938) was for a time almost as popular as Housman with the critics and the public, but his clearly expressed views on the necessity of religion and patriotism have made his work for the time less widely acceptable. He was the poet of the public-school code at its best and of the fighting services on land and sea. He wrote without undue emphasis on the subjects near to his heart and never forgot that he was a poet. The anthologists have made full use of his poems for the very good reason that he sang melodiously and never expressed himself in riddles. His *Poems New and Old* (1912) make a very small collection.

Newbolt provides a contrast to his more ambitious contemporary, Herbert Trench (1865–1923), who often attempted forms that were beyond his means. His odes show the influence of George Meredith, not always happily, and he survives only in a few short lyrics, of which the best known is "Trees."

Sir William Watson (1858–1925) was a poet whose work is difficult to estimate. Like Trench he essayed largely and there is some magnificent writing in his poetry, but he was unequal. He chose political themes which were frequently ephemeral, and his handling of them to present-day readers seems out of all proportion to their importance. The grand manner was congenial to the Victorians. It has been suspect ever since. For this reason some of the poems in Watson's *Lachrymae Musarum* (1892) are now almost forgotten, and this neglect is undeserved. The fact is that his promise was held to be so high when he began to write that he was considered as a possible successor to Tennyson for the Laureateship. He was never forgiven for failing to live up to this critical exaggeration of his early talent.

Two woman poets of the time are worthy of notice. Alice Meynell (1847–1922), who with her husband befriended Francis Thompson, was held in high regard by the writers of her day, both as poet and essayist. A devout Catholic, she expressed herself in prose and verse only after the most scrupulous self-criticism and revision. Her famous sonnet, "Renouncement," shows her at her best. Her *Collected Poems* appeared in 1923.

Mary Coleridge (1861–1907), an able poet, exploited the elegiac note with a large measure of success. Her verse is not always easily understood, but her *Poems Old and New* (1907) reveal her as a sincere and accomplished writer.

The decade of the 'seventies was rich in the birth of poets. In 1870 Hilaire Belloc, Thomas Sturge Moore and Charlotte Mew (1870–1928) were born.

Belloc's humorous verses for children were acclaimed in the 'nineties. Since then he has written sparingly in verse, but his sonnets, songs and ballades all show true poetic feeling and it is reasonable to wish that he had been able to devote more time to poetry and less to journalism and history.

Sturge Moore's poems reveal his strong interest in art. As a poet he is an individualist never easy to read but always worth reading. It was his practice to treat classical subjects in a manner of his own that shows little sign of outside influence. *The Vine Dresser* (1899) and the poetic drama *Absalom* (1903) are his most important works.

The poetry of Charlotte Mew is darkened by the tragedy that was her life. Her verse can be direct and intense. It can also be difficult and elusive. At her best she is among the few good English women poets. Her output was small and was published in *The Farmer's Bride* (1915) and *The Rambling Sailor* (1929).

One of the most disappointing of contemporary poets is Ralph Hodgson (b. 1871), whose two long poems, "The Bull" and "The Song of Honour," showed rare promise, a gift for narrative, and an exalted note which is not often heard in modern verse. With the exception of a few short lyrics Hodgson has published no other verse, but it is possible that he may yet surprise the world. The little that he has done shows him to be one of the most confident and able poets of his generation.

His contemporary, W. H. Davies (1871–1940), was a natural singer whose simple lyric gift expressed itself in numerous small volumes. His verses are clearly the work of a man who is at home with nature and who wandered happily, jotting down his poems as easily as though he was making entries in a commonplace book. Sometimes Davies erred on the side of over-simplicity. It is a small fault which detracts little from the unforced charm of his work.

In 1873 Walter De La Mare was born. An exquisite artist in poetry and prose, he is a true poet with a magic touch for the lyric and the power of evoking the strange and the sinister which is not matched by any of his contemporaries. He has the questioning mind of a child of genius. He is at home when he writes about children as they are at home when they read his poetry. He has created a twilight world, lying half in shadow and half in clear silver moonlight. He has fashioned also a hotly coloured oriental world shaped rather from the "shifting shining sovranties of dream" than from any known land of the East. But always the skeleton, the ogre, the corpse, the charnel house, seem to be round the corner, and for some years now the influence of Thomas Hardy has been perceptible in his verse. Both men can find real enjoyment, unhampered by any morbid feeling, in a graveyard.

De La Mare's prose fantasies, *Henry Brocken* (1904), *The*

Three Mulla Mulgars (1910), *The Return* (1910), and *Memoirs of a Midget* (1921), have a delicate and often thrilling beauty, but they are not somehow very easy to read. The poems express to perfection what the writer intends to convey. There are haunting cadences which run in the memory like half-remembered tunes. It is difficult to discuss the work of this writer without making use of the epithet "elusive." Second only to Yeats among recent poets as a writer of pure poetry, De La Mare was never swept up to popularity on the crest of a wave. He gradually won his way into popular affection and has surely strengthened his hold upon it. His reputation is not likely to give way before the assaults of time. His *Collected Poems* came out in 1942.

There is something Elizabethan about the poetry of both Gordon Bottomley and G. K. Chesterton (d. 1936), who were both born in 1874. Bottomley is not an easy poet. He has a great deal to say and his method is compressive. *Poems of Thirty Years* (1925) contains his best work, and his plays, *The Riding to Lithend* (1909), *King Lear's Wife* (1915) and *Gruach and Britain's Daughter* (1921), cannot be ignored.

Chesterton was never able altogether to sink the publicist and propagandist elements of his nature in the poet which he undoubtedly was. He was a master of the art of splendidly derisive ridicule in verse. He excelled at the ballade. His *Lepanto* is a highly coloured narrative. His rhythms are as virile and striking as his own mind was. His poems were collected in 1933.

It is not often remembered now that a tremendous stimulus to contemporary poetry was given by the publication in 1911 of the present Poet Laureate's poem, *The Everlasting Mercy*. John Masefield (b. 1878) was trained as a boy for the sea. He sailed before the mast and worked in an American mill besides earning his living with his hands in other capacities. He read deeply and variously and became a first-class reviewer, whose services were freely used by that stalwart of good reviewing, the *Manchester Guardian*. His first poems, *Salt-Water Ballads* (1902), showed the Kipling touch, but it also revealed a sensitive and serious singer. An admirer of Chaucer, and perhaps of Crabbe, Masefield astonished the world of letters by publishing in the *English Review* his long and violent narrative poem, *The Everlasting Mercy*. It is the fashion in smart literary cliques to deprecate Masefield's performance and merit to-day, largely because his faults are obvious and easily parodied. It is as if the poet regarded life as an inextricable compound of beauty and ugliness and had determined to mirror it in his verse. These lapses must not be allowed to prejudice the reader against Masefield's real and considerable achievement. He dared greatly and has accomplished much. His place is high among the English narrative poets. A love of melodrama, which permitted him to allow mere blood and thunder to encroach upon his serious work, has been a godsend to those who have been anxious to criticize him adversely, and yet when his work is considered as a whole it will be found that these purple patches occupy a surprisingly small part of it. When he follows the Chaucerian tradition, as in *Reynard the Fox* (1919), he is at his highly attractive and masterly best. In many of his sonnets and quieter poems he writes beautifully and soberly, and his *Collected Poems* (1932) show the wide variety of his accomplishment. Most worthily does he hold the office of Poet Laureate to-day.

The year 1878 also saw the birth of another poet who has excelled in narrative, Wilfrid Wilson Gibson. Preoccupied with the sufferings of labouring men and with the problems of industrial England in a machine age, Gibson's quietly written poems have drama and tragedy at their roots, though he too can write satisfactorily in a lyrical vein. His faults are a certain over-facility in composition and a pedestrian element which results sometimes in rather flat versification.

Edward Thomas (1878–1917), who had been known for many years as a literary journalist, sprang into prominence just before his death as a poet of the school of John Clare, but his muse was his own, and it is remarkable that one who spent most of his life in a literary atmosphere should have been able to shake off all influences in the composition of his thoughtful and friendly poems. As De La Mare has said, this poetry ennobles by simplification. Thomas's *Collected Poems* appeared in 1920.

Harold Monro (1879–1932) was a focal point for the "Georgians." That is not to say that he was the founder of that school of writers. The name "Georgian" was given by Sir Edward Marsh to a series of anthologies of contemporary poets, writing in the conservative tradition of verse and including some of the poets who have already been named. These were published by Monro at the Poetry Bookshop, which he had founded in Devonshire Street, Bloomsbury, in 1912, as a place where poetry could be read aloud and sold and where poets could live and meet each other. Thanks to Monro's generosity it was possible for an impecunious man of letters to rent a bedroom for three shillings and sixpence a week at the Poetry Bookshop before the last war. Monro's poetical output is small and uneven, but at his best he could write with a cool delicacy and could get inside the skin of domestic animals, especially cats. He deserves to be remembered for all that he did for poetry and for his fellow poets.

Two poets who have little in common, John Freeman (1880–1929) and Alfred Noyes (b. 1880), are contemporaries. Freeman was a sincere writer without any striking characteristics, a few of whose lyrics appear in anthologies. Noyes enjoyed a great popular success for his tales in verse which have no special characteristics either except a marked fluency.

Very different is the poetry of Lascelles Abercrombie (1881–1938), which might well be hewn from rock. He chose the difficult way and the unusual epithet, and this makes his verse hard to read. His resolute determination to avoid the ordinary did not lead him into any form of affectation, but it does not encourage the reader to turn to his poetry. There is something academic about it. He merits respect but there can be few readers of poetry who profess to love his work, which is mainly dramatic in intention and often depressing in subject-matter. His collected poems were published in 1930.

John Drinkwater (1882–1937) had a pleasant lyric talent and his unassuming verses, easily understood, have been widely read. Only occasionally, as in the fine poem called "The Midlands" and in the agreeable trifle "Mamble," did he succeed in stamping a poem with the impress of his personality.

Sir John Squire (b. 1884), who earned recognition first as an admirable parodist with *Steps to Parnassus* (1913) and *Tricks of the Trade* (1917), is a lyric poet of ability who has also been editor, journalist and reviewer. His work as editor of the *London Mercury* was invaluable as a rallying-point for sane and serious literature after the First World War. Regarding literature as an essential part of life and impatient of all poseurs and literary charlatans, Squire gathered round him a following of able young men of letters and helped them with all the influence at his command. In later days it will be found that Squire had a considerable influence on the literature of his time, and it will be found also that his influence was on the side of the angels.

In 1884, James Elroy Flecker was born. Like Rupert Brooke, he died young and it is difficult to say what he would have done had he lived. In the consular service, he worked for some years in the East, and his poetry is full of oriental colouring which may not be as authentic as it was thought to be when the poems appeared. He was no undisciplined singer of empty songs but a man who made beauty his aim and the choice of the apt epithet a life quest. In spite of this process of careful and conscious selection his poems flow very easily. They have great charm and no pretensions to depth of thought. The best description of Flecker is to be found in the first stanza of his poem, *To a Poet a Thousand Years Hence*:

> *O friend unseen, unborn, unknown,*
> *Student of our sweet English tongue,*
> *Read out my words at night, alone:*
> *I was a poet, I was young.*

His verse drama, *Hassan* (1922), which was eagerly anticipated, made a marked commercial success after the war of 1914–18, but it disappointed those who had looked for a great poetic play. *The Golden Journey to Samarkand* (1913) represents the height of his achievement in verse.

Humbert Wolfe (1885–1940), a busy civil servant, reviewer and author, wrote verse with great technical facility. His best-known volume was *Requiem* (1927), which sold well. Wolfe was a mannered poet with satirical powers which he hardly ever employed to the full.

A small group of writers who wrote for the most part in free

verse were the "Imagists." The leader of this movement,
T. E. Hulme, wrote less than half a dozen pieces. His inspiration seems to have been strongly felt by his followers, who
included T. S. Eliot, Ezra Pound, Richard Aldington, F. S.
Flint and "H.D." (Hilda Doolittle). Their poems were slight,
cool, clear and occasionally beautiful. The first *Imagist
Anthology* (1914) had some good things in it. Subsequent
collections did not maintain the standard and the movement
gradually died out.

It is convenient to mention Rupert Brooke (1887–1915) at
this point. When the war of 1914–18 broke out, at first the
poets were dumb. Then Hardy, Masefield, Kipling and others
of the senior poets had their say, which was usually on the
conventional lines of death or glory. Rupert Brooke, a young
man of charming personality and some academic talent—he
was a Fellow of King's College, Cambridge—wrote "The
Soldier" and his other famous sonnets. He had written poetry
before and had been noted as a promising young poet, whose
work showed the influence of Donne and had a slightly cynical
note. Exception must be made for the delightful poem "The
Old Vicarage," "Grantchester," "The Great Lover" and other
of his verses. "The Soldier" revealed Brooke as a man who
felt that the war gave his generation an opportunity to fight
for a better world and if necessary to die for it. He was only
twenty-eight when he died, but so great was the impression he
had made that when the news of his death reached England
there were those who could not rid themselves of the feeling
that the light of English poetry had gone out. Since that time
the pendulum has swung violently in the opposite direction and
it has become the custom to underrate Brooke now as stupidly
as he had been overrated just after his death.

A year or two of warfare with modern armaments and
among the Flanders mud made the poets change their tune,
and the first to express abomination and loathing of the
terrible waste of fine young life, almost entirely at the mercy of
machines, was Siegfried Sassoon (b. 1886). To Sassoon war
was a loathsome business. He disliked and distrusted profoundly the press "stunts" and sinister business interests which
were active behind the fields of battle, where young men were

slain and maimed. There used to be a French saying that for every soldier in the line the English had six men behind it making cups of tea for him, and Sassoon took a savage delight in pillorying old and inefficient staff officers, kindly but incompetent generals, and others who sacrificed young lives, while they, the old and paunchy, had a comfortable war at the base, whence, at the war's end, they would toddle safely home and die in bed. The full intensity of his poetic inspiration deserted Sassoon when the war was over and he has never written such vivid and memorable poetry since, but he made full amends with his superb autobiographical prose works of which the best are *Memoirs of a Fox-Hunting Man* (1928) and *Memoirs of an Infantry Officer* (1930). These recapture the atmosphere of an old, mellow, happy world as it appeared to a fortunate young man with enough money to be reasonably independent and able to indulge in the country pursuits that he loved. His prose account of his war experiences makes a valuable pendant to the author's poems. It lacks the bite of the verse but there is a gain in perspective. Among the prose literature of this century, *The Complete Memoirs of George Sherston* (1937), embodying the two books already mentioned, with *Sherston's Progress*, will occupy a deservedly prominent and enduring place.

Three other poets who first came into prominence in the last war can conveniently be mentioned here. They are Robert Graves (b. 1895), Robert Nichols (b. 1893) and Edmund Blunden (b. 1896). The first two wrote their best poetry in the war of 1914–18.

Graves is a true poet whose early songs were his best. Latterly he has written some careful and conscientious historical novels, and some highly experimental verses. He shares Sassoon's dislike for elderly incompetence, and he has a fine, fierce impatience which commands respect but not necessarily affection for his later poems. *Fairies and Fusiliers* (1917) shows him at his best as a poet with a delightful lyric gift. Nichols never recaptured the excellence of some of the poems in his *Ardours and Endurances* (1917). His "Fulfilment" is one of the best of English war poems.

The poetry of Edmund Blunden is essentially pastoral. He

can write happily of a countryman's pleasure in rural sights and sounds, and in his *Undertones of War* (1928), which has been considered by good judges as the best of the books produced by the last war, he wrote memorably in prose and verse of his experience as a fighting soldier.

Other war poets of the 1914–18 war generation, whose names survive as the writers of one or more satisfying poems, are C. H. Sorley (1892–1915), Julian Grenfell (1888–1915), F. W. Harvey (b. 1888), Francis Ledwidge (1891–1917), Isaac Rosenberg (1890–1918), Edward Shanks (b. 1892), W. N. Hodgson (1893–1916), Edward Wyndham Tennant (1897–1916), and Willoughby Weaving.

Of the Sitwells, Edith (b. 1887), Osbert (b. 1892) and Sacheverell (b. 1897), it is not easy to write. There is no doubt at all of their great gifts and remarkable ability. They might well have allowed these to speak for them, but they took delight in mocking the pompous and the inept. They even condescended to attack the toadies and hangers-on of literature and spent valuable time and energy in beating up nonenties which might have been expended more profitably on their own creative work. They are not only clever—they have genius. The anthology, *Wheels*, which appeared first in 1916 as a counterblast to the decorous and traditional *Georgian Poetry* collections of Sir Edward Marsh, show them and their collaborators as seekers after the perverse and unusual in verse. Undeniably these researches stirred up the placid and turgid-minded. Since those early days, Edith Sitwell has published a eulogistic critical study of Alexander Pope (1930), and some interesting anthologies and other work in prose and verse. Osbert Sitwell has revealed himself as one of the very best of contemporary prose writers in fiction and travel books, and Sacheverell Sitwell has written with charm and erudition on architecture and subjects connected with the arts. Almost all these writings deserve serious critical notice and are highly readable.

It was in 1918 that Robert Bridges published a selection of the poems of Gerard Manley Hopkins (1844–89), a volume which was to have considerable influence on the work of poets who wrote in the 'twenties and 'thirties. An enlarged collection appeared in 1930. It is important to notice that Hopkins never wrote for publication and that most of his verses were sent to Bridges in correspondence. He was an experimenter in verse, being especially addicted to the "spring-rhythm." He was also unconsciously responsible for introducing the cross-word puzzle mentality into modern poetry, and this resulted in many talented and not-so-talented young gentlemen paying overmuch attention to the construction of metrical pieces, in which the value of the content was obviously negligible. This cannot be alleged of Hopkins himself. Oliver Elton wrote astutely: "Hopkins is deliberately and invincibly queer; carries ellipse and compression to the limit; revels in new compounds; likes subtle alliterations and difficult rhymes with a difficult theory behind them." There have always been, and there always will be, young disciples eager to bite on theories but hardly any good poetry has ever been written within the rigid bounds of a theory, and there is no doubt that much of the obscurity and unprofitableness of the verse of the 'twenties and 'thirties must be brought home to Hopkins, who was unconscious of the dread harvest that others sowed and reaped in his name. He was a Jesuit, of deep learning, and possessed of the true poetic fire. If he had not followed his vocation he might have been a greater poet, but he would have lost the tremendous weight of religious experience which informs his fine devotional poetry.

Wilfred Owen (1893–1918), who was killed only a week before the Armistice, is another poet who has strongly influenced the younger generation by his attitude towards war. In the last year of his life he came into contact with Sassoon, and some of his poems are not very impressive imitations of the older poet's work. Serving as an infantry officer, he came to the conclusion that "passivity at any price" was the right ideal. "Suffer dishonour and disgrace but never resort to arms," he wrote, but this did not deter him from dying in the performance of his duty. His great gifts as a poet were maturing rapidly at the time of his death. He was a master of subtle harmonies in rhyme and consonance, but it is the temper of his mind and his strong anti-war feelings that endeared him especially to young readers after his death. His best-known poem, "Strange Meeting," in which two soldiers who have killed each other comment on the "pity of war," was congenial to a post-war generation, and his ability as a writer made for him a reputation which has endured.

It will be seen that the attention of the later war poets was concentrated on the futility of warfare and the massacre of youth. They were appalled by the wastefulness of it all. A few years afterwards, when it became apparent that civilization had gained little or nothing by the struggle and loss, and that the world's statesmen had been unequal to the opportunities presented to them for building a better world, a feeling of frustration became prevalent among people of imagination. They were to find an able, if humourless, exponent of their ideas in an American, Thomas Stearns Eliot (b. 1888), who threw in his lot with the British people and was naturalized in 1927. Always sincere, often obscure, sometimes arid, Eliot certainly expressed the intellectual mood of the moment, but he was essentially a writer of verse who was of the intelligentsia. His unquestionable sincerity gained a hearing for his verses, some of which are allusive and often pompously and unintelligibly annotated. The ordinary reader will not need to be told that the pith of a poem lies in the poem itself and not in a sheaf of notes, however relevant and enlightening these may be. In reading Eliot's poetry it is sometimes difficult to distinguish between the frustration and impotence he feels in the face of so much muddle and waste, and the doubt there may be lingering at the back of his mind as to the extent of his own poetic powers. He is not a natural, instinctive singer but a literary poet whose music is scanty, austere, and very occasionally lovely. Subsequent generations will judge Eliot's poetry not by its immediate message but simply as poetry. A few of his poems will stand this test. "Gerontion," "Ash Wednesday" and "The Waste Land" are likely to be among them. In a recent series of four poems, "East Coker," "Burnt Norton," "The Dry Salvages," and "Little Gidding," Eliot has shown signs of mellowing. His purpose is not always clear. His method continues unnecessarily tortuous but he seems to have found in religion an anodyne for the troubles of the time. Probably in after years Eliot will be regarded much as

Ben Jonson is regarded now, and Ben Jonson, who was venerated as a kind of literary dictator in his own time, survives only
in a few lyrics and some plays which are but rarely acted.
Between Jonson's accomplishment and Eliot's there can be
no comparison whatever, for Jonson was at his best a true poet
and an inspired singer who confined his genius within theories
and limitations of his own contrivance. There was a genial
element in Jonson to which Eliot would not pretend. It
is Eliot's misfortune that he had so many imitators who
might have done decent unobtrusive critical work but have
wasted their slender talents in an attempt to pose as creative
artists, a role for which their inconsiderable equipment made
them totally unfitted. Whatever of Eliot's work survives will do
so for the qualities in it which are least generally appreciated
now.

Eliot, Owen and Hopkins were claimed by Cecil Day Lewis
(b. 1904) as the "immediate ancestors" of himself, W. H.
Auden (b. 1907) and Stephen Spender (b. 1909), and these three
young poets received more critical attention and regard than
any other of the poets who began to write after the last war.
To the casual reader the work of the post-war poets, including
T. S. Eliot, presented superficial difficulties because melody and
magic were banished almost entirely from their poetry. Anything familiar and traditional either in content or metrical form
was taboo. They did not realize that a complete break with
tradition is bound to be harmful. Their scrannel pipings were
as unwelcome to the ear as were their ideological preoccupa-
tions to the mind. They were as imperfectly masters of their
medium as the average child is with his first box of chalks.
They received a recognition that was out of all proportion to
their achievement. In his valuable examination of their
writings, *A Hope for Poetry* (1934), Day Lewis examined
their social and literary influences, their aims and technique.

"The poet," he wrote, "is an artificer by profession, an
architect experimenting with a variety of materials, concerned
with levels and stresses, old foundations, new designs. Then,
suddenly, perhaps in one window only in the last of many
houses he has built, a light shows. An unearthly visitor has

taken up possession, the pure spirit of poetry. The works of great poets blaze with light from every story. But one single window so illuminated can justify a life's work, while a thousand structures of graceful design are vain and void without that fiery occupant. The poet is an artificer by profession, a poet by divine accident. The pure spirit that comes to possess him, for one minute maybe in twenty years, comes from regions over which he has no control. Between visits there is nothing he can do but work at his profession, so that, when next an angel arrives, he can better accommodate him. He may hope, but he cannot be certain, that the finer the tenement, the more likely it is to be tenanted."

This profession is sincere and deeply felt. Beginning with several honest and sometimes difficult volumes of verse which reveal Day Lewis working his way towards a method of self-expression in poetry which shall be both individual and satisfying, and drawing freely on the imagery of the machine and other contemporary industrial phenomena, he has arrived at the mature accomplishment of *Overtures to Death and Other Poems* (1938). The occasional obscurity of the earlier poems has been cast aside, and in "The Volunteer" Day Lewis wrote with a terse epigrammatic assurance reminiscent of Housman at his economical best. "The Nabara," a long narrative poem of a sea fight, revealed him as a master of assonance. This is one of the finest sea-pieces in the language. Whatever Day Lewis may do in the future he has already shown himself a true poet. In the future he may well free himself entirely from the harmful contemporary influences which have proved so great a handicap to the full development of Auden's talent.

There is no doubt that Auden possesses considerable accomplishment. That he is an authentic poet seems much less certain. That he has attracted so much attention is primarily due to the fact that he is a social critic, occupied deeply and sincerely with the problems of his time. In his pages is to be found an odd and irritating blend of obscurity, jazz, Marxism, cabaret, pacifism, psychology and balladry. The level of composition shown is extraordinarily uneven. It ranges from journalism, at the worst, to a wistful lyricism, which is for ever showing promise but does not attain a definite and satisfactory fulfilment. It is as though a lack of spiritual purpose stands between Auden and his work. Always conscious of dangerous shoals, he finds himself far out at sea in a small boat without steering-gear. In his *New Year Letter* (1941), with its elaborate and unnecessary apparatus of notes, he wrote as though he was helpless before the onset of the storm. This poem showed a deterioration of his accomplishment, which was at its best and highest in *Look, Stranger!* (1936) and *Another Time* (1940). It is possible that the future may reveal Auden as dramatist rather than poet, but if he is to succeed in the theatre he will have to subdue the restlessness and lack of sustained purpose which marred the great promise of *The Ascent of F.6*.

Stephen Spender has the greatest lyric gift of these three poets. He is the most introspective of them. He has been the most severely handicapped by the political chains with which he has bound himself and his muse. Day Lewis wrote: "It is always dangerous and impertinent to commend a poem for anything but its poetry." Spender, who comes of a family of politicians, seems to feel that he ought to have a message, but of its import he is still only half-aware. It is so imperfectly assimilated that he cannot pass it on in his poems. With a deep and tender regard for his fellow men, not altogether unlike that of Whitman, he combines a rare sensitiveness and a profound sincerity. The best of his verse is to be found in *Poems* (1933) and *The Still Centre* (1939). It has a grave music and sometimes a lovely radiance, as in the first stanza of the poem, "I think continually of those who were truly great":

> *I think continually of those who were truly great.*
> *Who, from the womb, remembered the soul's history*
> *Through corridors of light where the hours are suns*
> *Endless and singing, whose lovely ambition*
> *Was that their lips, still touched with fire,*
> *Should tell of the Spirit clothed from head to foot in song,*
> *And who hoarded from the Spring branches*
> *The desires falling across their bodies like blossoms.*

Spender is at his best when he is writing of youth or of children.

Like Auden, Louis MacNeice (b. 1907) is a critic of the world in which he found himself, a place made hideous by amoral publicity and sham civilization. A frustrated romantic with considerable dramatic powers, he is also a master of rhythm as in the cheerful, vigorous "Bagpipe Music." Possessing great vitality and a flair for outspoken, drastic criticism, MacNeice is one of the most interesting contemporary poets, but he has not yet found his bearings. *The Earth Compels* (1938), *Autumn Journal* (1939) and *Plant and Phantom* (1941) are his three most representative collections of verse. *Modern Poetry, A Personal Essay* (1938) and *The Poetry of W. B. Yeats* (1941) are two excellent critical works.

Roy Campbell (b. 1902) is an even livelier and more outspoken critic of European civilization to-day than MacNeice is. Campbell is a South African and perhaps the most considerable poet the Empire has yet produced; a vigorous satirist, who would be even more effective if he considered and revised his work more carefully before publication, Campbell in his early books, *The Flaming Terrapin* (1924), *The Wayzgoose* (1928) and *Adamastor* (1930) conveyed his impressions of the South African scene. Later he turned to satirize, first, London intellectual coteries in *The Georgiad* (1931), and then later, the Marxian concept of life against which he himself fought in the Spanish Civil War. This poem, *Flowering Rifle* (1939) showed his exultant, fiercely held nationalism at its fieriest. It also exhibited the virtues and defects of his satirical approach, with its indiscriminate and sometimes ill-considered condemnation.

Two older poets were brought into late notice by the great prominence given to them by W. B. Yeats in his ill-chosen anthology, *The Oxford Book of Modern Verse* (1936). W. J. Turner (b. 1889) wrote some charming lyrics, in which he invoked successfully the magic of romantic place-names. Herbert Read (b. 1893), who has been admired by the young intellectuals for what they consider to be the anarchical element in his verse, wrote quietly and realistically of war, and the waste of it. He is an able worker in assonantal verse forms.

Two poets who have not worried themselves with anything

H

but the writing of poetry and have essayed largely must also be mentioned here. Clifford Bax (b. 1885) wrote some thoughtful short lyrics and a colourful narrative poem, *The Traveller's Tale* (1921). Victoria Sackville-West (b. 1892) has a keen ear for music that can be made with verse and a heartfelt love for her native Kent. Her long pastoral poem, *The Land* (1926), gives full expression to both, and is altogether one of the most pleasant and satisfying poetic achievements of the century as it is also one of the best descriptive poems written by an Englishwoman. The work of both these poets may be recommended to those who ask for melody, lucidity and beauty in poetry and for subject-matter which does not insult the intelligence and is neither laboured nor obscure. Neither poet is obsessed by ideologies or social problems. Each has a conception of life which can be expressed intelligibly and profitably. A disproportionately small amount of attention has been paid to both of them by the intellectual critics of their time.

To turn from these limpid verses to the experiments of the young men of the last decade is like leaving the Thames at Henley and suddenly finding oneself in the middle of a Malayan jungle, thick, tangled, gnarled and twisted, but bereft of its tropical luxuriance. If literary theories and social ideologies obsess a writer to the extent that they choke his songs, leaving them half-strangled at the moment of utterance, there is little or nothing to be said for them. They cease to be matter for the literary critic and become the preserve of the social historian. Many of the young poets worshipped sedulously at the shrine of Eliot, and at the still more barren shrine of Marx, with the results that although they appear immensely important and rewarding to a small minority of the intelligentsia, they have no message and no music for the lover of poetry, who considers that poetry, if it is to be regarded as poetry, must have magic and melody in it. Eliot discovered the "Waste Land." The young writers who came after him ventured, many of them, far into an intellectual Sahara, from which there can be no return, unless the writer abjures his old faith, and finds refreshment in some traditional oasis, lying almost hidden from him by the accumulated sand of the years, and only found again after long and toilsome search.

The promise of some of the younger poets is undeniable. Unfortunately, their perversity is even more apparent than their promise. It is fair to add that this perversity is almost invariably due to the feeling that they have no faith or creed or party to cling to. They are understandably discontented and dissatisfied with life, and comparatively few of them, in their writings at any rate, seem able to stand up and face it. There is a great deal of clever criticism of systems, people, books and things. There is practically no sound constructive policy advanced by any of the young writers. Philip Sidney said that poets are the trumpets who sing to battle. It would be admirable if our young men would set about their rightful task of singing-in the new world. There has been, and still is, far too much written and said by young writers about being members of a "doomed" generation. They appear to be singularly ignorant of the facts of history, which would inform them that there have been comparatively few periods when writers have been able to pursue an even course untroubled by the world's alarms and excursions. It is for these young poets to find a new resolution and plunge into the struggle of life, armed and strengthened by a rediscovered faith. Eliot turned from the "Waste Land" to Anglo-Catholicism. The young writers would be happier men, better writers and more useful citizens if they too would grasp a stable faith. It is not only chance that some of the very best of verse by the young poets is religious verse. A remarkable little *Anthology of Religious Verse*, in the Pelican series, edited by Norman Nicholson, himself a real poet, may well point the way. Andrew Young, Clifford Dyment, John Short, Charles Williams, Anne Ridler, David Gascoyne, Ruth Pitter, are only a few of those who have written coherently. Andrew Young (b. 1885), a Scottish minister who has recently become a Church of England clergyman, is a singer of the natural world, a most sensitive observer and a traditionalist. He is a singer of exquisite songs, whose music is gradually obtaining a hearing. *Collected Poems* were published in 1936.

Among other young poets, Dylan Thomas, George Barker, Frederic Prokosch, Kenneth Allott, F. T. Prince, Julian Symons, Geoffrey Grigson, Sidney Keyes, Ruthven Todd,

Nicholas Moore, Henry Treece, G. S. Fraser, Tambimuttu, Alun Lewis, Alan Rook, Keidrych Rhys and J. F. Hendry have shown either promise or performance. Thomas's "In Memory of Ann Jones" (1938), Barker's "Calamiterror" (1937), and Rook's "Dunkirk Pier"(1942), all have merit, the last-mentioned being one of the few significant war poems written during this war.

Among the other writers of good verse, many of whom are accomplished workers in other literary forms, may be mentioned Richard Church, L. A. G. Strong, Edwin Muir, J. Redwood Anderson, Margaret L. Woods, Dorothy Wellesley, Sylvia Lynd, Rose Macaulay, William Plomer, Wilfrid Rowland Childe, Edward Davison, J. D. C. Pellow, Christopher Hassall, Laurence Whistler, E. R. Dodds, Richard Hughes, Oliver Gogarty, Frank O'Connor, Michael Roberts, William Empson, Charles Madge, F. R. Higgins and Ernest Rhys.

As in the last war, there have been collections made by young Service men showing reminiscent charm and promise, which have been greeted with unkindly eulogistic notice by benevolent and sentimental critics. There is little true achievement, and this is due to the poetic poverty of the age. The noise of party songs and ideological verses has almost silenced the singing poets. It is to be hoped that some singers in the great tradition, as Cecil Day Lewis and Andrew Young have shown themselves to be, may break through and banish the discords of to-day.

THE DRAMA

The nineteenth century was one of the leanest periods in the history of the English stage. A gleam of light was introduced by Tom Robertson (1829–71) with his naturalistic comedies. Only the last decade saw a lightening of the gloom when the technical efficiency of Sir Arthur Pinero (1859–1934) and Henry Arthur Jones (1851–1929) paved the way for the new frankness and freedom which were to be brought to the theatre by Ibsen and by George Bernard Shaw (b. 1856). Until these dramatists appeared, the world of the theatre had been completely divorced from life as we know it. In *The Second Mrs. Tan-*

queray (1893) Pinero, using the old-fashioned language of the stage, had employed a central situation which aroused a storm of controversy. Shaw, like Ibsen, used the drama as a medium for ventilating all manner of topics which preoccupied his fertile and versatile mind. He wrote quick and lively dialogue. His prose is admirable, clear, striking and forthright. If he had thought as clearly as he wrote, Shaw might well have been the second English dramatist. Unfortunately, there is a vein of irresponsibility in him which sometimes finds expression in the memorable phrase. Often enough this is exceedingly effective but the impression has been created at the expense of truth and accuracy. No one will quarrel with Mr. Shaw for his habit of shocking apathetic English audiences into attention with paradox and quip, or with his determination to take a serious or important matter and use it as material for a play. His powers are so great that he can make, and has made, the most unlikely subjects productive of good entertainment. It might be said that all his characters seem to belong to some vast debating society and that they do not possess an independent life of their own when the session is over. This impression is persistent and remains even after a reading of Mr. Shaw's careful and precise stage directions which sometimes give a brief biography of their subject. Another difficulty that Mr. Shaw has never overcome, indeed it is uncertain whether he has fought hard to expunge it, lies in the strong individuality of his thought processes. He cannot submerge his personality in that of a character. It is always Shaw who speaks, and for the most part the Shavian characters are the puppets animated by one able showman, who imitates all their voices as well. Shaw had much to say, and in his plays and prefaces he has expressed himself fully, but as he grew older he became less interested in the construction of his plays and more concerned with the dissemination of his ideas. The talk flowed on and at times degenerated into garrulity so that audiences of his later plays have often prayed for a little action after an act of unrelieved debate.

Born in Dublin, the son of an opera singer, who afterwards taught music, Shaw did not go to school. When he came to London at the age of twenty he soon became immersed in the world of ideas and was accepted with open arms by the Sidney Webbs and the Fabian Society. The Hampstead Parliament heard his young oratory and between 1879 and 1883 he published four novels. These may not have great merit as fiction but there is an air of integrity about them that promised well for the author's future. Musical criticism for the *Star* and dramatic criticism for the *Saturday Review* brought him still more into the public eye, and his defence of the plays of Pinero and Jones established him as a formidable controversialist with advanced and unconventional views. With the appearance of *Widowers' Houses* (1892), *Arms and the Man* (1894), *Candida* (1895) and *You Never Can Tell* (1899) it was clear that the stage had found a new master. Shaw gave to the English theatre dialogue which was a brilliantly magnified rendering of everyday conversation. He wrote with a punch. When the first book of his plays was published, in 1898, it was seen that the new dramatist, with his lengthy prefaces and picturesque and detailed stage directions, was the founder of a new school of dramatic literature. His approach to his medium was made with entire artistic reverence and tremendous gaiety and high spirits. Nothing was too difficult for him to attempt. Social problems, history, philosophy, fantasy, all came within his range, and all the time he was striving to get at the roots of things, to expose the causes of human failure and of human evils. He soon proved himself to be a master of satire.

Among his numerous plays, *Man and Superman* (1903), *John Bull's Other Island* (1907), *The Doctor's Dilemma* (1911), *Heartbreak House* (1919) and *St. Joan* (1923) are the most important, in addition to those already mentioned.

Two characteristics manifested themselves in Shaw's work about ten years after he began his career as a dramatist. A lessening of concern with the play's structure and action was one of them. The other was an inclination to take as subject-matter anything that occupied his mind at the moment and to treat it very fully not only in the play but also in the stage directions and in the preface. In the later plays it has sometimes seemed as though Mr. Shaw has forgotten what his audience will see and hear, and what will not be visible and audible to it, because they are tucked away in the preface and stage directions. Mr. Shaw became increasingly preoccupied with what he wanted to discuss and not with what his characters were to do and say when they were on the stage. The stage became his forum or a debating platform for the diversity of his ideas. As time went on, the Shaw plays had less to do with the theatre and more with the display of the author's amazingly ingenious dialectics. They became animated tracts.

It would be ungracious and ungrateful to end on this note. It is impossible to say yet how much the English stage and, indeed, the world's stage, owes to this writer. He blew away the Victorian cobwebs. He modernized the traffic of the theatre. He set men's minds to work on new lines. Apart from the tendency to wordiness which has been noted, Shaw's influence on the theatre has been all to the good.

Born in the same year as Shaw, Oscar Wilde (1856–1900) enjoyed a considerable success with his plays in the early 'nineties. By far the best of them is *The Importance of Being Earnest* (1895), a farcical comedy of great polish and consistent wit, which is rich in excellent comic situations: in this piece Wilde attempted no serious portrayal of life. He aimed only at entertainment, and it is doubtful whether within these limits there has ever been a more complete success. *Lady Windermere's Fan* (1892), the only other play by Wilde which is likely to be remembered, shows how weak he could be when he introduced serious emotions into the theatre. Something of the verbal felicity of the plays is to be found in Wilde's short stories collected in *Lord Arthur Savile's Crime* (1891) and in the novel, *The Picture of Dorian Gray* (1891). Among his poems only the moving *Ballad of Reading Gaol* (1898), calls for notice. *De Profundis* (1905) cannot be fairly criticized until the unexpurgated version is available.

Wilde's reputation as a writer has always been higher abroad than at home, because it has been felt by literary critics of other nations that Wilde had been persecuted on moral grounds in England, and that others could show that they were more tolerant to genius in adversity than the English were. An exactly similar attitude obtains abroad towards the poetry of Lord Byron.

Very little is heard now of the work of Stephen Phillips

(1864–1915). His experience as an actor and his talent for writing flamboyant verse enabled him to write several poetic plays which had a real success on the stage. The best known of them are *Paolo and Francesca* (1900) and *Herod* (1901), and it would be interesting to see how they would bear revival in the contemporary threatre without the expensive production lavished on them by Herbert Beerbohm Tree when they first appeared.

St. John Hankin (1869–1909), a writer of pleasant satirical comedies was unlucky during his lifetime, which ended tragically. Since his death *The Return of the Prodigal* (1905), *The Charity That Began at Home* (1906) and *The Cassilis Engagement* (1907) have enjoyed a sustained success in repertory theatres all over the British Isles. Hankin added to a real sense of the theatre a talent for writing easy, natural and amusing dialogue, and the ability to devise ingenious and diverting situations which he treated in an unconventional and convincing manner. It will not be surprising if his plays continue to be read and acted long after some of his better-known and more pretentious contemporaries are forgotten. He understood the nature of pure comedy.

Laurence Housman (b. 1865) has recently earned fame for his play, *Victoria Regina* (1934), which was fashioned from a series of short plays dealing with the life of the queen. Mr. Housman is at his best in the short episodic piece which has a religious or historical setting. He is at his happiest when his characters are real personages. With this reservation his achievement is notable, and he always writes with true literary distinction. His most important works are *Victoria Regina* (1934), *The Golden Sovereign* (1937), *Angels and Ministers* (1921), *Gracious Majesty* (1941) and *Little Plays of St. Francis* (1922; second series, 1931). The charming pierrot fantasy, *Prunella* (1906), written in collaboration with Granville-Barker, has been persistently successful on the stage.

The emergence of the Irish National Theatre Society in 1902 was the signal for the beginning of a literary and theatrical movement which has given to contemporary drama some of its most considerable plays. It came into being because George Moore (1852–1933), W. B. Yeats, G. W. Russell ("Æ"), Lady

Gregory (1859–1932) and Edward Martyn (1859–1924), felt that there ought to be a society for the production of great plays in Dublin. They were fortunate in finding in John Millington Synge (1871–1909) a national Irish dramatist, and so what had been founded as a vehicle for carrying great masterpieces of the stage to Dublin became in a very short time the means of introducing to the Irish playgoer a remarkable series of plays which soon spread the name and fame of the Abbey Theatre, Dublin, to the knowledge of audiences all over the world. It was Yeats who encouraged Synge to write for an Irish theatre. He had lived among the peasants of western Ireland and he reproduced their idiosyncrasies and charm in plays which abound in lively and dramatic situations and are written in a language which catches the authentic ring of Irish speech in a rhythm and cadence which are among its author's gifts to the drama. *Riders to the Sea* (1904) is a peasant tragedy in miniature, full of dignity and beauty. *The Well of the Saints* (1905) is an admirable comedy, which has as its theme the doubtful blessing of the restoration of sight to a pair of beggars. Finally, they reject it. *The Playboy of the Western World* (1907), the best and the best-known of Synge's plays, caused a tremendous hubbub when it was produced because local patriots found in it an attack upon Ireland and the Irish. So strong was this feeling that riots took place in the theatre when the play was acted outside Ireland. Needless to say, the author had no idea of making such an attack. He was only concerned with truth as he saw it, and when he wrote the play his great powers were at their height. Here are poetry and tragedy and humour beautifully blended, and the result is a great dramatic masterpiece. Like Yeats and "Æ," Synge treated the legend of Deirdre dramatically, and in this play he conjured up all the poetry and beauty that is to be got from "irishing" the English language. This is a method which can be carried so far and no farther, and no subsequent writer has succeeded as Synge did in using the idiom without becoming artificial and extravagant.

Edward Martyn used a more naturalistic method successfully in *The Heather Field* (1899) and *Maeve* (1899). He had a true dramatic sense and wrote good prose. His plays have not received their fair share of acclaim. Lady Gregory, who was

H*

largely responsible for Yeats's interest in the Irish theatre, was herself a comic dramatist without much stamina but with a real gift for relating a dramatic anecdote economically and with point. Her treatment of Irish peasant life in *Seven Short Plays* (1911) is a model of what this dramatic form can be at its best. Her book, *Our Irish Theatre* (1913), may be read with John Eglinton's *Irish Literary Portraits* (1935) as a corrective to George Moore's *Ave atque Vale*. The three books together give a comprehensive picture of an important literary and dramatic movement. A corresponding movement, the Ulster Literary Theatre, made its appearance in 1902. Its output never attained the same breadth and volume as the parent theatre did. "Rutherford Mayne" (Samuel Waddell) was the principal figure of the Ulster movement, and his best-known play is *The Drone* (1908). St. John Ervine (b. 1883), an Ulsterman by birth, who has made a considerable reputation for himself as playwright, dramatic critic and novelist, has written plays of Irish life. Best known of these are *Mixed Marriage* (1911), *The Orangeman* (1913) and *John Ferguson* (1915). He has since written many other plays. *Jane Clegg* (1911), in which Sybil Thorndyke gave a memorable performance, is among the best of them.

Two other Irish dramatists must be mentioned here. Sean O'Casey's (b. 1884) *Juno and the Paycock* (1926) has both comedy and tragedy. The slums of an Irish city are made to furnish rich and satisfying entertainment. Denis Johnston's (b. 1901) *The Moon on the Yellow River* (1931) gives a haunting picture of the "troubles."

One of the important influences in the Dublin theatrical circle was Miss A. E. F. Horniman, whose munificence was behind the Abbey Theatre for some years before she transferred her activities to the Manchester Gaiety Theatre.

When a new historian of the contemporary theatre takes up his pen he will find that there is a great deal to be written about Miss Horniman's influence upon the drama of the day. The same might be said of Harley Granville-Barker (b. 1877), who collaborated with J. E. Vedrenne (1867–1930) in some memorable repertory ventures at the Court Theatre, London, in 1904 and later. The most ambitious London repertory

venture was staged at the Duke of York's Theatre in 1910 by
the late Charles Frohmann, a most enterprising producer, who
was drowned in the wreck of the *Titanic*. In addition to plays
by Shaw, Galsworthy, Pinero, Meredith, Barrie, Granville-
Barker and Housman, a modern realistic play, *Chains*, by
Elizabeth Baker, was produced. This is the tragedy of a
clerk, who hates his environment. He is on the verge of
throwing up his job and following a friend to seek his fortune
in Australia, when his wife tells him that she is going to have a
child. The chains hold, and the clerk remains at his desk. In
this piece Miss Baker held her audiences with a play of ordinary
life, skilfully heightened just enough for stage use. Charles
McEvoy (1879–1929) adopted this method with some success
in *David Ballard* (1908), as did H. F. Maltby (b. 1880) in *The
Rotters* (1915). At the beginning of the century it looked as
though Granville-Barker would become the leading figure in the
English theatre. His early plays, *The Voysey Inheritance* (1905)
and *The Madras House* (1910), treated considerable social
problems worthily. A few years afterwards he retired from
the theatre and only his valuable *Prefaces to Shakespeare*
(1928 and later) and some translations from the Spanish, show
that he has retained his interest in it.

It was at the Court Theatre that *The Silver Box* (1906), the
first of John Galsworthy's (1867–1933) many plays, saw the
light. It made the point that there was one law for the rich,
another for the poor. Galsworthy always had a sympathy for
the underdog. He never tired of calling attention to abuses
which needed abolishing or to conditions of life which called for
radical alteration. To see or read *Strife* (1909) or *Justice* (1910)
to-day is to recall with surprise that when they first appeared
they were considered to be strictly impartial statements of the
cases which the author presented in them. Galsworthy's later
plays, such as *The Skin Game* (1920) and *Loyalties* (1922), both
of which achieved immense popular successes, were written with
considerable knowledge of the theatre and with less of a desire
to be a propagandist.

There is no doubt that Galsworthy always wrote with a fine
sincerity. It is equally certain that he often deceived himself
and was a victim of that sentimentality which was perceptible in

the earlier plays and often took charge of the writer in his later ones. Galsworthy had no remedies for the troubles of life in the twentieth century except understanding, patience and mercy. All human institutions, he felt, are the better for an infusion of the personal element. He had no sympathy for the complex mechanism of civilization unless it functioned with sympathy and tact so that the least of human creatures should not be wounded or crushed by it. He maintained that men and women in the mass are usually cruel and stupid. In effect, all Galsworthy's plays are a plea for greater gentleness and for the making of allowances. He would always give the benefit of the doubt but, as he showed in *The Pigeon* (1912), one can make any amount of concessions to people who are unworthy of them and the poor, misguided creatures will snatch any advantage they can. And who can blame them, he seems to add, when things are so utterly hopeless for them? Galsworthy was the mouthpiece of the world's unfortunates but neither he nor they seem able to explain how they are to be made happier.

Sir James Matthew Barrie, Bart. (1860–1937), who, like Galsworthy, was honoured by being made a member of the Order of Merit, was in his way as original a dramatic writer as is Bernard Shaw. A Scottish peasant by birth, he won his way to a university education at Edinburgh and passed by way of journalism in Nottingham and Fleet Street to his full career as a playwright and novelist. He satisfied a certain demand, which he did much to create, in the theatre of his day. The surface of his plays was garnished with a wistful humour, sometimes pawky, which lifted life right out of its normal drab colouring and made it rainbow-hued. As Denis Mackail showed in his *Story of J.M.B.* there was far more in Barrie than the escapist and wishful thinker, though it was largely through these qualities that he became so widely popular. There was a vein of hardness, almost of cruelty, which found expression in a few of his least-known plays. This was as much a part of the man as was the more attractive side of his genius. *Quality Street* (1902), an early nineteenth-century comedy, sentimental in the manner of *Cranford*, but tinged with great charm and humour, shows the author's remarkable knowledge of stage demands. *The Admirable Crichton* (1902) is one of Barrie's very best plays. The theme, which is that of the best man asserting himself in primitive surroundings, is treated with supreme tact and a mastery of presentation which does not fail until the last act. Two first-class one-act plays, *The Twelve-Pound Look* (1910) and *Rosalind* (1912) showed Barrie's mastery in this form and gave full play to the exquisite talent for light comedy of Dame Irene Vanbrugh. *Dear Brutus* (1917) is a sentimental but beautifully imagined story of lost opportunities. *Shall We Join the Ladies?* (1921), the fragment of a murder mystery, shows Barrie at his best, but it could never have been finished. The last play, *The Boy David* (1936), a version of the biblical story, is uneven, but in places very moving. It was not successful.

Barrie's greatest stage triumph is unquestionably *Peter Pan* (1904). In this piece Barrie achieved the extraordinary feat of adding a character to fairy mythology in the twentieth century. *Peter Pan* is a real play for children, to whom the central figure is now as familiar a friend as Lewis Carroll's "Alice."

It is too early to say yet how far Barrie's work is lasting. At the moment there is a reaction against whimsical humour and so his plays are temporarily under a cloud, always with the exception of *Peter Pan*, and in some nurseries he may be regarded as too delicate a creation for tough contemporary youth. Barrie's achievement rebels against classification, but it has made its mark in the theatre and, with the possible exception of A. A. Milne, no author who has attempted to imitate Barrie has emerged unscathed from the ordeal.

Barrie's other writings are less likely to survive. The most enduring are *Margaret Ogilvy* (1896), a biographical reminiscence of his mother, written with great feeling, and *The Little White Bird* (1902), stories of London children, in which Peter Pan made his bow.

To turn from Barrie to William Somerset Maugham (b. 1874) is to drop from the realm of fantasy to the hard earth. A highly successful and accomplished commercial playwright with a great talent for writing effective dialogue which is both witty and satirical, Maugham has written three plays which have both literary and dramatic merit. They have also affinities with Restoration comedy, possessing a glittering façade and an almost entire lack of feeling. These plays are *Our Betters* (1915), *The Constant Wife* (1923) and *The Circle* (1923), and they are his most convincing work.

Mention must be made of the dramatists who worked for Miss Horniman during her eventful tenancy of the Gaiety Theatre, Manchester, to which reference has already been made. It lasted from 1908 to 1921. The greatest publicity for Miss Horniman's work was obtained when a young Manchester man, Stanley Houghton (1881–1913) wrote *Hindle Wakes* (1912). This attracted widespread attention because it dealt with the unusual situation of a mill-girl who refused marriage with a man, economically and socially more prosperous than herself, because she thought that as a partner for life he would be thoroughly unsatisfactory, though he might pass muster as her companion during a holiday week at Blackpool. Magnificently acted by a cast which made the most of the Lancashire dialect, it created a stir out of all proportion to its merits. Two other Lancashire plays, *The Younger Generation* (1910) and *The Dear Departed* (1908), were also freshly written and unconventional for their period. Houghton's untimely death robbed literature of an interesting figure who undoubtedly possessed unrealized possibilities.

Harold Brighouse (b. 1882) knew the Lancashire scene and people as well as Houghton did, but after writing *Hobson's Choice* (1916), an entertaining play, he seemed to lose interest in the theatre, and turned his attention to other literary forms. Probably the most considerable of Miss Horniman's dramatists was Allan Monkhouse (b. 1858). Beginning life in a Manchester warehouse, he was taken on the staff of the *Manchester Guardian* as a commercial expert. In due course his flair for honest and discriminating literary criticism became widely recognized, and later he made a small reputation as novelist and playwright. He was prevented from obtaining wider recognition because of the austerity and over-economy of expression which characterized all his work. Of his plays the three best are *Mary Broome* (1911), *The Education of Mr. Surrage* (1912) and *The Conquering Hero* (1923).

Among the pieces which were given admirable performance by Miss Horniman's company, John Masefield's *Tragedy of*

Nan (1908) takes a high place. It is less popular now when a deliberately poetical treatment of a theme is out of fashion. Written in prose, with a poetical purpose evident in every line of it, the *Tragedy of Nan* clothes a sordid story of the Severn-side with a literary importance which the theme is hardly strong enough to carry. *The Tragedy of Pompey the Great* (1910), also written in prose, is a worthy treatment of one of the great events of history, which suffers a little from the author's delight in the short, direct sentence. In itself this is an obvious virtue, but Masefield has indulged in it so freely that the general effect of the play is mannered. It deserves revival. Masefield's later plays are experiments which have often only received private performance. He deserves well of the theatre because his contributions to it are always characterized by a thoughtful sincerity to which is added a tireless desire for sane experiment and sensible innovation. Numerous very young and very serious writers for the theatre would benefit by a study of Masefield's dramatic work. Its accomplishment and versatility deserve praise and notice.

Another poet, John Drinkwater, made an outstanding success with his chronicle piece, *Abraham Lincoln* (1918), which pro-bably attracted international interest because it is a play about a great American written by an Englishman. Drinkwater treated his subject soberly and competently. He was a man of the theatre and he avoided all the dangerous pitfalls, except in the rather platitudinous verses which were spoken by the chorus. *Abraham Lincoln* is an honest piece of homespun and no other play by Drinkwater met with similar success. A short war play in verse, $X = O$ (1917), has real beauty and is effective on the stage.

Drinkwater was closely allied with Sir Barry Jackson in his excellent work at the Birmingham Repertory Theatre, but no Midland school of dramatists sprang up round it, and Arnold Bennett (1867–1931), whose delightful *Milestones* (1912), written in collaboration with Edward Knoblock, was tremendously applauded, as was his dramatization of his novel, *Buried Alive*, called *The Great Adventure* (1913), never brought the Staffordshire people of his novels on to the stage.

G. K. Chesterton's peculiar blend of idealism and paradox found witty expression in one uneven play, *Magic* (1913), which nevertheless bears the unmistakable stamp of the author's genius.

As a dramatist, J. B. Priestley (b. 1894), won tremendous popularity with the stage version of *The Good Companions*, with which he was helped by Knoblock. Immediately afterwards he wrote his first play, unassisted, *Dangerous Corner* (1932), which is technically fascinating and flawless as a completely satisfying dramatic experiment. It has something in common with the "second chance" of Barrie's *Dear Brutus*, but the author's handling is entirely his own and the characterization is very able. *Eden End* (1934) has a North-country setting and some effective examples of dramatic portraiture. Flirting with J. W. Dunne's theories, Priestley has written several plays inspired by "time" themes. The best of these is *I Have Been Here Before* (1937). His most ambitious play, *Johnson Over Jordan* (1939), a modern pilgrim's progress, overweighted the writer, but it is deeply moving and has moments of true beauty. In it Mr. Priestley showed that he has the mind of a poet, without a poet's powers of expression.

Noel Coward (b. 1899) has an all-round talent for the theatre without compare and he also is an indefatigable experimentalist. After his immensely promising and amusing play, *The Young Idea* (1922), he wrote nothing of literary importance for some years. His deeply felt war play, *Post Mortem* (1931) has never been performed. *Cavalcade* (1934) is a remarkable panorama of English life in the first twenty years of the century. *Blithe Spirit* (1941) is a brilliant farce, which is by far the most polished piece of work he has done. Dealing with death and spiritualism, he manages to do so with such adroitness that he gives no offence and contrives situations at times so richly comic that they will stand comparison with those in *The Importance of Being Earnest*. The disciplined powers that he shows in this play may well foretell a richly fruitful phase of his maturity. Of his other light pieces, *Hay Fever* (1925) is the most satisfactory. *The Vortex* (1924) is a cleverly theatrical presentation of neurasthenics.

Until very recently, the intellectuals have not bothered themselves with the theatre. Aldous Huxley (b. 1894) wrote one promising play, *The World of Light* (1931), but since then he has not ventured into dramatic composition. It remained for T. S. Eliot to win a public for his *Murder in the Cathedral* (1935). Written for performance at the Canterbury Festival, this play, which George Sampson has rightly called a "modern exercise in the medieval manner," strangely lacks passion and deep feeling. The verse is arid but sincere. The story of Thomas à Becket had appealed to Tennyson, and it was found to have lost none of its compelling power when Eliot dressed it once again. Eliot's other plays, which, like his poems, seem to be exercises in proving to the author's satisfaction that almost any theme or blend of themes could be made to suit his poetico-dramatic approach, have not succeeded in proving this to the critics or the public. Some of the young writers who are his disciples have worked on the same lines, and two of them, W. H. Auden and Christopher Isherwood, working as collaborators, have written in *The Ascent of F.6* (1936) a play in verse and prose which is a real achievement, a highly satirical survey of bogus modern values and the abuse of publicity. It comes to grief completely in the last act, where the authors seem to have lost their sense of direction, but they have done enough for honour before the end is reached, and they may yet do great things for the theatre, if only they will discard obscure symbolism and wilful eccentricity.

In a short survey it is clearly impossible to mention the numerous accomplished authors who have had plays produced during the present century, but mention must be made of some of the more important of them. Before the last war, Cicely Hamilton wrote on feminist questions with authority and some success. Later, R. C. Sherriff in *Journey's End* (1928) and J. R. Ackerley in *Prisoners of War* gave us the two most effective war plays. "Clemence Dane" (Winifred Ashton) showed in her powerful and able *A Bill of Divorcement* (1921) the misery that can be caused by lunacy in married life and the law was subsequently altered. Clifford Bax has written several historical plays of which the best are *Socrates* (1930) and *The Rose Without a Thorn* (1931). There is more of permanence in these two dramas than in most of the work done by contemporary writers. They have beauty, poise and distinction in the writing. Rudolf Besier's *The Barretts of Wimpole Street* (1930) discussed the love affairs of the Brownings with dignity and sustained interest. Mr. Sutton Vane's *Outward Bound* (1923) handles death symbolically and with competent dramatic technique. In *French Without Tears* (1937) a very young writer, Terence Rattigan (b. 1912), showed that he could take a purely farcical situation and treat it with real dramatic accomplishment and gracious high spirits. Other dramatists who have done good and promising work include Ashley Dukes, "James Bridie" (Dr. Mavor), Reginald Berkeley, Lord Dunsany, C. K. Munro, Halcott Glover, H. F. Rubinstein, Gordon Daviot, Ronald Mackenzie, John van Druten and Emlyn Williams. James Bridie is an able and irritating writer, whose *Tobias and the Angel* (1931) is his one wholly satisfying play. With great powers of characterization and the ability to write effective dialogue, Bridie's most obvious weakness lies in his failure to develop a theme satisfactorily throughout a play.

It is too soon as yet to say much about a new kind of dramatic writing which has come to stay. Radio drama makes its appeal only to the ears. It is not always easy to distinguish between plays and "feature" programmes which often have a large element of drama in them. The three ablest exponents so far are J. B. Priestley, "Clemence Dane," Louis MacNeice and Eric Linklater, and there are others who have memorable and moving work to their credit.

It seems inevitable that a war should slow up the production of serious and important plays, but although no one would claim that we are living in one of the great periods of the theatre, the present era is full of hope and promise. There are able writers alive to-day who realize the essential demands which this form of writing makes, and who are not afraid to experiment freely and sensibly within it. The English theatre has been dying for a remarkably long time, according to the pessimists, and it is true that there are millions of young people who are cinema addicts and have never been inside a theatre. This competition is not in the least unhealthy. So far from discouraging managers, producers, writers and actors, it may well spur them on to fresh and more considerable efforts, and in those efforts lies the possibility of the future prosperity of English drama.

THE history of fiction from the much-discussed 'nineties to the present day is interesting but not heartening to admirers of this literary form. At the outset the most important feature was the appearance of the realistic novel, of which both George Gissing and George Moore produced notable examples. Gissing had a most unhappy life and he was not sufficiently armed against the arrows of misfortune to master the depression which pervades almost all his writings. Educated at Owen's College (now the University), Manchester, he makes the hero of his *Born in Exile* the product of a "new" university. *The Odd Women*, which came out in the following year, 1893, deals with the difficulties facing women without training and without income, as their lives are frittered away and there is no longer a possibility of marriage for them. By far Gissing's most popular book is *The Private Papers of Henry Ryecroft* (1903), a volume of reflective reminiscence, cast roughly in fictional form. It reveals Gissing's happiness in being able to escape the bondage of city life after years of poverty and writing to provide an income for himself. Curiously enough Gissing was inclined to make the most of his unhappiness. He would have attained higher stature as a novelist if he had not allowed himself at times to become obsessed by his misfortunes.

William Hale White (1829–1913), writing under the name of "Mark Rutherford", discussed the growing pains of the Dissenters in a series of admirably written novels. The best of these are *Mark Rutherford* (1881), *Mark Rutherford's Deliverance* (1885), *The Revolution in Tanner's Lane* (1887) and *Catherine Furze* (1894).

George Moore, the younger son of an Irish landowner, is an interesting and rather enigmatic literary figure. The history of his career is bound up with his search for a perfect style. In later years he rewrote some of his earlier books, robbing them of vividness and life in the process. His most notable novel, *Esther Waters*, was published in 1894. In its day this was as bold an essay in fiction as its contemporary, *The Second Mrs. Tanqueray*, was in drama. Moore was always experimenting, and it is only fair to say that he was often posing. His association with the pioneers of the Irish literary movement at the beginning of the present century gave him much of the material for his brilliant autobiographical trilogy, *Hail and Farewell* (1911–14). It is probably unfair to class this imaginative projection of Moore and his friends as fiction, but many of the characters portrayed in it have hotly denied that it is fact. It would be fair to call it a personal story and Moore is likely to be remembered by it, by *Esther Waters*, by the exquisite Irish novel, *The Lake* (1905), and by the long and carefully written Biblical tale, *The Brook Kerith* (1916). Moore passed from realism and the influence of Zola early in his career as a writer, and in his later phase concentrated as whole-heartedly upon the writing and construction of his books as did the older and more considerable artist, Henry James, the American, who honoured us by accepting the Order of Merit and also British citizenship at the end of his life.

The fiction of this writer will never be popular. He possessed a highly sensitive and acute intelligence. His work is finely wrought, too finely wrought for the taste of many perceptive readers, who feel that James interested himself too much in trifles. That is the great defect of much of his work. Born in America in 1843, a brother of the eminent philosopher, William James, he soon evinced a strong liking for Europe and the culture of the Old World. His early novels depict the impact of European life on the American mind, and prominent among them are *Roderick Hudson* (1876) and *Daisy Miller* (1879). James's approach to his medium was predominantly intellectual and analytical. He was concerned with the subtleties of the emotions, with the finer shades of conduct and behaviour, and in many of his novels there is a rarefied atmosphere which perplexes and provokes the reader who demands action in a story. There is no doubt that James excelled in what must be called for lack of a more concise term, the long-short story. He has left many exquisite examples of the storyteller's art in this form. *The Aspern Papers* (1888) is a lovely evocation of the spirit of Venice. *The Birthplace* (1903) comments shrewdly and humorously on a literary shrine and the wrong-headed intellectual snobbery which hovers about it. The loveliest of all his stories, *The Altar of the Dead* (1895), has the elements of great poetry in it.

All James's writings embody an idealization of the cultured life. They constitute an approach to a standard of humanitarianism which is too high to be achieved by any except quite unusual minds. These stories of James should be read slowly, discriminatingly. They are for the palate of the literary epicure. Among the novels, *The Turn of the Screw* (1898) and *What Maisie Knew* (1897), are two remarkable excursions into the supernatural. As his list of publications lengthened, James's style became more and more intricate and involved as his method became increasingly microscopic, so that most readers find his masterpiece, *The Golden Bowl* (1905), too subtle and protracted for them. It would be difficult to praise too highly the sincerity and integrity which inform all his work.

The same qualities are shared by a widely different writer, Rudyard Kipling, who was the first author of genius to bring home to the British peoples the immensity and diversity of their vast Indian Empire. Kipling's style is graphic, vivid, economical and forthright. The scents and colours of the Orient vivify his pages. His approach as a storyteller is as direct as possible. He was a very great Imperialist and, like Shakespeare, he did not hesitate to criticize his countrymen, though he did so usually by implication rather than by direct accusation. Like James, he excelled as a writer of the short story. Unlike him, he was quick to seize on the possibilities of the rapidly changing world in which he found himself. He found material not only in the tangled splendour of India and its many races and sharp contrasts, but also in the raw humanity and wisdom of simple people, schoolboys, soldiers and the like. He was fully alive to the almost endless possibilities awaiting the writer in the new machine age of which he became the prophet and historian. Born in India, and spending some years there as a journalist, his mind was trained to select the unusual and unfamiliar, which he presented to his readers in a form which they eagerly accepted. His quick, tireless mind turned also for refreshment to the best of English history and to the animal creation. The result is an impressive amalgam of different elements which makes his position as a writer difficult to estimate. It is only certain that he cannot be ignored now and that he is likely to be read far into the future.

Kipling's style, like that of James and of George Meredith, is almost impossible to imitate successfully. Its influence has been felt and shown more by twentieth-century journalists than by writers with more permanent intentions. Of his Indian writings, *Plain Tales from the Hills* (1887) and *Kim* (1901) are the best. The two *Jungle Books* (1894–5) and the *Just So Stories* (1902) are superb animal stories. *Soldiers Three* (1888–9) gives the author's highly individual idea of the British soldier. *Puck of Pook's Hill* (1906) and *Rewards and Fairies* (1910) contain episodes of English history, seen through his transfiguring eye. Perhaps the finest of all his short stories are *The Brushwood Boy* and *They*. They both have a supernatural element.

Like Rudyard Kipling, H. G. Wells (b. 1866) was quick to realize the possibilities of the machine age. In his first book Wells blended his scientific knowledge with fantasy, and during the 'nineties he occupied himself principally with romance and bold imaginative conceptions that showed a debt to the French writer, Jules Verne. *The Time Machine* (1895), *The Stolen Bacillus and Other Stories* (1895), *The Wonderful Visit* (1895), *The Island of Dr. Moreau* (1896), *When the Sleeper Wakes* (1899) and *The First Men in the Moon* (1901) were among them. As a boy, Wells's circumstances were humble. His mother was anxious that her son should reach the pinnacle of respectability to be attained by work as a salesman in a draper's shop. This proved so uncongenial that in *Love and Mr. Lewisham* (1900) and *Kipps* (1905) Wells wrote the first two of many sociological novels dealing with the life of the "little man," depicting the struggles of a sensitive mind in the uncongenial surroundings of modern industrial conditions. At this date unrest was in the air. Samuel Butler's *The Way of All Flesh*, a posthumous and devastating picture of some of the least happy aspects of Victorian family life, had appeared two years earlier. It formed a codicil to his two "Utopian" studies, *Erewhon* (1872) and *Erewhon Revisited*

(1901). George Bernard Shaw called attention to Butler's "fresh and future-piercing suggestions," and the beginning of King Edward VII's reign, now mistakenly regarded as a period of gross and complacent opulence, was in reality a time when heart-searching and dissatisfaction with prevailing conditions fully occupied many thoughtful minds. Wells, with his friends, Sidney Webb (now Lord Passfield) and Beatrice Webb, and George Bernard Shaw, formed the vanguard of this attack upon bad wages, inadequate living and industrial accommodation and indifferent education. Although Wells retained his interest in the progress of invention, he wrote voluminously in fiction and in other forms on the use and abuse of social and industrial life. He was especially concerned with the future of women. *Ann Veronica* (1909) dealt with the struggle of a girl anxious to "get away" from conventional life with no end in view except marriage. He showed the need for educating girls to earn a livelihood. His best novel, *Tono-Bungay* (1909), is a picture of the business world. It forecasts the decline of the landed aristocracy and the rise of the new ruling caste, the trade and newspaper magnates, with their craving for "publicity," their lack of principles, their often unscrupulous acquisition of wealth and power. This is the main theme, which with many variations Wells treated in a lengthy series of books. Frequently masquerading as novels, these grew gradually further away from the accepted idea of fiction. Narrative and story gave way to tremendous sermons, which conveyed the author's lively opinions on the subjects and problems which preoccupied him. Prominent among them are *The New Machiavelli* (1911), which contained the author's presentation of the Fabian socialistic circle with which he was associated; *The History of Mr. Polly* (1910), a diverting exercise on the "little man" pilgrimage, always so near to the author's heart; *Marriage* (1912), the adventures and fortunes of a reasonably prosperous young couple of more than average intelligence; and *Mr. Britling Sees It Through* (1916), which was Wells's fictional commentary on the last war.

John Galsworthy's approach to the problems of the period was conducted on very different lines. Galsworthy was an Englishman of the upper middle class, who had enjoyed a university education and was not without private means. Like Wells, he wrote easily and fluently, and he lived long enough to obtain an immense reputation at home and abroad as novelist and playwright. He is the historian of the class which he knew best. His mind was compassionate and sympathetic. There can be no question of his deep sincerity or of his desire for the welfare of his fellow creatures. His defects are a lack of humour and an over-facility in composition, and there is some want of consistency in the author's attitude towards his characters. This can be seen in his two main works, *The Forsyte Saga* (1922) and *A Modern Comedy* (1929). Each of these books is a collection of full-length novels depicting the vicissitudes of the propertied class over a period of about fifty years in the nineteenth and twentieth centuries. The title of Galsworthy's first novel, *The Island Pharisees* (1904), is sufficient proof of the author's satirical intention. As Galsworthy grew more familiar with the Forsytes and their circle, his critical attitude towards them became perceptibly modified. It is not to be supposed that when Milton began to write *Paradise Lost* he had the least idea that Satan would eventually become a creature who called for sympathetic treatment. Soames Forsyte, with his rigid code and stern marital demands, did not at first excite his creator's friendship but in the end Soames wins Galsworthy's suffrages and is by far the most memorable and living character in his novels. In his novels, as in his plays, Galsworthy gave ever-increasing scope to his dramatic sense with the result that although he was always a writer of integrity, he drifted unconsciously from the high ideals with which he had begun his career as a writer. The violent reaction against his great literary popularity, which set in after his death, may be temporary. A whole phase of English life is contained within his pages, and it is probable that posterity will not be satisfied until it has offered at least a passing salute to Soames and his relatives.

Enoch Arnold Bennett was Galsworthy's exact contemporary. He came from that great industrial district, the Staffordshire Potteries, and although he treated many aspects of English life in his novels, plays and critical writings, there is no doubt that he was most at ease with his own people. One of the most notable qualities that Bennett exhibited in all that he wrote is an unflagging zest.   He was a born journalist and diarist.   He had a masterly power in the use of significant detail and the knowledge that romance pulses in the most unlikely people and places.   Bennett had a curious inability to use humour in his serious fiction.   His two best novels are unquestionably *The Old Wives' Tale* (1908) and *Clayhanger* (1910), both Staffordshire tales.   So is his excellent comic fantasia, *The Card* (1911), which has given more pleasure to a great number of readers than either of them.   His increasing preoccupation with the mechanics of luxury was responsible for his exhaustive study of hotel life, *Imperial Palace* (1930).

Among the English novelists there is no more fascinating or enigmatic figure than Joseph Conrad, born Teodor Josef Konrad Korzeniowski (1857–1924).   He was a Pole from the Ukraine, in the south of Poland.   In May 1878 he first trod English soil, knowing nothing of the language.   In 1884 he became a master in the English Merchant Service.   In 1895 he published his first novel, *Almayer's Folly*.   This is an extra- ordinary record of perseverance towards the fulfilment of a long-held ambition.   Conrad himself said that "my faculty to write in English is as natural as any other aptitude with which I might have been born.   I have a strange and overpowering feeling that it had always been an inherent part of myself." Working in a foreign language, Conrad achieved a majestic, darkly brilliant mastery that stamps everything that he wrote. He was a poet among novelists, a tireless analyst of men's reactions when opposed to a fate best calculated to conquer them.   Most of his heroes are at grips with unseen powers as diabolical as those which confronted the protagonists in the great Shakespearean tragedies.   Above all, Conrad is a novelist of the sea, and his special interest was the men who went down to it.   Like Henry James, he excelled as the writer of the long- short story.   In addition to two magnificent books in the reminiscent vein, *The Mirror of the Sea* (1906) and *A Personal Record* (1919), Conrad's best fiction includes the three long stories published in *Youth* (1902), *Typhoon* (1903) and *The Nigger of the Narcissus* (1897).   His most ambitious and, in many ways, his best novel is the South American story,

Nostromo (1904), although it is overloaded with riches. Better known are *Lord Jim* (1900) and his first popular success, *Chance* (1914). *Lord Jim* allows Captain Marlowe, Conrad's narrator within the story, free rein, with the result that before the novel is over the reader feels that he is listening to a story-teller as tireless and pertinacious as Coleridge's Ancient Mariner himself. *Chance* is an example of Conrad's later method, when the hot and tangled splendours of the tropics had receded in his memory, and he was concentrating on the struggles of simple people against the world's infamies. There is far too much indirect narrative in this book and, like *Lord Jim*, its interest declines progressively towards the end.

Conrad was a great romantic, not in the popular sense of the term. Sir Walter Scott found romance in a Scottish child's funeral seen (and heard) at a distance across the snow. Conrad conjured up romance in the far places of the earth and sea, out of the perils and hardships of men, in the endless fight between man and the elements, and in the struggles of all poor, simple folk against the dark forces that beset them. His stories are of the stuff of poetry, and Browning has been cited as the writer nearest to him, but that judgment is of little import. What matters is that a Polish sea-captain in the English Merchant Marine grew to be a writer of fiction which turned men's minds away from the ephemeral problems of the day and out to the great eternal conflicts and verities, whose interest will endure so long as there are men and women left to read.

In a famous article on the novelists of the day, contributed by Henry James to *The Times Literary Supplement* in 1914, four "Juniors" were mentioned. No mention was made of J. D. Beresford, W. Somerset Maugham, Frank Swinnerton, E. M. Forster, or Oliver Onions, who had all written fiction ably.

Beresford (b. 1873) made his mark with the "Jacob Stahl" trilogy, three novels (*Jacob Stahl*, 1911; *A Candidate for Truth*, 1912; and *Goslings*, 1913) which dealt sensitively and capably with the life of a writer. *The House in Demetrius Road* (1914) is a haunting picture of alcoholism. The author has never touched the level of these four novels since.

William Somerset Maugham is a realist, with a cynical

turn of mind. Widely read, an admirer of French literature at its best and most economical, Maugham is also a
great traveller. Sparing in his use of words and scrupulously
economical in his use of emotion, he is a master of the prose of
narrative and dialogue. Plays, novels, travel books and short
stories have come from his pen, and are almost all of them
carefully fashioned and invariably well written. More than
most novelists Maugham draws on reality. "I think indeed,"
he wrote, "that most novelists, and surely the best, have
worked from life." His autobiographical novel, *Of Human
Bondage* (1915), is particularly direct and forthright. The skill
of the narrative is veiled by a deceptive simplicity and, like all
this author's writings, has a convincing air of realism about it.
Long, ambitious, and consistently readable, it is the best of his
novels. The admirable East Indian tale, *The Narrow Corner*
(1932), is almost as impressive. The Malayan short stories are
so cleverly wrought that their unfair emphasis on the weaker
side of human nature is not at first realized. This is the aspect
of life which has a strong fascination for this writer. His quiet,
low-toned expository method can point a cynical anecdote to
perfection, and he has an eye that never fails him for the
essentials of background. Most of Maugham's short stories
have been collected in one volume, entitled *Altogether*.

Edward Morgan Forster (b. 1879), James Joyce (b. 1882),
with Virginia Woolf (1882–1941) and Aldous Huxley, are the
four novelists who have exercised the greatest influence on and
have evoked the loudest plaudits from their younger contemporaries and from intellectual circles on both sides of the
Atlantic. Of the four Forster alone emerged as a full-fledged
novelist before the last war, when five of his seven books
of fiction had already been written. Like Maugham, Forster
writes precisely, but he is a more conscious and fastidious
writer, whose creative impulse is not a very strong one. He is
obviously more interested in life and letters than in the writing
of fiction, and it is curious that he should have attained such a
considerable reputation as a novelist on the strength of his
actual performance. Unquestionably he has great qualities as
a creator of character, within rather narrow limits. His
cultured spinsters, undergraduates and Anglo-Indians are

extremely well done, but the general impression produced on the reader is that Forster finds it rather tiresome to tell a story, and that he is entirely in his element when he is writing, as in the fascinating collection of literary essays, *Abinger Harvest* (1936), about books or people or cultural subjects untrammelled by the bonds that the discipline of the novel involves. When he attempts action he often achieves melodrama, but as a subtle and mischievous commentator on a relatively small cross-section of life he is outstanding.

The career of Oliver Onions (b. 1873) as a novelist is disappointing. He is a grim and forceful writer whose most complete success is the short novel, *In Accordance with the Evidence* (1912), which hinges on a successful and highly ingenious murder. A collection of eerie short stories, *Widdershins* (1911), reveals another aspect of his considerable talent.

It has been stated that Henry James selected four young novelists for special recognition in 1914. These were Compton Mackenzie, Hugh Walpole, Gilbert Cannan and D. H. Lawrence. They were all published by an enterprising newcomer, Martin Secker, whose influence upon early twentieth-century literature will be assessed one day at its proper value. Of the four there is no doubt that Compton Mackenzie (b. 1883) is the most remarkable personality, but it cannot be said that he has yet fulfilled the promise of his earlier performance. Beginning with a consistent pastiche of eighteenth-century life, *The Passionate Elopement* (1911), Mackenzie followed it up with a colourful novel of the theatre, *Carnival* (1912), which slipped towards its close into unconvincing melodrama. This was succeeded by his ambitious and vivid autobiographical story, *Sinister Street* (1913–14), and an appendage, *Guy and Pauline* (1915), which has often been praised as his most completely satisfying work of fiction.

In those early days Mackenzie's style was exuberant and glittering, but not sufficiently so to divert the reader's attention from the author's close and truthful reconstruction of the childhood, adolescence and youth of a sensitive young man at the beginning of the century. Few writers have portrayed public-school and university life so convincingly, and he is unrivalled as the delineator of the London *demi-monde* of the same period.

These novels show their author as an exponent of romantic realism and at the time he seemed to have a great literary future before him, but the first German war had a disruptive effect upon his talent. It also modified his romantic attitude towards life. *The Adventures of Sylvia Scarlett* (1918–19) is a further exercise in the *demi-mondaine* life, which the author prefers to his earlier novels, but there is a combination of sordid realism and farce in it which does not appeal so strongly because the author has not subjected his material to the process of transmutation which was at work so effectively in the other novels mentioned. Mackenzie has written many novels and books of reminiscence since, but he has never entirely fulfilled his first promise, probably because his interests are widespread and his talents are unusual and many-sided. He is a master of convincing farce, as he showed in a recent novel, *The Red Tape Worm* (1940), surely one of the funniest books of the century. A tremendous novel, *The Four Winds of Love* (1937–42), based on the period treated in *Sinister Street*, is in course of publication now, but although it has touches of the old magic it is diffuse and often unreal. Mackenzie is still young enough to write a novel in which he can harness his numerous talents and drive them as a team. Given a unifying control, it would be difficult to put a limit to the possibilities of this fascinating and sometimes irritating writer.

Sir Hugh Walpole (1884–1941) was one of the most deceptive of contemporary novelists. He wrote easily and with great confidence. He was influenced patently by fellow craftsmen. In the first stages of his career he went to school to Hawthorne, Henry James and Conrad. Later the similarity between his Polchester and Trollope's Barchester provoked a gratified chorus of recognition from the critics. They found it less easy to identify the sources from which Walpole drew inspiration for his "Herries" series, though the Waverley novels was clearly among them. A curious vein of cruelty was likely to obtrude itself in anything Walpole wrote. He professed himself unable to account for this, but it was in all probability derived from a period of exquisite unhappiness which he underwent as a small schoolboy, when his parents were away from England. Success is frequently belittled by professional literary critics.

Greeted at the outset by a chorus of approval from those eager
to be among the first to hail a young novelist who had been
recognized by James, Walpole's obstinate success provoked
sneers from writers who would have given a great deal to be in
his shoes.

Mr. Perrin and Mr. Traill (1911), a study of hatred in the
senior common room of a public school, has been acclaimed as
his best novel, and within its narrow limits it is completely
satisfying, but it is not as important as the first of two Russian
novels, *The Dark Forest* (1916), for which Walpole was able to
draw upon personal experience. *Fortitude* (1913) was praised
for its exaltation of courage in life, and it is to-day a very readable if rather melodramatic story with a picturesque background of Cornish and London life.

The Green Mirror (1918) has a similar setting and is more
ably constructed than its predecessor. Walpole's great natural
gifts as a storyteller were shown on a more ambitious scale in
his best-known novel, *The Cathedral* (1922). The hand of
Trollope lies heavy here, but the zest and the unflagging, if
mechanical, invention are Walpole's own, and there is an
infusion of the macabre which Trollope only attempted once,
in the death of Mrs. Proudie. Like other of Walpole's stories,
The Cathedral carries conviction when it is read, such is the
author's gift for narrative, but it does not bear reflection. It
owes its fame to the admirable fusion which the author
achieved of his own experience of close and cathedral life with
his knowledge of the Barsetshire novels of Trollope. The less
ambitious novel, *The Old Ladies* (1924), is artistically a greater
success. In his "Jeremy" stories, Walpole wrote with great
charm and understanding of children. His most ambitious
achievement is *The Herries Chronicle* (*Rogue Herries*, 1930;
Judith Paris, 1931; *The Fortress*, 1932; *Vanessa*, 1933).

When he was sitting in the muddy trenches near the Car-
parthians, during the last war, Walpole envisaged an English
chronicle "that would stretch without break from the days of
Elizabeth to our modern times." *The Herries Chronicle*
embodies the latter half of this vision, and *The Bright Pavilions*
(1940), set in Elizabethan days, is the first of four novels, three
of which the author did not live to write. They were to com-

plete this vast chronicle. To contemplate such a project indicates beyond fear of contradiction that Walpole was not afraid to attempt a great theme on the grand scale. Neither did he shirk from introducing real personages into his book, as Thackeray had done before him. Walpole's method in these Herries stories followed that of Scott. There is no attempt to dissect the characters. This spacious conception is an essay in the historical novel of tradition, "a loose, narrative, colloquial tradition" Walpole termed it. The Cumbrian background, beautifully painted, bears witness to another of the author's enthusiasms. Cumberland supplanted Cornwall and London in Walpole's affections.

There can be no doubt of Walpole's natural gift for fiction. He did not plumb the depths, but he knew what was significant and suitable for his purpose, and he wrote with a zest which carries the reader with him. The danger lay in his own enthusiasm and he did not always perceive it. He was not self-critical and did not easily tolerate criticism from others, although his native generosity often made him applaud and help the work of others, much less competent than himself, who wrote harshly about him. Time alone can decide the ultimate worth of his writings. That they have already given delight to thousands is evident. His books on Conrad and Trollope show that his own critical standards were scrupulous and high.

The third of James's promising novelists, Gilbert Cannan (b. 1884), has not been able to write since 1923 owing to illness, but he published no fiction of importance after 1918. Beginning as a disdainful realist of the Manchester school, Cannan achieved his greatest success with his third novel, *Round the Corner* (1913), a study of family life, vivacious, provocative and full of the author's opinions on many subjects. In his succeeding novels Cannan showed signs of the complaint from which H. G. Wells has suffered, the tendency to allow digressions and sermonettes to swamp the main purpose of the novel. Of his later books, *Mendel* (1916), the story of a painter, and *The Stucco House* (1918) are the best.

One of the most discussed of modern authors, D. H. Lawrence (1885–1930), is the last of James's quartet, and he was chosen unwillingly by James, who did not like his work.

Later generations may well find it hard to understand the immense veneration and equally strong antagonism which Lawrence roused in his lifetime. The son of a Nottinghamshire miner, he never seems to have been able to forget the grudge which he owed to his Creator for his humble birth. In fact he was more fortunate than millions. His mother was a remarkable woman whom her son adored. Lawrence was able to take a teacher's training course at Nottingham, taught for a little, and then soon made a reputation among the intellectuals by the publication of his early novels, *The White Peacock* (1911) and *The Trespassers* (1912). He reached his summit with *Sons and Lovers* (1913), an autobiographical novel of his own life up to his mother's death. After that his talent as a novelist fell away and he never regained it. The most suspicious and sensitive of men, Lawrence, who suffered from tubercular trouble, is almost determinedly unhappy and uneasy in his writings. His descriptive gift was immense, but he had little new to say in fiction, and the only reason that he was greeted as a prophet of a new way of living is that he showed the strongest possible conviction in his own views and opinions, which he reiterated loudly and, let it be admitted, vulgarly. Some of his travel books on Mexico and the Mediterranean show him at his best as a descriptive writer. He earned notoriety for *Lady Chatterley's Lover* (1928), a bad novel, made unusual by the use of impolite epithets and terms which contribute nothing to the story and only expose the weakness of its author's method. The best of this book, like the best of Lawrence's other writings, lies not in excursions into pseudo-psychology or eroticism, about which Lawrence was a perfectly honest and rather muddled thinker, but in his evocations of natural beauties, forthright narrative and descriptive pieces. His *Letters* will probably be read long after his novels, with the exception of *Sons and Lovers*, are forgotten. He could be a great writer but never for more than a chapter or two at a time. His temperament and peculiarly subjective approach to fiction prevented him from becoming a great novelist.

Francis Brett Young (b. 1884), like Lawrence, has something of the poet in him. A doctor, he has written with great conviction of his profession in *My Brother Jonathan* (1928), and this book, with the pleasant and leisurely picture of country life, *Portrait of Clare* (1927), forms his principal contribution to English fiction. Primarily a novelist, Young has no special message for his time and has, therefore, been neglected by the critics who have found him difficult to appraise. His other novels are uneven in quality and he betrays a tendency to repeat himself. The two novels mentioned rank among the best of their time. Brett Young has vision, a sane view of life, and an obvious regard for all that is best in the traditional English way of living.

Frank Swinnerton (b. 1884), well known as novelist, literary historian and critic, sat at the feet of Arnold Bennett and of the *Manchester Guardian* school of critics and journalists. By far his best novel is the justly praised *Nocturne* (1917), which is a beautifully conceived and executed miniature. In 1935, Swinnerton published *The Georgian Literary Scene*. This survey of his contemporaries, many of them known personally to him, has been consistently underrated by critics who were unable to understand Swinnerton's gay and honest approach to his subject. His autobiography, *Swinnerton* (1937), also contains interesting and useful sidelights on the literary world of the present century, which Swinnerton knows as well as any living man of letters, having worked in it as author, critic and publisher.

The twentieth century has seen an enormous increase in the number of women writers of fiction, and although many of them have made considerable reputations for themselves in their lifetime and some have been the victims of indiscreet adulation from small and temporarily powerful critical cliques, it is safe to say that there is no novelist of the first eminence among them. Elizabeth, Countess Russell (1866–1941) was an exponent of precise and lively irony, who did not disdain farce if it suited her purpose. At times she wrote beautifully. As humour seems always to be suspect among the critical panjandrums, she has never received the *réclame* to which her writings have entitled her. *Elizabeth and Her German Garden* (1898) established her popularity firmly with the reading public, and she maintained a high standard with her other novels over a period of forty years. Her early married life in

I

Germany filled her with a hearty dislike of the German people, whom she trounces with tremendous high spirits in *The Caravaners* (1909). Her last book, *Mr. Skeffington* (1940), shows that at the end of her life her talents were unimpaired.

The Irish stories of E. Œ. Somerville (b. 1861) and "Martin Ross" (Violet Florence Martin, 1862–1915) present a cheerful, unpretentious picture of a phase of Irish life that is over now. These collaborators wrote excellent English and they had a first-rate eye for the humours of hunting and country life. Their best books are *The Real Charlotte* (1894), *Some Experiences of an Irish R.M.* (1899), *Further Experiences of an Irish R.M.* (1908), and *In Mr. Knox's Country* (1915). "Martin Ross" wrote an excellent book of autobiographical essays, *Some Irish Yesterdays* (1906). Since Miss Martin's death, Miss Somerville has continued to write Irish novels, under the style of the collaboration, but these later books lack the exuberance and finish of those already mentioned.

A contemporary of these two writers and a delightful chronicler of the humours of village and country-house life, S. Macnaughten (1860?–1916), achieved her greatest success with *A Lame Dog's Diary* (1905), a later *Cranford*, marred a little by occasional descents into sentimentality, but true and convincing on the whole. Elizabeth Robins, well known also as an actress, wrote a number of thoughtful novels of which *The Magnetic North* (1904) deserves to be remembered.

The two women who obtained the highest critical regard in the early nineteen-hundreds were Edith Wharton (1862–1937), a careful disciple of Henry James, and May Sinclair (b. 1879), an earnest and strenuous writer, who has not been afraid to experiment. In 1914 May Sinclair published a novel, *The Three Sisters*, in which she took the Brontës for her subject. In the same year appeared her critical and biographical study, *The Three Brontës*. Miss Sinclair's writings have all had a strong psychoanalytical bias, not always to their advantage. The best of them is a short novel, *The Life and Death of Harriet Frean* (1922), remarkable for its economy of means and for an impressionistic method which may have owed something to Dorothy Richardson who, between 1915 and 1931, published ten novels, all parts of an immense work, *Pilgrimage*, devoted to the inner consciousness of the heroine. This is generally readable, but it does not produce in the reader an overwhelming impulse to go on reading. Extremely happy in its best moments of character revelation, it cannot be said that *Pilgrimage* shows in its author an irresistible urge of creation. It is more like a swollen commonplace book than an authentic novel.

Mary Webb (1883–1927) sprang into sudden popularity as the result of a mention of her work made by Earl Baldwin when he was Prime Minister. In *Precious Bane* (1924) and her other novels she wrote of the Worcestershire–Shropshire border country, which she knew thoroughly well. Her rustics are almost as convincing as Thomas Hardy's, and she had a true insight into the humours and tragedies of rural life. Her own integrity is evident in all that she wrote, but her style is mannered and sometimes over-intense. This blinded some to her very real merit. In a foreword to *Precious Bane*, Mrs. Webb wrote: "When antique things are also country things, they are easier to write about, for there is a permanence, a continuity in country life which makes the lapse of centuries seem of little moment." Firmly convinced of the importance of what she set out to do, Mrs. Webb succeeded in impressing a great many readers with the feeling that her books worthily caught and embodied material worthy of an able pen.

Constance Holme, whose works have earned the coveted honour of inclusion in the World's Classics series, has written eight straightforward novels, mainly about her native Westmorland. She also is a very sincere writer, but it is difficult to account for the tribute which has been paid to her.

The war of 1914–18 had little visible effect upon fiction, either at the time or afterwards. No great English war novel was written then or has been written since. In addition to those already mentioned, Wilfred Ewart's (1892–1922) *Way of Revelation* (1921), A. P. Herbert's (b. 1890) *The Secret Battle* (1919), a beautifully told and tragic story, J. B. Morton's (b. 1893) *The Barber of Putney* (1919), and *Peter Jackson, Cigar Merchant* (1919), a good example of popular fiction, by Gilbert Frankau (b. 1884), all deserve commendation. R. H. Mottram (b. 1883), a young Norfolk banker, began his career as a novelist with his *Spanish Farm Trilogy* (1924–27), of which the first part gave promise of possibilities which have never since been fully realized except in *Our Mr. Dormer* (1927), a well-told tale of a family bank in East Anglia.

Since the last war the history of the novel has not been a happy one. It may be that as a literary form it has had its day, though this seems unlikely. The fact remains that the post-war idols, E. M. Forster, Virginia Woolf, Aldous Huxley and James Joyce, have added little or nothing to the scope of the novel in spite of elaborate and sometimes tortuous attempts to do so. Virginia Woolf, a daughter of Sir Leslie Stephen, the well-known critic and essayist, was a subtle and consistent experimenter in the impressionistic form, much more discriminating in her approach than Dorothy Richardson has been. Her work has been likened by J. B. Priestley, to "rapid coloured films that have occasional moments of great poignancy," and the reader can have no doubt of her considerable intellectual ability. Virginia Woolf began her career as a novelist with a flying start. Her prowess as a thinker and talker were already acknowledged. There were critics ready to acclaim her first novel almost before they had read it. It is a fact too rarely noticed that few novels have obtained lasting popularity in this country which did not win considerable material success on their first appearance in print. The applause of a small but temporarily influential critical clique is not enough to establish a writer as an acknowledged expert in any form of writing, but it may influence public opinion over a period of years. Peacock, Meredith and James are three exceptions to this rule. Virginia Woolf will continue to be read by a number of readers not for her merits as a novelist but because she had a rare and subtle mind capable of catching and conveying delicate impressions in beautiful prose. Her two first novels, *The Voyage Out* (1915) and *Night and Day* (1919), achieve a definite pattern, but in her later fiction impressionism has clearly won the day at the expense of coherence. In *Orlando* (1928) the principal character experiences a change of sex in the course of the narrative. It would be impossible to define this book as a novel. It is a fascinating experiment which refuses to conform to any recognized type.

The creative power, the ability to present characters, was

never strong. When Mrs. Woolf allowed the strongly subjective side of her genius to take full charge, she was in her element, and for that reason her best book is *A Room of One's Own* (1929), a really delightful plea for women's economic independence, made in the academic atmosphere which was so congenial to the writer. In her two books of criticism, *The Common Reader* (1925 and 1932), she was most happily inspired. In fact, she takes rank without question as one of the few exceedingly good women essay writers. Time alone will show whether her reputation will ultimately rest on these three books and on other critical work which has yet to be published in book form.

Rose Macaulay has a mind more nimble and, perhaps, a little less subtle than Virginia Woolf's. She is both wise and witty, a poet with a very critical outlook on all human manifestations. She uses her great gift for satire with energy and verve. It is not her fault that, on putting down one of her excellent entertainments, the reader feels that he has been allowed to inspect a collection of diverting human oddities. It is the writer's habit of mind which seizes on the ludicrous and mocks it with a fine perception of what human values ought to be and most emphatically are not. If Rose Macaulay were ever to abandon her aloof attitude to novel writing and to concentrate her several talents within the framework of a single book, it might well be a memorable and enduring piece of literature.

It seems unlikely that James Joyce (1882–1941) will continue to enjoy the adulation which was showered upon him by critics who were obviously anxious to be regarded as heralds of the new dawn of fiction when *Ulysses* (1922) first appeared. A book of verse, a volume of sketches, and *A Portrait of the Artist as a Young Man* (1922) preceded it. The last-named is a conscientious essay in the psychological novel. It showed traces of the method which the author afterwards exploited for all and considerably more than it was worth in *Ulysses*, and in its even more unintelligible successor, *Finnegan's Wake* (1939).

Joyce was a musician. He had a remarkable sense of rhythm. He had read widely. He had an extensive and peculiar knowledge of certain aspects of Dublin life. He was very much a literary artist and experimenter. Unfortunately, he ignored one vital fact. A writer must conform to contemporary standards of intelligibility and comprehension. Joyce chose to disregard them. *Ulysses* deals with one day in the life of an Irish Jew who left his wife in the morning and returned to her at night, thus providing some small justification for the title. This brief summary gives no idea of the book's scope and contents. The "stream of consciousness" flows here in full and chaotic spate. Extraordinary outrages are perpetrated at the expense of the English tongue. It has been noted by one critic that Joyce tried to do "in printed prose what might be done by a combination of motion-picture and programme-music." No one can deny that there are flashes of genius in both books. They are both almost impossible to read. It is a relief to turn to the achievement of a novelist who has been content to use traditional forms.

J. B. Priestley is, to some extent, the victim of his own considerable versatility and of his immense success in various media. He has done well by fiction, drama, essay, autobiography and criticism. His most resounding triumph was won by the cheerful, happy story, *The Good Companions* (1929). At the time of its appearance the English novel was in the doldrums. Adventures in morbid psychology were the fashion and Mr. Priestley set himself deliberately to break down a vicious convention and went about his work with great enthusiasm. He assembles a small company of people, turns them into a concert party, and lets them loose over half England. It was an excellent device for his purpose. Humour, high spirits, and the belief that without courage and perseverance it is impossible to cope with life, animate every page of this compelling novel. Here and there the characterization is exaggerated, coincidence plays too large a part, and the author is too resolutely high-spirited. These are small blemishes on an excellent piece of work, which shows in many touches and descriptive passages examples of the essayist's habit of mind, which is a feature of Mr. Priestley's writings. *Angel Pavement* (1930), its successor, a more serious and ambitious work, is the author's most satisfying novel up to date, but his future is full of possibilities. For the work he has done already his reputation will probably grow rather than diminish. He would be a better novelist if he were not actively interested in many different literary forms.

The same criticism might be made of the work of A. P. Herbert, whose *Secret Battle* has been mentioned already. A humorist, writer of verse, barrister, M.P., libretto writer, he has written two other novels of some importance, *The Water Gipsies* (1930) and *Holy Deadlock* (1934). The *Water Gipsies* is a lively novel, full of well contrasted incident, set in London and on the English canals. *Holy Deadlock* is an able satire on the divorce laws which the author later helped to reform.

Exactly contemporary with J. B. Priestley, Aldous Huxley, member of the well-known literary and scientific family, seems to survey the contemporary scene with some of the detachment of Rose Macaulay. He appears to enjoy collecting oddities in his pages, and his early fiction, up to and including *Crome Yellow* (1921) shows clear traces of the influence of Peacock. An intellectual, very much alone in an uncongenial world, Huxley is an entertaining and provocative writer. He gives the impression of being uninterested in ordinary people. His three best novels, *Crome Yellow* (1921), *Point Counter Point* (1928) and *Those Barren Leaves* (1925) are full of brilliant conversation and stimulating opinions. Both of them are "menagerie" novels, exhibiting strange and remarkable fauna. Huxley is primarily a subjective writer, who does not appear to be greatly interested in the mechanics of fiction. *Brave New World* (1932) is a satirical glimpse into the future, which caused a great deal of comment at the time of its publication. As in the fiction of Virginia Woolf, the creative impulse does not seem to be strong, and Mr. Huxley's books are read principally for their author's thoughtful comments on men and things, expressed with a maximum of brilliance and wit. He is still comparatively young. His future development is a matter of considerable importance to English letters.

The last decade has witnessed a sad decline in the fortunes of the novel. Perhaps our race has grown less humorous than it used to be. Certainly it has shown a tendency to appreciate the portentous and the trivial, at the expense of the honest, the sane and the normal. The novels published during the period are, generally speaking, a reflection of the public taste. Loudly applauded by the intelligentsia is a newcomer, Christopher Isherwood (b. 1904), who can write with delicacy and precision and who is at his happiest when writing of the degenerate underworld of Berlin in the years which followed the last war. Best of his novels, *Mr. Norris Changes Trains* (1935), reveals a fascinated preoccupation with abnormal types. Some of his portraits are very cleverly done, but his books read more like slices of autobiographical reminiscence than original creative work.

Mention must be made of some other novelists who have written during the period. In the 'nineties, Mr. Arthur Machen (b. 1863) wrote *The Hill of Dreams* (1907) and other mystical stories. George Douglas's *The House with the Green Shutters* (1901) is a grimly effective Scottish novel. *South Wind* (1917), by Norman Douglas (b. 1868), is an interesting and amusing piece of Mediterranean amorality. James Stephens (b. 1882) wrote one delightful Irish fantasy, *The Crock of Gold* (1912), a sublime mixture of philosophers and fairies, and a short novel, *The Charwoman's Daughter* (1912), which gives beauty and humour to the Dublin slums. In 1917 Alec Waugh (1898) published *The Loom of Youth*, the most graphic story of public-school life to appear since *Tom Brown's Schooldays*. It was an extraordinary achievement for an eighteen-year-old boy. W. H. Hudson (1841–1922), the naturalist, published three works of fiction: *The Purple Land* (1885), a South American story, exquisitely set; *A Crystal Age* (1887), Hudson's contribution to the literature of Utopia; and the delicious *Green Mansions* (1904), the story of Rima, who became famous in another artistic medium. R. B. Cunninghame Graham (1852–1936) also had South American associations. His work is difficult to define, but he published several volumes of sketches, which may roughly be classified as fiction. Much of his best work is to be found in *Faith* (1909), *Hope*, (1910) and *Charity* (1911). Humour, beauty, irony and delicate colouring are to be found in these pieces, and the best of them may well be read for many years to come.

A number of contemporary authors have shown competence

in a variety of literary forms. Hilaire Belloc wrote several light political satires which have quality. Among the best of them are *Mr. Clutterbuck's Election* (1908) and *Pongo and the Bull* (1910). His friend and collaborator, G. K. Chesterton, threw off some stimulating fantasies, of which the best is *The Flying Inn* (1914). It contains some of the best of his lively verses. John Masefield is a most versatile writer. Nowadays the intellectuals are inclined to underrate him, but the fact is that his creative impulse in prose and verse is authentic and considerable, and he writes first-class narrative, quick and stirring. *Sard Harker* (1924) and *Odtaa* (1926) are tales of adventure which will thrill readers of exciting fiction for a long time to come. Perhaps the best of his novels is *The Bird of Dawning* (1933), a vividly realized picture of the China clippers, which has both pace and precision.

Another honest and able workman in this field was John Buchan (1875–1940), first Lord Tweedsmuir. His career was almost as romantic as his novels, of which the best is *Greenmantle* (1916), an exciting story of the last war. That he owed much to a fellow Scot, R. L. Stevenson, is certain. There may also be a debt to Sir Arthur Quiller-Couch (b. 1863), one of the most accomplished living men of letters, who showed in the immensely popular *Dead Man's Rock* (1887) and other stories that he possesses the genuine romantic quality. In *The Astonishing History of Troy Town* (1888), *The Delectable Duchy* (1894) and *Hocken and Hunken* (1912), "Q" established himself firmly as the best of the Cornish novelists. Writing a curiously archaic English, Maurice Hewlett (1861–1923) treated historical subjects with colour and animation in *The Forest Lovers* (1898) and other novels.

In recent years English fiction has shown a degree of technical competence and a lack of genuine inspiration. The public must take some share of the blame for this. If there are not enough novelists of supreme ability to supply the demand those who are available will naturally be called upon by publishers and readers to provide them with fiction. It must be emphasized that the creative impulse in fiction has not worked strongly since the war of 1914–18.

Richard Aldington (b. 1892), who showed promise as an

I*

Imagist poet, wrote one effective and vehement war novel, *Death of a Hero* (1929). His subsequent fiction has been much less impressive. Robert Graves turned from poetry and auto-biography to the composition of conscientious and carefully planned historical novels, of which *I, Claudius* (1934) and *Claudius the God* (1934) are the most satisfying. Graves writes strong, vivid prose and has vision. If his characterization was more memorable, there would be a future for these stories. Richard Hughes (b. 1900), who seems fascinated by meteorological vagaries, gave good examples of his individual talent in *High Wind in Jamaica* (1929) and in *In Hazard* (1938), a powerful tale of peril at sea. The Powys brothers, Llewellyn (1884–1939) John Cowper (b. 1872), and Theodore Francis (b. 1875), exhibited their psychological interests in some macabre studies of rural life, in which they showed narrative ability. William Mcfee (b. 1881) and James Hanley (b. 1901) wrote sea stories which are both exciting and authentic. Hanley's *Boy* (1931) is a terrible exercise in morbid psychology, and a haunting picture of unhappy boyhood. Forrest Reid (b. 1876), a sensitive writer, pictured adolescence in a series of novels, of which the best is probably *Pirates of the Spring* (1919). Graham Greene (b. 1904), one of the ablest of the younger writers, gave a vivid glimpse of the English underworld in *Brighton Rock* (1938). Charles Morgan, in one of his earlier novels, *Portrait in a Mirror* (1929), depicted shy and sensitive youth so ably that great things were expected from him. His later novels were overlaid with chunks of philosophy and mysticism, which seemed to indicate thought processes that were not altogether clear. This did not impair the novels' popular success. In a series of diverting and occasionally grim satirical novels Evelyn Waugh held up a mirror to the social follies of his time. *Vile Bodies* (1930), *Black Mischief* (1932) and *A Handful of Dust* (1934) are good examples of his engaging art.

A lively and unpretentious novelist, who wrote good, vivid prose, C. S. Forester (b. 1899), delights in tales of action, especially of naval action. *Brown on Resolution* (1929) was an early success. *The General* (1936) portrayed, without undue satire, one of those commanders who serve their country to its bitter cost. It is a revealing and truthful picture. *Captain*

Hornblower (1939), comprising the three novels, *The Happy Return*, *A Ship of the Line* and *Flying Colours*, is Forester's most ambitious work, and it is full of incident and sound characterization, but it is not as subtle a work as *The General*.

R. C. Hutchinson (b. 1907), a young novelist of undeniable gifts and considerable ambition, who is at his happiest in description and uses a large canvas, has not yet fulfilled the rich promise of *Unforgotten Prisoner* (1933) and *Testament* (1938). A. G. Macdonell (1895–1941) died regrettably young, and his death robbed the world of letters of a fiercely genial satirist, whose *England, Their England* (1933) poked fun and criticism in equal measure at many people and things south of the Border. His *Napoleon and His Marshals* (1934) is a colourful historical work. Wyndham Lewis (b. 1884) is both author and artist. He has written fiction and criticism. *Tarr* (1918) is the most satisfying and coherent of his novels, and it strikes an unfamiliar note. William Gerhardi (b. 1895) used a cosmopolitan background with ingenuity and resource in *Futility* (1922), *The Polyglots* (1925), and other novels.

Another Scottish satirist, Eric Linklater (b. 1899), wrote first a lively trifle, *Poet's Pub* (1929), then a serious and able novel, *White Maa's Saga* (1929). This was followed by *Juan in America* (1931), an excellent picaresque story showing a wide range of incidents and characters, which Linklater has never been able to equal since.

L. H. Myers (b. 1881) has written, among other novels, the fine trilogy, *The Root and the Flower* (1935), which includes *The Near and the Far*, *Prince Jali* and *Rajah Amar*. This is a leisurely and well written story of life in India years ago. A tetralogy which must be mentioned here is Henry Williamson's *The Flax of Dream*. This sequence of novels is idealistic, and sensitively written. Neil M. Gunn (b. 1891), who specializes in pictures of Scottish boyhood, has written with charm and authority in *Morning Tide*. R. C. Sherriff (b. 1896) presented two acutely observed studies of suburban life in *The Fortnight in September* (1931) and in the more mature *Greengates* (1936).

Two historical novelists, who have an eye for the romantic and can tell a story with point and fill in the background with authentic detail which does not impede the progress of their novels, are D. L. Murray (b. 1888) and Margaret Irwin. In *Regency* (1936), *A Tale of Three Cities* (1940) and *Enter Three Witches* (1942), Murray has written good, straightforward stories which show his powers of clear-cut characterization against a skilfully painted period setting. Miss Irwin is at her best in writing of Stuart times, and *Royal Flush* (1932) and *The Gay Galliard* (1941) are good examples of her honest workmanship.

Among the women novelists, E. M. Delafield (b. 1890) showed satirical ability in her early books, *Zella Sees Herself* (1917), *The War Workers* (1918) and *The Pelicans* (1918), but her most considerable and endearing work is her *Diary of a Provincial Lady* (1930), which gives a not unfriendly and invariably amusing picture of a country household, whose mistress, painted with careful self-depreciation, makes frequent appearances in literary circles. Miss Delafield is a keen critic of the pretentious and absurd. The *Diary* is much more important than are many more pretentious pictures of the period.

Miss Winifred Ashton ("Clemence Dane") began well with *Regiment of Women* (1917). She has considerable literary skill and a wide knowledge of human nature. The best of her later novels is *Broome Stages* (1931). Stella Benson (1892–1933), who spent some years of her life in China, created a strange, haunting world of her own in *I Pose* (1915), *Living Alone* (1919), *Pipers and a Dancer* (1924), and other books. A careful writer, whose impressions were always sharp, vivid and sometimes humorous, she wrote with tenderness and pity of the weaklings of life. Winifred Holtby (1898–1935), an able journalist and novelist, who also died young, had a radiant personality and literary powers, which only found expression in fiction with her posthumously published novel, *South Riding* (1936). Her charm and high spirits cannot be found in full measure in her novels, but the satirical *Mandoa, Mandoa* (1933) shows some of her sympathy with the unfortunates and her irony towards unimaginative administration. Margaret Kennedy (b. 1896) is remembered for her striking picture of a genius and his family in *The Constant Nymph* (1924), but she did not recapture in her later fiction the zest and creative enjoyment which she shows here. Elizabeth Bowen enjoys a considerable intellectual following and she has revealed a delicate talent for portraying human emotions, subtly analysed, in *Friends and Relations* (1931) and *Death of the Heart* (1938). Perhaps her best novel is *The Last September* (1929), with its nostalgically evoked picture of an old Irish country house. The descriptive work in this book is exquisitely done.

Among other women writers who have written workmanlike and, at times, satisfying fiction are Susan Goodyear, Storm Jameson, F. Tennyson Jesse, Rosamund Lehmann, Mary Butts, I. Compton-Burnett, E. Arnot Robertson, V. Sackville-West, Phyllis Bentley, Ann Bridge, E. H. Young, Sheila Kaye-Smith, Helen Waddell, Antonia White and Rebecca West.

When David Garnett's (b. 1892) first long-short story, *Lady Into Fox* (1922), was published, it was obvious that a new and delicate talent was maturing. His narrative of a fantastic transformation is told with a wealth of corroborative detail and strict attention to the business in hand. Unfortunately, this bold adventure in the fantastic could not be repeated, and in later books Garnett did not succeed in using subject-matter which proved as amenable to his method. Gerald Bullett (b. 1893) wrote good family-chronicle novels in *The History of Egg Pandervill* (1928) and *Nicky, Son of Egg* (1929). Louis Golding (b. 1895) convincingly depicted life in the Jewish colony of a north-country town in *Magnolia Street* (1932). L. A. G. Strong (b. 1896) is the author of a number of novels which are so good in places that it is difficult to say why they are so uneven. *The Brothers* (1932) and *The Last Enemy* (1936) show Strong's poetic imagination happily at work, and there is a lyric beauty in parts of *The Unpractised Heart* (1942) which is full of good promise for the future. Another poet-novelist, Richard Church (b. 1893), has written with confidence and sincerity of contemporary life, and *The Sampler* (1942) shows constructional ingenuity. Rex Warner (b. 1905), who has obviously been influenced by the German, Kafka, created an odd, harsh world in *The Aerodrome* (1941), which reveals him as an original thinker and a novelist of promise. Joyce Cary (b. 1888) has shown ability to understand the child mind in *A House of Children* (1941) and *Charley is My Darling* (1940).

Of the many American writers whose books are popular in

England now, Sinclair Lewis (b. 1885), Ernest Hemingway (b. 1898), Frederic Prokosch (b. 1909) are the most prominent.

Sinclair Lewis created an unforgettable character in *Babbitt* (1922), the simple, unimaginative, Middle-Western business man. The popularity of this book here proved that the type was not peculiar to the United States of America. In *Main Street* (1920), a story of a small town, Lewis's ironical pen was also very much at home. Ernest Hemingway excels in depicting the field of battle. There is plenty of romance and brutal action in his best novels, the memorable war stories, *A Farewell to Arms* (1929) and the less satisfactory *For Whom the Bell Tolls* (1941). Frederic Prokosch presented a strange oriental world of his own imagining in *The Asiatics* (1935).

Short stories in book form have never been popular in England, with very few exceptions. An American, "O. Henry" (1862–1910), managed humour and pathos with equal dexterity in a number of volumes which caught the public fancy over here. Recently, William Saroyan (b. 1908), who is more of an intellectual than "O. Henry," has shown in *The Daring Young Man on the Flying Trapeze* (1934) and other books that a new master has arrived, and in his adroit use of American idiom reveals once more that it is particularly well suited for the swift, laconic anecdote. William Faulkner (b. 1897), an irritating, powerful, and often obscure writer, gave a vivid picture of aspects of American life in *Go Down, Moses* (1942) and other collections of short stories. His genuine talent is increasingly threatened by his unconscionable wordiness.

At the beginning of the century, St. John Lucas (1879–1934) published two books of short stories, which had great promise. They were *Saints, Sinners, and the Usual People* (1912) and *The Lady of the Canaries* (1913). Some of these tales had a graceful irony which no other English writer has approached. *The Unfortunate Saint* and *The Little Friend of St. Hilarius* may owe something to the writings of Anatole France. They have a nicely pointed wit. Stacy Aumonier (1877–1928), writer, painter, actor, had a great sense of character and an ardent pleasure in odd types, coupled with an instinct for the dramatic, sometimes, unfortunately, the melodramatic, moment. His short stories represent a varied achievement.

Katherine Mansfield (1888–1923), who was at her best when she wrote about children, excelled in presenting a scene and the people in it. She did not often attempt to develop plot or character. Her short stories are curiously static, and can be wearying. She had a notable talent for description, seen at its best in *Bliss* (1920), *In a German Pension* (1911) and *The Garden Party* (1922). A. E. Coppard (b. 1878), whose approach was not dissimilar, attracted critical attention with *The Field of Mustard* (1926). He is an accomplished writer, whose stories do not linger in the memory. H. E. Bates (b. 1905) has a more varied range and can hit off the humours of rural life very happily, as in *My Uncle Silas* (1939). Earlier collections include *Thirty Tales* (1934) and *Through the Woods* (1936).

In *Some People* (1927) Harold Nicolson (b. 1886) made the dangerous and altogether successful innovation of introducing real people into his stories. This is a notable book, in which the author's urbanely polished style conveys exactly what he sets out to say. An incident in the life of Lord Curzon, *Arketall*, is one of the best English short stories. It is also a remarkable vignette of the statesman himself.

English readers have always refused to take their humorous writers seriously. It is difficult to understand why, as this form of writing calls for altogether exceptional powers in the author and gives very great pleasure and refreshment to the reader. Presumably, comic and lightly satirical stories are accepted by the public as trifles, which have amused the author as much as they have pleased his audience. This point of view is highly fallacious, as the amount of concentration, invention and resourcefulness needed by the writer to ensure success in this specialized form of composition is considerable. Kenneth Grahame (1859–1932) commands a wide following for his sketches of child life, *The Golden Age* (1893), and its sequel, *Dream Days* (1898), though his most popular story is *The Wind in the Willows* (1908), a fantasia of animal life.

W. W. Jacobs (b. 1863) depicted the humours of mariners and longshoremen of the Thames and of the countryside in a series of stories. He excels in the short tale and has an eye for a well-crusted character. Of his many collections of stories, *Many Cargoes* (1896) and *The Lady of the Barge* (1902) are representative. He has also written some peculiarly successful studies in the horrible, of which the best known are "The Monkey's Paw" and "The Well."

H. H. Munro (1870–1916), who wrote under the pen-name of "Saki," is probably the best English exponent of light humour and satire. Within sharply defined limits his sense of comic characterization and witty dialogue find entirely satisfying expression, and it is significant that his popularity grows with the passing of the years. *The Chronicles of Clovis* (1911) and *Beasts and Superbeasts* (1914) are the liveliest of these collections of tales, but in *The Unbearable Bassington* (1912) Munro essayed the satirical novel with considerable success. His death in action was one of the greatest losses our literature sustained during the last war. He was completely equipped for what he set out to do. His writing is informed with a deceptive ease and polish, which must have been the result of close thinking and remarkable concentration. If Munro had been a Frenchman his work would have been greeted with a chorus of applause on its appearance. He has had to wait until after death for the recognition which he richly earned. Future generations are likely to add to the praises of his brilliant work.

P. G. Wodehouse (b. 1881) couples great comic inventiveness with the ability to involve ludicrous characters in most amusing situations. His dialogue is all his own, crisp, unexpected, the very language of the larger lunacy. Wooster, Jeeves, Psmith, Mr Mulliner and others of his people have become part of the nation's humorous currency.

During the period the cult of the detective story assumed extravagant proportions. Sir Arthur Conan Doyle (1859–1930), the author of several sound historical novels and of one charming book of literary essays, *Through the Magic Door* (1908), created a demand with his Sherlock Holmes stories. Sherlock Holmes is one of the few fictitious personalities known to everybody, and his scientific approach to the solution of criminal problems paved the way for a host of fictional detectives with laboratories and elaborate equipment. G. K. Chesterton, in his "Father Brown" tales, mingled piety, high spirits and crime in his own inimitable manner. E. C. Bentley (b. 1875), also well known for his delicious biographical quatrains, produced in *Trent's Last Case* (1913) the best detective story of the century. Various other writers have brought true literary ability to the detective story, with the result that the novels of Dorothy Sayers, Agatha Christie, Josephine Bell, Ngaio Marsh, G. D. H. and M. Cole, Nicholas Blake, Margery Allingham, A. E. W. Mason, Austin Freeman, Freeman Wills Crofts, Francis Beeding, Francis Iles, Milward Kennedy and others, are appreciated by many readers who find a crime story uninteresting unless it is told by an author who pays careful attention to characterization and plot and is, in fact, a thoroughly competent novelist. Lord Peter Wimsey, Poirot, Inspector French and Dr. Thorndyke do not rival Sherlock Holmes in popular regard, but they have all become widely known and have deserved this widespread recognition.

Since the last war it cannot be said that fiction has enjoyed a widening of its functions or any outstanding practitioner. There has been a dearth of novelists possessing wide invention and first-rate powers of character creation. The immense popularity of autobiographies and travel books revealing in the frankest possible manner the author's habits, inclinations, loves and humours is a hallmark of an age spoonfed by irresponsible newspaper proprietors who have raised among the English reading public an apparently insatiable appetite for personal gossip. It would be too much to say that the decline of fiction is due to this new fashion. Whatever the reason, there is no doubt that at this moment the English novel is in the doldrums, and there is no sign as yet to show if or when it will emerge from them.

THE ESSAY

The eighteenth and nineteenth centuries both had periods when the essay flourished. The Romantic Revival at the beginning of the last century was a time of productivity in this literary form which has never been equalled or surpassed. Although it would not be reasonable to assert that the present day can provide the equivalents of Charles Lamb and Hazlitt it can be stated without reservation that the essay is flourishing to-day, although many excellent examples are tucked away in the pages of periodicals with small circulations and do not afterwards find a more permanent form.

In no other branch of literature, except honest autobiography and poetry, is it possible for the writer to get into closer touch with his readers. He must be frank about his tastes and aspirations, his hatred of cold veal, his love of apple dumplings, his hopes of Heaven, and his fears of Hell. Nothing is too trivial, nothing too important to figure in his confessions. The outstanding feature of the English essay is the frank intimacy shown by the writer, and yet he must always exercise the nicest tact in all that he says.

There is no doubt that the revival of interest in the essay in modern times was largely due to the great popularity of Robert Louis Stevenson's essays. On publication these won the acclaim of critics and public. Their style was warmly praised, and so was the author's avowed determination to find a suitable style for himself by imitating other authors. There is no inevitability about Stevenson's style. His essays are not easily identified as their author's work, except where his natural Scottish mother-wit and humour break through.

To succeed, an essay must be a part of the man who made it. His style must be himself and not a conglomeration of bits and pieces taken from other men.

Sir Max Beerbohm (b. 1872) has a prose style which is exquisitely his own. Delicately mannered, it is an accurate reflection of its author's personality. Educated at Charterhouse and Oxford, a contributor to the *Yellow Book*, an affected and aesthetic periodical of the 'nineties, Beerbohm's first literary experience was as dramatic critic to the *Saturday Review*. His first book, *The Works of Max Beerbohm* (1896), revealed him as an essayist of great ability but with a limited appeal. In "Diminuendo," one of the essays in this book, he sketched his life's plan. He would devote his life to contemplation, to a close scrutiny of the more sensational pages of the newspaper, and of any beauty and oddity that might come his way. Ever since, he has done so, and has recorded his experiences almost invariably with delicious and sometimes with devastating effect. Never has there been a less obviously didactic writer and never one with a more scrupulous regard for the accurate and even sympathetic portrayal of eccentrics, ranging from the fictitious Enoch Soames, an obscure poet of the 'nineties, who is commemorated in Beerbohm's delicious book of short stories, *Seven Men* (1919), to the remarkable Mr. "Romeo" Coates, who was "so fantastic an animal that Oblivion were indeed amiss. If no more, he was a great fool. In any case, it would be fun to have seen him." Beerbohm shows an Olympian detachment in these portraits, and not one of them is more delicate and memorable than the study of Swinburne and Watts-Dunton in "No. 2 The Pines" (*And Even Now*, 1920).

Beerbohm's talent is intensely personal, though he is never obtrusive. It is so personal that it is the despair of translators (just as Charles Lamb's is), and it is full of gaiety and scorn, urbanely and courteously expressed, for the pedants and drones of life and literature.

It would be an excellent thing for younger writers who aim at achieving effects of irony and satire to take lessons in literary deportment from Sir Max Beerbohm. He is an artist whose work at a first scrutiny gives delight. Further readings reveal nuances of meaning which increase the reader's respect and liking. *The Works of Max Beerbohm* was followed in three years by *More*, and later by *Yet Again* (1909) and *And Even Now*. Two high-spirited fantasies, *The Happy Hypocrite* (1897) and *Zuleika Dobson* (1911), in which the very soul of Oxford is captured, must also be mentioned. *A Christmas Garland* (1912) is prose parody at its best and wittiest. Beerbohm's collected dramatic criticisms read to-day as freshly as when they were first written in the 'nineties. Beerbohm is also one of the few people who have succeeded in making literature out of a broadcast talk. Although many writers wrote essays in the 'nineties, among them Augustine Birrell (1850-1933), whose graceful *Obiter Dicta* show that he was more at home in his library than in politics, there is not one of Beerbohm's contemporaries whose work has endured, although great claims were made for the essays of Alice Meynell on their publication. She wrote a very careful, studied prose, which had rhythm and contained the result of much scrupulous observation

Her works lack the touch of intimacy which is essential for success in this kind of writing. The personality of the writer must come through to the reader. Alice Meynell's did not—she was too reserved for this to be possible. Her essays are seldom heard of to-day, but they have merit, and with Jane Jewsbury (1800–1833) and Virginia Woolf, Alice Meynell takes her place among the scanty group of women essay-writers. England has produced no woman essayist of the first rank. Lord Grey of Fallodon (1862–1933) commented urbanely on literary and other topics in *The Fallodon Papers*. His small book on *Fly-Fishing* (1899) is a classic of angling. Earl Baldwin (b. 1867) is another politician who wrote finely in praise of his native land and of literature in *On England* (1926), and other volumes of collected papers.

Edward Verrall Lucas (1868–1938) is known as the bio-grapher of Charles Lamb (1908). His interests were wide and varied, and he wrote too abundantly and freely on many of them. The vintage was thin and did not keep well, though at the time of their publication, *Character and Comedy* (1907) and *Loiterer's Harvest* (1913) received serious and laudatory critical appreciation. Most of Lucas's work was contributed to the periodicals, whose pages have seen the work of the essayists to be noticed next. For many years Bernard Darwin (b. 1876) has written about golf in *The Times* and *Country Life*. His knowledge of Dickens and of other Victorian novelists is extensive. No one has quoted Dickens more aptly than he does. He can rival Hazlitt himself when he writes about games, and he has the tactful and intimate approach of the born essayist. His collected papers, *Out of the Rough* (1932) and later volumes, appeared mainly in the columns of *The Times*, but they are made of the stuff that endures. He has also written two delightful autobiographical studies, *Life is Sweet, Brother* (1940) and *Pack Clouds Away* (1941). Some years ago a critic referred to Neville Cardus (b. 1889) as the "Saint-Beuve of the cricket field," and it is true to say that he writes about cricket so that he will make a reader enjoy his essays who would make a detour to avoid a cricket field. It is chance and inclination which made Mr. Cardus a writer about the game. He is in grain an essayist and a literary stylist.

His *Days in the Sun* (1924) and *The Summer Game* (1929) rank in merit with Mr. Darwin's writings. Another journalist, A. G. Gardiner (b. 1865), wrote with charm, simplicity and good sense on life and literature. *Pebbles on the Shore* (1917) is representative of Gardiner's ability.

A delightful and most consistent essayist is Robert Lynd (b. 1879), though it is not surprising that one who has written an essay weekly for well over twenty-five years should only rarely touch the peaks. At his best he has charm, wit and urbanity, and is notably sincere. *Y.Y.: Selected Essays* (1933), is the best introduction to his work. Even more satisfying at their best are the essays of Hilaire Belloc, whose prose, when it is not marred by carelessness or restlessness or controversial violence, can be matched with that of any of his contemporaries. Widely travelled and a scholar of parts, Belloc has written many books of essays on varied themes. Among the best are *Hills and the Sea* (1906), *On Nothing* (1908) and *On Everything* (1909). Strongly opinionated though he can be at times, Belloc excludes his delight in controversy from many of his essays and his moderation in doing so is their gain.

Since the appearance of Sir Max Beerbohm he had no rival until the early nineteen-twenties, when J. B. Priestley, just down from Cambridge, began to write for the *Saturday Review* and afterwards for the *Week-end Review*. Priestley has established a reputation for himself in several fields, but he has done nothing better than the best of his essays. These are to be found in *Open House* (1927), *Apes and Angels* (1928) and *The Balconinny* (1929), and the author has collected a number of them in *Self-Selected Essays* (1932).

Priestley's approach to the essay is disarming. He depicts himself as a frank, guileless, ordinary chap, who likes his pipe, pint of beer, slippers, and a quiet seat in the corner. The reader who has not read *The English Comic Characters* (1925), one of the best books of critical appreciation in English, might conceivably be bluffed for a time by the author's oft-repeated protestation of his ordinariness. The illusion will not last long. There is a universality of appeal in these pieces which will not be perceptibly blunted by time. The range is wide.

In *Seeing Stratford*, Mr. Priestley wrote one of the most

perfect things of its kind that we have. After debunking the traditional approach to the literary shrine, all slow music and forced gravity, the author goes on in a final passage to tell where and how he found beauty and reality in Stratford, and this is exquisitely done.

In *The Mancroft Essays* (1923), Arthur Michael Samuel, Lord Mancroft (1872–1942) showed a flair for the literary pastiche and a curious erudition on such things as bells, pepper, coal tar and Norwich shawls. A mannered writer, he was a true essayist.

To conclude this section mention must be made of a curious by product of the essay which Logan Pearsall Smith (b. 1865) used in his *Trivia* (1918). These finely polished pieces, which mingle the qualities of the aphorism, the *conte* and the essay, have some happy moments, but it is unlikely that the author will be the founder of a new literary form.

XV. PROSE OF INFORMATION

BIOGRAPHY

IN common with history and autobiography, biography put on a brighter and more highly coloured dress in the new century. Lord Macaulay and J. A. Froude had paved the way, and although the scholiasts plodded along laboriously, and eulogistic two-volume "lives," which commemorated their subjects in piously misleading tribute, were still a familiar feature, there were signs of impatience among their readers. The tremendous Victorian reticence was wearing thin at last. It had become almost transparent. It only remained for some outstanding writer to pluck it cheerfully aside and then get on with the congenial business of idol-smashing or "debunking," a process which has been continuously carried on ever since.

The year 1886 saw the appearance of the *Dictionary of National Biography*, which was first edited by Leslie Stephen and later by Sidney Lee. It has now been taken over by the Oxford University Press. Factually, the *D.N.B.* is an admirable compilation. The English Men of Letters series, first under the editorship of Lord Morley and now under that of Sir John Squire, inaugurated the fashion for short monographs, most of them very well done. The E.M.L. series is sane, critically and biographically. The Great Lives series of Messrs. Duckworth, though less ambitious, has also these good qualities.

The century began solidly with the *Life of Gladstone*, by John Morley (1902), which has a cold clarity that is not endearing. The *Life of Disraeli* (1910–20), by W. F. Monypenny and G. E. Buckle, is a much livelier affair, possibly because the subject was more volatile and various a man than Gladstone. Sir Edmund Gosse published his *Father and Son* in 1907. This study of a clash of temperaments is a piece of enduring literature because the author realized as few Victorians did that life is an extraordinary blend of grave and gay. Philip Gosse, the biographer's father, was a distinguished zoologist. He was also closely connected with a dreary Nonconformist sect known as the Saints. His wife died young and Gosse had to bring up his young son without much help. Edmund Gosse is remarkably fair in presenting incidents which must have been almost unendurably painful to him when they happened. He has given an unsurpassably vivid picture of a cross-section of Victorian society. *Father and Son* is a model of intimate biography and of clever and unobtrusive construction. It is also a triumphant vindication of the selective method of biographical writing.

Lytton Strachey (1880–1932) did more than anyone else to change the face and the direction of biography in his time. Writing a clear, ironical prose, and possessing a keen sense of the ludicrous, Strachey wrote his first biographical work, *Eminent Victorians* (1917), at a moment which was ripe for the outburst of irreverence against Victorian idols. Cardinal Manning, Dr. Arnold, Florence Nightingale and General Gordon came in for some rough handling by Strachey, and there is no doubt that he provided a considerable public entertainment from which justice was excluded. Encouraged by popular applause and the discovery by the uninformed reader that historical portraiture could be positively amusing, Strachey went on to attempt a Life, which he intended to write on similar lines, but at greater length, of the principal Victorian, the Queen herself. *Queen Victoria* (1921) showed clearly that the biographer who had come to scoff remained to applaud, and Strachey, who thought that he had chosen a subject peculiarly well suited to his great powers of irony, had to admit that he had found his mistress. The book presents a remarkable picture of the Sovereign. There is plenty in it to amuse the reader, but he closes the book with a feeling that this little woman, though opinionated and not equipped with outstanding mental ability, was somehow a great Queen. Her strength of character compensated her for the qualities she lacked. *Queen Victoria* is the best of Strachey's biographical works. *Elizabeth and Essex* (1928) fails because the author was not able to draw on the wealth of material which he had to work on for his more modern subjects. He excelled as an ironical commentator on documentary evidence, and the evidence available for the Tudor period was not of the kind best suited to his method. The impression made on the reading public and on contemporary writers by *Eminent Victorians* and by *Queen Victoria* was immense. Imitators of Strachey's approach sprang up like mushrooms. Ever since the air has been loud with the harsh sounds of idol-smashing, and there is hardly an eminent historical or literary personage who has not suffered from the irony and ridicule of one of the tribe of Strachey. At its best the method has much to be said for it. History lives. Remote monarchs and statesmen and writers and men of war become human beings. They are stripped of their trappings and are not often very impressive without them.

Philip Guedalla (b. 1889), the most important of Strachey's disciples, is a historian of great industry and real ability. Apart from a rather tiresome tendency to overwrite, he has an excellent popular style, as is shown in *The Second Empire* (1922), *Palmerston* (1926) and *The Duke* (1931). This is a most moving and stirring book which gives a brilliantly sympathetic portrait of the first Duke of Wellington. *The Duke* deservedly takes a place among the best examples of English biographical writing. *The Hundred Years* (1936) is a study of international life at the time of the abdication of King Edward VIII. It is also an example of clever special pleading.

It was André Maurois (b. 1885) who, with *Ariel* (1923), his fanciful study of Shelley, set the fashion for a number of literary biographies. He also wrote an able *Disraeli* (1927).

Winston Churchill (b. 1874) wrote a good life of his father, *Lord Randolph Churchill* (1906), and twenty-seven years later embarked on a full-length study of his greatest ancestor, *Marlborough: His Life and Times* (1933–8). Mr. Churchill is equally a man of action and of words. He delights in the ceremonial parade of history. Probably he is a greater master of the spoken than of the written word, but his biographical talent is considerable. His interest in historical biography is shared by Hilaire Belloc, who has also touched life at many different points. He excels in the short biography, of which his best examples are *Danton* (1899) and *Wolsey* (1930). A staunch Catholic, his faith colours all his serious works. He is among the most able publicists of his day.

John Buchan, Lord Tweedsmuir, wrote some honest and readable biographies which effectively mirror his own widespread interests. Midway between the colourful works of Strachey and the scholarly arid monograph, Buchan contrived to be a biographer of ability with a reasonably popular appeal. The best of his biographical writings are *Sir Walter Scott* (1932), *Montrose* (1928), *Julius Caesar* (1932), *Oliver Cromwell* (1934) and *Augustus* (1937).

Harold Nicolson has shown himself an adept at literary and political biography. His works on Byron, Swinburne, and Tennyson are both subtle and engaging. The smooth surface of his prose conceals a pleasantly malicious humour and he has an evident pleasure in the eccentricities of the great which does not affect his admirable sense of proportion in dealing faithfully with them.

Professor J. E. Neale's (b. 1890) *Queen Elizabeth* (1934) is not remarkable for its style, but the author's learning and patient research have made this work the leading monograph on the subject.

Duff Cooper's (b. 1890) *Talleyrand* (1932) is a lively portrait.

His *Haig* (1935–6) shows that he was much less happy in dealing with a contemporary.

Among the younger biographers, Arthur Bryant (b. 1899) occupies an honourable place. His study of the life of *King Charles II* (1931) won him popular acclaim and a reputation among serious historians. His excellent life of Pepys (begun 1933), not yet completed, proves that there was much to be said about that remarkable man which cannot be found in the pages of his diary. Not only the man himself but Stuart London comes to life in these pages.

Evelyn Waugh (b. 1903), in a serious vein, wrote a strong monograph on *Campion* (1935). Lord David Cecil (b. 1902) showed great delicacy of perception in *The Stricken Deer* (1929), a study of the life of Cowper, which he followed with a sympathetic portrait of Lord Melbourne (1939). Peter Quennell's (b. 1905) *Byron: The Years of Fame* (1935) and *Byron in Italy* (1941) deserve mention, and so does the late E. F. Benson's (1867–1940) valuably informative *Charlotte Brontë* (1932). Christopher Lloyd filled two gaps on the library shelves with his careful and readable lives of *Fanny Burney* (1938) and *Captain Marryat and the Old Navy* (1939). One of the most accomplished of the younger biographers, A. J. A. Symons (1900–41), died after completing only one full-length biography, *Quest for Corvo* (1934), an elaborate and beautifully constructed study of one of the least admirable figures of the 'nineties. His short *H. M. Stanley* (1933) is a perfect biography in miniature. Fragments of the life of Oscar Wilde, upon which he was engaged when he died, showed that it promised to be the best of his writings.

The period has provided four examples of intimate biography which must be noted here. Virginia Woolf's sensitive *Roger Fry* (1940) is a discerning comment on an unusual personality. Vera Brittain's *Testament of Friendship* (1940) commemorates vividly and sympathetically her relationship with a remarkable woman, Winifred Holtby. E. M. Forster, in his acute and delicate study of *Goldsworthy Lowes Dickinson* (1934), and H. E. Wortham (b. 1884), in his too little known and altogether admirable *Oscar Browning* (1927), have produced academic lives which do not smell of the lamp. It was in 1918 that a *Manchester Guardian* reviewer in a notice of *Eminent Victorians* referred to this "unusually interesting volume in a department of literature which, in England, had fallen to a grievously low level." Two books which appeared in the early nineteen-forties, in addition to those which have been mentioned here, would certainly make him optimistic about the state of biography to-day. The complex personality and divided allegiances of Father Joseph, Richelieu's adviser, gave Aldous Huxley his first biographical subject in *Grey Eminence* (1941). A fascinating picture is painted of Joseph's varied activities, but the mystery of his personality is not solved.

The latest adherent of the school of Strachey, George Dangerfield (b.1904), shows complete mastery of his method and a brilliant handling of a difficult subject in *Victoria's Heir: The Education of a Prince* (1942).

Many other writers, Edith Sitwell, Rose Macaulay, Lord Charnwood, Lord Lytton, and St. John Ervine among them, have shown that they understand how the biographical art should be practised. In fact, biography in England to-day is one of the most flourishing of the literary forms.

AUTOBIOGRAPHY

One of the most marked features of twentieth-century literature is the development of the autobiography, due primarily to two causes, the increase in outspokenness and frankness of expression, which occurred naturally in the reign of King Edward VII with its more tolerant moral standards, and the growth of popular journalism with its never-ending quest for "personal" stories and tittle-tattle about the celebrities and notorieties. Lord Northcliffe, who founded the halfpenny *Daily Mail* in 1896, changed the tone of the Press. It has become increasingly a purveyor of news which aims at the literate rather than at the educated. The so-called education which so many English people receive does not appear to teach them to think and for the last forty years "tabloid" journalism has been in the ascendant. A growing preoccupation with other people's private lives has been one of its most marked characteristics, and for some years now the public has been informed of the condemned man's breakfast on the day of his execution and of the snug domesticity of a glamorous film-star's home. At the back of this fatuous and sometimes unpleasant prying curiosity there is a perfectly sound human instinct—the desire to know how other people, and particularly people in the public eye, live. Numerous writers have realized this, with the result that as the years pass autobiographies and reminiscences have tended to become ever franker and more revealing, and matrimonial and love affairs are described by participants in them with a minimum of reserve. Among a great many books which are completely worthless are to be found others which are important and are, indeed, literature. The autobiography has come into its own during the present century.

The year 1911 saw the publication of George Moore's entertaining literary autobiography, *Ave atque Vale*. Moore was an artist. When life did not give him the exact and exciting pattern which he thought was his perquisite, he would shape an unsatisfying experience and turn it into something undeniably readable and something which the author might well be proud to have lived through and subsequently to write about. There is no doubt that Moore subjected actual experience to a drastic process of transmutation, which kept his mind at full stretch as he compiled these Irish Nights' Entertainments. He realized the importance of being factual, and always conveys the impression of frankness and intimacy. He is not afraid of caricature, and W. B. Yeats, Edward Martyn and "Æ" all suffered at his hands. It would not be a great exaggeration to say that *Ave atque Vale* reads more like good fiction than any of the novels which its author wrote. In *Memoirs of My Dead Life* (1906) and other autobiographical volumes Moore adopted the same technique with success.

W. H. Davies's (1871–1940) *Autobiography of a Super-Tramp* (1908) is a poet's life-story which provides a strong contrast to Moore's elegant recollections by reason of its unstudied sincerity and simple style.

Autobiography written since the last war is closely linked

with journalism. When a censorship has been in operation for a prolonged period its removal naturally causes a scramble to exploit the new situation. The newspapers replaced the horrors of war by the horrors of crime and passion. The new frankness influenced the writers of personal reminiscence, but it was not until 1929 that Robert Graves really broke the post-war ice with his *Good-bye to All That*. This book seems to have unsealed the lips of other authors. Graves was thirty-four when he wrote it. He shows a remarkable detachment in relating most intimately the story of an eventful life. His book is both brave and honest. Before it appeared, two talented women had published autobiographical books. Dame Ethel Smyth (b. 1858) is an outstanding personality, and she writes as she talks. Female suffrage, music, friendship, copious letter-writing, games and sports, all play a part in her life and in her books. A full pleasure in life in as many of its manifestations as possible is the thing, and in *Impressions That Remained* (1919) she allows her many enthusiasms full play. It must be left to later generations to discover whether Dame Ethel excels as writer or as composer.

Lady Oxford and Asquith's *Autobiography* (1920) is vivid and imperious. The only claim she makes for it is "natural directness," but her life has brought her into contact with many interesting and eminent people and she is a formidable conversationist. Her book is matter for the historians and it is also good entertainment.

Thirteen years later, Vera Brittain published her much-discussed *Testament of Youth* (1933). In it she set out to do a clearly defined piece of work, to show what the whole war and post-war period meant to the men and women of her own generation. A certain lack of humour does not detract from a sincere, high-minded and accomplished piece of work. In 1934 Mabel Lethbridge wrote *Fortune Grass*, which has a claim to be considered the most remarkable autobiographical writing by a woman in English. To Miss Lethbridge life is a drama. At the age of sixteen she ran away from her Ealing home to be a nurse in a war hospital in Bradford. Subsequently she made munitions and had a leg blown off. Her career has been eventful ever since. Her extraordinary story would be even more effective if it was less melodramatic in the telling. With a little more restraint and literary skill this would have been a great book.

Dr. Axel Munthe's *Story of San Michele* (1929) has had a profound influence on writers who followed him. The brilliantly episodic autobiography probably inspired Halliday Sutherland's (b. 1882) *Arches of the Years* (1933) and numerous other medical autobiographies. Doctors and priests see more of human nature with the veneer off than anyone else does, and the strictness of professional etiquette in the past exercised a restraining effect which has robbed the world of many valuable books. During the last decade medical men seem to have been making up for lost time.

In a series of volumes of reminiscence dealing with his experiences in the Middle East during the war of 1914–18, Compton Mackenzie showed an agreeable shrewdness and humour, coupled with a welcome regard for perspective and great competence in characterization. *Gallipoli Memories* (1929) is as good as any of them. These qualities are also to be found in Mr. Priestley's *Midnight on the Desert* (1937) and *Rain Upon Godshill* (1939). They are not formal presentations of his life. Their form is elastic. They present experiences which seem to the author to be significant and important. Mr. Priestley convinces as a critic of life and literature because his standards are sincere and informed by his natural good taste.

Another man of letters, Howard Spring (b. 1889), excels as a descriptive writer. His *Heaven Lies About Us* (1939) is the narrative of his early boyhood in Cardiff, where his father was a jobbing gardener with a family of nine children. It is peculiarly strong in the happy expression of small and highly significant incident. Spring continued his reminiscences in *In the Meantime* (1942).

Equally sensitive in its depiction of sensitive childhood and adolescence is *Apostate* (1926), a book of reminiscence by Forrest Reid, the novelist.

H. G. Wells, whose varied literary and scientific activities have been so vast that they defy computation, wrote in *Experiment in Autobiography: Discoveries and Conclusions of a Very Ordinary Man* (1934) a record of his life, which completely disproves the title. It is as provocative as might be expected, but it is also extremely sane and closely reasoned. It is written with the greatest discretion.

E. F. Benson completed just a week before his death *Final Edition: An Informal Autobiography* (1940), which reveals an experienced and urbane man of letters at his best. As a detached and amused commentator on the social scene of his time Benson is unsurpassed. No writer has ever had a keener perception of the ludicrous than he had. He commemorated Edwardian extravagances as no one else has done, and *Final Edition* and *As We Were* (1930) provide a rich quarry for the social historian.

Freshness and zest are the outstanding merits of Hugh Walpole's *Roman Fountain* (1940). This autobiographical fragment allows the writer to discuss some eventful personal experiences with sane self-criticism and lively revelation. It provides an interesting contrast to the Poet Laureate's *In the Mill* (1940), an austere record of the writer's early life in America.

The great number of contemporary authors who have practised the autobiographical form makes it impossible to consider them in detail, but the names of the more prominent must be mentioned. Winston Churchill, Somerset Maugham, Arthur Waugh, Clifford Bax, Rudyard Kipling, Eric Gill, Lord Berners, Air-Commodore L. E. O. Charlton, George Orwell, F. Yeats-Brown, B. L. Coombs and Christopher Isherwood have all written important books in this form. Isadora Duncan's reminiscences pulse with the energy of an astonishing personality.

It is not unfair to say that with the prevailing standards of frankness and outspokenness we may expect in the near future many more autobiographies which will enlarge men's knowledge of the varieties of human experience.

HISTORY

It is one of the curiosities of literature that in spite of the excellent example set by Macaulay, Motley, Prescott, Napier and others, numerous nineteenth-century historians churned out a drab and muddy stream of historical fact without paying the slightest attention to the presentation of material or to literary style.

The greatest historical achievement of this century has been the publication of the great Cambridge Histories, forty volumes by different expert hands dealing fully with Ancient, Medieval and Modern History. They are not remarkable for literary accomplishment. The Cambridge History of English Literature, edited by Sir Adolphus William Ward (1837–1924) and Alfred Rayney Waller (1867–1922), must also be mentioned here. It is the only great, full-length treatment of English literature in existence, and in *The Concise Cambridge History of English Literature* George Sampson (b. 1873) has boiled down its contents and brought the record almost up to date in a book of 1,092 pages, which is a little masterpiece of compression, graced by wit and wisdom.

James, Viscount Bryce (1838–1922) wrote his best-known work, *The Holy Roman Empire*, when he was only twenty-six, and it has remained in popular favour ever since. His other standard work, *The American Commonwealth* (1888), was revised in 1920. His style is clear and forthright but has no special distinction.

Industrial problems which formed an unpleasant legacy from the Victorian era are discussed in three volumes by J. L. Hammond (b. 1872) and his wife, Barbara Hammond (b. 1873). These are *The Village Labourer, 1760–1832* (1911), *The Town Labourer, 1760–1832* (1917) and *The Skilled Labourer, 1760–1832* (1919). They carry on their history in *The Rise of Modern Industry* (1925) and *The Age of the Chartists* (1930).

The fame of Sidney Webb, Lord Passfield (b. 1859) and his wife, Beatrice Webb (b. 1858) is already almost legendary. Their achievement consisted largely in their great work for the underdog and for the working classes generally. Their researches put a great mass of carefully co-ordinated material at the disposal of social workers and historians, and their tireless struggle for better working conditions, as shown by their work for the Fabian Society and by other public activities, will long be honoured and remembered. Among their principal works are *The History of Trade Unionism* (1894), *English Local Government* (1906–22), *English Poor Law History* (1927–9) and their great book on the U.S.S.R. (1935).

H. G. Wells, who was for many years associated with the Webbs in the Fabian Society, made a notable attempt in his *Outline of History* (1920) to sketch the evolution and progress of mankind through the ages. This book has the advantage of being consistently readable.

The most considerable historical work of the twentieth century is the *History of Europe* (1935), by H. A. L. Fisher (1865–1940). This remarkable survey mirrors the lucidity and erudition of its author's mind. There is no doubt that immediately on publication it took rank with the great English histories. Other writings from Fisher's pen are invariably informed with grace and a sense of perspective. His profound scholarship is matched by a masterly power of presentation. Among other notable books from his pen are *Napoleon* (1913) and a critical examination of Christian Science, *Our New Religion* (1929). The other historian who worked in the great tradition is George Macaulay Trevelyan (b. 1876), son of Sir George Otto Trevelyan (1838–1928) and great-nephew of Macaulay; chief among his works are his Garibaldi trilogy (1907–11), his Queen Anne trilogy (1930–4) and his concise and vivid one-volume *History of England* (1926).

Most ambitious of contemporary historians, Arnold Joseph Toynbee (b. 1889), chronicled the rise and fall of all great human civilizations in his *A Survey of History* (1934–9). On this work alone Toynbee takes his place with the great historians of the past.

Dr. G. G. Coulton (b. 1858) employed his great learning on medieval and religious subjects, and his pictures of life in the Middle Ages are unequalled. Among them are *Five Centuries of Religion* (1923–6), *Life in the Middle Ages* (1928–30) and *Medieval Panorama* (1938).

Of the chroniclers of the last war, mention must be made of two who wrote good short histories, C. R. M. F. Cruttwell (1887–1941) and B. H. Liddell Hart (b. 1895). Cruttwell's *A History of the Great War* (1934) and Liddell Hart's *The Real War* (1930) have considerable merit. Adequate justice has not been done to *The History of the Great War* (1921–2) by John Buchan. In its original form this work came out book by book while the war was still in progress. Buchan always wrote

K

attractively and in this comprehensive survey he shows great gifts of arrangement and sound judgment. It is hardly necessary to add that he wrote with a disciplined enthusiasm worthy of his great theme. Intended originally as a month by month record of the struggle, this history has qualities far removed from a merely ephemeral record. Winston Churchill's *The World Crisis* (1923–31), which is equally readable, must always be consulted by future historians of the period.

The Oxford one-volume *History of India* (1923), by V. A. Smith (1848–1920), is a good example of the virtues of discreet compression and sound scholarship.

In addition to the works of major importance which have been noticed here, this century has seen the publication of numerous first-rate specialized historical works and "tabloid" histories. There has never been a time when so much sound and readable history has been available both for the specialist and for the general reader. It is one of the penalties of war that difficulties of publishing, printing, and especially of binding, restrict the issue of works of this kind, whose study can only conduce to the knowledge and wellbeing of mankind.

BOOKS OF TRAVEL AND EXPLORATION

There has always been a demand for travellers' tales and the vast improvement in transport during the last century has made great stretches of the world attainable and an increasing volume of travel literature has been published.

Standing out like a rough and rocky eminence among travel literature is C. M. Doughty's *Travels in Arabia Deserta* (1888), which has been termed by competent critics the best of all our travel books. Living for some years among the Arabs, Doughty won their confidence and respect. His name is still venerated by them to-day. In his book, which is written in rugged, closely packed prose, Doughty gave the story of the life and habits of a remarkable people. He made no concessions to his readers, so that his book can never be widely popular, but it has greatness stamped on every page, and it has deeply influenced many since it was published, including T. E.

Lawrence, who contributed an introduction to the reprint which appeared after the last war.

It would be almost impossible to find a greater contrast in style than is provided by the austere prose of Doughty and the polished, reflective periods of Henry James. His *A Little Tour in France* (1885) is a miniature masterpiece. Less well known but equally satisfying is *English Hours* (1905), which embodies the fine freshness of the author's earlier impressions of this country. It is worthy of note that James's travel writings inspired at least two other authors to set down impressions of their own. The promising young *Manchester Guardian* critic, Dixon Scott (1881–1915), wrote a florid but charming little book on *Stratford-on-Avon, Warwick and Leamington*, which should be more widely read by visitors to Shakespeare's birthplace. Rebecca West's (b. 1892) *Black Lamb and Grey Falcon* (1942) is an elaborately written account of European travel in which the author's keen and nimble mind is the decisive factor. More mannered but full of information and charm are Maurice Hewlett's *Earthwork out of Tuscany* (1895) and *The Road in Tuscany* (1904). A literary traveller who delighted the young intellectuals in the early years of the present century and continues to entertain innumerable readers since, is Hilaire Belloc. Beer and ballads, fine descriptive writing, virile conversations, deep, unaffected piety, and long days' marches are the most prominent features of *The Path To Rome* (1902) and *Four Men in Sussex* (1912). Belloc founded a school of disciples who wrote in a similar style. By far the best of them is J. B. Morton, whose *Pyrenean* (1938) has liveliness and gusto.

Joseph Conrad's two reminiscent books, *A Personal Record* (1912) and *The Mirror of the Sea* (1906), are exquisite examples of his work. Nowhere else did he write with such passionate frankness about the sea and about the varied experiences and encounters of his life. It may be doubted whether any English writer has equalled the subtlety and perception shown by the Polish ex-sea-captain in these delightful evocations of his past.

W. H. Hudson's (1841–1922) autobiography, *Far Away and Long Ago* (1918), is memorable. Writing a calm, unim-

K*

passioned but sometimes lovely prose, Hudson commemorated the English rural scene in numerous pleasant books. Born in South America, he also wrote with great feeling of his childhood there. Among his other books, *A Shepherd's Life* and *The Land's End* (1908) are notable. His contemporary, the Scot, R. B. Cunninghame Graham was a romantic figure, who had also a love of nature and an even greater love for human nobility. His work has been mentioned elsewhere.

Also interested in South America, a fine descriptive writer, H. M. Tomlinson (b. 1872) commemorated his brief experience there in *The Sea and the Jungle* (1912) and his sensitive reactions to travel are to be found in numerous other books, especially in *Old Junk* (1918), *London River* (1921) and *Tidemarks* (1924). He was much less happy as a novelist, as he seemed to find that a plot was an encumbrance to him.

An enigmatic figure among his contemporaries, Norman Douglas showed polish and a curious erudition in his reflective and discursive travel books, of which the best are *Siren Land* (1911), *Fountains in the Sand* (1912), *Old Calabria* (1915), *Alone* (1921) and *Together* (1923). An autobiographical excursion, *Looking Back* (1933), relating experiences in many parts of the world, shows him as a resourceful traveller, able to win the confidence of all sorts of people.

Of the many books which treated autobiographically of travel during the last war, the most notable are T. E. Lawrence's (1888–1935) *Seven Pillars of Wisdom* (1926), H. W. Nevinson's (b. 1856) *The Dardanelles Campaign* (1918), John North's (b. 1894), *Gallipoli: The Fading Vision* (1936), and Francis Brett Young's *Marching on Tanga* (1918).

Lawrence, who as an undergraduate came under the influence of D. G. Hogarth (1862–1927), author of *A Wandering Scholar in the Levant* (1896), kept the Arabs together, and was made wretched when the politicians made terms which in his opinion betrayed them. *Seven Pillars of Wisdom* is a laborious account of his campaign with them, written with tremendous care and much detail, but curiously disappointing in its failure to give a living portrait of the man himself. Possibly the strong attraction which he felt for Doughty's method hindered him from writing a personal revelation of his experiences, but it is more likely that his reserve was due to psychological problems of his own.

His namesake, D. H. Lawrence, wrote his descriptive pieces with a rich intensity which is impressive. At his best he was a great painter in words. There is a dark brilliance in his writing which was his personal contribution to our literature, and it is nowhere more strongly marked than in a late work, *Mornings in Mexico* (1927). Some of the best of his writing can be found also in *Twilight in Italy* (1916) and *Sea and Sardinia* (1917).

In *The Voyage of the "Bonaventura"* (1922) Edmund Blunden's limpid prose is seen to great advantage in a description of a trip to the Amazon. Among women travellers, Dame Ethel Smyth, Freya Stark and Ella Maillart have all written memorably of their experiences. Dame Ethel's *A Three-Legged Tour in Greece* (1927) reveals her fine, impartial curiosity about statues and sanitation, to mention only two of her widespread interests. The other two ladies dared more greatly but their pens cannot be matched against Dame Ethel's.

Evelyn Waugh has been largely responsible for the shape which travel books have taken since his *Labels* appeared in 1930. *Labels*, subtitled "A Mediterranean Journal," is an extremely sophisticated chronicle. It contains the blend of self-mockery, cocksureness and beauty, which with the addition of some really good comic stuff served the author, Peter Fleming, and other writers very well in a number of books published during the 'thirties. *Waugh in Abyssinia* (1936) gave a frank account of the Italian war in that country.

In *Brazilian Adventure* (1933) Peter Fleming (b. 1907) wrote the most representative travel book of the between-wars period. None of his later work shows the same high spirits or zest for the comedy of life which made *Brazilian Adventure* consistently entertaining. In this account of a some-times dangerous expedition the author described his experiences in a book which is deeply tinged with irony and bubbles over with humour that spares neither himself, his companions, nor the people and events of this South American journey. *One's Company* (1934) and *News from Tartary* (1936) are both admirable accounts of hazardous adventures.

As entertaining is the *Hindoo Holiday* (1932) of J. R.
Ackerley (b. 1896). Going out to a small Indian native
state as tutor to the Maharajah's two-year-old son, he became
the companion and confidant of this peculiar potentate, of
whom he has painted a picture that is both exceedingly funny
and very sympathetic.

Dr. Walter Starkie (b. 1894) is another lively traveller whose
Raggle Taggle (1933) and *Spanish Raggle Taggle* (1934) show
him as a literary descendant of Borrow, a true Bohemian of
travel.

Among twentieth-century records of polar exploration
Captain Robert Falcon Scott's (1868–1912) *Journal* (1913)
holds a unique place. The author could write good prose, and
the last entry, written when the author was dying, is as memorable as it is moving. Shackleton's books and Apsley Cherry-
Garrard's (b. 1886) *The Worst Journey in the World* (1922) are
not without interest, but they cannot be compared for literary
importance with Dr. F. D. Ommanney's (b. 1903) *South
Latitude* (1938). There has never been a better account of
Antarctic life than this. The author is outstanding as a descriptive writer, and his other book, *North Cape* (1939), which
recounts his life as a deck-hand on a Grimsby trawler, is full of
realism and beauty.

Two men of letters who described their travel experiences
with point and polish are W. Somerset Maugham and Osbert
Sitwell (b. 1892). Maugham's precise prose is agreeable
to read. His books do not satisfy altogether because the
author is assiduous in collecting morbid or acid anecdotes
to season them. The best is *The Gentleman in the Parlour*
(1930). Sitwell's *Escape With Me* (1939) is a beautifully
written record of a journey from England to China, including
a diversion to Angkor. Another writer who has drawn upon
Far Eastern experiences is R. H. Bruce Lockhart (b. 1887).
A romantic and arduous life has furnished him with material
for several "personal stories," of which the best known is the
admirably told *Memoirs of a British Agent* (1932). Lockhart
is a born traveller. He can settle down in a place as though he
was a native of it, and although he writes about himself with
a complete lack of reserve, he manages to do so without offence

or vulgarity. His *Return to Malaya* (1936) gives a notably accurate picture of life in that country before the war of 1939 broke out.

Bruce Lockhart and Negley Farson (b. 1890), an American writer whose *Way of a Transgressor* (1935) is a frank narrative of personal and international experiences, were the founders of a large school of journalist authors. Their work provides a significant comment on the public taste of the time. They reveal almost without reserve their love affairs and adventures, and their books embody the "personal, human stories" so dear to the hearts of the editors and readers of the popular press. Douglas Reed's *Insanity Fair* (1938) and John Gunther's *Inside Europe* (1936) are able examples of this kind of book. There is no doubt that they succeeded in arousing in numerous complacent citizens' minds an interest in international affairs which could not have been kindled by any less picturesque treatment. During the last two generations the British public has become increasingly irresponsive to a sober presentation of fact. The flagging appetite can only be stimulated by the appetizing concoctions dished up by fluent and resourceful journalists.

Other men of letters have added to the library of travel books during the last twenty years. Among the young intellectuals Auden has been particularly active. With MacNeice he wrote *Letters from Iceland* (1937), a rather arid holiday record in prose and verse. MacNeice's own *I Crossed the Minch* (1938), an account of his journey to the Western Isles, is much livelier. *Journey to a War* (1939), the story of a voyage to China by Auden and Isherwood, is more revealing as a picture of the authors than as an informative book about China. *The Lawless Roads* (1939) gave Graham Greene the opportunity to sketch a haunting picture of Mexico, and in several books Philip Guedalla gave vivid impressions of South America. The West Indies provided material for Aldous Huxley in *Beyond the Mexique Bay* (1934) and for Alec Waugh in *The Coloured Countries* (1930). An ex-civil servant, Maurice Collis (b. 1889), has written out of his personal experience in a series of fascinating books on Burma and China.

Most popular of all with the general public have been the

travel books, often written with a religious setting, of H. V. Morton. A shrewd journalist and a most able descriptive writer, Morton found himself among the best-sellers with his *In the Steps of the Master* (1934) and *In the Steps of St. Paul* (1936), *In Search of England* (1927) and others. Full of useful information, tactfully conveyed, the reason for the wide sale of these books is easy to see.

An able writer, Sean O'Faolain showed a keen knowledge of Ireland and his native scene in his delightful *An Irish Journey* (1940), which took a very high place among recent books of travel, and Moray Maclaren, in the Belloc tradition, wrote pleasantly of Scottish experiences in *Return to Scotland* (1930). Neither has the English scene gone unnoticed in the twentieth century. Messrs. Macmillan's "Highways and Byways" series contains two books of particular merit: *Sussex*, by E. V. Lucas (1904), and *Essex* (1939), by Clifford Bax. Sir Arnold Wilson (1884–1940), who died in air action at the age of fifty-five as a rear-gunner, was a man of many talents and activities. Soldier, administrator, M.P., expert on a variety of subjects, and above all, a great Christian, Arnold Wilson had the ability to make his fellow countrymen and women talk. In his journeys at home and abroad it was his custom to keep a record of people and things interesting to him. He amassed a vast amount of information and anecdote, which he used in his *Walks and Talks* (1934), *Walks and Talks Abroad* (1936), *Thoughts and Talks* (1938) and other books. There is something of Cobbett in the style. It is forthright, like Wilson himself. He was loath to believe evil of any man, and this streak of guilelessness in his nature sometimes led him into bad errors of judgment. For a time he was blind to the darker side of the Nazi regime. He was a tireless critic of present-day standards of business and political morality. He detested red tape. He wrote well. His books should endure. So should J. B. Priestley's *English Journey* (1934). He has an eye for the essentials of the national character which few of his contemporaries possess. He has also a sense of place, which enabled him to see and depict the industrial tracts of England as easily as the urbanities of Norwich. There is true English humour and realism in *English Journey*, which is a very personal and companionable book. These qualities shown within narrower limits characterize a charming picture of a holiday: *Water Music* (1939), by Sir John Squire, and *The London Perambulator* (1925) and *The Edinburgh Perambulator* (1926), by James Bone (b. 1872), a great journalist and a fine writer.

MISCELLANEOUS PROSE

It is impossible in the limits of this section of a small history of literature to do more than chronicle the most important of the many and varied works which have appeared in the last fifty years. Samuel Butler (1835–1902) was a satirical humorist who delighted in controversy and wrote with a brilliant, witty and often savage pen. Science, literature, music, religion and travel all came within his scope. His sense of perspective was remarkably weak and his theories and conjectures were often more remarkable for their originality than for their good sense. In addition to the novels, his principal works are *Life and Habit* (1877), *Alps and Sanctuaries of Piedmont and the Canton Ticino* (1881), *The Authoress of the Odyssey* (1897), and the posthumous *Note-Books of Samuel Butler* (1912). This delightful collection of jottings from his manuscript collections is the most rewarding and stimulating of all his works. An excellent biography of this curious and embittered personality was written by his friend, Henry Festing-Jones.

Among the philosophers, F. H. Bradley, O.M. (1846–1924), who was hailed by some as the leading exponent of idealism, wrote several works in admirable prose. The best known is *Appearance and Reality* (1893). Hardly less eminent, John McTaggart (1866–1925) was venerated as a teacher by many of his Cambridge pupils. He had not the ease and clarity in exposition of Bradley. His most notable work is *The Nature of Existence* (1921–7). A leader among the Pragmatists and the possessor of a very lucid style, William James (1842–1910), brother of the novelist, is still much read to-day, especially in his *Varieties of Religious Experience* (1902). The foreign philosophers, Schopenhauer, Nietzsche, Benedetto Croce and Henri Bergson, were all in fashion for a time, but it is unlikely that they profoundly affected English philosophical thought.

The twentieth century has produced a number of scientists able to write and expound theories and lines of research and investigation very readably. Learned works intended for the specialist are outside the scope of this survey. Sir Oliver Lodge (1851–1940) included among his studies problems relating to wireless. He was tireless in his psychical researches. He was convinced that communication could be established with the dead, and after the death of his son, in the last war, he wrote *Raymond, or Life and Death* (1916), which is still the subject of much questioning and debate. Bertrand Russell (b. 1872), a student of the philosophy of mathematics, wrote also on more general subjects. His *Mysticism and Logic* (1918), *The Analysis of Mind* (1921) and *An Outline of Philosophy* (1927) need only be noted here. A. N. Whitehead (b. 1861), a great mathematician, wrote his most significant work, *Science and the Modern World*, in 1926. Alive to the fact that science cannot stand alone, he discussed wider questions in *Religion in the Making* (1927), *Process and Reality* (1929) and other books. He wrote clear expository prose. Professor Lancelot Hogben wrote a mathematical best-seller in his *Mathematics for the Million* (1936).

Following on the now outmoded popular works on astronomy of Sir Robert Ball (1840–1913), other distinguished astronomers have written clearly and acceptably for the general reader. Sir James Jeans (b. 1877) achieved a remarkable degree of intelligibility in *The Stars in Their Courses* (1931). *The Mysterious Universe* (1930) was even more popular. Sir Stanley Eddington (b. 1882), writing with less regard for the popular market, published *Stars and Atoms* (1927) and, taking a more general philosophical view, *The Nature of the Physical World* (1928) and a sequel, *New Pathways in Science* (1935). Among various works on the Atom may be mentioned Professor da Costa Andrade's *The Structure of the Atom* (1927). Problems of time were treated by J. W. Dunne (b. 1875) in his *An Experiment with Time* (1927), of which a revised edition appeared later. Biology found many able exponents. Sir Arthur Thomson (1861–1933), writing in collaboration with

Sir Patrick Geddes (1854–1932), published *Life: Outlines of General Biology* in 1931. Other biologists whose writings have more general implications and are not beyond the powers of the educated reader were John Scott Haldane (1860–1936) and his son, J. B. S. Haldane (b. 1892), Julian Huxley (b. 1887) and Sir Francis Galton (1822–1911). Sir Arthur Shipley (1861–1927) wrote profitably on parasitology and infection. Among geologists, Professor W. J. Sollas (1849–1936), and among botanists, Sir Albert Seward (1863–1941) and Sir Frederick Keeble (b. 1870), advanced the study of their respective subjects.

A leading anthropologist, whose literary powers won for him a wide circle of readers, was Sir James George Frazer, O.M. (1854–1941). His great work, *The Golden Bough*, which was begun in 1890, proved to be the most popular of all studies of comparative religion, as it is the most comprehensive and ambitious study of the subject.

In spite of the oft-repeated cry that the churches were empty, interest in the study of religion and in the literature of devotion has remained at a high level through the century, rising to a peak in each of the war periods. The public taste for these books is markedly ephemeral, which is due to two causes. First, a popular preacher may create an interest for his writings by a purely personal appeal. His books usually have no lasting value. Few theologians have possessed notable literary gifts. Secondly, religious approach varies with each generation, and a theological work popular in one decade has gone out of fashion in the next. In recent years the foreign theologians, Nicholas Berdyaev (b. 1874) and Jacques Maritain (b. 1882), have attracted considerable attention in England. Christopher Dawson (b. 1889), an impressive and sometimes difficult theologian, has gathered a large following among Catholics with his *Progress of Religion* (1931), *Religion in the Modern State* (1935) and other works. The present Archbishop of Canterbury, William Temple (b. 1881), has published many wise and scholarly works, and among them perhaps his short and popular *Christianity and the Social Order* (1942) is the most important. A companion volume, *Christianity and World Order* (1940), by the Bishop of Chichester, G. K. A. Bell, the

K**

able biographer of Archbishop Randall Davidson, is a brilliant summary of the functions of Christianity in the world to-day. Other theologians whose works will repay study are Charles Williams, A. G. Hebert, Bishop Charles Gore, and the young writers who have contributed to the "Signpost" series. T. S. Eliot's *Idea of a Christian Society* (1939) is stimulating and has been widely read. C. S. Lewis (b. 1898), who became a Christian in later life, has written two notable books full of sound thought and good writing, *The Problem of Pain* (1940) and *Screwtape Letters* (1942).

The army of books devoted to literary criticism, biography and history is large and impressive. W. J. Courthope's (1842–1917) *History of English Poetry* (1895–1909) has not been superseded. Oliver Elton (b. 1861), a readable and learned critic, wrote *A Survey of English Literature* (1912–28), which contains a masterly summary of the literature written between 1730 and 1880. Among his other books, *The English Muse* (1933), which gives a survey of English poetry up to recent years, also shows his great gift for terse and epigrammatic statement. Elton's other books and essays all show that learning can be presented gracefully and acceptably.

George Saintsbury (1845–1933) had an immense and, on the whole, a superficial range of knowledge. He wrote conversationally. For a historian he was a discursive and opinionated writer. He tackled a variety of literary subjects cheerfully and with great energy. His most important works are *A History of Criticism* (1900–4), *A History of English Prosody* (1906–10), *A History of English Prose Rhythm* (1912) and *A Short History of English Literature*, which was issued in a revised edition in 1937. His occasional writings are companionable and entertaining. No one has ever written better about Thackeray than he did in his *A Consideration of Thackeray* (1936).

W. P. Ker (1855–1923) was a student of early language and literature. His style is clipped and precise and yet readable. He immersed himself in the writings of the periods which he studied and his best books are *Epic and Romance* (1896) and *English Literature: Medieval* (1912).

There has been much good writing about Shakespeare since the time of the Romantic Revival. Edward Dowden (1843–

1913) wrote a thoughtful *Shakspere: A Critical Study of His Mind and Art* (1875) which may be profitably compared with the eager extravagance of Swinburne's approach to the Elizabethan playwrights, illuminating though Swinburne sometimes was. A. C. Bradley (1851–1934) published only five books, of which the two best are *Oxford Lectures on Poetry* (1909) and *Shakespearean Tragedy* (1904). This is a noble and illuminating critical exposition of the four great tragedies. No critic since Coleridge had written so satisfyingly about Shakespeare, and *Shakespearean Tragedy* is likely to remain for many years unsuperseded as an approach to his conception of the essentials of tragic drama.

A Miscellany (1929) includes among other literary studies a salient analysis of the character of Feste the Jester. Bradley's researches into the tragedies have been matched by J. B. Priestley's excellent papers on the Shakespearean comedies in *The English Comic Characters* (1925). Priestley may be a light-weight of criticism. He gets to the root of the matter in this book. Professor A. W. Pollard's (b. 1859) *Shakespeare's Fights with the Pirates* (1917) deals interestingly with special literary problems of Shakespeare's day.

Oxford and Cambridge were fortunate in their professors of English literature, both newly appointed at the beginning of the century. Sir Walter Raleigh (1861–1922) will live by the admirable *Letters* (1926) which were published after his death. They are the best of contemporary correspondence, wise and witty. His great inspirational qualities were never fully transmitted in his books. He had little patience for writing, but at his best, in the short *Shakespeare* (1907), *Romance* (1916), *The English Novel* (1893), *Six Essays on Johnson* (1910) and *Some Authors* (1923), he conveyed to his readers some of the rich pleasure he derived from the authors he discussed in these books and which he transmitted inimitably to successive generations of undergraduates. Sir Arthur Quiller-Couch, who won a reputation for himself as poet, critic and novelist—he completed Stevenson's unfinished romance, *St. Ives*—brought to the consideration of literature from an academic chair a wide and extensive knowledge of the problems of the writer's craft. Like Raleigh, he has always worn his scholarship debonairly.

The two men believed that literature is a necessary part of civilized life, and in all their appreciative criticism they stated their faith no less effectively because they did so unobtrusively. In the reprinted books of his Cambridge lectures Quiller-Couch proved himself a superb literary evangelist. He was able to persuade any person of average intelligence that he could, and would, enjoy books which had been comprehensively damned for them by being classified as "classics," a wicked term which has been responsible for much terror among the simple-minded. Quiller-Couch's most notable works of critical appreciation are *On the Art of Writing* (1916), *Shakespeare's Workmanship* (1917), *Studies in Literature* (1918, 1922, 1929), *On the Art of Reading* (1920), *Charles Dickens and Other Victorians* (1925) and *The Poet as Citizen* (1934).

Two small books worthy of note here are the *Popular History* of English Poetry (1936), by T. Earle Welby (1881–1933), a persuasive critic and essayist, and *English Prose Style* (1931), by Herbert Read. *The Development of English Biography* (1937), by Harold Nicolson, is an able piece of compression. Among works dealing with Old and Middle English periods, C. S. Lewis's *The Allegory of Love* (1936) is an imaginative piece of literary history, beautifully done. Sound and lively writing on Chaucer may be found in books published by G. K. Chesterton (1934) and by J. L. Lowes (1934). Prof. R. W. Chambers' *Sir Thomas More* (1935) is both scholarly and readable. Saintsbury's *Elizabethan Literature* (1890) is a good introduction to the period. Less reliable, but vivid and stimulating, is John Addington Symonds's *Shakespeare's Predecessors* (1884). On Shakespeare's plays, in addition to the writers already noted, Harley Granville-Barker's *Prefaces to Shakespeare* (1937–40) explain the approach of a practical man of the theatre. John Masefield's *Shakespeare* (1911) is a first-rate handbook. In *The Essential Shakespeare* (1932) J. Dover Wilson (b. 1881) embodied much patient research. *A Companion to Shakespeare Studies* (1934) is invaluable to the student.

Sir Herbert Grierson, Sir Edmund Gosse, Allardyce Nicoll and Bonamy Dobrée have all written well on seventeenth-century writers, and the eighteenth century found its literary historians in George Saintsbury, Gosse, Nicoll, Austin Dobson, ·Leslie Stephen, Elton and Thomas Seccombe (1866–1923), whose *Age of Johnson* (1899) is only a small reminder of its author's great erudition. Saintsbury's *The Peace of the Augustans* (1915) contains some of his best critical writing. Elton continues as the chronicler of the first eighty years of the nineteenth century, to which C. H. Herford (d. 1931) made a useful contribution with his *Age of Wordsworth* (1897). Grierson's *Lyrical Poetry from Blake to Hardy* (1928) is remarkably well informed. G. K. Chesterton's *The Victorian Age in Literature* (1913) is genial, colourful and erratic.

Many critics have written fully on the nineteenth- and twentieth-century authors. Only a few of them can be named. Arthur Symons's *The Romantic Movement in English Poetry* (1909) contains thoughtful essays on the various writers of the time. Lord David Cecil's *Early Victorian Novelists* (1934) deals fairly with some great names. B. Ifor Evans covers a later period with *English Poetry in the Later Nineteenth Century* (1933). General histories and appreciations of the work of the twentieth century are few and far between, obviously because of the great difficulty which the historian must find in obtaining a proper perspective of his subject. An attempt was made by A. C. Ward (b. 1891) in *Twentieth-Century Literature, 1901–1940* (1940), which is informative but inevitably incomplete. *Axel's Castle* (1931), by a leading American critic, Edmund Wilson (b. 1895), is worthy of notice. Among books devoted to individual writers, Grierson's *Sir Walter Scott* (1938), M. Lascelles's *Jane Austen and Her Art* (1939), J. L. Lowes's *The Road to Xanadu* (Coleridge), revised edition, 1940, H. W. Garrod's *Keats* (1926), G. K. Chesterton's *Dickens* (1906), Michael Sadleir's *Trollope, a Commentary* (1933), G. M. Trevelyan's *The Poetry and Philosophy of George Meredith* (1920), Raleigh's *R. L. Stevenson* (1895), are only a few among many which might be mentioned. The dangerous 'nineties found excellent historians in Holbrook Jackson (b. 1874), *The Eighteen-Nineties* (1913), and Osbert Burdett, *The Beardsley Period* (1925). G. M. Young (b. 1882), an urbane and learned critic, has written with spirit and discrimination in *Victorian England: Portrait of an Age* (1936), *Daylight and Champaign* (1937) and other works. I. A. Richards (b. 1893), in *Practical Criticism* (1929) and *Principles of Literary Criticism* (1924), dealt, sometimes satisfactorily, with the problems confronting teachers of English literature. Stephen Potter (b. 1900) has done so more effectively and amusingly in *The Muse in Chains* 1937).

In 1927 *A New English Dictionary on Historical Principles*, popularly known as *The Oxford Dictionary*, was completed. It had been begun in 1884 under the editorship of Sir James Murray (1837–1915), and the work was carried to completion by a corps of learned philologists and lexicographers. It stands unrivalled as the greatest English dictionary. Among its editors was Henry Bradley (1845–1923) who wrote *The Making of English* (1904), an invaluable little book which is still widely read. Others associated with the work were H. W. Fowler (1858–1933) and his brother, F. G. Fowler (1870–1918), who compiled from the parent work *The Concise Oxford Dictionary of Current English* (1924), which is adequate for all ordinary purposes. H. W. Fowler was also responsible for *A Dictionary of Modern English Usage* (1926).

Among other authors who have written memorably on literary and allied subjects during the period, J. W. Mackail (b. 1859) takes a prominent place. His biography of William Morris (1899) is among the best English "Lives." His *Select Epigrams from the Greek Anthology* (1890) is a superb rendering. Gilbert Murray (b. 1866) has done admirably as scholar, translator and man of letters. As translator, Murray won for his verse translations of Euripides, Sophocles, Aeschylus and Aristophanes a place in the contemporary English theatre. Among his other works, which appealed almost as much to the general reader as to the scholar, his *History of Ancient Greek Literature* (1897), *Rise of the Greek Epic* (1907) and *Euripides and His Age* (1918) are all valuable and most readable. Another scholar who caught the public ear was Goldsworthy Lowes Dickinson (1862–1932), whose *The Greek View of Life* (1896), *Letters from John Chinaman* (1901) and *A Modern Symposium* (1908) influenced their readers so much that Dickinson's ideas penetrated far beyond the immediate circle of those who had read them.

A critic in the Jamesian tradition, Percy Lubbock (b. 1879) wrote *The Craft of Fiction* (1921), a colloquial appreciation which was based on his master's teaching. Lubbock wrote good, conversational prose in this book and in *Earlham* (1922), a nineteenth-century picture of a Norfolk house, in *Roman Pictures* (1923) and in *Shades of Eton* (1929), a delightful evocation of his schooldays. Lubbock always shows himself to be an artist in words.

A scholar, Dr. W. R. Inge (b. 1860), for many years Dean of St. Paul's, wrote important works, such as *The Philosophy of Plotinus* (1918) and *The Platonic Tradition* (1926), but he is best known for his collections of reprinted journalism, *Outspoken Essays* (1919, 1922), which discussed a wide range of subjects of immediate interest in a vein of gloomy and witty irony. This gave them a wide appeal. They belong to the ephemeral literature of the period. At the time of publication they were effective and influential. Edward Carpenter (1844–1929) was also ordained but did not take up work as a clergyman. He made his name with *Towards Democracy* (1889–1902), a long Whitmanic poem extolling comradeship between men of all classes in a manner which seemed almost revolutionary when it appeared. He also wrote frankly and helpfully on sex problems in *Love's Coming of Age* (1896). His influence cannot be compared with that of Henry Havelock Ellis (1859–1939), whose great work, *Studies in the Psychology of Sex* (1897–1910), to which a supplementary volume was added later, was at first refused publication in this country. It is unrivalled for a thorough and comprehensive treatment of sexual phenomena and it will not be replaced for many years. Ellis was a recorder and not a theorist. For this reason more attention has been paid by the experts to the much less valuable work of Freud and others. Ellis was also a writer on other scientific subjects and a literary critic and editor of great accomplishment. He edited *The Mermaid Series: The Best Plays of the Old Dramatists* (1887–9) and so made available to his contemporaries the works of the Elizabethan dramatists. *The New Spirit* (1890) is interesting as an almost contemporary view of Ibsen, Whitman and Tolstoy. *Affirmations* (1897),

Impressions and Comments (1914, 1921, 1924), contain Ellis's speculations and opinions on many artistic, literary and scientific subjects. Ellis more than other better-known publicists helped to mould the thought of his time, and he was always a salutary influence.

Among numerous specialists on economic problems, Lord Keynes (b. 1883) sprang into popularity with his post-war study, *The Economic Consequences of the Peace* (1919).

The literature of the theatre in this period is small but select. It begins with the stimulating criticisms of Sir Max Beerbohm and George Bernard Shaw, ably supplemented by William Archer (1856–1924) and A. B. Walkley (1856–1926). The criticism of Shaw and Beerbohm has been reprinted in book form. Shaw's *Quintessence of Ibsenism* (1891) has never been superseded. Walkley, an urbane and discursive writer, is best represented by his *Playhouse Impressions* (1892) and *Drama and Life* (1937). The emergence of the repertory movement was responsible for P. P. Howe's *Repertory Theatre* (1910) and the lively interest in the drama carefully fostered by the critical staff of the *Manchester Guardian*, headed by C. E. Montague (1867–1928), found expression in Montague's excellent little book, *Dramatic Values* (1911), which has become a critic's *vade mecum*. A highly stylized writer, much influenced by George Meredith, Montague wrote one amusing journalistic novel, *A Hind Let Loose* (1910), a remarkable book on war and its effects, *Disenchantment* (1922), some short stories, *Fiery Particles* (1923), and other works, all of which testify in mannered prose to his ability as a writer and thinker. Montague was one of the most interesting journalistic figures of his time and his books are fresh and forceful now.

Another old member of the *Manchester Guardian* staff, J. E. Agate (b. 1877), afterwards became the best known dramatic critic of his day. Writing with tremendous gusto and strong prejudice, Agate is never dull, often delightful, and at times irritatingly provocative. At his best he has some of the zest which informs Hazlitt's writings. Agate's range is wide. He could communicate his own enjoyments, and did so in a series of autobiographical books, entitled *Ego*. A young disciple of Agate, Alan Dent (b. 1905), has published one book of reprinted criticisms, *Preludes and Studies* (1942), which show real literary and appreciative powers. He has the right approach to his subject. Desmond MacCarthy (b. 1878), a scholarly and sincere critic, has for many years written most ably on the theatre and on literature. His interests are wide but not popular. Some of his critical writings were collected in *Portraits* (1930) and later volumes. At his best, as in his writings on Henry James and Samuel Butler, he is unequalled by any contemporary, but he never had the unique ability shown by Sir John Squire in the days when he wrote a weekly article on books for the *Observer*, of persuading the general reader to read anything that he recommended. Squire has a great talent for sharing his enthusiasms with his readers. His sense of humour, hatred of pretence and great critical and appreciative faculties are apparent in his *Sunday Mornings* (1930), papers reprinted from the *New Statesman* and the *Observer*. Arnold Bennett's *Books and Persons: Being Comments on a Past Epoch, 1908–1911* (1917), essays reprinted from the *New Statesman*, have considerable zest, but they lack Squire's humour and wide range. Bennett is seen to greater advantage in his *Journals* (1932–3). At the moment, with the exception of MacCarthy, no critic of the first rank is writing regularly in the English periodicals, though Cyril Connolly (b. 1903) is doing excellent work for the younger writers in his monthly periodical, *Horizon*, and John Lehmann has published some important recent work in *New Writing*. The *Times Literary Supplement* continues to be unrivalled as an impartial and unbiased guide to current literature, and the review pages of *The Sunday Times* and *Observer* are conducted with integrity and distinction.

T. S. Eliot, whose critical writings have attracted among the intelligentsia almost as much attention as his poetry, is invariably sincere, scholarly and often laboured. In his appreciative criticism, of which *Dante* (1929) is the best example, he can be an admirable guide. In his destructive vein, as when he writes of Matthew Arnold or of his own immediate predecessors, he can be petulant and pompous. *Essays Ancient and Modern* (1936) and *Elizabethan Essays* (1934) are the best of his other critical works.

Robert Graves in *On English Poetry* (1922) and Lascelles Abercrombie in *The Idea of Good Poetry* (1925) and other books, have written sensibly and practically about the poet's approach to his work. An amusing squib is Ralph Straus's *A Whip for the Woman* (1931), which describes the evolution of a novel, without too much exaggeration.

Good musical criticism of the period is rarer and less well written. In this field, too, Bernard Shaw has done well. Sir Donald Tovey (1875–1940) revealed a literary gift and great knowledge in *Essays in Musical Analysis* (1935–9). Mr. Ernest Newman exercised a lively pen, which seemed occasionally to have been dipped in vitriol, in his critical writings on music and musicians. Bernard Shore, a member of a great orchestra, most ably advanced the case for the executant in *The Orchestra Speaks* (1938) and A. H. Sidgwick (1882–1917) honoured a great musical institution worthily and humorously in *The Promenade Ticket* (1914).

The literature of art and architecture is vast and varied and there is room here only for the mention of the names of Roger Fry, Clive Bell, Sacheverell Sitwell, C. R. W. Nevinson, Sir William Rothenstein, Sir Kenneth Clark, Geoffrey Scott, R. H. Wilenski and that original and quaintly amusing writer of prose and poetry, John Betjeman.

A feature of the last twenty-five years has been the interest taken in the older diarists. This has led to the publication of several, which, though going back a century or two, have only become part of English Literature in our own times. *Parson James Woodforde's Diary* (1924–31), edited by John Beresford, gives a charming picture of the life and activities of a country clergyman in the eighteenth century. *Kilvert's Diary* (1938–40), edited by William Plomer, is a much more passionate and intimate record of the life of a nineteenth-century country parson. The *Memoirs* of Charles Greville (1794–1865), secretary to the Privy Council, portray vividly Court and political life in the Georgian and early Victorian periods. A new edition, edited by Lytton Strachey and Roger Fulford, came out in 1938. Thomas Creevey, a politician and acute observer and recorder, who was in Brussels at the time of the Battle of Waterloo, left a copious diary from which selections were published in *The Creevey Papers* (1903) and *Creevey's Life and Times* (1934). The lively Anglo-Indian *Memoirs of William Hickey* (1913–25), edited by Alfred Spencer, which are as good reading as any other personal records, have been compared not without reason to the writings of Cellini, Defoe, Smollett and Fielding. They emerge unscathed from these comparisons and there is no doubt that they have not attained their full popularity yet.

A curious, lonely figure, Bruce Cummings ("W. N. P. Barbellion," 1889–1917) in *The Journal of a Disappointed Man* (1919) combined the exact observation of the scientist with an intense and detached study of his emotions as the victim of an incurable disease.

The *Journals and Letters of Viscount Esher* (1934–8), a courtier and confidant of many, who might have been a great statesman, are profoundly discreet, but they give glimpses of life behind the scenes in Court circles which have considerable historical and human interest.

An allusion to the excellence of Sir Walter Raleigh as a letter-writer has already been made elsewhere. Among other notable correspondents were Gertrude Bell, whose wide knowledge of the Middle East is embodied in her *Letters* (1927) and *Earlier Letters* (1937). Another lover of that region, T. E. Lawrence, revealed as much of himself as is ever likely to be known in *The Letters of T. E. Lawrence* (1938), edited by David Garnett. His namesake, D. H. Lawrence, was also an admirable correspondent, as his *Letters* (1932), edited by Aldous Huxley, clearly show.

Two fascinating books, showing both sides of a correspondence, are *Ellen Terry and Bernard Shaw: A Correspondence* (1931) and *The Pollock-Holmes Letters* (1942), in which two eminent men, Sir Frederick Pollock and Mr. Justice Holmes, kept up an interchange of letters across the Atlantic, leisurely, scholarly and pungent, in which all manner of things and people were discussed for sixty years. It was agreeable to have this reminder that the art of letter-writing is not yet dead.

Three writers who have specialized in the literature of the countryside and farming, George Bourne (1863–1927), A. G. Street (b. 1892) and Adrian Bell (b. 1901), have written with deep understanding of their subject. Bourne was a recorder of village life. *The Bettesworth Book* (1901) and other books commemorate the struggles of the poor, simply and effectively. *The Wheelwright's Shop* (1923) brings to life a village craft. *A Small Boy in the Sixties* (1927) describes the writer's childhood. A. G. Street gave a vivid picture of agricultural life in *Farmer's Glory* and later books. Adrian Bell's *Corduroy* (1930), *Silver Ley* (1931) and *The Cherry Tree* (1932) survey the same subject with authority and charm. Commanding a clear and pleasant style, Eric Parker (b. 1870) has written of the countryside and of bird life in a series of books that bear witness to his admirable powers of observation. *The World of Birds* (1941) is representative of his work.

Humorous journalism has reached a high level during the period. In a series of short leading articles in *The Times*, afterwards reprinted in book form as *Light and Leading*, Douglas Woodruff (b. 1897), a brilliant wit, made nonsense of numerous contemporary foibles. These short pieces are literature.

Some years ago, D. B. Wyndham-Lewis inaugurated the "Beachcomber" column in the *Daily Express*. Here he was able to invent comic and preposterous characters, tilt at abuses, charlatans and poseurs, and introduce scraps of verse. His successor, J. B. Morton, an able historian, author of *The Bastille Falls* (1936) and *The Dauphin* (1937), has carried on the tradition for many years and has maintained a consistently good standard. A first collection of his papers appeared in *By The Way* (1931) and there have been others since.

Other writers who have succeeded in this kind are Nathaniel Gubbins and Maurice Lane-Norcott. All four have deserved well of their fellows and their humour will have its historical value for succeeding generations.

Through all the years *Punch* has gone serenely on its way. Always conservative in its humour and maintaining an almost irreproachable taste, it has been the means of introducing some admirable humorists to the public. Stephen Leacock (b. 1869) was a contributor. Born in England, and for many years a university professor in Canada, he combines, at his best, a logical and diverting silliness with a talent for parody which is pure burlesque. *Literary Lapses* (1910), *Nonsense Novels* (1911) and *Frenzied Fiction* (1918) show him at his funniest.

E. V. Lucas and C. L. Graves (b. 1856), both constant contributors, tilted amiably at contempoary idiosyncrasies in *Hustled History* (1908) and *Wisdom While You Wait* (1903), with the able pictorial assistance of the *Punch* artist, George Morrow. In his youth, A. A. Milne (b. 1882), who won a vast popularity for his children's verses, *When We Were Very Young* (1924), published *The Day's Play* (1910) and other light humorous pieces which caught the carefree spirit of the years before the war of 1914–18 and can still be read with wistful pleasure by the mature. E. V. Knox (b. 1881), now editor of *Punch*, wrote one good volume of parody, *Parodies Regained*, (1921), and several books of good comic verse. His predecessor Sir Owen Seaman (1861–1936), was a parodist and verse writer of ability. A. P. Herbert, a versatile man of letters with the tireless spirit of the born reformer, added to the gaiety and to the common sense of the nation with his *Uncommon Law* (1935), *Trials of Topsy* (1928), *Topsy, M.P.* (1929), *Misleading Cases* (1927), *Honeybubble & Co.* (1928) and other books of humorous verse and prose.

Best known of all the *Punch* humorists of this period was "F. Anstey" (Thomas Anstey Guthrie, who showed his knowledge of the Cockney scene in *Voces Populi* (1890), and in *Vice Versa* (1882) revealed the essential incompatibility of father and son when viewed from the curious angle of the Victorian middle class. George (1847–1912) and Weedon (1854–1919) Grossmith's *Diary of a Nobody* (1894), the supposed diary of an extremely respectable city clerk of the 'nineties, still makes people laugh to-day. Two later *Punch* humorists, R. J. Yeatman (b. 1897) and W. C. Sellar (b. 1898), drew lavishly on their own sense of humour and knowledge of English history and character to write *1066 and All That* (1931) and other diverting and ludicrous reconstructions.

Among the enormous quantity of books for children which have been published in ever-increasing numbers annually up to 1939 there have been many showing literary accomplishment and some which are literature. It would be ridiculous to include in the second category the stories for boys, excellently suited for young readers' tastes when they appeared, of G. A. Henty (1832–1902), G. Manville Fenn (1831–1909), Gordon Stables (1840–1910), "Herbert Strang" and many others. Richard Jefferies's *Bevis* (1882) and *Wood Magic* (1881), delightful nature stories, still hold their places. Kipling's *Jungle Books* (1894–5), *Just So Stories* (1902), *Puck of Pook's Hill* (1906) survive heartily with them. Daisy Ashford wrote, as a child, *The Young Visiters* (1919), which children still love to-day. E. Nesbit (1858–1924) excelled in writing the kind of story that appealed equally to boys and girls, and Arthur Ransome (b. 1884), a critic and expert on Russian literature, has become even more popular with his tales of cruising and other holiday adventures. The secret of Ransome's appeal to children is that he never writes down to them, shows them how to make things, and introduces some good, straight thrills which are not too horrific for young readers. Other serious writers who have succeeded with children's books are John Masefield, Richard Hughes, L. A. G. Strong, Howard Spring, Noel Streatfeild, Enid Bagnold, Richmal Crompton, Martin Armstrong and Walter De La Mare. For very young children, Beatrix Potter's *Peter Rabbit* books are still supreme, although their popularity has been challenged by Hugh Lofting, whose resourceful *Doctor Dolittle* tales, which appeal also to older children, are perfectly calculated to achieve their object.

Increasing knowledge of the habits of the animal world has given opportunity to a number of authors to write books which have become nursery classics. Fortescue's *The Story of a Red Deer* (1897) was followed by Felix Salten's *Bambi* (1928) and Henry Williamson's *Tarka the Otter* (1927) and *Salar the Salmon* (1935) which appeal to children and grown-ups. Introductions to art, music, literature and religion are now an integral part of the children's library. It may be said with confidence that if the children of to-day care to avail themselves of the opportunities offered to them they should become wiser and better men and women than their parents.

So many war books, official and unofficial, were written between the two wars that it is possible to refer here to only a few of them. Enid Bagnold's *A Diary Without Dates* (1917) gives a glimpse of the 1914–18 war as a nurse saw it. F. A. Voigt's vivid *Combed Out* (1929) is unforgettable for its picture of the impact of war's horrors on the sensitive and unwilling participant. Among the numerous narratives of prisoners of war, *The Road to En-dor* (1919) by E. H. Jones, and *The Escaping Club* (1921) by A. J. Evans take an honourable place. "Ian Hay" (Major-General J. H. Beith) has rightly earned the gratitude of several generations for his amusing stories of youth, and he applied his light-hearted method with notable success to *The First Hundred Thousand* (1915) and its successors. Charles Manning's *Her Privates We* (1930) gives a well written account of experience on the Somme and Ancre fronts in 1916.

Among the books of actual experience by airmen, the best are probably *An Airman's Outings* (1917), by Alan Bott, *Sagittarius Rising* (1936), by Cecil Lewis, and the breath-taking, anonymous *Fighter Pilot* (1941).

The period has been rich in excellent translations from the literature of other countries. Some of them have been mentioned in other sections. Constance Garnett did invaluable work when she translated the works of Turgeniev, Tolstoy and Dostoieffsky into English. Aylmer Maude's versions of Tolstoy are also excellent. Charles Scott-Moncrieff's renderings of Stendhal and Proust have become classics in their own right. Eric Sutton's version of Henri Fauconnier's *Malaisie* contains lovely prose. Its English title is *The Soul of Malaya* (1931). Lengthy and lumbering German novels have been given graceful English dress by a small army of competent translators. In these works exactness of reproduction has gone hand-in-hand with literary merit. André Maurois has been particularly happy in his translators. The standard of accuracy in sympathetic translation was never higher than it is to-day, although the flowery grace of Florio's *Montaigne* is neither sought nor required.

In these last sections of this book it has not been our purpose to criticize so much as to present, leaving the choice and the decision to the reader, but indicating where we feel that a profitable choice may be made. The vagaries of literature are tortuous and at times astonishing. One thing is clear. To be modern is not to be meritorious. To break entirely with tradition is usually to achieve a stillborn birth. There are certain great truths of form and matter which run through the literary histories of every country. It has been our aim to call attention to those writers, both ancient and modern, whose work seems to us to contain these indispensable elements. Without them the books of the past could not have survived. Authors who write to-day will be well advised to ponder these things and act upon them. If they do not, their books will be added to the library of limbo, where books that were silly and ephemeral lie alongside the majestic tomes of the pompous and pretentious by authors who would not, or could not, learn that without something that had to be said, without humour, humanity and a true knowledge of the hearts of their fellow-men, their books, if they were intended for posterity, had no chance of survival.

INDEX

*Main references only are given in this index,
and casual allusions have been omitted.*

Abercrombie, Lascelles, 183, 276
Ackerley, J. R., 209, 262
Addison, Joseph, 894
"Æ" (George William Russell), 175, 200
Aelfric, 11
Agate, James E., 274
Akenside, Mark, 78
Aldington, Richard, 185, 233
Alfred, King, 4
Allingham, Margery, 241
Allott, Kenneth, 195
Ancrene Riwle, 11
Anderson, J. Redwood, 196
Andrade, Edward N. da Costa, 266
Anglo-Norman Literature, 11
Anglo-Saxon Chronicle, 4, 7
Anson, George (Lord Anson), 91
Anstey, F. (T. A. Guthrie), 279
Apollonius of Tyre, 4
Arblay, Madame d' (*See* Burney, Frances)
Archer, William, 274
Armstrong, Martin, 280
Arnold, Matthew, 125, 126, 161
Ashford, Daisy, 280
Ashton, Winifred (*See* Dane, Clemence)
Asquith, Margot (Lady Oxford and Asquith), 253
Auden, W. H., 190, 191, 192, 209, 263
Aumonier, Stacy, 238
Austen, Jane, 116, 117

Bacon, Francis, 28, 33, 34, 35
Bagehot, Walter, 167
Bagnold, Enid, 280
Baker, Elizabeth, 203
Baldwin, Stanley (Earl Baldwin) 227, 244
Ball, Sir Robert, 266
Ballads, 24, 25, 26
Ballantyne, Robert Michael, 149
Barbellion, W. N. P. (Bruce Cummings), 277
Barker, George, 195, 196

Barrie, Sir James Matthew, 204, 205
Bates, H. E., 239
Bates, Henry Walter, 152
Bax, Clifford, 194, 209, 255, 264
"Beachcomber" (J. B. Morton) 278
Beaumont, Francis, 56, 57
Beckford, William, 98
Bede, The Venerable, 3, 4
Beeding, Francis, 241
Beerbohm, Sir Max, 242, 243, 274
Beith, Major General J. H. (*See* Hay, Ian)
Bell, Adrian, 277, 278
Bell, Clive, 276
Bell, G. K. A. (Bishop of Chichester), 267
Bell, Gertrude, 277
Bell, Josephine, 241
Belloc, Hilaire, 179, 233, 245, 249, 259
Bennett, Enoch Arnold, 207, 216, 217, 275
Benson, E. F., 250, 255
Benson, Stella, 236
Bentham, Jeremy, 156
Bentley, E. C., 240
Bentley, Phyllis, 237
Beowulf, 1, 2
Berdyaev, Nicholas, 267
Beresford, J. D., 218
Beresford, John, 276
Berkeley, George, 98, 99
Berkeley, Reginald, 210
Berners, Lord, 40
Berners, Gerald (Lord Berners), 255
Besier, Rudolf, 210
Betjeman, John, 276
Bevis of Hampton, 10
Bible, The, 32, 33
Birrell, Augustine, 243
Black-eyed Susan, 81
Blake, Nicholas, 241
Blake, William, 83
Blunden, Edmund, 186, 187, 261
Blunt, Wilfrid Scawen, 176.

Boccaccio, Giovanni, 17, 18
Boëthius, 4
Bone, James, 265
Book of Common Prayer, 32
Book of the Rhymers Club, 169
Borrow, George, 139, 140, 155
Boswell, James, 94, 95
Bott, Alan, 281
Bottomley, Gordon, 181
Bourne, George (George Sturt), 277, 278
Bowen, Elizabeth, 236
Boyle, Robert, 85, 86
Bradley, A. C., 269
Bradley, F. H., 265
Bradley, Henry, 272
Bridge, Ann, 237
Bridges, Robert, 172, 173, 187
Bridie, James (James Mavor), 210
Brighouse, Harold, 206
Bright, John, 168
Brittain, Vera, 250, 253
Brontë, Anne, 140, 141
Brontë, Charlotte, 140, 141
Brontë, Emily, 140, 141
Brooke, Rupert, 185
Brown, T. E., 175, 176
Browne, Sir Thomas, 64, 65
Browning, Elizabeth Barrett, 124
Browning, Robert, 122, 124, 125
Brunanburh, 5
Bryant, Arthur, 250
Bryce, James Viscount, 256
Buchan, John (Lord Tweedsmuir), 233, 249, 257
Buckle, G. E., 247
Buckle, Henry Thomas, 165
Bullett, Gerald, 237
Bunyan, John, 65, 66, 67
Burdett, Osbert, 271
Burke, Edmund, 97, 101
Burney, Frances (Madame d'Arblay), 91
Burns, Robert, 82, 100
Burton, Sir Richard Francis, 153
Burton, Robert, 65
Butler, Joseph, 98
Butler, Samuel, 214, 265
Butts, Mary, 237
Byron, George Gordon, Lord, 104, 110, 111, 112.

Cædmon, 3
Calverley, C. S., 130

Cambridge Histories, 256
Campbell, J. F., 80
Campbell, Roy, 193
Campbell, Thomas, 110
Campion, Thomas, 58
Cannan, Gilbert, 220, 223
Cardus, Neville, 244
Carew, Thomas, 60
Carlyle, Thomas, 161, 162, 163
Carols, 24
Carpenter, Edward, 273
Carroll, Lewis (Charles Lutwidge Dodgson) 149
Cary, Joyce, 237
Caxton, William, 23, 28, 29
Cecil, Lord David, 250, 271
Cervantes-Saavedra, Miguel de, 93, 142, 143
Chamberlain, Joseph, 168
Chambers, R. W., 270
Chapman, George, 40
Charlton, L. E. O., 255
Charnwood, Lord, 251
Chatterton, Thomas, 80
Chaucer, Geoffrey, 16, 17, 18, 19, 20, 21, 22, 35, 36
Chesterfield, Earl of (Philip Stanhope), 90
Chesterton, Gilbert Keith, 181, 208, 233, 240, 270, 271
Child, Francis James, 25
Childe, Wilfred Rowland, 196
Christie, Agatha, 241
Church Hymnary, 81
Church, Richard, 196, 237
Churchill, Winston Spencer, 248, 255, 258
Clark, Sir Kenneth, 276
Cloud of Unknowing, 12
Cobbett, William, 116
Cole, G. D. H., 241
Cole, Margaret, 241
Coleridge, Mary, 179
Coleridge, Samuel Taylor, 104, 105, 106, 114
Collins, Wilkie, 138
Collins, William, 79
Collis, Maurice, 263
Compton-Burnett, I., 237
Congreve, William, 74
Connolly, Cyril, 275
Conrad, Joseph, 217, 259
Cook, Captain James, 91, 92
Coombs, B. L., 255

Cooper, A. Duff, 249
Coppard, A. E., 239
Coulton, G. G., 257
Courthope, W. J., 268
Coverdale, Miles, 32
Coward, Noel, 208
Cowper, William, 78, 81, 91
Crabbe, George, 77
Crashaw, Richard, 60, 61
Creevey Papers, 276
Crofts, Freeman Wills, 241
Crompton, Richmal, 280
Cruttwell, C. R. M. F., 257
Cummings, Bruce (*See* Barbellion,
    W. N. P.)
Cynewulf, 3

Dane, Clemence (Winifred Ashton)
    209, 210, 236
Dangerfield, George, 251
Darwin, Bernard, 244
Darwin, Charles Robert, 152, 157,
    158
Davison, John, 175
Davies, W. H., 180, 252
Daviot, Gordon, 210
Davison, Edward, 196
Dawson, Christopher, 267
Defoe, Daniel, 87, 88
Delafield, E. M., 236
De la Mare, Walter, 180, 181, 280
Dent, Alan, 274
Deor's Lament, 2
De Quincey, Thomas, 115
Dickens, Charles, 55, 135, 136,
    137, 138
Dickinson, Goldsworthy Lowes,
    272
Dictionary of National Biography,
    246
Disraeli, Benjamin, 138, 168
Dixon, Richard Watson, 170
Dobrée, Bonamy, 270
Dobson, Austin, 176, 270, 271
Dodds, E. R., 196
Dodgson, Charles Lutwidge (*See*
    Carroll, Lewis)
Dolben, Digby Mackworth, 170
Doolittle, H. ("H. D."), 185
Donne, John, 59
Dostoieffsky, Fyodor Mihailovich
    281
Doughty, Charles Montagu, 171,
    172, 258

Douglas, Lord Alfred, 176
Douglas, Gavin, 22
Douglas, George, 232
Douglas, Norman, 232, 260
Dowden, Edward, 268
Dowson, Ernest, 169, 170
Doyle, Sir Arthur Conan, 240
Dream of the Rood, 4
Drinkwater, John, 183, 207
Druten, John Van, 210
Dryden, John, 72, 73, 74, 75
Dukes, Ashley, 210
Dunbar, William, 22
Duncan, Isadora, 255
Dunne, J. W., 208, 266
Duns Scotus, John, 11
Dunsany, Lord, 210
Dyment, Clifford, 195

Edda, 2
Eddington, Sir Arthur Stanley,
    266
Eglinton, John (William Kirk-
    patrick Magee), 202
Eliot, George (Mary Ann Evans),
    142, 143, 144
Eliot, T. S., 185, 189, 190, 194,
    195, 209, 267, 275
Elizabeth (Elizabeth Mary Beau-
    champ, Countess Russell), 225
    226
Ellis, Henry Havelock, 273
Elton, Oliver, 268, 270, 271
Empson, William, 196
English Men of Letters Series, 247
Ervine, St. John Greer, 202, 251
Esher, Viscount, 277
Etheredge, George, 74
Evans, A. J., 281
Evans, B. Ifor, 271
Evans, Mary Ann (*See* Eliot,
    George)
Evelyn, John, 87
Everyman, 24
Ewart, Wilfred, 227
Ewing, Mrs. (Juliana Horatia
    Gatty), 148

Fanshawe, Sir Richard, 40
Farquhar, George, 74
Farrar, Frederick William, 149
Farson, Negley, 263
Fauconnier, Henri, 281
Faulkner, William, 238

Fenn, G. Manville, 280
Fielding, Henry, 92, 93, 132
Fighter Pilot, 281
Filmer, Sir Robert, 86
Finlay, George, 165
Finnsburh, 2
Fisher, H. A. L., 256, 257
Fitzgerald, Edward, 127
Flecker, James Elroy, 184
Fleming, Peter, 261
Fletcher, John, 56, 57
Flint, F. S., 185
Ford, John, 57
Ford, Richard, 155
Forester, C. S., 234
Forster, E. M., 219, 220, 250
Fortescue, Sir John, 20
Fortescue, Sir John, 280
Fowler, F. G., 272
Fowler, H. W., 272
Fox, Charles James, 101
Frankau, Gilbert, 227
Franklin, Sir John, 154
Fraser, G. S., 196
Frazer, Sir James George, 267
Freeman, Austin, 240
Freeman, Edward Augustus, 165
Freeman, John, 183
Frohman, Charles, 203
Froissart, Jean, 40
Froude, James Anthony, 165, 166, 246
Fry, Roger, 276
Fulford, Roger, 276

Gaimar, Geoffrey, 8, 9
Gallienne, Richard le, 169
Galsworthy, John, 203, 204, 215, 216
Galton, Sir Francis, 267
Gardiner, A. G., 245
Gardiner, Samuel Rawson, 166
Garnett, Constance, 281
Garnett, David, 237, 277
Garrard, Apsley Cherry-, 262
Garrick, David, 97
Garrod, H. W., 271
Gascoyne, David, 195
Gaskell, Elizabeth Cleghorn, 142
Gatty, Juliana Horatia (*See* Ewing, Mrs.)
Gawain, Sir, and the Green Knight, 12
Gay, John, 77

Geddes, Sir Patrick, 267
Geoffrey, Arthur (*See* Geoffrey of Monmouth)
Geoffrey of Monmouth, 8, 9
Georgian Poets, 183
Gerald of Barry (Giraldus Cambrensis), 8, 9
Gerhardi, William, 235
Gesta Romanorum, 4
Gibbon, Edward, 84, 100, 101
Gibson, Wilfrid Wilson, 182
Gilbert, William, 33
Gilbert, Sir William Schwenk, 130
Giraldus Cambrensis (*See* Gerald of Barry)
Gissing, George Robert, 211
Gladstone, William Ewart, 168
Glover, Halcott, 210
Gogarty, Oliver St. John, 196
Golding, Louis, 237
Goldsmith, Oliver, 77, 83, 96, 97
Goodyear, Susan, 237
Gore, Charles, 268
Gosse, Sir Edmund, 176, 247, 270
Gosse, Philip, 247
Gower, John, 21
Graham, R. B. Cunninghame, 232, 260
Grahame, Kenneth, 239
Granville-Barker, Harley, 200, 202, 203, 270
Graves, C. L., 279
Graves, Robert, 186, 234, 253, 276
Gray, Thomas, 79, 91
Great Lives Series, 246
Green, John Richard, 166
Greene, Grahame, 234, 263
Greene, Robert, 45
Gregory, Lady Isabella Augusta, 201, 202
Grenfell, Julian, 187
Greville Memoirs, 276
Grey of Fallodon, Lord, 244
Grierson, Sir Herbert J. C., 270, 271
Grigson, Geoffrey, 195
Grossmith, George, 279
Grossmith, Weedon, 279
Grote, George, 163
Gubbins, Nathaniel, 278
Guedalla, Philip, 248, 263
Guevara, Antonio de, 40
Gunn, Neil M., 235
Gunther, John, 263

Guthrie, Thomas Anstey (*See* Anstey, F.)
Guy of Warwick, 10

Hakluyt, Richard, 33
Haldane, J. B. S., 267
Haldane, John Scott, 267
Hamilton, Cicely, 209
Hammond, Barbara, 256
Hammond, J. L., 256
Hankin, St. John, 200
Hanley, James, 234
Hardy, Thomas, 146, 147, 170, 171
Hart, B. H. Liddell, 257
Harvey, F. W., 187
Hassall, Christopher, 196
Havelok, 10
Hawes, Stephen, 21
Hay, Ian (Major-General J. H. Beith), 281
Hazlitt, William, 114, 115
Hebert, A. G., 268
Hemingway, Ernest, 238
Hendry, J. F., 196
Henley, William Ernest, 175
Henry, O., 238
Henryson, Robert, 21, 22
Henty, G. A., 280
Herbert, A. P., 227, 231, 279
Herbert, George, 60
Herford, C. H., 271
Herrick, Robert, 60
Hewlett, Maurice, 233, 259
Hickey, Memoirs of William, 276
Higden, Ranulph, 8
Higgins, F. R., 196
Highways and Byways Series, 264
Hobbes, Thomas, 67, 68
Hoccleve, Thomas, 21
Hodgson, Ralph, 180
Hodgson, W. N., 187
Hogarth, D. G., 260
Hogben, Professor Lancelot, 266
Holland, Philemon, 40
Holme, Constance, 227
Holmes, Mr. Justice, 277
Holtby, Winifred, 236
Homer, 40
Hood, Thomas, 130
Hooker, Richard, 62, 63
Hopkins, Gerard Manley, 187, 188
Horizon, 275
Horn, 10
Horniman, A. E. F., 202, 206

Houghton, Stanley, 206
Housman, A. E., 177, 178
Housman, Laurence, 200
Howard, Henry, Earl of Surrey, 36
Howe, P. P., 274
Hudson, W. H., 232, 259
Hughes, Richard, 196, 234, 280
Hughes, Thomas, 149
Hugo, Victor, 129
Hulme, T. E., 185
Hume, David, 99, 100
Hunt, Leigh, 115
Hutchinson, R. C., 235
Huxley, Aldous, 209, 219, 231, 251, 263, 277
Huxley, Julian, 267
Huxley, Thomas Henry, 159
Hymns, Ancient and Modern, 82

Iles, Francis, 241
Imagist Anthology, 185
Inge, W. R., 273
Irish National Theatre Society, 200
Irwin, Margaret, 236
Isherwood, Christopher, 209, 232, 255

Jackson, Sir Barry, 207
Jackson, Holbrook, 271
Jacobs, W. W., 239
James I of Scotland, 21, 22
James, Henry, 212, 213, 218, 259
James, William, 265
Jameson, Storm, 237
Jeans, Sir James, 266
Jefferies, Richard, 160, 280
Jesse, F. Tennyson, 237
Jewsbury, Jane, 244
John of Salisbury, 11
John of Treves, 8
Johnson, Lionel, 169, 170
Johnson, Samuel, 77, 94, 95, 96
Johnston, Denis, 202
Jones, E. H., 281
Jones, Henry Arthur, 196
Jones, Henry Festing, 265
Jonson, Benjamin, 44, 45, 52, 54, 55, 56, 58, 190
Joyce, James, 219, 229, 230

Kaye-Smith, Sheila, 237
Keats, John, 104, 112, 113
Keble, John, 150, 168

Keeble, Sir Frederick, 267
Kennedy, Margaret, 236
Kennedy, Milward, 241
Ker, W. P., 268
Keyes, Sidney, 195
Keynes, Lord, 274
Kilvert's Diary, 276
Kinglake, A. W., 155
Kingsley, Charles, 138
Kingsley, Henry, 138
Kingston, W. H. G., 149
Kipling, Rudyard, 176, 177, 213, 255, 280
Knoblock, Edward, 207, 208
Knox, E. V., 279
Kyd, Thomas, 45, 46

Lamb, Charles, 115
Lamb, Mary, 115
Landor, Walter Savage, 116
Lane, Edward William, 154
Lang, Andrew, 176
Langland, William, 13, 14 19, 20
Lascelles, M., 271
Lawrence, D. H., 220, 223, 224, 261, 277
Lawrence, T. E., 259, 260, 277
Layamon, 9
Leacock, Stephen, 278
Lear, Edward, 130
Ledwidge, Francis, 187
Lee, Sidney, 247
Lehmann, John, 275
Lehmann, Rosamund, 237
Lethbridge, Mabel, 253
Lever, Charles James, 139
Lewis, Alun, 196
Lewis, Cecil, 281
Lewis, Cecil Day, 190, 191, 192, 196
Lewis, C. S., 268, 270
Lewis, D. B. Wyndham, 278
Lewis, Wyndham, 235
Lewis, Sinclair, 237
Lindsay, Sir David, 23
Linklater, Eric, 210, 235
Livingstone, David, 154
Lloyd, Christopher, 250
Locke, John, 86, 87
Lockhart, John Gibson, 121
Lockhart, R. H. Bruce, 262, 263
Lodge, Sir Oliver, 266
Lofting, Hugh, 280
Lovelace, Richard, 60

Lowes, J. L., 270, 271
Lubbock, Percy, 273
Lucas, E. V., 244, 264, 279
Lucas, St. John, 238
Lydgate, John, 21, 22
Lyell, Sir Charles, 157
Lyly, John, 40, 41, 45
Lynd, Robert, 245
Lynd, Sylvia, 196
Lytton, Lord Bulwer-, 138
Lytton, Lord, 251

Macaulay, Rose, 196, 229, 251
Macaulay, Thomas Babington, 94, 95, 163, 164, 168, 246
MacCarthy, Desmond, 275
M'Carthy, Justin, 167
Macdonell, A. G., 235
McEvoy, Charles, 203
McFee, William, 234
Macgregor, Sir James, 80
Machen, Arthur, 232
Mackail, Denis, 204
Mackail, J. W., 272
Mackenzie, Compton, 220, 221, 254
Mackenzie, Ronald, 210
Maclaren, Moray, 264
Macnaughten, S. 226
MacNeice, Louis, 193, 210, 263
Macpherson, James, 80, 81
McTaggart, John, 265
Madge, Charles, 196
Maillart, Ella, 261
Maine, Henry James Sumner, 167
Maitland, Frederic William, 156
Maldon, Battle of, 2
Malory, Sir Thomas, 10, 23
Maltby, H. F., 203
Malthus, Thomas Robert, 103, 158
Mancroft, Lord (Arthur Michael Samuel), 245
Manning, Charles, 281
Mansfield, Katherine, 239
Map, Walter, 10
Marie de France, 9
Maritain, Jacques, 267
Marlowe, Christopher, 41, 43, 44, 46, 47, 48
Marryat, Frederick, 149
Marsh, Sir Edward, 183
Marsh, Ngaio, 241
Marshall, Alfred, 156

Martin, Violet Florence (*See* Ross, Martin)
Martyn, Edward, 201
Marvell, Andrew, 60, 61
Masefield, John, 181, 182, 207, 233, 255, 270, 280
Mason, A. E. W., 241
Massinger, Philip, 57
Matthew, Thomas, 32
Maude, Aylmer, 281
Maugham, W. Somerset, 205, 206, 218, 219, 255, 262
Maurois, André, 249, 281
Mavor, James (*See* Bridie, James)
Mayne, Rutherford (Samuel Waddell), 202
Meredith, George, 144, 145
Mermaid Series, 273
Metrical Psalms, 82
Mew, Charlotte, 179, 180
Meynell, Alice, 179, 243, 244
Mill, James, 156
Mill, John Stuart, 156, 157
Miller, Hugh, 160
Miller of Dee, 81
Milman, Henry Hart, 165
Milne, A. A., 279
Milton, John, 58, 61, 62, 68, 69, 70, 71, 72, 157, 216
Miracle Plays, 24
Moncrieff, Charles Scott, 281
Monkhouse, Allan, 206
Monro, Harold, 182, 183
Montagu, C. E., 274
Monypenny, W. F., 247
Moore, George, 200, 211, 252
Moore, Nicholas, 196
Moore, Thomas, 110
Moore, Thomas Sturge, 179
Morality Plays, 24
More, Sir Thomas, 29, 30, 31, 32
Morgan, Charles, 234
Morier, James, 121
Morley, John, Viscount, 247
Morris, William, 127, 128
Morrow, George, 278
Morton, H. V., 264
Morton, J. B., 227, 259, 278
Mottram, R. H., 227, 228
Muir, Edwin, 196
Munro, C. K., 210
Munro, H. H. (*See* Saki)
Munthe, Axel, 254
Murray, D. L., 236

Murray, Gilbert, 272
Murray, Sir James, 272
Myers, L. H., 235

Nairn, Lady, 100
Neale, J. E., 249
Neale, J. M., 81
Nesbit, E., 280
Nevinson, C. R. W., 276
Nevinson, H. W., 260
Newbolt, Sir Henry John, 178
Newman, Ernest, 276
Newman, John Henry, Cardinal, 81, 150, 151
Nichols, Robert, 186
Nicholson, Norman, 195
Nicoll, Allardyce, 270, 271
Nicolson, Harold, 239, 249, 270
Norcott, Maurice Lane, 278
North, John, 260
North, Sir Thomas, 40
Northcliffe, Lord, 251
Norton, Thomas, 45
Noyes, Alfred, 183

Observer, The, 275
O'Casey, Sean, 202
Ockham, William of, 11
O'Connell, Daniel, 168
O'Connor, Frank, 196
O'Faolain, Sean, 264
Omar Khayyám, 127
Ommanney, F. D., 262
Onions, Oliver, 220
Orosius, Paulus, 4
Orwell, George, 255
Ossian, 80, 81
Otway, Thomas, 74
Owen, Wilfred, 188, 189
Oxford and Asquith, Lady (*See* Asquith, Margot)
Oxford Book of Modern Verse, The 193
Oxford Dictionary, The, 272

Paine, Thomas, 102
Painter, William, 40
Paris, Matthew, 7
Park, Mungo, 152
Parker, Eric, 278
Passfield, Lord and Lady (*See* Webb, Sidney and Beatrice)
Paston Letters, 26, 27
Pater, Walter Horatio, 167

Patience, 12
Patmore, Coventry, 170
Pearl, 12
Pecocke, Reginald, 20
Peele, George, 45
Pellow, J. D. C., 196
Pepys, Samuel, 87
Percy, Thomas, 26
Phillips, John, 77
Phillips, Stephen, 199, 200
Piers Plowman, Vision of, 13, 14
Pinero, Sir Arthur Wing, 196
Piozzi, Hester Lynch (Mrs. Thrale), 96
Pitt, William, the Elder, Earl of Chatham, 101
Pitt, William, the Younger, 101, 102
Pitter, Ruth, 195
Plomer, William, 196, 276
Pollard, A. W., 269
Pollock, Sir Frederick, 277
Pollock-Holmes Letters, 277
Pope, Alexander, 75, 76, 77
Potter, Beatrix, 280
Potter, Stephen, 272
Pound, Ezra, 185
Powys, John Cowper, 234
Powys, Llewellyn, 234
Powys, T. F., 234
Priestley, J. B., 208, 210, 230, 245, 254, 264, 269
Prince, F. T., 195
Prior, Matthew, 77
Prokosch, Frederic, 195, 238
Proust, Marcel, 281
Psalms, 32
Punch, 130, 278, 279
Purchas, Samuel, 33
Purity, 12
Puttenham, George, 40

Quennell, Peter, 250
Quiller-Couch, Sir Arthur, 233, 269, 270

Raleigh, Sir Walter, 64
Raleigh, Sir Walter Alexander, 269, 271
Ramsay, Allan, 100
Ransome, Arthur, 280
Rattigan, Terence, 210
Read, Herbert, 270
Reade, Charles, 138
Reed, Douglas, 263

Reid, Forrest, 234, 254
Religious Verse, Anthology of, 195
Reynolds, Sir Joshua, 97
Rhys, Ernest, 196
Rhys, Keidrych, 196
Ricardo, David, 156
Richards, I. A., 272
Richardson, Dorothy M., 226, 227
Richardson, Samuel, 92
Ridler, Anne, 195
Robert de Boron, 10
Robert of Gloucester, 9
Roberts, Michael, 196
Robertson, E. Arnot, 237
Robertson, Tom, 196
Robertson, William, 100
Robin Hood Ballads, 26, 32
Robins, Elizabeth, 226
Rolle, Richard, 11, 12
Roman de la Rose, 17
Rook, Alan, 196
Rosenberg, Isaac, 187
Ross, Martin (Violet Florence Martin), 226
Rossetti, Christina, 127
Rossetti, Dante Gabriel, 127
Rothenstein, Sir William, 276
Rubinstein, H. F., 210
Ruskin, John, 161, 162
Russell, Bertrand, 266
Russell, Countess (*See* Elizabeth)
Russell, George William (*See* "Æ")
Rutherford, Mark (William Hale White), 211

Sackville, Thomas, 36, 45
Sackville-West, Victoria, 194, 237
Sadleir, Sir Michael, 271
Saintsbury, George, 268, 270
Saki (H. H. Munro), 240
Sally in Our Alley, 81
Salten, Felix, 280
Sampson, George, 256
Saroyan, William, 238
Sassoon, Siegfried, 185, 186
Sayers, Dorothy, 241
Scale of Perfection, 12
Scott, Dixon, 259
Scott, Geoffrey, 276
Scott, Robert Falcon, 262
Scott, Sir Walter, 115, 117, 118, 119, 120, 121
Seaman, Sir Owen, 279
Seccombe, Thomas, 271

Secker, Martin, 220
Sellar, W. C., 279
Seward, Sir Albert, 267
Sewell, Anna, 148
Shackleton, Sir Ernest, 262
Shakespeare, William, 31, 41, 42, 44, 47, 48, 49, 50, 51, 52, 53, 54, 109
Shanks, Edward, 187
Shaw, George Bernard, 196, 197, 198, 199, 215, 274, 276, 277
Shelley, Percy Bysshe, 104, 113, 114
Shelton, Thomas, 40
Sheridan, Richard Brinsley, 83, 101
Sherriff, R. C., 209, 235
Shipley, Sir Arthur, 267
Shirley, James, 57
Shore, Bernard, 276
Short, John, 195
Sidgwick, A. H., 276
Sidney, Sir Philip, 35, 39, 40
Signpost Series, 267
Sinclair, May, 226
Sitwell, Edith, 187, 251,
Sitwell, Osbert, 187, 262
Sitwell, Sacheverell, 187, 276
Smith, Adam, 102, 103
Smith, Logan Pearsall, 246
Smith, V. A., 258
Smollett, Tobias George, 93, 94, 100
Smyth, Dame Ethel, 253, 261
Sollas, W. J., 267
Somerville, Edith Œ., 226
Sorley, C. H., 187
Southey, Robert, 109, 110
Speke, John Hanning, 153
Spencer, Alfred, 276
Spencer, Herbert, 159
Spencer, Sir Walter Baldwin, 154
Spender, Stephen, 190, 192, 193
Spenser, Edmund, 18, 19, 35, 36, 37, 38, 39
Spring, Howard, 254, 280
Spurgeon, C. H., 168
Squire, Sir John Collings, 183, 184, 265, 275
Stables, Gordon, 280
Stanhope, Lady Hester, 155
Stanhope, Philip (See Chesterfield, Earl of)
Stanley, Arthur Penrhyn, 167, 168

Stanley, Sir Henry Morton, 154
Stark, Freya, 261
Starkie, Walter, 262
Steele, Sir Richard, 89
Stendhal (Marie-Henri Beyle) 281
Stephen, Leslie, 246, 271
Stephens, James, 175, 232
Sterne, Laurence, 94
Stevenson, Robert Louis, 148, 175, 242
Strachey, Lytton, 247, 248, 276
Strang, Herbert, 280
Straus, Ralph, 276
Streatfeild, Noel, 280
Street, A. G., 277
Strode, William, 21
Strong, L. A. G. 196, 237, 280
Stubbs, William, 166, 167
Sturt, George (See Bourne, George)
Suckling, Sir John, 60
Sullivan, Sir Arthur Seymour, 130
Sunday Times, The, 275
Sutherland, Halliday. 254
Sutton, Eric, 281
Swift, Jonathan, 77, 88, 89
Swinburne, Algernon Charles, 128, 129, 130
Swinnerton, Frank, 225
Symonds, John Addington, 167, 270
Symons, A. J. A., 250
Symons, Arthur, 169, 170, 271
Symons, Julian, 195
Synge, J. M., 201

Tambimuttu, 196
Temple, William (Archbishop of Canterbury), 267
Tennant, Edward Wyndham, 187
Tennyson, Alfred, Lord, 122, 123, 124
Terry, Ellen, 277
Thackeray, William Makepeace, 131, 132, 133, 134, 135
Thomas, Dylan, 195, 196
Thomas, Edward, 182
Thomas the Norman, 10
Thompson, Francis, 170
Thomson, Sir Arthur, 266
Thomson, James, 78
Thomson, James ("B.V."), 175
Thrale, Mrs. (See Piozzi, Hester Lynch)

Times Literary Supplement, The, 275
Todd, Ruthven, 195
Tolstoy, Leo, 281
Tom Bowling, 81
Tomlinson, H. M., 260
Toplady, Augustus, 81
Tovey, Sir Donald, 276
Toynbee, A. J., 257
Treece, Henry, 196
Trench, Herbert, 178
Trevelyan, George Macaulay, 257, 271
Trevelyan, Sir George Otto, 257
Trollope, Anthony, 134, 135
Turgeniev, Ivan, 281
Turner, W. J., 193
Tweedsmuir, Lord (*See* Buchan, John)
Tyndale, George, 31, 32

Udall, Nicholas, 44

Vane, Sutton, 210
Vaughan, Henry, 60, 61
Vedrenne, J. E., 202
Vega, Lope de, 43
Vinogradoff, Sir Paul, 156
Voigt, F. A., 281
Voltaire, F. M. Arouet de, 95

Wace, 8, 9
Waddell, Helen, 237
Waddell, Samuel (*See* Mayne, Rutherford)
Wakefield, Edward Gibbon, 154
Walkley, A. B., 274
Wallace, Alfred Russel, 157, 158
Waller, Alfred Rayney, 256
Walpole, Horace, 90, 91, 97
Walpole, Hugh, 220, 221, 222, 223, 255
Walton, Izaak, 65, 87
Ward, A. C., 271
Ward, Sir Adolphus William, 256
Warner, Rex, 237
Waterton, Charles, 152
Watson, Sir William, 179
Watts, Isaac, 81
Waugh, Alec, 232, 263
Waugh, Arthur, 255
Waugh, Evelyn, 234, 250, 261
Weaving, Willoughby, 187
Webb, Mary, 227

Webb, Sidney and Beatrice (Lord and Lady Passfield) 215, 256
Webster, John, 57
Welby, T. Earle, 270
Wellesley, Dorothy, 196
Wells, H. G., 214, 215, 254, 257
Wesley, Charles, 81
Wesley, John, 91
West, Rebecca, 237, 259
Westminster Shorter Catechism, 64
Wharton, Edith, 226
Whistler, Laurence, 196
White, Antonia, 237
White, Gilbert, 90
White, William Hale (*See* Rutherford, Mark)
Whitehead, A. N., 266
Whymper, Edward, 154
Wilde, Oscar, 169, 199
Wilenski, R. H., 276
William of Malmesbury, 7
William of Ockham, 11
Williams, Charles, 195, 268
Williams, Emlyn, 210
Williamson, Henry, 235, 280
Wilson, Arnold, 264
Wilson, Edmund, 271
Wilson, John Dover, 270
Wodehouse, P. G., 240
Wolfe, Humbert, 184
Woodforde's Diary, 276
Woodruff, Douglas, 278
Woods, Margaret L., 196
Woolf, Virginia, 219, 228, 229, 244, 250.
Worde, Wynkyn de, 28
Wordsworth, William, 104, 105, 106, 107, 108, 109
Wortham, H. E., 250
Wyatt, Sir Thomas, 36
Wycherley, William, 74
Wyclif, John, 14, 15, 16

Yeatman, R. J., 279
Yeats, William Butler, 173, 174, 175, 193, 200
Yeats-Brown, F., 255
Yellow Book, The, 242
Young, Andrew, 195, 196
Young, Edward, 78
Young, E. H., 237
Young, Francis Brett, 224, 225, 260
Young, G. M., 271